Introduction

Welcome to the Pyramid Football Guide to Non-League 2004/05. This is the second edition of our annual publication that was first released last year and is a complementary addition to the already popular and well established Pyramid Football website, which has been running since July 2000. Once again we have had our loyal and hardy band of reporters travelling the length and breadth of the country over the past year and, once again, they have been an invaluable part of piecing the guide together.

The 2004/05 edition appears after one of the most transitional years in the non-league game's history. The enormous re-structuring has seen many clubs moving leagues as the Conference has added North and South sections under its main Nationwide Division, with the three Premier Divisions of the three feeder leagues now falling underneath. This means that, in most cases, there are more promotion places up for grabs which will no doubt make the individual leagues much more competitive (something that was perhaps lacking last season with the champions of the Dr Martens, Ryman and Unibond Premier divisions all enjoying large winning margins). The restructuring has been met with approval from most, if not all quarters, with many clubs and representatives from the Ryman League quick to voice concerns over potential demotions and increased travelling costs due to the league covering a wider geographical area.

On the pitch, it was certainly a season to remember. Chester returned to the Football League after winning the Conference title, while the Play-Off system for the second promotion place once again proved a success, with Shrewsbury bouncing straight back into Division Three after victory over Aldershot.

The non-league once again flew the flag proudly in the FA Cup as Telford (whose financial plight sadly saw them go out of business at the season's end) claimed the scalp of Crewe Alexandra before losing to eventual finalists Millwall in Round Four while Accrington and Stevenage both claimed Football League scalps. However, the real headline makers were Scarborough as they disposed of Southend before setting up a now famous David and Goliath meeting with Chelsea in the Fourth Round.

Wessex League champions Winchester City lifted the FA Vase after beating AFC Sudbury in the Final (this time held at Birmingham City's St Andrews ground), to complete a fine double, while the FA Trophy again went outside the Conference after unfancied Hednesford upset the odds by beating Canvey Island in a thrilling match at Villa Park.

For many, season 2004/05 will be a case of 'the proof of the pudding is in the eating' as the logistics of the new restructured non-league format are put to the test. Whatever the outcome, Pyramid Football will no doubt continue to be enthused by the game at this level and, although it is a level of the game that does get regularly swept under the carpet by the money and media surrounding the Premiership and Football League, there are many who are fully aware of the value, history and unique nature of the English Non-League game. It is a culture that you would struggle to find anywhere else in the world and whose praises we should all be keen to sing. Here's to a harmonious season.

Joe Bush

Pyramid Football July 2004

The Non-League Football Website
PyramidFootball.co.uk

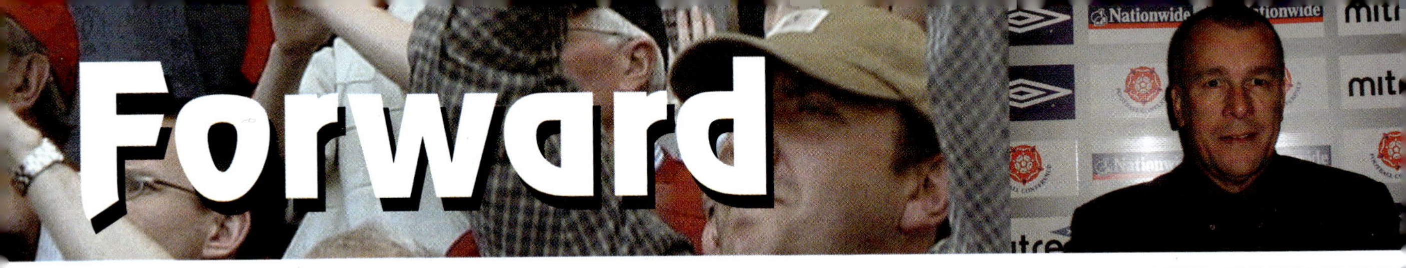

Forward

Since 1979 when the Alliance Premier League was first formed, the Football Conference has had a significant impact on the national game. Clubs all over the country have set their sights on progressing to the top level of the football pyramid to the Conference and over 70 clubs have achieved that aim in the past 25 years.

Now the time has, however, arrived for further changes to the national structure of the game to provide wider equality of progress and opportunities for promotion for those ambitious clubs and to ensure that geography does not prevent a club attaining its aims and objectives.

Season 2004/2005 sees the National Leagues Structure being subject to the largest change for 25 years. The Conference has led the project and, as part of the changes, has expanded the competition from 22 to 66 member clubs in a national and two semi-national competitions. The football pyramid now reflects a truly national structure with an equal number of promotional steps from step seven to step one, in whatever part of the country a club is located. Supporters of the national game will for the first time in many years now have the opportunity to visit new grounds and make new friends within the structure while the game itself will be very exciting with increased promotion opportunities and more Play-Offs.

The new structure sees two clubs promoted from the Nationwide Conference into Division Three of the Football League with four clubs contesting the end of season Play-Offs for the second promotion place. In the Nationwide North and Nationwide South, the champions are automatically promoted with eight clubs contesting a third promotion place through a series of end of season Play-Offs.

In the newly formed Isthmian Premier, Northern Premier, and Southern Premier Divisions, the promotion opportunities are again increased with the introduction of end of season Play-Offs. The next stage in restructuring will be at county level to ensure that they are treated equally across the pyramid to again allow for equality for all at this important level of the game.

While the agony and excitement of Play-Offs will be long debated, there can be no doubt they offer more opportunities to progress than ever before in the national game. Play-Offs also guarantee the winner promotion to the next step in the game which 42 matches in a season does not always provide.

The Pyramid of Football is where 95% of the game is played and it provides an opportunity for those wishing to progress to achieve their goals while those who pay to enjoy the game as supporters or players are the backbone of the national game.

There can be no doubt that restructuring of the national game will bring new challenges and opportunities and continued debate up and down the country. To all involved, we can all look forward to season 2004/05 with renewed interest and enjoyment in the game we all love.

John Moules

Chief Executive
Nationwide Conference

Contents

The Non-League Football Website
PyramidFootball.co.uk

ISBN 1 904 778 062

Published by IBS Publishing

11 Mount Street, Hythe, Kent CT21 5NT, UK
Tel. +44 (0) 1303 262636 Fax. +44 (0) 1303 262646
Email: info@pyramidfootball.co.uk
Web site: www.pyramidfootball.co.uk

PyramidFootball Reviews

2003-04

Once again our team of reporters has done a sterling job to get this year's publication together, writing reviews, articles and features and working to a tighter deadline than last year.

Thanks to Steve Hawdon, Jeremy Biggs, Peter Dagger, Geoff Wilkinson, Ken Clarke, Steve Greenfield, Ian Parker, Carl Field, Martin Whybrow and Howard Milton for their efforts for the feature articles and thank you to all the clubs whose contributions to the club pages were invaluable.

A special commendation goes out to Gerard Butler, Alan Percival and Michael Pilcher who have once again shown their dedication and commitment to making the guide a success.

DB = David Bauckham
DBL = David Balheimer
MB = Mick Brennan
JB = Joe Bush
GB = Gerard Butler
RC = Richard Chamberlain
MC = Murray Craig
MF = Mark Farrell
CF = Carl Field
SF = Steve Field
SG = Steve Greenfield
MJ = Mike Jarvis
RK = Richard Kilner
CL = Chris Laker
HL = Hugh Larkin
SL = Simon Larkins
IL = Ian Lewis
HM = Howard Milton
PM = Paul Minister
RM = Richard Murrill
AP = Alan Percival
MP = Michael Pilcher
JR = John Reidy
JRI = James Riley
DS = David Stowell
MT = Mike Tunningley
MW = Martin Whybrow
TW = Tony Whybrow
SW = Steven Wood

Once again the guide has featured some excellent photos of last season and, once again, without them, the book would not look as attractive as it undoubted does. We would like to offer a big thank you to everyone who has contributed any pictures to the guide - they are as follows:

Article photos

Main League Reviews
Chester City - Chester City FC
Canvey Island - Kieran Galvin
Hucknall Town - Jamie Foster
Crawley Town - Mark Farrell
Yeading - Tim Fuell
Lewes - Carroll Bailey
Kings Lynn - Lynn News
Redditch United - Lynn News
Hyde United - Adrian Hunt

Feeder League Articles

AFC Sudbury - Anthony Simpson and Chris Jones
AFC Wimbledon - Paul Willatts
Beaconsfield SYCOB - Brian Southam
Bideford - Brian Saunders
Brackley Town - Brian Martin
Chichester City United - Martin Smith
Clitheroe - www.clitheroefc.co.uk and Peter Ryan
Concord Rangers - Anthony Smith
Dunston FB - Malcolm James
Leighton Town - Brian Kidd
Ossett Albion - Neville Wigglesworth
Rocester - Alf Hawksworth
Spalding United - Ted O'Connor
Winchester City - Andy Stevenson

Match Photos

FA Cup: Scarborough v Chelsea - Robert Jarvis
FA Vase: Winchester v Sudbury - Sherry Chen
FA Trophy: Dave Linney
Four Nations Tournament: Duncan Brown

Ground Photos

Special thanks to
David Bauckham
Chris Bushe
KIPAX

Also

Ian Morsman
John Murray
www.pyramidpassion.co.uk
Chris Patton
Martin North
Ken Hunt
Mike Curtis
www.dunstabletownfc.co.uk
www.eastleighfc.net
Dave Johnson
www.redditchunited.com
www.rugbyunited.co.uk
www.yorkcityfc.com
Rob Wilkinson
www.guiseleyafc.com
Steve Jones
Graham Wallhead
Mark Syder

Special Articles - Premier League Players Article

www.billericaytownfc.co.uk
www.harrogatetown.com
Ian Leech
www.youngterras.co.uk

Derby Days

Dorset Echo
Eastbourne Herald

Lee Boylan Article

Kieran Galvin

Apologies to anyone we have inadvertently missed

Thank you

Joe Bush - Editor

Conference Review

With two sides relegated to the Conference for the first time, the competition for the Championship and Play-Off spots was likely to be fiercer than ever. And so it proved. Exeter City and Shrewsbury Town began their Non-League career with 1-1 home draws against Halifax Town and Margate respectively, whilst Tamworth started their Conference adventure with a defeat. The opening programme also featured the classic pairing of Aldershot Town and Accrington Stanley - both opening their Conference seasons after winning promotion the season prior. Aldershot won that one, and it would be December before they would taste defeat at the Recreation Ground. It was Hereford United who led the table through to November, with the Shots just behind them in the fledgling table. The top pairing met on Bank Holiday Monday - Hereford prevailing by the odd goal in seven in an exciting encounter. At the other end of the table, Gravesend & Northfleet had a nightmare start to the campaign with four straight defeats, but a 2-1 win at Farnborough got them off the mark, even though they stayed bottom of the pile.

A strong run by Chester City saw them rise to second following six wins from eight matches, but the September manager of the month award went to Barnet's Martin Allen as key wins had firmly established the Hertfordshire side in the Play-Off chase. Giuliano Grazioli, signed on a free transfer, just couldn't stop scoring. Some way behind this pair were Dagenham & Redbridge, who, far from being the title challengers they were expected to be, were woefully inconsistent. However, there was better news for Gravesend, as Rob Howarth proved the inspiration for a 3-1 win over Leigh which dragged them out of the relegation zone. Hereford continued to be the frontrunners, as the strike rate of Steve Guinan, Ben Smith and David Brown made them a formidable outfit, particularly on the road. However, they suffered their first reverse on 20th September, 4-1 at Burton. Meanwhile, the Play-Off challengers were taking shape, as Chester, Barnet, Aldershot and Morecambe made up the top five, whilst the struggle to avoid relegation saw Margate claim a key 3-1 win over Northwich. Steve Davis left the Vics to be replaced by Alvin McDonald soon afterwards.

With Farnborough still winless going into October, Tommy Taylor departed Cherrywood Road to be replaced by chairman Vic Searle and veteran front man Ken Charlery. Exeter City seemed to have turned off-the-field problems into a galvanising force as, through the goals of Sean Devine, they began to threaten the top five. Meanwhile, Morecambe's bid was beginning to wobble as their home form, usually a strong point, became slightly hit and miss. The 18th of the month was key at both ends, as the top pairing of Chester and Hereford shared a scoreless draw, and there were celebrations in Hampshire, as Farnborough

collected their maiden win at the 15th attempt against a Telford side who had failed to challenge for the Play-Offs as expected.

Continuing poor form saw Mark Patterson resign as manager at Leigh RMI, with the outstanding form of striker David McNiven the only saving grace and, as is so often the case when a new manager takes the helm, his former charges rallied and produced the shock of the season. Phil Starbuck took temporary charge and oversaw a 1-0 win at Hereford United which was a defining moment as the balance of the Championship swung delicately Chester's way. The Bulls saw their lead cut to a solitary point, and there were now a trio of clubs on their tail, with Aldershot and Barnet entering the fray. This was definitely the point at which the title was at its most open. By the middle of the month, City had eased into a two point advantage following the vital 1-0 success against Barnet, as their virtually impenetrable defence was proving the underpinning factor at this point. Exeter and Shrewsbury completed an all ex-Football League top six. There were changes at the bottom as well, as a pivotal win for Farnborough at Northwich saw their Cheshire hosts drop to bottom spot, where they would stay to the end of the season.

Hot on the heels of the Barnet game, Chester travelled to Aldershot and were held to a 1-1 draw, which meant City's lead was trimmed to a single point. However, Hereford were suffering a relative loss of form. Despite enjoying a 7-1 thumping of Halifax, they contrived to lose at home to struggling Tamworth in mid-December. Despite that, the last Saturday before Christmas provided the first hint that this was going to be a two horse race, as Chester won 5-1 at Tamworth, and Hereford hit seven again, at Forest Green Rovers. However, three of the other chasers, Aldershot, Barnet and Exeter were all defeated at home by struggling opposition. For Chester, specifically, the festive period was the time that they became more prolific, as single goal wins became rarer and Daryl Clare's push for the golden boot ignited, as the team scored 16 goals in three matches, including eleven in the double header against Leigh.

There was still the odd surprise, though, as Forest Green, now under the charge of Tim Harris, handed Chester a 2-1 reverse on 17th January. Despite this, City enjoyed a bit of luck that weekend, as only Aldershot of the teams in the top nine managed to win. Dagenhams inconsistency was now of baffling proportions as the side who had lost to Leigh twice recorded an impressive 4-2 win at Barnet that week. Leigh slipped to second from bottom as Farnborough beat them 2-0, but improvements in home form had been the main reason for Tamworth and Gravesend's moves away from trouble. Farnborough's steady improvement continued with a shock 4-0 win over Aldershot, and Leigh struck again as their response to five straight losses was a 3-1 defeat of Morecambe.

Whilst narrow wins were the Autumn trademark of Chester, by February they had developed a liking for late winners, none more important than on the seventh of that month when a stoppage time goal not only enabled them to beat Farnborough, but to strengthen their lead in the wake of Hereford's home loss to Burton. In contrast, the steady form of Aldershot, Barnet and Shrewsbury, three sides containing effective blends of youth and experience, made them consistent fixtures in the Play-Off zone, with Barnet claiming a particularly important 3-1 success at Morecambe towards the end of the month. Two weeks after the Farnborough success, Chester did it again, as Dagenham were defeated by a late goal, and Woking, a side who also salvaged many points in a similar manner, won at Hereford. This meant City had an eight point lead. However, Hereford then recorded a superb 9-0 win at Dagenham, which not only grabbed the headlines, but marked the first of eleven straight wins which would make the final title race much much closer.

Hereford had a good opening to March as a 3-0 win at Telford United, struggling after defeat in the FA Cup, narrowed the gap at the top to a far less daunting five points. As the month progressed, the top two matched each other point for point. Meanwhile, there was upheaval at Barnet, who were shocked when Martin Allen surprisingly defected to Brentford. However, morale was restored as Chester's run of six straight wins was halted at Underhill in a 0-0 draw, allowing Hereford to close the gap further to three points following a win at Margate.

As March came to a close, a significant 2-1 win for Hereford against Shrewsbury Town, and the postponement of Chester's game, meant the Bulls were top of the table briefly for the first time since November. However, City held their nerve and regained first place after a win at Telford the following Tuesday. Although the bottom three looked all but settled, Halifax Town were in danger as an alarming slide from the turn of the year had brought just a solitary point from eleven games, but they recovered just in time as a Good Friday win against Leigh saw the Railwaymen assured of a bottom three finish. A crucial Easter Weekend saw wins for both Chester and Hereford. The Monday saw Hereford win at Aldershot, but Chester's 0-0 draw at Shrewsbury meant that a win against Scarborough in the next game would guarantee City the title, and would avoid a winner takes all clash on the last day as Chester travelled to Hereford. Barnet, now under the control of Paul Fairclough, struck a priceless 88th minute winner against Burton to nudge Exeter out of the top five as the Grecians lost a lead in a home reverse to Woking.

The penultimate weekend of action saw Chester duly beat Scarborough to take the title, meaning Hereford's tenth straight win, 5-0 at Leigh RMI, was in vain. Shrewsbury Town sewed up third place, but a series of surprising results meant the Play-Off composition would be decided on the final day. Barnet needed a late leveller again in a 1-1 draw at Northwich, whilst Morecambe lost a lead in the same scoreline at Margate. Aldershot put their place in jeopardy by losing 3-1 at Forest Green Rovers. Exeter, though, suffered a 2-1 reverse at Tamworth, which meant that their destiny was no longer in their own hands, and they would have to rely on other results. However, there was good news for Farnborough, who confirmed third-from-bottom spot, and a reprieve from relegation if, as expected, the Northern Premier League was unable to provide a promotion candidate.

So, enter the final frantic day, Hereford beating Chester meant that City's final margin was only a point. However, the main focus was on the sides who would be trying to deny the Bulls promotion through the Play-Offs. Shrewsbury were assured of third place, but their opponents, Morecambe, needed to win and hope that other results went their way. Neither happened as the sides drew 3-3. Barnet trailed to Leigh early on, but a timely equaliser and winner by Grazioli secured their place. Aldershot cut it finer, as they went behind to Tamworth and were grateful to Lee Charles for rescuing the solitary point that they needed. That meant heartbreak for Exeter, who looked likely to slip into the top five at some points of the afternoon, but ultimately, their thrilling 3-2 success against Accrington Stanley proved in vain. However, not as much heartbreak as for Telford, whose 4-2 home reverse to Farnborough Town proved to be their last game as the financially crippled club finally went under. This meant that Northwich were reprieved along with Leigh who also found themselves remaining in the Conference, as Margate took demotion to Conference South due to problems with the rebuilding of Hartsdown Park, which dominated their whole season.

So to the Play-Offs, which were dominated by penalties of one kind or another. Hereford were paired with Aldershot Town, and it seemed to be going to plan in the seventh minute of the First Leg when David Brown put the Bulls ahead. However, Roscoe D'Sane levelled from the spot on the stroke of half-time for a final score of 1-1. Meanwhile in Hertfordshire, Barnet drew first blood against Shrewsbury through Ben Strevens' penalty, and though Luke Rodgers' spot kick made it level, it was advantage Barnet as Simon Clist netted a first leg winner deep into stoppage time. Cue the Second Legs, and Aldershot played out a goalless draw at Edgar Street to squeeze out the favourites in a penalty shoot out, whilst Shrewsbury did the same to Barnet after another Luke Rodgers penalty won the second leg 1-0. Aldershot went ahead in the Final through Aaron McLean, but Duane Darby rescued the Shrews, again just before the break. They returned to the Football League after just a one year absence with a 3-0 penalty shoot out win.

Gerard Butler

Dr Martens Review

So much for my predictions. If you take a look back in last year's edition of this tome, you will notice that I predicted this season's two leading protagonists, Weymouth and Crawley Town, to finish around mid-table. How wrong I was.

You will have seen how Weymouth's season panned out (sort of) on the recent BBC Television programme, Football Diaries, that was aired on BBC2. Chairman and Observer journalist, Ian Ridley, had brought in friend and much travelled centre forward, Steve Claridge, as player-manager and, while the according hype which was afforded to the move no doubt dominated much of the early press, Claridge got to work quickly by moulding the remnants of the team he inherited and introducing experienced faces such as those of midfielders, Paul Buckle and Martin Barlow, together with winger Lee Philpott and forward Luke Nightingale.

Of course, the rest of the non-league world automatically thought the Terras were splashing their money around. There was some irony here, considering the club was at one time £250,000 in debt. With the spotlight on the Wessex Stadium for much of the year, Claridge did well to cajole his charges into an eight-point lead by the New Year. It could not last and the Terras slowly but surely blew a gasket.

Injuries started to strike the thin squad and, when they suffered a 1-0 home defeat to Crawley in the early part of this year during an encounter in which the visitor's goalkeeper, Andy Little, had been sent off and Claridge failed to convert a penalty, the impetus quickly went with the Sussex side.

Claridge's main bone of contention was he couldn't strengthen when he needed to, but with no extra money forthcoming, the former Weymouth player - he had turned out in their colours in the late eighties - had to make do and, as a consequence, their form took a turn for the worse.

By March, the situation at the top of the table was tight and it took Crawley's 2-1 win over Weymouth at the Broadfield Stadium for the Sussex side - who had been eyeing the top position with increasing interest - to finally hit first position. It was an advantage which they were never to relinquish.

The Reds' manager, Francis Vines, was then able to strengthen his squad at a crucial time following that Weymouth game which was watched by a record 4,500+ crowd and that ultimately proved to be the difference between the two sides. Vines - a former minor non-league player - should take the credit as well, as he kept his side motivated where necessary and displayed the tactical acumen to more than match the other sides in the division.

There had been a fair share of apprehension when he took over the Broadfield Stadium reins in Spring 2003 but his shear commitment to the cause drove the club to the title charge and promotion into the Conference top division. And to think the Reds had only initially taken two points from the opening three games. For the large part of the opening months of the season they had pottered in and around the seventh position they had finished in the season before and a dodgy Christmas and New Year period

was only enlivened by that win down on the South Coast. Two of their eventual six defeats came during the early months of 2004, at which stage Crawley were still not looking like promotion material.

However, the Weymouth express was quickly coming off the rails and, combined with Vines' team collecting 36 out of 42 available points from the start of February, another defeat of Weymouth and the addition of players such as Rob Traynor and Fiston Manuella brought the Championship to Sussex on Easter Bank Holiday Monday with a win at Welling United, with leading scorer Charlie MacDonald amongst the goals.

In contrast, the Terras limped into second place, which was only confirmed on the last day when they overcame relegated Grantham while Stafford Rangers - the nearest challengers - achieved one point from their final two games, at Weston-super-Mare and Dover.

That is not to say the 2003/04 campaign wasn't a bad one for Phil Robinson's Stafford outfit either as they frequently challenged the leading two. Despite having the dangerous Danny Davidson and Neil Grayson - the veteran was signed towards the end of the season - Robinson had only a small squad to play with and the lack of numbers ultimately told in the final finish.

An anticipated title challenger, Nuneaton Borough, had an indifferent return to the Southern League. The former Conference side began the season well, with manager Alan Lewer leading his experienced side into contention. However, a behind the scenes falling out coupled with some indifferent results saw the ex-Telford boss eventually depart, to be replaced by the much travelled Roger Ashby.

Worcester City experienced problems of a different kind, namely financial, but still managed a finish of fifth, while Hinckley United and Newport County filled the next two positions. Former St Albans boss, Gary Roberts, enjoyed a good season with his Cambridge City side, while Welling, managed by former Manchester United star Paul Parker, flattered to deceive by ending up the season in ninth.

Frank Gregan used all his experience and know-how from years guiding sides around the non-league scene to manoeuvre Weston-Super-Mare into tenth. But that was not without a controversial end, as their home game late in April with Stafford was called off after a match official injured himself. The two teams could not decide on a replacement.

As it was, they eventually replayed the game on Thursday at the end of the season and Weston won 5-1 against a tired Rangers side. This was a move which was looked on dubiously by other sides who were jostling for that top 13 finish and qualification for one of the new Conference regional divisions.

Indeed, that factor meant there was a lot to play for right up until the final whistles across the country, with only five points separating ninth to 17th positions. Eastbourne Borough - promoted from the Eastern Division the previous season - together with Havant & Waterlooville and Moor Green all made the cut on the final day while Merthyr fell into the unpredictability of the Play-Offs with a 3-1 loss at another Play-Off side, Chelmsford, on the final day.

Those two sides were joined by Tiverton, Bath City and Dorchester Town and, in the end, Western Division Champions, Redditch United. The latter joined in the end of season dogfight after battling their way past Eastern title winners, Kings Lynn. Redditch produced a stunning 3-0 victory at Merthyr to qualify for Conference North. Meanwhile Tiverton edged past Chelmsford, and Dorchester came through a difficult away tie at Bath - who had won five of their last five regular league games - 4-2 to set up a tense final play-off.

That play-off game was played at St James Park, Exeter because Tiverton had accidentally arranged a rock concert at their Ladysmead ground on May 8th and the lack of home advantage told as Dorchester's golden oldies, Paul Wood and Matty Holmes, played a large part in their 3-1 victory.

Joining Merthyr, Chelmsford and Tiverton in dropping down a level are Dover (a rapid slide, having been playing Conference football two years ago), FA Trophy winners, Hednesford, Chippenham and Grantham. Meanwhile, the Dr Martens League Cup went to champions Crawley who achieved a 2-0 win at Moor Green to deservedly take the double.

In the Eastern Division, a three-way season-long battle eventually saw the title head towards Norfolk and champions Kings Lynn. It proved to be a strange season, as they had lost the services of manager Peter Morris mid-campaign but joint assistant bosses, Kevin Boon and Darren Bloodworth, maintained the momentum to seal the title at Fisher Athletic with a 2-0 victory on the final day of the season. Forwards Dale Watkins and Dave Staff had supreme campaigns and contributed much to the final goals for total of 90 and an FA Trophy run which ended in defeat to former league side Exeter City.

Kings Lynn had their work cut out through, because East Anglian neighbours, Histon, under the charge of former Cambridge player, Steve Fallon, went unbeaten for much of the opening months of the season, with the brothers Ian and Adrian Cambridge proving effective along with names such as Neil Munns and Jamie Barker.

There is no doubt the small Cambridgeshire club have the capacity to challenge in the Dr Martens Premier Division next year, while Tonbridge Angels fans will be deeply disappointed at how events turned out following a season in which they sat in top spot for so long. They were hit by financial problems after the loss of their main sponsor, leading to management and player defections, but they still hung on for much of the rest of the season, only to run out of puff late on.

The clubs from fourth to eighth also qualified for the Premier set-up and one of those, Eastleigh, made the perfect step up from the Wessex League last season by finishing fourth and were well ahead of Nick Holmes' Salisbury City, Folkestone Invicta - who included a 20+ unbeaten game run in their year - and Stamford.

In contrast to the Premier Division, the clamour for a top eight position was less tight as seven points divided seventh to ninth where Burgess Hill - the defending Sussex League Champions - made an impressive adjustment to a higher standard of football. Elsewhere, Sittingbourne - managed by former Leeds goalkeeper, Mark Beeney - made a late late run for the top eight finish, but just left it a bit too late, while Bashley and Ashford Town (Kent) all had chances for the top half of the table but flattered to deceive right at the end.

Towards the bottom, former Premier Division side Hastings Town suffered a surprisingly poor season while Newport (IOW) hit severe cash flow problems and only just survived the season by the skin of their teeth. Bottom two sides Erith & Belvedere and Fleet Town were both cast adrift right from the season's start and were undoubtedly the division's poorest sides.

In the Western Division, champions Redditch did their hardest work in the opening months of the season and, by the time anyone noticed, had stretched out what appeared to be an unassailable lead. Every team has bad spells sometime during the eight-month league campaign and United chose theirs towards the close of the year. In the end it took a final day win at one of the league's front runners, Cirencester, coupled with Gloucester's loss at home to Ilkeston, to finally decide the destination of the Western Division gong for the 2003/04 campaign.

In fact, as mentioned, United took so much heart from their last day win that they overcame Kings Lynn in the first of the end of season play-offs and then surprisingly won at Merthyr Tydfil to shoot up two levels of the newly reconstituted pyramid and win promotion to the new Conference North division.

Chris Burns' Gloucester City side performed a late charge towards the top spot but failed at the last moment, with midfielder Jimmy Cox again shining out, while four other clubs earned a foot up into the Premier Division. Amongst them were Halesowen who lost manager Brendan Phillips but recovered to regain their Premier status at the first time of asking, and the students of Team Bath who followed their Western League promotion with a sixth place finish. Bromsgrove, where experienced manager George Rooney lasted less then three quarters of the campaign, and Ilkeston just missed out from finishing in those coveted positions.

Elsewhere in the league, Mangotsfield waved goodbye to Andy Black and said hello to former Tiverton assistant boss, Martyn Grimshaw, and their season was epitomised by their final goals for and against record of 70-70 and their last day 9-0 defeat of relegated Shepshed Dynamo.

Of the other sides making up the numbers, Swindon Supermarine got through three managers including former Chippenham boss, Tommy Saunders, while Yate Town slowly acclimatised to being back in Southern League football having spent some years in the Cherry Red set up.

The fact that Cinderford Town and Shepshed finished bottom was hardly surprising as the lower rung of the famous league prepares for a new start and a refreshed constitution. This season the whole of the Southern league heads into the unknown. Many will be pondering what is just around the corner?

Howard Milton

Ryman Review

It was a case of fourth time lucky, as Jeff King led Canvey Island to the Ryman Premier Division Championship and into the Conference by a whopping 19 point margin and with seven games to spare. Lee Boylan claimed the golden boot yet again with 42 of the team's 106 strikes but, in an intriguing Autumn, there was little to indicate the eventual magnitude of their lead. Back in August, all eyes were on Essex, as Grays and Hornchurch, (the latter replacing Marsden with former Aldershot boss George Borg in the close season), both looking likely to provide a stiff challenge to the Gulls as they announced their move to full-time. However, it was Bognor Regis Town who got off to a flyer on the first day by beating Braintree 4-1, with Hitchin Town also getting off to a good start. Much fancied Kettering Town were shocked on the Bank Holiday weekend as Braintree recorded their first win of the season at Rockingham Road and, by the 1st September, Carshalton, tipped by many to be relegated, led the table, with Bognor and Hitchin just behind. Both Harrow and Heybridge had yet to register a win, whilst Hayes were yet to be beaten.

Carshalton showed their sticking power with one of the matches of the season as they came from 2-0 down to beat Kettering 3-2 on 8th September. However, it was to be a much tougher start for rookie managers Justin Edinburgh and John Dreyer, who found their respective Billericay and Maidenhead charges struggling at the foot of the table. Bedford Town followed on from their impressive close to the previous year by making a good start this time around. However, the following month would see Kevin Wilson make the surprise switch to Aylesbury. Carshalton's run of five wins in seven, which saw them head the table, came to a surprise halt at Heybridge as the Swifts ran out 4-0 winners, a mere two weeks after the Kettering comeback. Canvey had started to shift through the gears as they moved into second by the end of September, closely followed by Bognor and Hornchurch. Further down the table, Kettering were stuttering, there was a first win for Harrow, and the poor form of St Albans City (pacesetters at this time last year), would soon lead to the departure of Steve Cook.

By early October, Canvey were top as Premier Division new boys Carshalton began to falter. At the other end, Harrow's run of three straight wins hauled them away from trouble, as Bishops Stortford began to be sucked into the basement. Moving into November, there was another managerial change, as Eddie Stein left Harrow, after a 3-2 home loss to Braintree Town, who had just dismissed Gary Bellamy. Canvey won their most important game so far as they claimed a 2-0 success at Carshalton in mid-November, allowing Hayes to take second place. Hornchurch, Hendon and Thurrock made up the remainder of the top six. Hornchurch gave indications that they were not overawed by their first season in the Premier Division as they recorded a significant scoreless draw with free-scoring Canvey in late November. However, their local rivals Billericay continued to struggle at the bottom.

Many people look for a pivotal moment when analysing how a title was won and lost, and, for me, that day seemed to be the 13th December. Canvey travelled to Basingstoke and won 2-1 with a goal deep into stoppage time, and with nearest challengers Hornchurch, Hendon and Hayes all finding their games postponed, the Gulls opened up a seven point lead over Carshalton at the top, and were in a more comfortable position than Aldershot at the same time the season before. However, there were many other sides going for promotion through the top 13 as well, with Heybridge Swifts catching the eye, as strong Autumn form took them from the bottom four and into the top half. A week later, while Canvey were increasing their lead to ten points, Kevin Wilson's honeymoon period at Aylesbury was definitely over as he resigned after only two months, following a damaging 1-0 home reverse to Northwood; he would soon appear at Kettering Town, his third Ryman League club of the season.

Moving into the New Year, it was looking ominous for the rest, as none of Canvey Island's challengers were able to keep up with their remarkable consistency. Meanwhile, Billericay were becoming a tougher nut to crack and looked like they may reach the Play-Offs, and Mark Nicholls, the former Chelsea striker, was inspiring Northwood to better form. St Albans City, under Steve Castle, were still flirting with the bottom four, however, and Hayes were in free-fall as a goal drought kicked in. By 7th February, the table toppers found themselves an astounding 21 points clear, and the only question seemed to be - How many would they win it by? Bishops Stortford were making a sustained Spring bid for the Conference South, but Aylesbury, winless since December, were beginning to be cut adrift. Valentine's Day saw the continuation of Sutton's free-scoring form, and the debut of Steve Watts for St Albans in a significant 4-2 win at Braintree - he would be the key figure as the Saints claimed a place in the Conference South via the Play-Offs.

With the top of the table more or less settled as the season entered March, eyes turned to the sides hoping to feature in Conference South. Hayes arrested their slide with a winning run to all but assure their place, and borderline cases such as Maidenhead and Bedford Town had an encouraging month too. Graham Roberts made a return to the Ryman Premier Division as manager at Braintree Town, and led his new side to a 1-0 win at Billericay in his first game. However, he couldn't prevent the Iron finishing in the bottom four, and they parted company at the end of the season. There was a shock on the 13th March, as Sutton gave Canvey their first home loss of the season, 3-1, although the Gulls were still sitting pretty on top of a huge lead. However, teams such as Kettering and Basingstoke were less happy as they continued to oscillate either side of the vital 13th place.

By early April, though, the picture was becoming clearer, as Thurrock, Sutton, Carshalton, Grays, Hayes and Hornchurch had all but booked their Conference South berths. Canvey made the title officially theirs by winning 2-1 at Thurrock on Good Friday. By Easter Monday, with three games left to play, six teams were chasing four spots: Ford, Basingstoke, Kettering, Bognor, Bedford and Maidenhead. The following Saturday, Bognor took their place, as Bedford dropped out of contention and, the last day, 1st May, saw a number of issues settled, as Maidenhead and Ford beat Basingstoke to the last two automatic spots, but Town would join them following Hendon's withdrawal. Sutton, who couldn't stop scoring, climbed above Thurrock and Hendon to take second in the final table, while Grays and Hornchurch, the sides with the best defences in the league, sat in fifth and sixth respectively. Hitchin edged ahead of Northwood to take the final Play-Off spot.

DIVISION ONE NORTH

Cheshunt, fresh from their Division Two championship win, opened the new season with a 1-0 win against a Tilbury side who struggled at the foot of the table in the early stages. They soon followed this up with a stunning 7-3 win at Hemel Hempstead Town, struggling to live up to their pre-season billing. Yeading, who won the Bryco Cup the previous season, and gave a good account of themselves in defeat to Aldershot in the Charity Shield, were also challenging, accompanied by good starts from Dunstable Town, promoted from the Spartan South Midlands League. Chesham United, another side tipped to do well, had a woefully inconsistent start. Defeats, sprinkled with big wins such as the 8-2 beating of Wivenhoe, highlighted their inconsistency. Cheshunt

were proving particularly lethal on the road as the season entered September as Darrell Cox and Leon Archer were carrying on where they had left off the season before when their partnership had yielded 40 goals. Their promoted colleagues, Leyton, were also building a reputation as a side who were hard to beat, as the three promoted outfits were all giving an excellent account of themselves. It wasn't until September that Enfield entered the fray, as they were suspended from league action because of problems with their ground-share at Boreham Wood. However, they still managed to beat Hemel Hempstead in the FA Cup in late August.

Moving into November, Cheshunt were top. Yeading, Dunstable, Harlow and Leyton were just behind, and Hemel Hempstead were recovering from a poor start to challenge for the top six. Boreham Wood, who were always a threat with former Kingstonian frontman Sammy Winston contributing 32 goals, stayed in contention as well. However, the team to watch in the run-up to Christmas were Chesham United. They brought John Lawford back to lead the line, and he formed a devastating partnership with Gary Sippetts as they combined for an outstanding 56 goals by the time the season ended. There was also a surprise appearance for Wingate & Finchley in the top six as the North London side made a concerted bid for promotion. At the midway point of the season, Cheshunt remained top.

However, the New Year saw something of a shift. As injury affected the Cox-Archer strike-force at Cheshunt, the Ambers began to lose consistency, whilst Yeading gained it, helped by the 33 league goals of Golden Boot winner DJ Campbell. Leyton had also entered the equation and slowly became the West London club's main challengers following a 2-1 win over Cheshunt in February. Looking at the top six, the challenges of Wealdstone and Wingate were rapidly fading, but Boreham Wood's change of manager, bringing in ex-Barton Rovers chief Ian Allison, looked to be reaping dividends, as Allison's arrival was followed up with several important wins. By the end of the month, it was only the top three who looked in contention for the title.

As the season moved into March, there was a significant change at the wrong end of the table, as Barking & East Ham United moved off the bottom (following an impressive 2-1 win at Wealdstone on the 13th) at the expense of Enfield. A week later, Wealdstone embarked on a stunning run of nine wins in eleven to achieve promotion via the Play-Offs. At the time, Arlesey looked a decent bet to join them, as a fine run of free-scoring form saw them enter the top six. Easter Monday's results left Yeading needing to win two of their last four games to take the title, with Leyton the only remaining challengers. However, it was an intriguing battle for the remaining spaces, as Wealdstone's priceless win at Arlesey had seen them enter the top six, and significantly boost their goal difference in an 8-0 win the following week at Enfield (scoreless at half-time!). With a week left, Yeading won the title by winning 2-1 at Leyton, but Wealdstone's late run looked to have been in vain as a home reverse to Hemel put them out of the top seven, with one match left. However, a complex last day saw Chesham secure promotion with a 4-0 win at Barking, Dunstable added promotion to their Bryco Cup Final place and, by a quirk of the fixtures, Hemel's victory over Arlesey allowed Wealdstone into the top seven after their win at East Thurrock United.

DIVISION ONE SOUTH

Lewes were the early pacesetters, now under the charge of Steven King, after going very close to gate-crashing the top two the previous season. Hampton & Richmond Borough, who were tipped to do well under Alan Devonshire, started their campaign with a 0-0 draw at Ashford Town (Middlesex). As the season neared the completion of its first month, Lewes stayed in pole position, but Croydon Athletic were surprisingly challenging as well, whilst Staines Town, expected to be near the top under the new management of Steve Cordery and Craig Maskell (fresh from Aylesbury), had a slower than expected start. Slough Town, now ground-sharing with Windsor & Eton after the lease expired at Wexham Park, found themselves in the early chasing pack alongside their landlords.

Early September saw Dulwich Hamlet

emerge as real challengers after going so close the previous season, as the 28 goals of Omari Coleman kept them in contention (almost) until the end. The most important match of the season so far was on 22nd September as Windsor & Eton hosted Lewes and lost 2-1, not only allowing the East Sussex side to strengthen their lead but, significantly, the only reverse the Royalists would suffer in the first 31 league games. Staines had recovered to move up to second, with Worthing tucked in behind. Croydon Athletic beat Slough to maintain their surprisingly lofty standing. As the Autumn progressed, Lewes stayed on top, but the struggling trio of Metropolitan Police, Corinthian Casuals and Epsom & Ewell found wins hard to come by. The usual suspects were around the top in early November: Windsor & Eton, Hampton & Richmond, Staines and Worthing but, buoyed by the form of Mark Tompkins, who would eventually contribute 26 goals, Whyteleafe were also in the top six.

Windsor & Eton and Lewes slowly began to pull away, as it seemed they would sew up the top two places. How wrong that prediction was. Hampton & Richmond Borough, who were proving hard to beat, kept their hopes alive with a key 3-1 win at Worthing on 6th December. However, a week later, Staines announced their arrival by handing Lewes a then rare 3-1 reverse. Ian Hodge set the tone for a prolific second half of the season in which he would claim the golden boot by hitting four in Slough's 7-1 win against Epsom & Ewell. On the Saturday before Christmas, there were significant developments as Windsor & Eton went top following a 2-0 win over Staines after Lewes' match fell foul of the weather. Whyteleafe, meanwhile, had gone into freefall to be replaced by a Leatherhead outfit in red-hot form, and their challenge would continue well into the New Year. Windsor & Eton also held the lead of the division in mid-February until their second league defeat of the season, 3-0 at Ashford Town (Middlesex), ushered in an unnerving period for both of the top two, as their lead shrunk alarmingly as they struggled for any sort of consistency. Dulwich and Hampton sensed a chance of the title, but didn't always take full advantage of the top pair's slip-ups. Lewes' 6-1 reverse at Banstead was probably the pick of them all. The Royalists were just about clinging to top spot going into March as their defence was better than Lewes, but injuries to key players, particularly Keith Scott, began to affect their strike rate. Despite that, the title seemed to be theirs when they recorded a priceless 2-1 win at Lewes. However, they failed to push on, and Worthing were emerging as a new challenger, eventually nipping ahead of Windsor for second, who really stuttered towards the finish line. Lewes, having sorted out their defence, recovered to take the title. With two weeks left, the top seven was confirmed, and it was just a case of who would face who in the Play-Offs. Lewes took the title with a game left, and Staines Town jumped in front of Dulwich for the final automatic spot on the last day.

THE PLAY-OFFS

With the Ryman objection to restructuring lodged in October and thrown out in late February, the Play-Off to decide the final Conference South participants went ahead, but not without its problems. The action started with Lewes travelling to Division One North champions Yeading, and winning 1-0 through Whiteman. On the evening of that May Day Bank Holiday, seventh in Division One South and North clashed at Champion Hill, as Wealdstone earned the spare Premier Division place by winning 5-4 on penalties after a 2-2 draw with Dulwich Hamlet. Lewes progressed to an away tie at Basingstoke, coming from behind to win 4-1 (although Basingstoke would still qualify for the Conference South after Hendon's withdrawal). Bedford Town knocked out Hitchin 3-1 in a derby match, and Harrow were edged out on penalties after a scoreless draw with Kingstonian and Heybridge were undone by ten man St Albans City who enjoyed a last gasp 4-3 extra-time win. Confusion ensued as the final pairings were changed just a day before the games were played, but the Saints surpassed themselves as they trailed 3-1 to Bedford Town at the break but snatched a Conference South place with an amazing 5-4 win. Warren Haughton ensured Lewes' elevation with the only goal against Kingstonian.

Gerard Butler

Unibond Review

Back in August, the hot favourites for the Unibond Premier Division title were Southport. Although they had suffered in the Conference the year before, the Sandgrounders still had impressive resources, and were expected to bounce back. An opening day win away at Wakefield & Emley looked like setting the tone for their season, as they overcame an Emley side with six debutants after a turbulent close season at Belle Vue. Newly promoted Spennymoor United also got off to a strong start, winning 3-1 away at Marine. There was a 0-0 draw against Altrincham for Alfreton Town, but they quickly found some form and won their next three games in style, beating Gainsborough Trinity 4-2, Whitby Town 4-0 away, and local rivals Hucknall Town 1-0 to move top of the table. Blyth Spartans were showing impressive if somewhat surprising form as they won their opening three games to keep pace with Southport, but there was no such luck for Lancaster City, expected to do well, but without a point from their opening three games.

As September came, the Dolly Blues were still struggling as they went down 3-0 to the pacesetters, Alfreton, who stayed ahead of Southport only because they had played a game more. The Sandgrounders inflicted Whitby Town's fourth straight defeat to maintain their 100% record. After a slow start, Vauxhall Motors showed their potential with a 6-0 thrashing of Bradford Park Avenue as Terry Fearns netted a hat-trick. Gary Sampson did likewise as Play-Off-winners Radcliffe Borough breezed past Emley, who were already struggling badly under Ian Banks.

Southport's winning run came to a sudden end a week later when Hucknall beat them 4-0, but Alfreton remained out in front after another away win at Marine. Harrogate Town's strong start continued at the expense of Lancaster as they won 4-1, while Vauxhall looked to have found their scoring touch, netting six again as they beat the fast-fading Blyth 6-3. Despite an inauspicious start, Droylsden were quietly accumulating points, and a 2-0 win over Burscough moved them into the top six before their progress was dented with a 4-1 defeat at Southport. Hucknall were also stuttering, as struggling Lancaster beat them 3-1. Spennymoor were suffering no such problems though, and they continued their good form at the expense of a disappointing Stalybridge Celtic. A week later, they even took three points off Alfreton, allowing Hucknall to take full advantage and go top of the table by virtue of a 1-0 win over Harrogate. Southport stuttered again as Ashton United became the latest team to beat them. The Sandgrounders parted company with boss Mickey Walsh at the end of September, and would appoint Liam Watson by mid-October.

Moving into October, Alfreton - struggling since the departure of Ryan France to Hull - stalled again, as bottom club Burscough shocked them with a 4-1 win. Hucknall could only draw against Marine, meaning that Barrow were the main beneficiaries after they came from behind to beat Emley. Droylsden also stayed in touch after putting four past Frickley Athletic. Worksop had been slow to deliver on pre-season expectations, but they saw off Vauxhall in a seven-goal thriller to move up on the leaders. Radcliffe were surprising a few people as well, and a Jody Banim hat-trick gave them a 3-1 win over high-flying Harrogate. A week later, Hucknall and Alfreton did get some breathing space at the top as the chasing pack all drew, with Harrogate and Droylsden sharing the points from a thrilling 4-4 draw.

Barrow's charge towards the top was halted in early November as Hucknall beat them to extend their lead at the top. Worksop went sixth as they defeated a fading Southport side and Vauxhall fans were again treated to a feast of goals, but they wouldn't have enjoyed most of them as they lost 6-2 to struggling Bradford Park Avenue. A week later, it was all change at the top as Alfreton and Hucknall were both held to draws, allowing Droylsden to sneak through and go top after a win at Spennymoor. Emley finally got a win - their first in eight - when they saw off Lancaster 1-0, but they couldn't move off the bottom as Burscough picked up a point at Whitby Town. Jody Banim fired his 20th goal of the season to give Radcliffe a win over Stalybridge, but with the player attracting interest from bigger clubs, Radcliffe would eventually succumb and sell him to Shrewsbury Town.

Alfreton fell further off the pace with a shock defeat at Frickley and, with Droylsden losing the East Manchester derby at Ashton United, Hucknall once again closed up the lead with a win over Vauxhall Motors. Life after Banim began badly at Radcliffe as they lost 4-1 at Altrincham, and it got worse a week later when Hucknall put six past them. Emley at last moved off the bottom after they came away from their trip to Stalybridge with a point.

Droylsden weren't enjoying games against their local rivals, and dropped another two derby points at the hands of Ashton. Southport boss Liam Watson came under increasing pressure as they were held to a 1-1 draw at home to Emley, now under the new management duo of Ray Dennis and Paul David. Meanwhile, after briefly sparking into life in October, Vauxhall had dipped almost as far as the bottom three, and weren't helped by a 1-1 draw against lowly Whitby. With a number of games called off because of bad weather, Barrow were able to move fourth with a win over Gainsborough. They may have sold their best striker, but it was the defence that was the main concern for Radcliffe as they again shipped a hat-full, losing 4-1 against Worksop. Emley showed little resolve to get off the bottom as they threw away a 2-0 lead to draw with Burscough.

February brought a little respite for Watson at Southport as they thrashed Whitby 5-0 but they remained eighth in the table. Lancaster's recovery from a poor start was going well and they posted a warning to others with a 6-0

win over Spennymoor to move into the all important top 13. Droylsden were getting desperate for their run of Tameside derbies to end as Stalybridge were the next to take points off them, allowing Hucknall to pull away at the top with a 1-0 win over Blyth. However, a week later, the Bloods' form was no better out of Manchester, and they lost at Lancaster to allow Hucknall to open up a four point gap.

Early March saw some top v bottom clashes as Hucknall saw off Burscough, but Droylsden came from behind to beat Emley and keep up the pressure. Harrogate beat Barrow to go level on points with the Cumbrians in third. Alfreton's 4-0 win over Marine helped them stay in touch in fifth. Wins for Stalybridge, Vauxhall and Radcliffe put all three sides into serious contention for the Conference North slots. As the month went on, Hucknall played their games in hand, and opened up a seemingly unassailable eleven point lead, aided by Droylsden's defeat at the hands of Altrincham. Southport moved back into the top six with a win over Harrogate, whose challenge was dented further by a 3-1 defeat by Droylsden a week later. Hucknall's lead was cut to nine points after they were beaten by Barrow. Burscough defeated Blyth to move out of the bottom three, while Spennymoor's spell near the top of the table became a distant memory as defeat against Lancaster saw them slip into the drop zone. Emley's fate at the bottom of the table looked sealed after they threw away yet another lead as they lost 5-3 to Runcorn.

Hucknall's lead at the top allowed them to wrap up the title over the Easter weekend with a 3-0 win over Worksop on the Saturday. Monday's visitors, second placed Droylsden, could do nothing to close the gap but they did their best to spoil the party by holding the champions to a 1-1 draw. By then, both teams knew that they wouldn't be promoted because of ground regulations, which left the door open for Barrow if they could overtake Droylsden and move second. However, a 1-1 draw against Ashton dented their charge. Emley eventually succumbed to the inevitable with a 2-1 defeat at the hands of local rivals Frickley Athletic. Vauxhall enjoyed a 4-3 win over Stalybridge before Terry Fearns' 35th goal of the season eased them past Marine and secured their place in the Conference North. Despite the defeat, Celtic joined them in the new league after beating Southport.

Barrow maintained their push for promotion with a 4-2 win over Worksop, moving to within three points of Droylsden. Hucknall were able to ease off the gas with a 0-0 draw against lowly Bradford. Southport drew 0-0 with Ashton and Lancaster lost 1-0 to Gainsborough, but other results meant that both they and Harrogate were guaranteed a Conference North place. Altrincham edged past Whitby Town 1-0 to hold on to the last qualifying spot.

By the time the final day came, a midweek defeat against Alfreton had ended Barrow's promotion hopes, and they threw in the towel by surrendering a 2-0 lead at Stalybridge who came back to earn a draw. Ashton missed out when they finished on the wrong end of a seven goal thriller against Harrogate, pushing them into the Play-Offs. A last minute goal against Radcliffe earned Burscough a place in the Play-Offs at the expense of Blyth and Frickley.

Despite having narrowly avoided straight relegation, Burscough went into the Play-Offs as the form team, and they saw off Marine 3-1 in the Quarter-Finals. Ashton needed extra-time to see off Division One Champions Hyde 2-1, while Bradford got the better of Spennymoor. After a goal each in extra-time, Whitby and Radcliffe were tied at 2-2 and the game was eventually decided on penalties, 8-7 to Radcliffe. In the Semi-Finals, Burscough's form held as they beat Radcliffe 2-0, while Bradford edged out Ashton. The Final at Bradford finished 0-0 in normal time, but extra-time goals from Stephen Oleksewycz and James Russell took Bradford Park Avenue into the Conference North.

Division One

Newly promoted Prescot Cables were the first team to fall victim to the charge of Matlock Town, as they set out their stall on the opening day. However, another new side in the league, Bridlington, took a significant scalp, beating eventual champions Hyde United 3-1. Ossett Town got a warning of a difficult season ahead as they were thrashed 7-0 by Workington.

Bishop Auckland were among the sides making the early running as Hyde continued to struggle early on. After three wins, Matlock's good run came to an abrupt end when they lost 5-2 at Lincoln United. However, Prescot Cables, undefeated on their way to promotion into Division One, bounced back from the opening day loss to post three wins together in August.

Leek Town were also going strong, and they beat struggling Kendal Town to move top of the league early in October. Matlock, meanwhile, were still there or thereabouts, beating Farsley Celtic to stay in touch.

It was Hyde who needed to play catch up, and they beat Workington Town to take advantage of Matlock's defeat at Witton Albion. Bridlington Town had started well but lost ground with defeat at Bamber Bridge.

Matlock opened up a gap at the top after they won their six-pointer against second placed Leek Town, while Gateshead were up to within a point of Leek after beating Witton Albion. Bridlington's defeat at the hands of Belper Town let in Prescot Cables who saw off Farsley.

In early December, Hyde moved up to second as they beat Belper to take advantage of Matlock's defeat at Bishop Auckland. Nearer the bottom, the league's whipping boys Ossett Town delivered a reverse dose as they saw off Colwyn Bay to begin a rapid change of form, having been stuck on five points long into the season.

Matlock and Hyde began to pull away at the top as several games were called off over the Christmas period, and when Matlock lost 2-0 at Chorley, Hyde moved top with a 5-2 win over Ossett. With Leek and Lincoln sharing the points in a 1-1 draw, Hyde went six points clear.

In early March, Hyde beat Matlock 2-1 to move four points clear, with Lincoln moving second after a 4-0 win at Rossendale United. Bishop Auckland's enforced ground-share with Spennymoor got off to a bad start as they lost their opening two games at Brewery Field to slip away from the leading pack. Farsley Celtic were having no such trouble though, and victory over Lincoln helped them into second place. When Matlock were held to a draw by Colwyn Bay, Hyde moved five points clear, while Lincoln went third with a win over Workington. Ossett Town's charge for a Premier Division place continued with a 2-0 win over Gateshead, but results above them meant that it was beginning to look as though they had left it too late. They had three points deducted for a breach of the rules, and that was looking as if it would be extremely costly. Leek Town were the next to fall victim to their charge and, as Lincoln were held to a draw by Bishop Auckland, the top three pulled away. A week later, Hyde lost 1-0 at Chorley to allow Matlock to pull level. When Matlock were held to a 1-1 draw at Bridlington, Hyde regained the initiative with a 2-1 win at Rossendale. Farsley remained third, but their hopes of catching the leaders were dented by a 3-3 draw against Gateshead. Lincoln were assured of fourth despite a 0-0 draw with Bishop Auckland after Leek lost at Chorley.

On the final day, Hyde romped home with a 4-0 win over North Ferriby United, while Matlock were held to a 0-0 draw by bottom side Kendal Town. Farsley beat Leek to stay third ahead of Lincoln who signed off with a 5-0 win over Workington. Ossett's brave bid fell three points short - the same number they were deducted - after a 2-1 win at Chorley. However, following Telford's demise, Ashton were promoted to the Conference North, allowing Ossett (who finished 14th in the league) to join the Premier Division.

Ian Parker

FA Trophy Review

For the second season in succession, the FA Trophy Final was contested by two teams from outside the Conference and again it was the year of the underdog, in this case Hednesford Town, who defied the odds to lift the trophy and deny their so-called classier opponents an unprecedented league and cup double. Who would have thought it?

Indeed, Hednesford's stunning 3-2 win against Canvey Island at Villa Park brought back memories of the 2003 Final when Burscough, who had struggled all season in the Unibond Premier League, rose to the occasion to beat Tamworth 2-1, a side that had stormed to the Dr Martens Championship and gained promotion to the Conference, and in turn denied them an historic double.

On paper Canvey were overwhelming favorites and, for a side who basically had the Ryman League title wrapped up by Christmas, a side that could boast a century of goals and points to show for a breathtaking campaign, and a side that boasted 47-goal hitman, Lee Boylan, it would have taken a brave punter to back against them.

On paper Hednesford might as well have not turned up and, after an awful campaign in the Dr Martens Premier Division, not many would have given them a prayer against their record-breaking counterparts. But football is not played on paper and Hednesford obviously did not read the script. They duly rose to the occasion, defended doggedly, controlled the ball in the middle of the park and were sharp in the final third and thoroughly deserved to take the spoils and did so with a magnificent 3-2 win.

Although the showpiece finale at Villa Park is given intense media spotlight with a nationwide audience on Sky television, avid followers of the Non-League game know that the excitement and passion starts from the Preliminary Round in November. Each year more than 200 clubs enter the competition and this season was no different, with local pride also at stake, for example when Telford and Shrewsbury locked horns in the Quarter-Final. It made for one of the most exciting competitions in years. The competition began with a bang as the Preliminary Round got under way. Almost 200 goals were scored in an action packed round. There was an impressive win for Guiseley who put seven past Kidsgrove Athletic. Enfield, twice previous winners of this competition, also found their shooting boots in a 7-3 win over Epsom & Ewell. Meanwhile, Team Bath, the university side that grabbed the media spotlight with a fantastic run in the FA Cup in 2002/03, continued their knockout competition success with a 2-0 win against Banbury.

The road to Villa Park for Hednesford began at the First Round stage and a tricky tie on an awkward pitch at Shepshed Dynamo, who themselves had come away with a 2-1 victory at Solihull Borough in the previous round. However, Mark Danks latched onto a poor back pass from Steve Prindiville, to guide the ball over the line and send his side through to Round Two. Other highlights saw Runcorn destroy Bishop Auckland 7-0. Weymouth, managed by former Leicester City and Millwall striker, Steve Claridge, make it through with a 5-2 win over Merthyr Tydfil. Meanwhile Kingstonian, who are one of only seven clubs to have won the Trophy twice, began their search for a third success with a 2-0 win over Stamford. Another one of those seven clubs, Altrincham, also made it into Round Two after a 2-1 win at Gateshead. There were also victories for Yeading and Wealdstone against Dulwich Hamlet and East Thurrock United respectively.

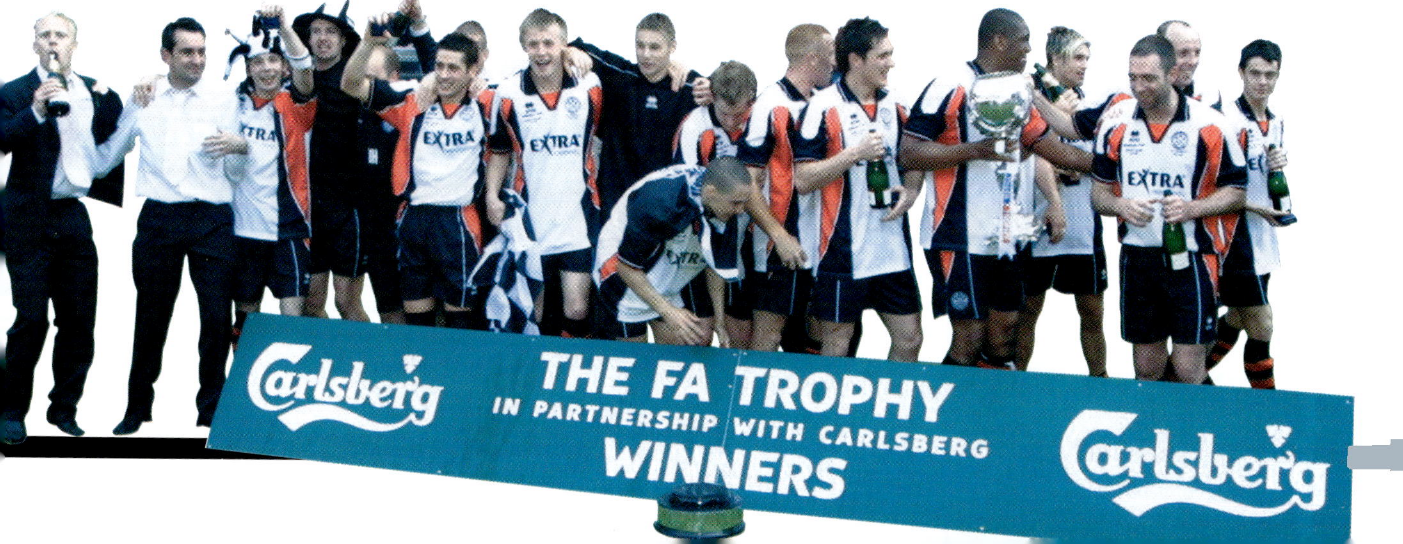

Lifting the trophy would have been the last thing on Hednesford's mind as they struggled past Lancaster City in Round Two. Steve Anthrobus' headed equaliser saved their blushes after Tony Sullivan had put Lancaster in front and on course for the Third Round. The replay at Keys Park was another close affair but, in the end, a Steve Evans goal was just enough to send them through. No such problems for eventual beaten finalists Canvey Island on the other hand, who entered at the Second Round stage as they edged past Windsor & Eton. Jeff Minton stole the show with two second half goals as they eventually ran out 3-1 winners. There was also an exciting finale in the clash between Crawley Town and St Albans City. After a goalless first encounter, the replay was deadlocked at 1-1 after 90 minutes. Home advantage eventually told for Crawley, and three goals in extra-time sent them spinning into the Third Round. Meanwhile, previous winners Kingstonian's brief flirtation with the FA Trophy ended at this stage after a 2-0 home reverse at the hands of Bishops Stortford.

The Third Round brought the introduction of the Conference clubs. But one tie in particular jumped out when the draw was made. A repeat of last year's final between holders Burscough and beaten finalists Tamworth at Victoria Park. Revenge was sweet for Darron Gee's men as Rob Warner's strike gave Tamworth the victory and gained some retribution for their 2-1 defeat last May.

So, with the holders gone, attentions turned elsewhere and the performance of the round without doubt went to Canvey Island, after tearing apart Conference side Farnborough 6-0 at Park Lane. Lee Boylan and Ollie Berquez both grabbed hat-tricks as Canvey ran riot and, in truth, probably could have reached double figures, they were simply that good on the day. It was all a far cry from Farnborough's era under Graham Westley, who had led them out at Highbury in the FA Cup just a season prior. But Jeff King had no sympathy for sorry Farnborough. 'We thrashed them. That was probably our best performance of the season. Without exaggerating, we could have scored 12 or 15! Even the Farnborough people admitted that.'

Meanwhile, Hednesford eased into Round Four with a 2-0 home win against Gresley Rovers. Craig Dean's stunning volley set them on their way and Mark Danks duly rounded things off and sealed a comfortable victory.

To win any cup competition, a team needs some luck along the way and Hednesford's success did not go without the odd hiccup. A tough task awaited them in Round Four against a resolute Worthing side. After taking the lead through Danks, continuing his impressive record in the competition, they were pressed back and took a 'battering' according to manager Barry Powell and, after Sam Francis had levelled things up for Worthing, the two sides were forced to do it all over again in a replay. It mirrored the first game, as Francis cancelled out a Danks opener. The game was headed for an extra half hour before Steve Anthrobus put Hednesford into the Fifth Round with a late header.

Canvey Island progressed into the next round, with a 2-0 win at Stafford Rangers as they overcame a difficult pitch to sneak through, Lee Boylan and Chris Duffy on the score sheet.

There was also no shortage of shock results as Conference sides Stevenage and Forest Green crashed out against Hornchurch and Dover respectively. Also

heading out were Dagenham after going down 4-2 to Arlesey Town after a replay. Meanwhile Paul Barnes, who was so instrumental in helping York City dispatch Manchester United in the League Cup at Old Trafford in 1995, continued his love affair with cup competitions, as he smashed a hat-trick to help last season's beaten finalists Tamworth on their way to a 4-0 win at Marlow.

With the Ryman Premier Division all but in the bag, Canvey Island were starting to entertain the prospect of a return to Villa Park and the chance of repeating their 2001 FA Trophy success against Forest Green Rovers (and also the possibility of an unprecedented league and cup double). And they did that scenario no harm whatsoever with a resounding 4-0 success against Stalybridge Celtic - Lee Boylan grabbing a brace. However, they did not have it all their own way it has to be said, this win coming after they were forced to play out a goalless draw in the original tie but made sure with a marvellous display in the replay. Hednesford also sealed their place in the last eight with a 1-0 win against Dover. It was a tie that looked tricky on paper, seeing as Dover had dispatched Conference opposition in the previous round. However, not for the last time in the competition, Hednesford proved a few doubters wrong and Steve Anthrobus duly obliged to send the Midlanders marching on.

There were also wins for Aldershot, who got past season 2002/03 runners-up Tamworth, and Telford eased through at the expense of Margate to set up a mouthwatering Quarter-Final against local rivals Shrewsbury Town, who themselves won through by beating Altrincham.

After a 1-1 draw at Gay Meadow, the stage was set for a titanic battle at the New Bucks Head. And, on this occasion, home advantage paid dividends as goals from Rob Hulbert and Tony Naylor sealed a 2-1 win, to set up a two-legged Semi-Final clash with Ryman League Champions-elect Canvey Island who sealed their passage into the last four as they easily brushed aside ten-man Maidenhead United 4-0.

The other Semi would be contested between Aldershot, who came through a tricky Quarter-Final against Exeter, and Hednesford. Barry Powell's side continued to impress, seeing as they were having a torrid time in the league. Mark Danks, Chris Brindley and Danny McGhee were all on target as they put three past Hornchurch at Keys Park. The visitors bowed out in the last eight but can hold their heads high after shocking Conference outfits Stevenage and Burton Albion in earlier rounds.

So then to the last four. There was a possibility that the game between Telford and Canvey might not actually take place due to the periless financial position of the Staffordshire side. Jeff King referred to it as being 'a harrowing day for everyone'. The game did finally take place after quite a delay but, in the end, both sides played out a goalless draw. So, it would be winner takes all back at Park Lane - and it did not disappoint with some end to end, goal-mouth action. The two sides exchanged blows in 90 minutes, Telford drawing first blood only for Boylan to haul Canvey level. He then looked to have won the tie in extra-time only for Telford to draw themselves level with a glorious free-kick in the dying seconds. It would have to be decided on penalties to see who would go forward to Villa Park and a chance of lifting the Trophy, and it was Canvey who edged through after an emotional shootout.

For Telford it was heartbreaking. A side that had also reached the dizzy heights of the FA Cup Fourth Round, before bowing out to eventual finalists Millwall. A shame too for Mick Jones, who had worked tirelessly to get Telford where they were, but it was all in vain. Due to the club's sorry state, he would lose his job days later as Telford headed towards liquidation.

So, Canvey advanced to the final, but who would oppose them? Aldershot, third in the Conference, would clearly fancy themselves against a struggling Hednesford outfit. However, Barry Powell's men had other ideas, and goals from Mark Danks and Anthony Maguire stunned the Shots into silence, as the underdogs ran out comfortable 2-0 winners in the First Leg. Any hopes of a Shots comeback in the Second Leg was quashed just nine minutes in as Maguire netted again, to surely send the home side to Villa Park. Not even a late flurry from Aldershot could stop the Pitmen who sealed a 3-1 aggregate win.

So, to Villa Park and the 35th anniversary of the most prestigious

competition in Non-League football. Canvey were clear favorites, of that there no was question. Man-for-man, Canvey had the superior advantage. Not to mention a resounding Championship success and wins over Conference outfits Farnborough and Telford en route to the Final. They were hoping for a repeat of 2001 when they overcame Forest Green Rovers to lift the FA Trophy and were bidding to become only the eighth club in history to win it twice. Also at stake was that league and cup double, that would cap-off a tremendous record breaking season for them. King named five of the side that played in that 2001 Final.

One of the key talking points prior to kick-off was how Hednesford's Chris Brindley would match-up against Canvey goal machine Lee Boylan, with 47 goals going into this one, not to mention nine goals already in the competition.

A crowd of just over 6,500 witnessed this epic battle, as did viewers on Sky television. However, they must have been left scratching their heads at the interval, as Hednesford went in ahead thanks to a goal just before the half hour mark through Anthony Maguire.

It was expected that Canvey would stage a fightback and, no sooner had Lee Boylan restored parity just a minute after half-time, they went in front. Boylan was again involved, Ryan Young attempted to clear Boylan's chip and Chris Brindley could only help it over the line.

Many people would have thought, at that stage, that it was game set and match to Canvey. Not so. Les Hines' curling free-kick five minutes later squared it all up again at 2-2. With the game heading for extra-time, Chris Brindley stepped up and produced one of those special moments that will be talked about for years to come. With eight minutes to go, he unleashed a stunning volley into the top corner of the net to seal a remarkable 3-2 win. Barry Powell was ecstatic: 'To come here as a manager and to lead the team that you have built to victory is a fantastic moment and I am a proud man.'

Carl Field

FA Vase Review

The FA Vase culminated at Birmingham City's St Andrew's Stadium where, in a splendid advertisement for football at this level, Winchester City became Hampshire's first winners of the tournament as their sweet passing, panache and enterprising attacking play earned them a 2-0 victory over perennial bridesmaids, AFC Sudbury.

The entertaining final was a fitting conclusion to a competition that is very much on the up in terms of popularity and financial reward. This season saw 475 entrants, over twice the number of clubs involved when the competition replaced the old FA Amateur Cup in 1974. Prize money for this season's competition had likewise increased dramatically with the overall prize money for the tournament as a whole rising from £153,000 to £350,000. In reaching the final, Winchester and Sudbury each secured £15,700 and eventual winners, Winchester, would receive a further £15,000 payment for lifting the Vase, a full two-thirds increase on the remuneration received by Brigg Town for their triumph over Sudbury in last season's final.

Sudbury, as last season's beaten finalists, were hoping to go one better this season as they entered the competition at the Second Round Proper stage and, in a terrific start to the tournament, they disposed of league rivals, Lowestoft Town, with Andy Claydon grabbing a hat-trick in a 5-1 home victory. In a more inauspicious start, Winchester City, beaten Quarter-Finalists in their initial foray into the Vase last year, also entered the competition in the Second Round with the pouring rain ultimately failing to dampen their spirits, despite fielding a depleted line-up. However, City had to rely upon the award of a penalty kick to notch their first goal in the 2003-4 competition, duly converted by Michael Dean, before an own-goal doubled their advantage in their triumph over Hamworthy United.

Elsewhere, the Second Round saw holders, Brigg Town, sent crashing out of the tournament, losing by the only goal of the tie at home to Buxton in their initial game in the competition. AFC Wimbledon meanwhile were 3-0 victors over Wooton Blue Cross in front of 2,307 fans, the newly constituted Dons having already negotiated two rounds after entering the Vase in the First Qualifying Round stage.

Winchester were drawn away for the Third Round but, with the prolific forward partnership of Andrew Forbes and Ian Mancey restored to the starting line up, along with inspirational midfielder, Gary Green, they swept aside Whitehawk, taking a three goal lead before conceding an injury-time consolation goal to their hosts.

In the same round, AFC Sudbury were at home for their tie but it was a case of familiarity breeding contempt as they played Harwich & Parkeston for the third time in as many weeks. Each side had a man sent off as Sudbury carved out a hard fought victory after extra-time, by three goals to two.

There was a fair amount of concern in the Winchester City camp when the draw for the Fourth Round was announced and they were given the task of travelling to play the North West Counties league leaders, Mossley. Indeed City boss, Neil Hards, rated the game as their toughest test on the way to the final, stating, 'To get a result in their own back yard was terrific', and describing City's victory by two goals to one as, 'A great team performance'. After taking a deserved one goal first half lead through Forbes, City were put under the cosh in the second half with Mossley eventually equalising with 17 minutes left to play. However, seven minutes later City's Forbes popped up again to meet Liam Green's free-kick and head home and, in a 'backs to the wall' finale, City resolutely defended their lead.

Desborough Town were the visitors for AFC Sudbury and they stunned their hosts by taking an early lead. Sudbury team supremo, Gary Harvey, admitted that with the team still trailing at half-time and not playing well, their Vase dream looked like it could be over. However, an improved second half display orchestrated by Gary Bennett and a hat-trick in the last half hour of the game by Sam Banya saw Sudbury through to the next round. Sudbury's relief was apparent as Banya's opener was followed by the muscular striker diving onto manager Harvey who promptly crumpled under the impact!

However, by far the biggest crowd of the Fourth Round went home largely disappointed as AFC Wimbledon were eliminated by Colne in front of a home crowd of 3,215. Both of the eventual finalists triumphed away from home in the Fifth Round as their defences held firm. Winchester netted three times without reply against Wroxham, Danny Smith notching a double separated by another Forbes strike as City extended their run of successive victories in league and cup games to eleven. Sudbury also kept a clean sheet as goals from Claydon and Neil Calver settled matters in their favour at Congleton Town.

The Suffolk side had a rather more torrid time in their next tie, having to endure extra-time to progress to the semi-final in a tense encounter away to Kent's Cray Wanderers. Neither Sudbury nor their hosts could break the deadlock in normal time in a game where crowd disorder also caused a suspension in play of some 15 minutes late in the second half. In extra-time, though, Sudbury struck twice through Dean Francis and Paul Betson to secure a Semi-Final slot.

Winchester had been eliminated at the Quarter-Final stage last season but made no mistake this time around as they whacked Wessex League rivals, Andover, by five goals to one, setting a record home attendance of 933 in the process. First half goals by Smith, Forbes (pen) and a spectacular overhead kick by Mancey gave Andover a mountain to climb. Forbes scored again after the break as did Lloyd Webber, both men incidentally ex-Andover players. The visitors were then reduced to ten men in the final minute but did snatch a consolation goal in stoppage time.

With 'Cup Fever' rife in the city, Winchester were paired with Bideford for the Semi-Final with the first leg to be played away.

An anonymous sponsor approached the club to provide funding to meet the team's expenses for their overnight stay in Devon. City then proceeded to twice surrender a two goal lead in the face of a spirited Bideford fight back. It was not a happy occasion for City's Gary Green who had a 'goal' disallowed with City leading three goals to two. Green was later sent off and immediately afterwards Bideford equalised. In the final ten minutes, City were grateful to keeper Simon Arthur for keeping the scores level in a thrilling encounter.

For the second leg, Premiership neighbours Southampton provided ten stewards as City smashed their attendance record set in the Quarter-Finals with 1,818 packed into witness them crush Bideford by four goals to nil. Two goals at the end of the first half - first from Mancey then a Forbes strike in injury-time - knocked the stuffing out of Bideford. Four minutes after the restart, Mancey struck again, while a handball on the line reduced Bideford to ten men allowing Forbes to hit home from the spot for his 70th goal of the season. The visitors were reduced to nine men as frustration got the better of them as City strolled into the final.

Wimbledon's conquerors, Colne, visited Sudbury's Kings Marsh Stadium for the first leg of the other Semi-Final and they must have thought that they were on their way to St Andrew's as they dominated the first half and took a two-nil lead into the break. Sudbury though re-emerged reinvigorated and attacked relentlessly. Nevertheless, it was not until the 81st minute that they pulled a goal back through Bennett. A

minute later and they were level through substitute Banya and then, in injury-time, another of their substitutes, Francis, notched their third for a remarkable comeback.

In the second leg in Lancashire, both sides had to contend with gale force winds. Sudbury boss Gary Harvey admitted that his team, 'were grateful to see half-time at 0-0'. The wind dropped after the break but Harvey conceded that when his side took the lead with ten minutes to play it had been against the run of play. The scorer once more was 'Super Sub', Sam Banya. Five minutes from time Colne equalised but it was too little, too late and once more Sudbury had reached the final.

Both clubs promised an attacking display for the fans for the competition's conclusion and did not disappoint. On a beautiful sunny afternoon in Birmingham, Winchester started brightly with snappy passing, using the width of the Premiership pitch through wing-backs Sean Dyke and Matthew Bicknell and always looking dangerous with the dynamic duo of Forbes and Mancey up front.

Mancey saw an early effort strike the Sudbury post with Sudbury keeper Dean Greygoose beaten. City continued to be the more inventive and, when Mancey linked with strike partner Forbes, he took Mancey's return ball to shoot low across goal. Greygoose got a hand to it but couldn't prevent Forbes putting City ahead with his 76th goal of a remarkable season for the Wessex League Champions.

While City were having the best of things, Mancey spurned a great opportunity when Dyke's cross found him near the penalty spot and he failed to get hold of his shot allowing Greygoose to make an easy save. As the half came to an end, Sudbury bogan to get into the game more as City looked as if they might tire and City keeper, Simon Arthur, had to pull off a terrific save to deny Lee Owen.

Both sides attacked in the second half as play flowed from end to end. However, the game was settled with 15 minutes left to play when Sudbury substitute, Neil Calver, pulled back City captain, Danny Smith, and conceding a penalty, being sent off into the bargain. Sean Dyke capped a fine personal display by converting the penalty and the Trophy was on its way to Hampshire for the first time.

Sudbury creditably never gave up and the ten men almost snatched a consolation in stoppage time when Gary Bennett's shot cannoned off the City post. However City's triumph was well-deserved and they merited the applause of their fans as the celebrations began at the final whistle.

Steve Greenfield

FA Cup Review

There are two certainties in the FA Cup: that little-known clubs will be thrust into the national spotlight, and that there will be shocks a-plenty, and these two components were in abundance in an intriguing campaign. Names such as Hornchurch, Shildon and Thurrock raised their profile, whilst a pair of clubs reached the fourth round: for different reasons, it will be something Scarborough and Telford will never forget.

Back on 23rd August, Skelmersdale United took the Extra Preliminary Round headlines by beating Glasshoughton Welfare 7-2, but this round was to mark the beginning of a stunning run by Northern League side, Dunston Federation Brewery, who would come within touching distance of the First Round Proper.

Moving into the Preliminary Round, there were shocks and high scores in equal measure, as Liversedge of the Northern Counties East League accounted for Gateshead of Unibond One, 3-1. Eventual Vase finalists, Winchester City, won 2-0 at Ryman One South, Banstead Athletic, and an intriguing local derby saw Banstead's colleagues, Walton & Hersham, despatched at home by the same scoreline by Combined Counties' Walton Casuals. Fellow CCL side, Bedfont, got in on the act as they won 4-3 at Dr Martens Eastern strugglers, Fisher Athletic, whilst Ryman One North basement club, Barking & East Ham United, lost 2-1 at United Counties side, Yaxley. It was Ryman One North which provided the most intriguing story, as Enfield, who had been prevented from starting their league campaign due to ground issues, were allowed into the FA Cup and borrowed Haringey Borough's Coles Park. Against all odds, they held Hemel Hempstead Town to a 1-1 draw before winning the replay 3-2. More comfortable victories saw seven teams hit seven or more. Eventual Ryman One North champions, Yeading, were humbled 7-0 at Histon; Flixton conceded eight with no reply at Bishop Auckland.

On to the First Qualifying Round, and whilst the scorelines were a lot more measured, the shocks weren't, although this stage saw the competition wave goodbye to Harrogate Railway Athletic, who had reached the Second Round Proper in 2002/3. It is rare that one of the round's biggest shocks is also the one with the greatest margin of victory, but AFC Sudbury's 9-0 win at Berkhamsted Town, again of Ryman One North, had both of these characteristics. It was a good round for AFC's fellow Ridgeons League clubs, as Lowestoft Town won 2-1 at Aveley and Soham Town Rangers claimed victory at Wivenhoe Town, two more Ryman One North clubs. Maltby Main had a notable success in defeating Unibond Colwyn Bay 4-2, whilst Winchester City continued their impressive form as they won 3-2 at Ryman One South strugglers, Metropolitan Police. Their fellow Wessex League side, Lymington & New Milton, enjoyed a giant-killing too, as Erith & Belvedere of Dr Martens Eastern were dispatched by a single goal.

With the dream of meeting a League club drawing ever closer, along came the Second Qualifying Round. There were several notable results in the Midlands. Congleton Town, of the North West Counties, beat eventual Unibond League winners, Hucknall Town 3-2 after extra-time in a replay, whilst another side who did well in that league, Alfreton Town, lost by a single goal at local Northern Counties East rivals, Gedling Town. Shildon continued their run by defeating another Unibond side, Frickley Athletic, 5-1, whilst Lymington & New Milton celebrated their progress to this stage by demolishing Clevedon Town, 8-2. Whilst most of the other Premier Division sides in all three leagues survived, there were some exceptions, as AFC Sudbury struck again with a 4-2 win at Ryman strugglers, Northwood, Heybridge lost out in a replay at Worthing, and Hednesford Town, who would reach the Trophy final, were knocked out 2-0 by a Bromsgrove Rovers side a league below them in the Dr Martens.

The trend of sides from lower divisions beating teams in the higher division of their own league proved a key theme of the Third Qualifying Round. A replay saw Ryman One North title chasers Leyton and Boreham Wood account for Bedford Town and Hayes, the latter after a replay, whilst a trio of Dr Martens outfits upset the natural order: Salisbury City won 4-2

at Havant & Waterlooville, Mangotsfield United collected a stunning 6-3 success at Newport County, and Gloucester City undid struggling Chippenham Town, 4-1. Buxton, from the NCEL, drew the largest crowd of the round, as an astounding 1,416 witnessed their 2-1 defeat of Radcliffe Borough, of the Unibond. Dunston Federation Brewery continued to advance with an impressive 2-1 away win at Marine, whilst Screwfix Western challengers Paulton Rovers claimed the impressive scalp of Ryman One South side, Hampton & Richmond Borough, 2-1. The most eventful game of the round saw a Canvey Island side, who went on to win the Ryman League at a canter, trailing 3-0 to Dover Athletic of the Dr Martens League, only to roar back for a 4-3 win.

Enter the Fourth Qualifying Round, and the Conference clubs, most of whom progressed unscathed. However, there were some notable exceptions, as perennial giantkillers Dagenham & Redbridge travelled to Ryman Premier side, Thurrock, with their collection of ex-Daggers, only for the Ryman outfit to win 2-1. Margate were edged out on penalties following two thrilling 3-3 draws with Grays, but there was no problem for then Conference leaders, Hereford United, who brushed aside the challenge of Ryman League Harrow with a 6-1 win at Earlsmead. The tie of the round saw Shrewsbury Town make nonsense of Morecambe's strong home record by winning 4-2 on the Lancashire coast, whilst basement side Northwich Victoria enjoyed the break from a nightmare league season by beating Halifax Town by the only goal of the game. There was a fright for Woking who were held to a 1-1 draw at East Thurrock United, before two late goals won the replay, but Burton Albion eased through, as brave Buxton's run came to an end, 6-0. Dunston Federation Brewery reached the end of the road too, as Stalybridge Celtic handed them a 1-0 home loss, but fellow Northern Leaguers, Shildon, surged into the competition proper as they thumped Unibond One side, Stocksbridge Park Steels, 6-0.

Thus, 32 sides took their places in Round One, and the national consciousness. There were a fairly small number of shocks this time, the most notable being Hornchurch, who marked their first ever appearance in the proper rounds by extending their stay with a 2-0 win over Darlington, struggling in Division Three. Steve West and Vinnie John got the historic goals. Stevenage Borough renewed acquaintances with Sammy McIlroy, one time manager of Macclesfield Town, former challengers with Boro' for the Conference title. It wasn't a happy return for McIlroy as Dino Maamria's double meant Boro' beat his new Stockport County charges 2-1. Scarborough welcomed back Doncaster Rovers, who would achieve promotion from Division Three, beating them 1-0 through Karl Rose's late goal, and the only away shock saw Burton Albion win at fellow promotion chasers Torquay United, 2-1, through Steve Woods' own-goal and a Robbie Talbot winner. If Team Bath and the Farnborough tie with Arsenal were the abiding non-league images for the wider population the previous season, then this time around it was the 1980s milk commercial which suggested that children who didn't drink the white stuff 'wouldn't be good enough to play for Accrington Stanley'. In the First Round, yet another Division Three promotion chaser, Huddersfield Town, found they weren't good enough to beat them, as Andy Gouck's late goal gave them a 1-0 win.

A number of sides must have wondered 'if only', as stoppage time winners by Cambridge United at Lancaster City, Leyton Orient at Grantham, and Scunthorpe United at home to Shrewsbury, saw the League sides escape, whilst Essex pair Canvey Island and Thurrock went out in replays to Southend United and Luton Town respectively, following 1-1 draws. Ford United held out until extra-time in a home replay with Port Vale, before losing 2-1, having secured it with an impressive 2-2 draw in the Potteries. The remainder of the League sides got through comfortably with some heavy scorelines in their favour, Blackpool beating Boreham Wood 4-0, Shildon seen off 7-2 at Notts County, Brentford hitting seven against Gainsborough, Bishops Stortford losing 6-0 at Mansfield, Sheffield Wednesday netting four without reply against Salisbury City, Bristol City winning 5-2 at Bradford Park Avenue, and the coastal battle between Hartlepool and Whitby ending 4-0 to the hosts. More modest scorelines saw Hereford United edged out 2-0 at Peterborough and Northwich 2-1 at Kidderminster.

There remained six all-non-league affairs, as Weston-super-Mare sprung the biggest shock by winning 1-0 at Farnborough Town through Billy Clark with a fifth minute goal. Barnet needed a replay to dispose of Stalybridge Celtic, but Chester City found themselves beaten 1-0 at home by a Gravesend & Northfleet side then in poor form. Grays lost after taking the lead as a Roscoe D'Sane double rescued a 2-1 win for Aldershot Town in Essex, whilst Telford United recovered from 2-0 down at home to eventual Dr Martens title winners, Crawley Town, to win 3-2. Woking had a comfortable 3-1 passage against Histon, who were challenging for the top in Dr Martens Eastern.

Ten sides from the non-league had made it into the Second Round, including Weston-super-Mare from the Dr Martens Premier and Hornchurch from the Ryman League. There were to be three survivors, in a variety of circumstances. Scarborough travelled to Port Vale on the Sunday, with Ashley Sestanovich's fine second half strike earning the Seadogs a 1-0 away win, building on Telford United's progression the following day when Christian Moore's hat-trick had seen them beat Vale's Division Two colleagues Crewe 3-0. Accrington Stanley had to wait to extend their run, despite John Mullin heading them into a ninth minute lead at AFC Bournemouth, with Marcus Browning earning the hosts another bite of the cherry with a 56th minute equaliser. However, Stanley won the replay 5-3 on penalties after a scoreless 120 minutes. Gravesend & Northfleet would have been hopeful of joining them, as Steve Perkins gave them a 42nd minute lead against Notts County, only for the Magpies to equalise and then snatch a stoppage time winner to leave their hopes dashed.

A series of narrow defeats eliminated most of the remainder, as Swansea City beat Stevenage Borough 2-1 despite Anthony Elding's goal for the visitors, and Burton Albion were nudged out 1-0 at home by Hartlepool United. Aldershot Town travelled to Colchester United only to lose to a late goal when a scoreless draw seemed likely, and Woking would have probably expected to have done better than a 3-0 home reverse to Division Three strugglers Kidderminster Harriers. Hornchurch fell to a controversial 1-0 home loss to Tranmere Rovers, whilst Weston reached the end of the road, 4-1 at Northampton, as did Barnet, 5-1 at Yeovil Town.

Round Three saw the three survivors compete in a trio of tight ties. The only one to be settled on the day was Telford's short trip to Crewe Alexandra, as Lee Mills' second minute header settled the game 1-0 to the Bucks, in what was probably the biggest FA Cup result involving a non-league team since Dagenham's games with Charlton in 2000/1. Accrington Stanley held Colchester United to a scoreless draw, and could have won it, but for an exemplary display from U's keeper, Simon Brown. Two goals from Joe Keith in the eleventh and 84th minutes won the replay for Colchester, with Mullin netting a late consolation. It had looked bad for Scarborough when Southend went ahead in the ninth minute through Jay Smith, but Scott Kerr got a priceless 74th minute leveller to bring the Shrimpers back to the East Coast; Mark Quayle completed the task as his goal in the 83rd minute was the winner. This of course earned the type of tie which all of the clubs involved dreamt of, a home tie with multi-millionaires, Chelsea. Unlike Arsenal and Farnborough last year, there was no ground switch, as 5,379 crammed into the McCain Stadium for this classic David and Goliath Fourth Round tie. Without descending into cliche, the Seadogs did themselves proud as John Terry's tenth minute header proved the only difference between the sides. Indeed, the hosts were denied a penalty in the dying stages when William Gallas appeared to handle. In contrast, Telford's home match with Millwall was fraught with difficulty, as poor weather meant it was postponed twice, and when it did go ahead, goals from Paul Ifill and Dennis Wise ended the dream, albeit against a side who went on to contest the final.

Gerard Butler

Feeder Leagues

MIDLAND ALLIANCE LEAGUE

As in previous seasons the competitive nature of the Midland Football Alliance meant that the championship was not decided until the last game of the season with Rocester winning the title for the second time and Willenhall Town finishing in second place. Virtually to the end of the season several clubs were in contention, with Stratford Town, Quorn and Studley all at times during the season looking as if they would be real contenders for the title.

Following the revision of the Non-League football pyramid, both Rocester and Willenhall Town gained promotion. Under the new system clubs from the Midland Football Alliance are considered for promotion to either the Northern Premier League or the Southern League and both of the league's promoted clubs were placed in the Northern Premier League.

Whilst the revised system has done away with some anomalies, particularly in the south of the country, again the opportunity was missed to create a Midlands Premier League. It cannot be sensible for clubs at the new step 4 of the pyramid to have to travel to Cumbria and North Yorkshire in the north or Middlesex and Somerset in the south when there are so many clubs within the midlands conurbation.

For the first and hopefully the last time the League Cup Final between Rushall Olympic and Stratford Town had to be postponed because of a waterlogged pitch.

Once again the performance of the league's clubs in the FA Cup and FA Vase were disappointing with the exception of Studley who reached the last 16 of the FA Vase before losing at Gosport after a replay. In the County Cup competitions Alvechurch must be congratulated for winning the Worcestershire Senior Vase.

Prior to the start of the season the match for the Joe McGorian Trophy competed for by the previous season's League Champions and League Cup winners saw Stratford Town take the trophy after defeating Stourbridge.

Three clubs, Loughborough Dynamo, Malvern Town and Romulus have been promoted to the Midland Football Alliance for season 2004/2005. The bottom two clubs, Stafford Town and Pelsall Villa, have both been relegated to the West Midlands (Regional) League with the third relegation place being taken by Grosvenor Park who resigned from the league. This saved Cradley Town from relegation as they had finished third from bottom and were due to be relegated until the demise of Grosvenor Park.

Finally, on a sad note, this season saw the death of the League President Bernard Davis. Bernard had been the main instigator in persuading Interlink Express to be the first sponsors of the league in 1994 and for several years had also personally sponsored the league cup. He was a great supporter of the Midland Football Alliance and will be greatly missed. We were also shocked to hear of the death of Steve Cooper, Player/Coach with Studley FC, who collapsed at his home following the club's return from Gosport after playing in the FA Vase.

Peter Dagger (General Secretary)

SPARTAN SOUTH MIDLANDS

Beaconsfield SYCOB put many near misses behind them, as their consistency proved the decisive factor in them taking the title by an eight point margin, and achieving promotion to Division One East of the Southern League. The league contained just 19 teams as Milton Keynes City folded just before the season started (ironically at the time of the Wimbledon relocation to the Buckinghamshire town), and, in happier circumstances, Dunstable Town were promoted to the Ryman League's Division One North. As a result, Holmer Green, the basement side in 2002/03, earned a reprieve. SYCOB started the season as they meant to go on with an opening day 3-1 win at Broxbourne, followed up by a 7-0 success at Holmer, as Leon Callender in particular made an early impact. The sides promoted into the Division, Hertfordshire pair Leverstock Green and Harpenden Town, both started their campaigns with defeats.

As September began, some sides were still winless but, by the end of the month, Broxbourne Borough, Hillingdon Borough, Ruislip Manor and Holmer Green had all collected their first three point hauls. Meanwhile, Beaconsfield had won all of their games up to that point, as Callender hit a hat-trick in a 4-1 victory at Haringey Borough. Their main challengers at this point were Potters Bar Town - not as free-scoring as SYCOB, but who boasted five different scorers in a 5-1 win at Royston. The game of the season so far was at Potters Bar as the hosts played out a 1-1 draw with the leaders, who dropped their first points as a result. The momentum from that saw Town's challenge ignite with a 6-1 midweek win versus Broxbourne. SYCOB dropped points again the following week in a surprise home stalemate with Ruislip Manor. Another crushing win for Potters Bar, this time against Holmer Green, meant Beaconsfield's lead was cut to three points.

However, it was Beaconsfield who capitalised in mid-October as Potters Bar crashed to a 4-3 loss at Greenacres, whilst the leaders won at Bedford United & Valerio to stretch their lead again at the top. At the other end of the table, Holmer Green were slipping back into trouble as they failed to build on two straight wins by collecting just a solitary point in a run of seven matches through to early November. As Autumn progressed, Brook House staked their claim as title contenders after a run of five straight wins. However, the leaders were still undefeated, unlike Potters Bar, who fell further off the pace as they lost 3-0 at a St Margaretsbury side who would eventually pip them to third spot.

The challenging trio of Potters Bar, St Margarestsbury and Brook House were all prone to small bouts of inconsistency, meaning that, significantly, none of them were able to overhaul the leaders at the top of the table. Town still headed the queue, and gained a real scoring touch in November as they hit five at Holmer Green and seven at Broxbourne in back-to-back away wins. At the vital post-Christmas halfway point, there was a shock double defeat at the top as SYCOB fell to their first reverse of the season, 3-0 at home to Harefield, whose strong second half of the season would see them take fifth spot. And even more surprising was Potters Bar's 2-0 home loss against Bedford United. Brook House, by now second, took full advantage by winning at Holmer Green, whilst St Margaretsbury hit the only goal of the game against Broxbourne.

In another crunch clash soon after, Beaconsfield came out on top as they beat Potters Bar 1-0, whilst an important result saw Brook House win 2-1 at St Margaretsbury. Brook House continued to put sustained pressure on the

leaders with a run of wins, until a shock Valentine's Day defeat at Broxbourne, whilst Potters Bar began to re-emerge after a damaging sequence of just three points from five games. The eagerly awaited game at Brook House saw Beaconsfield handed only their second loss of the season in a 2-1 defeat, which blew the title race wide open. In the struggle to avoid the drop, Haringey and Holmer Green looked destined for the bottom as they had long winless streaks. The end of February saw St Margaretsbury as the team to watch as, off the back of their strong defence, they were gaining results.

As the season reached its climax, Beaconsfield were dropping points but, perhaps more significantly, were still not losing. Brook House were the side snapping at their heels but, yet again, in the recurring theme of the season, when a side looked poised to overtake the leaders, a defeat to struggling opposition dashed their hopes: this time it was a 2-1 reverse at Royston Town. A nightmare week for Brook House also had Potters Bar scratching their heads and wondering what might have been as they cruised to a 5-0 away win in West London. However, their focus was now the top three and potential promotion, which was hindered when their main rivals for third, St Margaretsbury, collected a point from their visit to Potters Bar. The leaders, meanwhile, had a comfortable and consistent run in, and ended their season with five straight wins as they took the title with something to spare. Holmer Green lost to Haringey Borough with a week to go, meaning Boro finished second from bottom, and Green were destined for the wooden spoon for the second successive season. Brook House finished second, and moved sideways to Ryman Division Two, whilst St Margaretsbury, Potters Bar, Harefield and Hanwell completed the top six - all will be back next season to challenge again.

Gerard Butler

RYMAN DIVISION TWO

Leighton Town found the net a remarkable 111 times during the 2003/04 season to take them to the Ryman League Division Two championship with the impressive total of 91 points from their 42 league matches. The Bell Close club lost on just seven occasions on their way to securing the title, but their success wasn't confirmed until the last day of the season, when a 2-0 victory over Kingsbury Town made it impossible for Dorking to overtake them.

The Surrey outfit also only tasted defeat seven times throughout the campaign, and even a five-game winning streak at the end of the season failed to take them to the title as Leighton ended their campaign brilliantly to match them every step of the way. Dorking finished the season on 89 points, just two behind the champions, but their second place still secured them a place in Division One for next term.

Hertford Town will remain in Division Two after finishing in a distant third place, eight points behind Dorking. Kevin Cooper netted 34 times over the course of the season to help the Blues' promotion push, but Leighton's late surge was ultimately to deny them.

Fourth-placed Chertsey Town scored more goals than Hertford - 75 to the Blues' 74 - but a more leaky defence meant they ended the season on 75 points, six behind the top three. Flackwell Heath completed the top five, winning 22 times on the way to recording 71 points.

Spa Road-based Witham Town completed their league campaign with a comprehensive 3-0 victory over Wokingham Town, but it wasn't enough for the Essex club to overhaul Flackwell, who beat Clapton 4-2 to preserve their one point advantage over Witham.

The top six were effectively in a different league to the remainder of the division, and come the end of the season, Witham held a 17 point lead over seventh-placed

Kingsbury Town. The Silver Jubilee Park side would have finished the season closer to Witham had it not been for their woeful form in the season's closing stages, but they still held off the challenge of Ware, Abingdon and Camberley to end the 2003/04 campaign in seventh with 14 victories.

Ware also claimed 14 three-point hauls to come eighth and Abingdon Town, one place further back, saw goals flying in at both ends during a remarkable season. The 83 goals they netted made them the third highest scorers in the division, but their own net was breached on 81 occasions to ensure the Town were never anything more than middle-markers. They claimed 51 points, exactly the same as Camberley Town in tenth, but Abingdon's vastly superior goal difference meant that the Surrey outfit couldn't break into the top nine.

The lower reaches of the table start with Wembley in eleventh position. 20 defeats and 13 victories from 42 starts left them with 48 points, five more than Wokingham Town could manage. Edgware Town and Chalfont St Peter ended a point down on Wokingham, but a six-goal advantage in Edgware's favour meant they escaped the bottom two.

London club Clapton were the unfortunate side to be cut adrift in last position. 129 goals were conceded in a season which saw them win on only eight occasions. Their 29 points meant they were a huge 13 points shy of Chalfont St Peter in front of them.

Leo Tyrie

NORTHERN LEAGUE DIVISION ONE

In a season where Dunston Federation Brewery finished as champions, six points ahead of Durham City and seven ahead of Bedlington Terriers, it was another disappointment to North East teams that no clubs would take the plunge and leap up a division, once again leaving the Northern League stagnant at the top.

At the other end of the table Washington, Marske United and Penrith battled bravely against relegation but, in the end, to no avail with Hordon finishing above all three with several points to spare. The lack of points condemned Washington, who only picked up eleven on the road all season with a crushing minus 30 goal difference on their travels to boot.

The first day of the League season saw a continuation of a recent trend. In previous season's the reigning champions were defeated on the opening day. So this meant it was Brandon's turn. The fixture list had paired them with a new-look Durham City. Durham had made many changes to their squad during the Summer, bringing in players of considerable talent and experience. Many observers were intrigued to see how this newly constructed team would fare, especially after an impressive pre-season campaign, most notably against a strong Kilmarnock team despite losing 4-1. In the league opener, Durham won the tie 2-1, in what proved to be a fiery encounter with their near neighbours. Last season's fixture between these teams was an explosive contest, and this was a no less entertaining encounter. The vastly experienced Sam Kitchen and Andrew Shaw scored the goals. Brandon's season didn't improve too much as they finished a disappointing eighth.

Bedlington Terriers, champions for five successive seasons from 1998 to 2002, won their opening game for the first time in three seasons - a two-goal blast from John Milner being enough to defeat Esh Winning 2-0. Was this an early indication that they would be near the top once again come the end of the season? Only one game finished level in Division One on the opening day, and that was the clash at Dean Street between Shildon and Dunston Fed. The game was goalless until the 74th minute when Lee Ellison opened for Shildon, but within a minute, Dunston responded with a goal by Stephen Pickering to rescue a point for the would-be champions.

The next few weeks showed many that Dunston Fed could challenge for the title with victories over Brandon United and then Durham City. Further wins against Hordon Colliery Welfare and Esh Winning were to also come. Champions Brandon United lost 3-2 at Federation Park on the 25th August. They led at the interval after Andy Purvis' eleventh minute strike proved the only goal of the opening half. However, Dunston went into a 3-1 lead in the second half with two goals from Ray Booth and a third by David Southern before Brandon got a second consolation goal from Chris Neil with a header from a corner on 78 minutes.

On the same day Durham City beat local rivals Chester-Le-Street 3-1, with all the goals being scored in a rampant first half spell. Justin Keegan, Stephen Halliday and Robert Herbert all netted within the first ten minutes to give City a 3-0 lead. Martin Bowes managed to pull one goal back on 42 minutes but unfortunately it didn't spark a comeback for Chester-Le-Street. Durham City were then visited by Dunston Fed at the Archibald's Stadium on the 6th September and saw two goals

go past Paul Gilmore in the first half. It appeared that Durham could allow goals past them just as quickly as they could score them as it took Shore four minutes to stretch his leg out to score from a left wing cross. Paul Hollier made it 2-0 on 41 minutes from a low drive from inside the post after Anthony March sent a long pass forward from inside his own half.

October proved to be a very fruitful period for Durham City and they picked up 14 points from a possible 21 in an unbeaten month. It started well with a 5-1 home victory over Billingham Town despite going behind in the first minute thanks to a Craig Skelton goal. Lee O'Donovan and veteran Willie Moat gave Durham the half-time lead and Stephen Halliday scored a goal either side of Ray Stinger's 69th minute header to complete the rout.

The soon to be relegated Marske were then beaten by Durham on their own turf 4-1 with goals by Herbert and Canavan either side of an O'Donovan brace. There was a win against Whitley Bay before two one-all draws against Esh Winning and relegation endangered Washington before a 2-1 victory over bottom side Penrith saw Durham pick up the maximum three points again. Gavin Mudd became the hero after Barry Irvine had cancelled out his opening goal on 62 minutes. With just three minutes left on the clock, Mudd scored his second with a 20-yard chip over Penrith keeper James Holland. Durham then ended the month with a 1-1 draw at Guisborough with the Durham goal scored by Michael Dunwell.

Dunston were going quietly about their business while Durham stole the Northern League headlines. They were showing good form as they defeated Washington 4-0 in November and fellow title contenders Bedlington Terriers 3-1 at Welfare Park. Paul Hogg gave the visitors the lead in the first half and then Richie Pitt scored a second after half-time - a goal that will surely go down in Dunston history as it notched up their 1000th league goal. Ian Dixon gave Bedlington some hope but it wasn't enough as Michael Farrey slotted away a penalty after Danny Anderson brought Paul Hollier down inside the area.

Durham City put themselves firmly in the championship driving seat on the 10th January when they faced Dunston at Federation Park. A goal by Glen Robson in the first half and a second by O'Donovon in the second 45 minutes was enough to give Durham the three points.

However, the defeat in the key clash against Durham only served to spur Dunston on. Their first game after the defeat against Durham was played on the 24th January and it ended 2-2 against Esh Winning. This was the first of 13 matches without a defeat for Dunston and, with wins over Thornaby, Tow Law, Penrith, Washington, Chester-Le-Street, Billingham Town, Jarrow Roofing, Guisborough Town and Marske Town (with just three draws in-between), Dunston were right back in the hunt.

The 6th April saw last season's Division Two champions Penrith relegated back from whence they came after just one year in the top division as they crumbled against Shildon and lost 2-1. Although it was mathematically possible for both Marske Town and Washington to survive, their fates were decided within the final weeks of the season.

Although their unbeaten run was clearly a lucky 13 for Dunston they came up short in game number 14 against Billingham Synthonia at Federation Park on the 10th April. However, the leaders saw their nearest rivals for the title, Durham City, slip up at home to Shildon. The Railwaymen had proved to be something of a bogey team for Durham that season, having met each other four times in all competitions: Shildon won all four of the contests.

I think that there would be few who would disagree that Shildon deserved to win this latest encounter between the two teams. A large crowd assembled to see the contest between the teams lying second and fourth in the table and, in the opening exchanges, Shildon repeatedly threatened the home goal. However, they only had to wait until the sixth minute before Gary Barnes opened the scoring. The visitors could, and should, have increased their lead before Durham got back on level terms just before the half hour with a fine goal from Glen Robson.

The second half was a more even, if a slightly subdued affair, but certainly a point would not have satisfied Durham City, who saw their championship hopes fading fast as the minutes ticked by. Worse was to follow as Barnes added two more goals in the last ten minutes of the game, to complete his hat-trick and take his personal tally to a staggering 53 goals for the season, as Shildon ran out 3-1 winners.

The other result of significance in Division One on that Saturday was at Horden, where Tow Law Town were the visitors. The game looked to be ending goalless, although the visitors had already had the ball in the Horden net once, but it was ruled offside. The deadlock was finally broken in the last few minutes when Beasley scored for Tow Law, for what was the game's only goal. The result meant that Tow Law Town were safe in Division One for another season, but Washington and Marske United dropped to Division Two.

Dunston Fed were crowned champions of the Northern League for the first time in their history on the 20th April following a 2-0 victory over Billingham Town. Goals by Paul Hogg and David Southern ensured the trophy was theirs. They were presented with the championship trophy before their home game with Peterlee Newtown on the 24th - a game they then went on to claim another three points from in what had been a remarkable season for the Fed. It was another clean sheet, their 18th of the campaign as they went on to win 2-0.

Dunston Federation Brewery had a remarkable season lifting not only the league title but also the league cup - beating Durham City to the trophy. It took a golden goal by David Southern (who also scored the regulation time goal for the Fed), to win the match. Craig Lake had given Durham the lead with a header after Dunston keeper Tom Phillips fumbled from a corner but, after seeing Jamie Howe sent from the field, the game was made easier for Dunston, who put keeper Adam Dowell under immense pressure throughout the match.

Alan Percival

COMBINED COUNTIES LEAGUE

From the very start of the season, AFC Wimbledon were destined to take the league championship. From the point they opened up their league campaign on the 16th August (with a 2-0 victory at Feltham), the fans of the club never looked back and ran through the entire season unbeaten.

Their final record of played 46, won 42, drawn 4, lost 0, goals for 180, goals against 32, points 130 will take some beating in years to come. Having operated on average 2,500 crowds and taken over the Kingsmeadow ground they shared with Ryman League side Kingstonian, in comparison to other sides in the Combined Counties League, the club were the Chelsea of the division.

That's not to disparage their efforts either in a season when they took the league's Premier Challenge Cup in front of a 3,000 plus crowd on a late April night at the Kingfield Stadium in Woking. The 4-1 defeat of North Greenford United saw ace goal getter Kevin Cooper notch a double.

The year was not without controversy, however, as manager Terry Eames lost the job as Dons boss in the New Year following accusations that he allegedly acted against the best interests of the club during various business and football deals.

The club were also the odds on favourites for the FA Vase, but in their first year of competition they surprisingly slipped up to Colne in a game which was marred by several confrontations including one in the tunnel, but Eames' former assistant, Nicky English, ensured their unbeaten league record did not come under threat with a first game 9-0 victory at Chessington United.

The side immediately responded by hitting eight against Bedfont and the AFC Wimbledon train continued on the right tracks having been threatened with a diversion down the slow line. All of which meant, no one could hope to get near the side that were packed full of former Ryman League players who had regularly plyed their trade in the Premier Division.

Chipstead threatened early on, but fell away after manager Stuart Massey departed for Whyteleafe, while Southall, who play out of Chesham United's ground, remained there or thereabouts, but could never get near enough. However, having taken a while to get going, old foes AFC Wallingford lifted themselves up to end the year in second position with 103 points.

AFC Wimbledon's title was ensured with a 3-0 win at Walton Casuals on Easter Monday, with nine games to spare. Goals from Everard and a predictable double from Cooper confirmed the honours. And perhaps it was fitting that the Dons' last game in the league was against Wallingford as a 2-1 win was secured thanks to goals from Jamie Taylor and Gareth Graham who cancelled out Bradley Ward's equaliser. Dave Crowdy's side even had to play both of their league games at

Kingsmeadow and undoubtedly gave Wimbledon their hardest games of the two years they were members of the league with that last day defeat and 1-1 draw in the away game in March covering their encounters in 2003/04.

While it will be interesting to see how AFC get on in the Isthmian league set-up next season, with former Hendon boss Dave Anderson the new incumbent in the Dons hot seat, Wallingford will find it a hard task to continue their challenging form of previous years.

Indeed a mid-winter run of 13 games without even dropping a point did much to move Crowdy's men up to their final finishing position with strikers Stuart Beavon and Ray Spence scoring 51 goals between them.

Behind them a last day 3-1 win over Chessington & Hook manoeuvred Reading Town, formerly managed by ex-Manchester United star Neil Webb, into third position, while Southall's largely impressive run through the season only ended in a finish of fourth mainly because of their occasional inconsistency.

Forwards Donal O'Sullivan and Andre Robinson proved to be the side's main goal getters and an early highlight was a 5-1 thrashing of Walton Casuals. They would end the season with a goals for total of 121, a reflection of the side's goal scoring ability.

A 4-1 reverse at lowly Westfield proved to be a sign of things to come and prevented any lengthy challenge to the top two. However, there's no doubt the nomads can be in amongst the top four when next season comes around. Sandhurst improved last season to move up one to fifth with a solid season and had the second best goal scorer in Mark Anderson who knocked in 37, one fewer than Wimbledon's Cooper.

Former champions Cove occupied bottom spot and finished the year with a 4-0 loss, a performance which summed up much of what had gone before for the troubled club. Chessington United, despite losing a Surrey Senior Cup game 14-1 to Woking, scrambled to second from bottom but still may suffer relegation to the new Division One, depending on how many sides come into the Premier Division.

Farnham Town, who have a certain Geoff Chapple as a board member, finished just behind last season's Champions Withdean 2000 who themselves were hit by the mass defection of their title winning team and manager to Worthing before the start of the campaign. So the season was always going to be about bare survival and that is exactly what happened.

Elsewhere during the season, many competitive games were played between clubs who themselves emphasise what English non-league football is all about. Many would not exist if it were not for the many volunteers who gladly lend their time to the cause of staging a football match. Quite simply they do it for the love of the game.

The league will also have to find a new sponsor after Seagrave Haulage ran into financial difficulties and pulled out of the second year of their sponsorship deal in all but name. Withdean 2000 unexpectedly withdrew from the CCL, intending to play only at youth level next season. They will seek to regroup in the next few years, following the gutting of their Championship side of 2002/03.

However, next season promises to be a more even contest, following AFC Wimbledon's unparalleled run this year. One aspect of the Dons' involvement that will be missed is the support and extra finance their supporters brought to the league when they regularly bolstered average crowds of 60 well into four figures. They will be missed.

Howard Milton

SUSSEX COUNTY LEAGUE

Chichester City United claimed the Division One title by six points ahead of their nearest challengers, Rye & Iden and East Preston, to close out a successful 2003/04 season. The capturing of the Championship pennant was their first in over a decade and represented the desired improvement for manager Adie Girdler based on the previous season's fourth place finish.

United, based in the west of the county, found themselves in contention throughout much of the campaign and began the season with 1-1 draw with 2002/03 Division Two winners, Rye & Iden United, who were to eventually finish in second.

Girdler's men kept up their fine start in matching league favourites, Horsham YMCA - who had finished second behind Burgess Hill the year before - by sharing a 1-1 draw in a September meeting at Church Road, a game the match officials proclaimed to be the best they had officiated up to that point. Paul Thomas and Jamie Price shared the goals.

The side remained unbeaten until November 29 when they slipped up 3-1 to mid-table Hailsham, but they then had the

fortune to come up against lowly Pagham the following week and got back on form with a 4-1 victory thanks to a Jamie Laidlaw hat-trick and Scott Murfin goal. And from then on the Lilywhites maintained pole position, with an 8-1 away thrashing of Sidlesham providing a highlight. The lead was retained despite three quick fire losses in the early part of 2004 that had Girdler sweating on their top position.

However, the team always remained there or thereabouts as the title race evolved into a four way scrap with, at one point, Eastbourne Town getting in on the act. A late April thrashing of Shoreham brought the glory even closer but Girdler and his squad had to put a hold on the celebrations until the last day of the season when strikes from Lee Preston, Paul Thomas and Louis Denimore saw off Sidley; Rye were three points behind and hoping for a United slip up but crashed 2-1 at Pagham to make May Day one to remember for the club who were struggling for its very existence at the end of the last decade.

Girdler told the club website in May: 'It has been a hard slog this season, this is a tough league to win and at one stage everyone thought we had blown it when we had a bad spell after Christmas. But the players have shown a lot of character - I've brought in one or two experienced players but a lot of these lads have come up through our junior sides. They've worked hard, sometimes they've played when not fully fit and taken their turn on the substitute benches, they've done me proud and they deserve their success.'

Meanwhile, Rye continued their miraculous rise. Just two seasons ago, they were down in the Third Division but two successive title wins almost became a third, although they didn't quite have enough to keep up with Chichester. New boss, Ryan Light, and his charges deserve credit for keeping up the pressure throughout, even though their Fish Market Road ground isn't remotely fit for a higher standard of football.

An early test for Rye was that opening day draw at Chichester, while a 2-2 at eventual third placed outfit, East Preston, meant a brief rise to first position. During this time Rye suffered an FA Vase exit - perhaps unsurprisingly to AFC Wimbledon - and slipped out of the RUR Cup to Oakwood coupled with a predictable John O'Hara Cup 8-1 thrashing of Shoreham, a run that was to end in failure in the final to Arundel 3-1. In fact, they would not have picked up the John O'Hara trophy due to the fielding of an ineligible player in an earlier round.

By the New Year they had slipped down to sixth in the league and original manager, Glynn White, stepped down. As March arrived over Sussex, the side manoeuvred themselves back into contention, with a seven-goal thriller with Sidlesham proving a highlight. United's chance of top honours only ended in the final weeks when a late goal from Three Bridges' Simon Funnell dished out defeat and ended the club's dreams. Elsewhere, East Preston took third spot, having at one stage been only one point off the lead with a game a hand. They hit the top when coming back from 3-1 down to defeat Redhill 4-3 at the end of the following month but, as they and Chichester swapped positions throughout the final months, the crunch finally came when Preston lost 1-0 at the eventual title winners, courtesy of a last minute Tony Stephens' goal.

Amongst the other clubs throughout the division, there were the usual highlights, lowlights and newsworthy stories to light up any season. Multimillionaire and Sussex based non-league football nut, Victor Gladwish, handed Horsham YMCA a £95,000 sponsorship deal in September, which was thought to be the biggest in the County League history. Later in the year, he tried to set up a non-league Super Cup competition between the clubs that his land sales business had sponsored. When he failed, he took over as chairman of Third Division side Forest and threw his money in the direction of Haywards Heath instead.

The 2003/04 season was also the year of quick goals. In September, Redhill's Luke Jones scored an opener against Sidlesham after nine seconds; St Francis' Martin Schlieder then topped that with a seven second goal in October, while Chichester's Murfin joined the ranks by hitting the goal net with 13 seconds on the clock in a game in the early part of 2004.

By then, former Dr Martens side St Leonards had resigned from the league, due to a Customs & Excise order for £18,000, which was a sad end for a club who took the non-league headlines in the mid-nineties when they were named Stamco and enjoyed a couple of runs in the FA Vase. The Redhill and Arundel clash made the local headlines back in the first month of the new year when a massive brawl ten minutes from the end saw six players sent off. A late tackle from the home side's Paul Whithead sparked scenes more akin to a wrestling contest as referee Warren Lester dismissed the visitors' Josh Sutcliffe, Stuart Hack, Jon Tucker and Dan McLaughlin and Redhill's Whithead and Herve King. Down at the bottom, Selsey - who got through three managers - and penniless Shoreham slipped into Division Two, while Littlehampton completed a Division Two league and cup double by returning to the league from whence they came. Worthing United joined them.

Pease Pottage also took the headlines in that division, by regularly conceding double figures through the early stages of the campaign, including scorelines of 0-18 and 1-15. Gradually the village outfit scrambled out of the clutches of relegation to finish third bottom, although they conceded 119 goals for their troubles.

Crowborough Athletic were another side that completed the League and Cup double in Division Three and were joined in promotion by St Francis Rangers who swapped places with Lancing and Haywards Heath from Division Two.

It was a good season for Sussex football as a whole, with Football League side Brighton reaching and winning the Division Two play-offs and Crawley Town achieving promotion to the Conference as champions of the Dr Martens League, while 2002/03's County League champions, Burgess Hill, adapted well to Southern League football by achieving a top ten finish in the Eastern Division, albeit just failing to make the top seven which would have seen them move into the newly reconstituted Dr Martens Premier League.

Howard Milton

WESTERN LEAGUE PREMIER

Bideford and Paulton Rovers started the season as joint favourites to take the league title, and they kept everyone guessing until the last two weeks of the campaign. Bideford hit top spot after their first match and stayed there for most of the season. Paulton Rovers showed well early on but dropped away, mainly due to cup involvement.

Mid-season saw Paulton Rovers move back to challenge Bideford and the battle was strong for the rest of the season. Frome Town turned out to be the side that decided the Premier Division championship, and they did it by defeating Paulton Rovers twice within eight days. Until they faced Frome Town, Paulton sat in second place and needed six points to apply pressure on table-topping Bideford. Bideford were on track for most of the season to take the treble of FA Vase, League Championship and Les Phillips (League) Cup, but fell at the FA Vase Semi-Final hurdle at Winchester - but still ended up with the double. It was fitting that Paulton Rovers were Bideford's cup final opponents, after their season-long rivalry, and the North Devon side lifted the cup with the only goal of the game.

Paulton Rovers had indicated early on in the season that they were seeking membership of the realigned Southern League for season 2004/05, and set out to prove their worth. A club record run in the FA Cup gave the club national recognition, but they went out in the Fourth Qualifying Round - still further than any other Western League club last term. With Bideford deciding to remain as a Western League club the door was held open for Paulton Rovers to realise their dreams and take the step up to the Southern League.

Elsewhere in the top division many clubs were laying the foundations for a shot at the championship next season. Frome Town and Backwell United came from lowly positions in mid-season to finish in third and fourth slots. Frome Town suffered from a disastrous home run - until they brought in a white witch to reverse their fortunes. Local TV and radio had a field day with the story, but the spell was cast to good effect. Exmouth Town equipped themselves well in their first season back in the top flight and finished a worthy fifth. Bridgwater Town disappointed with a poor set of results as winter set in, after starting the season brightly. Brislington finished seventh, and could have challenged for a top two place with a little more luck. The top seven were, realistically, the only teams with enough strength in depth to look for honours.

Welton Rovers, Odd Down, Barnstaple Town and Torrington turned in some good performances and produced some surprise results, but none of them could find the consistency to move out of mid-table. Both Torrington and Keynsham Town fared well in the FA Vase, and made friends from other leagues along the way. Bridport, Devizes Town and Melksham Town struggled to find form throughout the season but did enough to stay away from the danger zone. To most neutral observers Keynsham Town finished in a false position, but they could just not convert pressure into goals and faced a worrying last few matches starring at relegation. Even deeper trouble faced Bishop Sutton who struggled to find form all season, but they produced more than enough points in their last four matches to pull away from the threat of relegation.

Dawlish Town certainly considered themselves unlucky to end up as a relegated club. After turning the club's fortunes around, following a dreadful start, the new regime were bitterly disappointed not to find enough points to finish in a safe position. Elmore never looked like being able to produce a run of results to justify Premier Division survival and ended the season with an unlucky 13 points in the basement position.

Ken Clarke

HELLENIC PREMIER LEAGUE

There was a thrilling climax to the Hellenic League Premier Division, as it was settled on the last day, with only four points separating the leaders and fifth place. In the event, it was Brackley Town who won the title on goal difference and a place in the Southern League Eastern Division for next season. However, their success seemed unlikely back in the early months of the campaign, following a distinctly modest start which had seen just two wins from their opening eight, but they had managed to record a 3-1 success over highly fancied Didcot Town.

However, there was a stunning change as October came, as the goals flew in from all areas of the pitch which, indeed, proved a crucial part of their staying power in the title race. The 4th October saw the start of a nine game winning streak, including a 3-2 win over Southall Town, which was to prove so crucial in the final reckoning. A pair of draws broke the sequence, but with all areas of the team being in such fine form, another four wins in a row emerged, and it wasn't until the 24th January that they tasted defeat, 3-1 at the hands of a Hungerford Town side who had switched from the Ryman League at the start of the campaign.

The eagerly awaited return clash at Southall Town saw a 2-2 draw, but yet again the Northamptonshire side bounced back by winning the next eight games without conceding a solitary goal - a factor that was key to their goal difference come the end of the season. A couple of defeats crept into their run-in, most notably a 2-1 reverse at home to Slimbridge, but they recovered by taking ten points from the last twelve of the season to secure the title on goal difference. Crucial to their last day success, which saw a 6-2 win at Fairford Town, was the distribution of goals throughout the whole team. Slinn was Town's top scorer with 22 goals from 19 matches with Miller, Baird and Dunkley all reaching double figures in support. However, a total of 15 other players netted at least one goal, meaning someone was always likely to pop up with a goal, and usually did.

Southall Town chased them all the way, and indeed, but for their goal difference, had an identical record of 28 wins, eight defeats and six losses, but there was a bitter aftermath, as just after the club's promotion to the Southern League Eastern Division had been confirmed, the club folded, having only existed since 2000. Town had made a fairly promising start, although a title challenge didn't really seem to be on the cards at this stage. Christian Glynn set the tone for the season with an opening day hat-trick against Fairford Town and Michael Meaker, the former QPR and Bristol Rovers forward, joined in with four goals in the 7-3 win against Abingdon Town, as the team won four from its first six. The West London club then surged into title contention by recording eleven straight wins deep into January, with two further hat-tricks by Meaker along the way.

The defeat that ended that run proved to be isolated, as it heralded another sequence of ten without loss featuring important draws with Brackley and Bishops Cleeve and a 4-0 demolition of Didcot, all of which seemed to have set them up well for the final straight. The 3-2 home reverse to Slimbridge seemed costly, but it was the back to back scoreless draws against mid-table opposition which proved to be their undoing in the thick of the run in. They recorded a 5-0 win at Almondsbury on the last day which, in the event, proved to be in vain. However, the Town had claimed their highest ever league placing, as Michael Meaker (25) and Christian Glynn (22) had contributed a combined 47 goals between them.

Bishops Cleeve finished just three points behind the top two and had got off to a better start than both of them, but fell just short because of their modest form when playing fellow challengers: in the eight games against the other members of the final top four, they won just once (1-0 at Didcot). However, one defeat in their opening seven showed great promise. They remained hard to beat, but didn't achieve the long winning runs of the other sides: five straight wins in November forming their best sequence. Although they closed the campaign eight unbeaten, the significant 1-1 draw with Southall meant the title was out of their hands on the final day despite recording a 4-0 home win. They were unusual in that despite scoring 94 goals, their top scorer claimed a relatively modest 14, suggesting they lacked the devastating finisher to settle the tight games against fellow challengers although, on balance, having six players contributing nine or more goals seemed to work in their favour.

Slimbridge joined the Bishops on 89 points, but had to make do with fourth place. This was despite having the best defence in the league, with just 29 conceded. However, their goals for tally of 85 was the smallest of the top six. This relative lack of goals didn't seem a problem, though, when they won their second game 8-0 at Pewsey Vale, but early September brought an important home loss to Southall Town. However, the 22nd November witnessed the start of an impressive 20 match unbeaten run, which included 15 wins, and took the Gloucestershire club into the closing weeks of the season. This had put them in an outstanding position with just three games left, but a return of four points from the final three games was perhaps disappointing, when maximum points would have handed them the title.

Completing the quintet were Didcot Town, whose problem was the opposite of Slimbridge's ...too few draws. They won

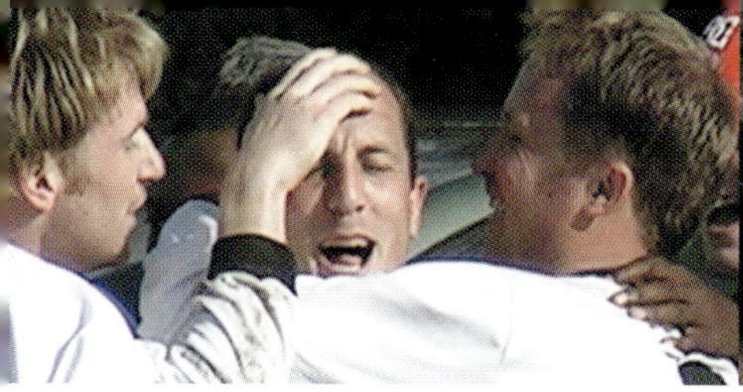

the same number of matches as the top two but had some of their ten defeats been rescued into draws, they would have gone closer. However, it looked very promising in the Autumn as they won ten of their opening twelve, with games in hand because of their ongoing cup commitments, and the 3-1 win at Brackley was particularly key. With Ian Concannon in inspired goalscoring form, they enjoyed four straight wins, as November became December. However, hopes were hit with three straight losses at the end of 2003, including damaging reverses to challenging colleagues, Bishops Cleeve and Brackley. With their defence in good form, seven wins in eight repaired some of the damage, but in mid-February, with the other title hopefuls in superb form, Didcot began to slip off the pace, with one win from six. Although they closed strongly, and recorded a win at Slimbridge, there was fractionally too much to do, and their title hopes fell before the final day. Unlike the other teams, it was very much a one-man show in the scoring stakes, as Concannon scored 29 goals.

Gerard Butler

ESSEX SENIOR LEAGUE

Far from it being a one horse race, the Essex Senior League title challenge was one of the most thrilling around, despite the eventual winning margin of Concord Rangers being five points. Back in August, alongside Town, Basildon United had been tipped to do well, and seemed to justify this by handing the Champions Enfield Town a 4-1 opening reverse, but they failed to sustain their challenge and dropped into mid-table. However, Enfield Town's wobbly start continued with only one win in their first four matches, including a crunch 2-2 draw with Romford, for whom Kevin Clark was making an early impact as they put in a challenge.

The opening days of September saw Town pick up as they welcomed the League's new side, London All Peoples Sports Association. This is a community club with its roots in the Asian community of Newham, but playing their home matches at Aveley. Fresh from their first ever win at this level, 2-1 at Waltham Abbey, Enfield Town beat them 2-1 in the first of six straight wins which would propel them to top spot after a home success against struggling Stansted on the 24th September.

This had provided a real platform for them, particularly as Romford hit something of a sticky patch in October. However, the significance of Town being held to a 1-1 draw by Concord Rangers on 11th October would only become clear later. Indeed, when the Middlesex side went on to draw with Ilford the following midweek, it set a trend which would see them struggle to win the crunch games, and fail to build any advantage over their rivals.

This meant that the top of the table would frequently change hands, with Ilford in particular always in contention. Romford announced their return to form in some style in November as they recorded back to back wins against Basildon and away to Enfield Town, drawing a close to the latter's long unbeaten run. At the other end of the table, London APSA were finding the going tricky, as were Hullbridge Sports, who added to some encouraging displays in the cups by recording their first league win, on the 15th November versus Stansted.

After the turn of the year, title hopefuls Enfield Town went head to head with Concord Rangers - again Town failed to win a six-pointer as Rangers scored a last gasp equaliser which would prove priceless in the final reckoning. However, the team of the moment were undoubtedly Romford whose stunning run of nine wins and a draw from ten games saw them surge to the top of the table, after Ilford and Enfield Town shared a 2-2 draw in the then clash of the top two.

Romford would hold the leading spot for two months, as Town hit a bad streak with wins again hard to come by, including a shock home defeat to Waltham Abbey in February, and an

entertaining 5-5 draw at a Brentwood side destined for the bottom three. However, as March arrived, there were several sides in contention, although the balance began to shift with some crucial results emerging, particularly as most clubs had games in hand on the current leaders. Romford's hopes were dealt a decisive blow with a damaging double defeat in early March as they fell to two 2-1 losses at the hands of Ilford and Concord in the space of a week. Enfield Town, holders of the Gordon Bradsted Memorial Trophy, were surprisingly eliminated from it in a surprise 1-0 reverse at London APSA, while Ilford, Sawbridgeworth and Romford were all level at the top on 53 points.

However, both Romford and Enfield Town bounced back, but for the latter, a late burst of form came too late, and a late scoreless draw with Sawbridgeworth meant they missed out on a top three berth, although there was some silverware as they lifted the League Cup. Early April saw Romford move back to second with a key success at Sawbridgeworth and a crushing win over Burnham, as well as winning the Memorial Trophy, 3-0 against Ilford, with both sides still in the promotion race.

A burst of wins by Concord Rangers had not gone unnoticed, though, as they were clocking up points from their games in hand, with an unbeaten run stretching back to late February. Their eventual winning streak numbered ten games, the ninth of which saw them lift the title with a commanding 4-0 success against Romford on the 20th April. They had the League's best strike rate with 75 goals scored, of which ESL golden boot winner Danny Heale contributed 32. And, whilst that long winning run was the decisive factor, they did very well by winning the important games. Ironically, both Ilford and Enfield Town lost fewer games than the champions but failed to gain the crucial advantage by drawing too often. Concord's title success was their second, following their triumph in 1997/98 under current East Thurrock manager, Lee Patterson, but unfortunately Ben Embery, who had masterminded the repeat, parted company with the club when they opted not to take promotion to the Ryman League. Ironically, Embery had won the Essex title with Canvey Island in 1986/87, and so had succeeded with both of the Island's clubs.

The final table saw a stray game on the 1st May, in which Ilford beat London APSA to take second place, with Sawbridgeworth and Enfield Town making up the top four. The restructuring saw Enfield Town offered a place in Ryman Division Two, only for the invitation to be withdrawn just a couple of weeks later, and extended instead to Ilford, who will now be the team to leave the league.

Gerard Butler

EASTERN COUNTIES PREMIER

AFC Sudbury retained the Eastern Counties Premier Division title for a fourth consecutive season, the first team to achieve this feat since Lowestoft Town in the 1970s, but they would be the first to admit that this was far from a formality, particularly in an intriguing first half of the season. It had been all change at the Kings Marsh, as Keith Martin announced his departure at the end of the previous season, with assistant Gary Harvey stepping in, and most of the players staying as well, including the trio of Gary Bennett, Sam Banya and Andrew Claydon, who would contribute around 60 goals of the team's final 123 league tally.

There was an early hiccup with a surprise home reverse to Newmarket, but then a 14 match unbeaten run ensued through to early December, which featured a 6-0 win at Stowmarket and a 7-0 home win in the return fixture. Former manager Martin was helping out at Wroxham, and it was this side who handed AFC a 5-1 defeat on the 6th December but key to their eventual success was their ability to bounce back from defeat. With strong closes to the season a feature among all the challengers, a sequence of one loss in 14 (to Wroxham again) to the end of the season saw them take the title with a 1-0 win at Dereham Town - Sam Banya popping in yet another crucial goal with a 93rd minute winner meaning they could relax with three games left.

However, relaxation was certaintly not on the agenda for AFC in an intriguing Autumn as, for a long time, their hopes of retaining the title looked in real jeopardy thanks to Robert Fleck's Diss Town. After an inconsistent August, which brought only one win in four, Diss then hit form and went on a 17 match winning streak in the league, which at one point saw Diss twelve points clear of their rivals at the top. The last match in the run came exactly three months later, when Diss' 4-0 success against Lowestoft saw them nine points clear of AFC Sudbury, after the latter's loss at Wroxham, but crucially the defending champions had two games in hand. With the league intriguingly poised, the top two met in Suffolk, with Diss rescuing a point in a 2-2 draw. The Norfolk side hit a wobble with two straight defeats allowing AFC to hit the top. However, Diss returned to pole position two weeks later, and they re-built a twelve point advantage thanks to six straight wins in February.

It was looking good for Diss. However, 'Beware the Ides of March' seemed an appropriate comment, as their challenge inexplicably collapsed in that month. They collected a solitary point from the four games played, including costly losses at home to Wroxham, as well as at Maldon. Although Coren Hardy and Stuart Jopling contributed an aggregate 60 goals by the

season's end, Town had hit a real goal drought at this stage, and the run of defeats stretched into April, their 4-2 loss at Newmarket being a fifth straight reverse. With chances of the title long gone by now, it was now a bid for second place, and whilst three late wins against Stowmarket, Histon Reserves and Halstead boosted morale, these hopes were extinguished in home defeats to Maldon and Sudbury, and they had to make do with fourth.

With AFC Sudbury declining promotion, it was Maldon Town who took second place and a spot in the Southern League Eastern Division. They had made a strong start to the season, but were a little too inconsistent to push the leaders any closer, with some disappointing results in November and December one of the key factors, particularly a 2-1 home loss to a Tiptree side who would eventually be relegated.

However, after that surprise, they would only lose two of the remaining 25 games, and those against AFC Sudbury and Wroxham. After that potentially devastating Wroxham result, they closed the season with twelve wins and three draws, including seven straight maximum hauls at the end of the season. They also led the table briefly at the end of March following a 5-0 crushing of Diss, but in the event, AFC Sudbury's games in hand proved a decisive factor. Wroxham's season was incredibly similar to the side which nudged them into third, as they too had a bright start with four wins out of the first five, before a September slump yielded just two points from a quartet of matches, including a significant home loss to Diss. The side bounced back to keep in touch with some particularly miserly defending over the Autumn and, in their last 25 games, their only defeat was a shock one at the hands of Halstead. There were crunch wins over the rest of the top four to savour, particularly the 4-1 home success against Maldon. They could also boast a 2-0 win at AFC Sudbury, thus completing the double over them, and a 3-1 victory at Diss, as they concluded the season in free-scoring form.

However, with all of those goals flying around, there were bound to be some strugglers and, in particular, it was a season to forget for Fakenham who only collected eleven points (and two wins) all season, letting in 130 goals and only scoring 30. However, their companions in the bottom three were not much better, as Tiptree accumulated 34 points, but having let in 95 goals and only scoring 40, they would always struggle, and two wins in the last 13 was a distinctly modest run-in. Gorleston's poor end to the season was also the main factor in their 20th place finish, as a twelve match sequence without a win rendered their last day success at Tiptree academic, but Stowmarket Town and Dereham Town both got key wins in March and April to pull clear, the latter getting a particularly noteworthy 1-0 win against fifth-placed Soham Town Rangers.

Gerard Butler

UNITED COUNTIES PREMIER DIVISION

The big game experience of Spalding United proved the key factor in the United Counties League Premier Division championship race as the Tulips claimed their fifth title and an immediate return to the higher level.

Following their relegation from the Dr Martens League, Spalding opted for an almost complete change of personnel, hiring manager Dick Creasey who had led neighbours Holbeach to the 2002/03 crown. Two-thirds of the successful Tigers squad followed Creasey to the Halley Stewart Field and, with vast experience in their ranks in the shape of skipper Nick Keeble, midfield powerhouse Steve Appleby and experienced strikers Micky Nuttell and Lee Hudson, Spalding always looked set to be major contenders.

They overcame a dismal December, which saw them pick up just a single point from four home matches, to emerge all the stronger after the turn of the year, and the late season signing of the league's top marksman - Ian Dunn from Yaxley - proved a managerial masterstroke as the striker scored nine goals in nine games to nudge Spalding across the finishing line and promotion - but to the Unibond League rather than the old haunts of the Dr Martens, following the restructuring of the top levels of the Non-League game.

Twelve months earlier Holbeach had timed their run to perfection to burst past long time leaders Newport Pagnell. In 2004 Spalding, featuring many of the same players, did likewise to inch ahead of Buckingham who were unable to maintain a blistering early pace which saw them win 16 of their first 17 matches. Their only slip in that sequence was a 2-0 home defeat by Spalding which ended the Robins' ten match winning start.

The pivotal moment in Buckingham's season was a controversial Vase defeat at Lymington in December. The Robins had four players red carded in the New Forest, and when the suspensions took effect they coincided with injuries to key players. Buckingham's winning habit deserted them, a series of draws enabled the chasing clubs to close the gap, and even when back to full strength, Buckingham never quite recaptured their early season sparkle. A sequence of four defeats in April saw them overhauled by Spalding and, at season's end, their only tangible reward was the Baker Perkins Trophy awarded to the highest scoring team - no surprise given the impressive array of striking talent on board at Ford Meadow, with Meshach Cole, Darren Harmon, Reuben Max-Grant and Abdul Abdi all boasting double figure goal tallies.

Top flight new boys Harrowby finished third in their Premier Division debut, with striker Martin Wormall catching the eye in his first season at the level as several professional clubs kept tabs on his progress. The Arrows had plenty of higher grade experience in their ranks with Lee Sharp, Wayne Hallcro, Lee Marshall and Richard Holmes among the quality players recruited by managerial pocket dynamo Graham Drury. A fixture backlog damaged St Neots' title hopes. They reached three cup finals and the last 32 of the Vase with the consequence being that their late season burst into honours contention ran out of steam in the final furlong. Star performer for the Saints was Steve Kuhne who scored goals galore in the first half of the season before switching to defence with good effect.

At the wrong end of the table Daventry finished six points adrift of nearest rivals Long Buckby but both retained top flight status. Daventry were surprise strugglers after four wins in the first six matches, but amidst injuries and suspensions they won just once thereafter. Buckby underwent a traumatic season which saw Geoff Green, Kevin Townsend and finally Aidy Mann have spells in the hot seat. The trio called on the services of 95 players between them in a search for the right blend.

Northampton Spencer and Desborough both spent much of the campaign in the relegation scrap. The Millers pulled themselves to safety in March and early April as goalkeeper Oliver Urquhart kept six successive clean sheets, Spencer picking up 16 vital points. Ar Tarn's first half of the season form contrasted sharply with impressive cup results but Simon Rielly's appointment as manager saw the arrival of some influential players and a move up the table.

Jeremy Biggs

NORTHERN COUNTIES EAST LEAGUE

It was an exciting season in the Premier Division, with the destination of the League title only decided on the last day, and then only on goals scored, as the top two had the same goal difference. Ossett Albion were crowned champions after scoring three more goals than Eastwood Town. Albion made a very solid start to 2003/04, with the veteran Micky Norbury making an early impact with two goals in the decisive 3-2 success at Brigg Town. The West Yorkshire club began to wobble slightly, though, as they suffered consecutive reverses against in-form Eastwood and Buxton.

However, they got back on track with a five match winning streak, including a 5-1 victory at struggling Borrowash, 5-0 against Hallam, and most importantly of all, 3-1 against Goole. Their good form continued into the spring, but February saw the potentially costly loss of a lead against Brigg in stoppage time, with both sides in the thick of the promotion race. It did indeed knock them off course slightly, as the wins didn't flow quite as easily as they became inconsistent, though still enjoying some heavy wins against weaker opposition. Mid-March witnessed some important results against fellow hopefuls, as they claimed a point after being two-down at Buxton and shared a scoreless draw with Eastwood. Three 1-0 wins on the bounce against struggling opposition gave them new momentum, and though the goals had dried up, their unbeaten run meant they could hang on to top spot with a 3-0 success against Borrowash on the last day clinching a place in Unibond Division One.

The side who had to be content with second, but still joined them in the Unibond League, were Eastwood Town, a comparative rarity, as they bounced straight back after relegation the previous year under the continued charge of Bryan Chambers. However, despite winning their first game 3-0 at home to Harrogate, promotion seemed a long way away, as they collected just a solitary point from their next four games,

including a heavy loss at Brigg Town. Having overcome this, however, they recorded an impressive nine straight wins, beating Ossett 3-1 along the way, their success built on a miserly defence which saw just four goals conceded and five clean sheets during this run. Once this good run was brought to an end, though, their form at the turn of the year was decidedly mixed as they were defeated by Selby and Buxton, both firmly in the promotion race themselves.

However, there was a lifeline for the Nottinghamshire club, as their continued involvement in the Vase meant they were accumulating games in hand which would firmly put them in the promotion picture if used to good effect. Would they do this? The answer was a resounding 'yes' as February 14th's 2-1 win at Selby marked the start of a superb run-in, which saw twelve wins, four draws and just two losses from the remaining 18 contests. Once again, their defensive record was formidable, boasting twelve shut-outs in this time.

Brigg Town, the reigning Vase holders, completed the trio of clubs joining the Unibond League as the astounding 37 years that Ralph Clayton had spent with the club ended brightly. Town made a strong start, recording an eight match unbeaten start before suffering two defeats in three against Thackley, and crucially, Ossett Albion.

However, eight wins in a row, including successes against Pickering and Goole, catapulted them right into the title picture. Although they never quite managed to regain this form, it was this sequence that was to prove the foundations on which their promotion was built. However, they opened 2004 on an encouraging note with a single goal win against Selby. A lean spell ensued in the spring, as they collected just a pair of wins from nine games, as hopes of the title receded. They rescued the season, though, as a burst of free-scoring form led them to four wins and two draws, which was a decisive factor in seeing off the challenges of Sheffield, Pickering, Goole and Buxton, with Brigg's promotion only secured with a win over the last of these. Sheffield claimed fourth place but, despite expenditure on ground improvements, found themselves ineligible for promotion, amid wider surprise that a fourth side was not promoted from the NCEL, as had seemed likely at an earlier stage. They had done exceptionally well in games against their closest rivals, having won at both Brigg and Eastwood, as well as taken a point at Ossett, but they suffered from too many draws and a lack of consistency at times. Of the other unsuccessful challengers, the fall from grace of Selby, who were eighth in the final table, was the most dramatic. They were one of the teams of the Autumn, as they started the season off with seven wins and two draws to occupy a leading position in the league, and their excellent form kept them in a title chasing position into the new year, with the win at Eastwood on the 27th January particularly noteworthy. However, as they entered February, a single point against rivals Eastwood, Ossett and Buxton began a 15 match winless run, which would see the Robins plummet out of contention, and enjoy just one more win. Goole were unsettled by the early departure of Steve Richards to Ossett Town, to be replaced by former Harrogate Railway manager Paul Marshall; their away form was on a par with the champions, but modest home form and too many draws were their undoing. The same applied to Buxton - one place below them. Pickering's fifth spot, four points below Brigg, was built on an excellent home record, but their poor away record left them thinking what might have been. There were no sides leaving by the other end of the division, as Brodsworth and Borrowash found themselves reprieved.

Gerard Butler

KENT LEAGUE

At the finale, Cray Wanderers pulled ahead of a close chasing pack to win their second consecutive league title. This time around, the club that claims to be the second oldest in the country, applied for promotion. With a well established ground-share at Bromley's Hayes Lane, the step up was duly accepted, so Cray have bade farewell to the Kent League, following in the recent footsteps of Chatham Town and Folkestone Invicta.

It was widely agreed that Ian Jenkins' Cray were deserved winners. Despite a pile up of fixtures, largely due to a fine run that took them to the Quarter-Finals of the FA Vase, they seldom faltered. They started at a canter, drawing at Hythe Town on a sweltering first day of the season and then winning their next twelve matches, at the end of which they had scored 49 goals and conceded a mere eight. They did not lose a league match until early December, a surprise 3-1 home reverse against Greenwich Borough.

While Cray clearly showed they would be the team to beat once more, there was no doubt that Maidstone United would also be there or there-abouts. Although not on the scale of AFC Wimbledon, this revival of a former league club attracts strong support (average gates of 250 or so) and has relatively deep pockets in comparison to most Kent League clubs. What they do miss at present is their own ground; they ground-share with Sittingbourne, and the distance of this 'home' from the town of Maidstone means their way upwards is blocked at present. A return to a new ground in Maidstone is a top priority. One other

thing that the Stones lacked last season was consistency. In the end, ten league draws was a telling statistic. Unglamorous Thamesmead Town pushed Cray closest. Manager, Paul Blade, made the best use of his limited resources but, for the third consecutive season, the club could not quite maintain their challenge. This time around, they did gain the consolation of victory over Cray in the Kent League Cup final at Folkestone in May.

One club that flickered for a while but then faded was Greenwich Borough. This was an example of that non-league phenomenon - an injection of money by a local benefactor, but in Greenwich's case the backer had upped and left by the end of the season, taking his finances to Fisher Athletic. Another of the south-east London sides, VCD Athletic, had a strong season, while Whitstable Town put together a great run and could have been champion contenders but for an indifferent start to the season. Hythe Town showed a similar purple patch in the second half of the season, winning ten consecutive matches late on. Both sides could be strong contenders this season.

Two clubs joined the Kent League at the start of the 2003/04 season and had mixed fortunes. Sevenoaks Town were promoted from the Kent County League and settled well at the new level. One quirk of their season was a reluctance to draw matches - they had only one draw in the league all season. Sporting Bengal United had been a more surprising addition to the league. They are the representative team of the Bangladesh Football Association (BFA) UK and moved up into the Kent League from the London County League. Playing at Mile End in Tower Hamlets, this was stretching the boundaries of Kent somewhat but the truth of the matter is that the Kent League does not have strength in depth (17 clubs last season, once Sporting Bengal had been added) and was keen to welcome any newcomers, within reason. The newcomers proved to be out of their depth and took some thumping defeats along the way, but they won friends with their warm welcome for visiting teams and there was widespread glee when, in March, they won their first match as a Kent League side - 4-0, no less, at Tunbridge Wells (the glee outside of Tunbridge Wells was partly because no one had wanted to be the first to be defeated by the newcomers). It was no more than they deserved because they did not have their share of luck, being pipped late on in a fair few games. It is to be hoped that they can now progress, as their final record does not make happy reading: five points from their 32 games, 26 goals scored and 110 conceded.

At the other end of the table, Cray gained the points they needed to win the title on a Monday evening in late April, with a 3-1 win at home to Hythe. This saved them from having to pick up points from their last two fixtures, both of which were against Maidstone. It was an achievement to savour for Jenkins, a consummate club man. Last season was his twelfth with the club, having started as a player, and he had scored in each of the previous eleven campaigns. This time he limited himself to a few appearances on the substitutes' bench. His charges beat most of their rivals at least once and were top-scorers in the league, thanks to the efforts of Jamie Kempster (over 30 goals from midfield in the season), Ricky Bennett and Jamie Wood. Other clubs had impressive goalscorers (John Main at VCD, Sam Prett at Whitstable, and Richard Sinden at Maidstone) but Cray Wanderers had more contributors as well as impressive youngsters such as Danny Whelan at right-back and Sam Wood on the wing. They will be missed by the Kent League, especially as Erith & Belvedere gained a reprieve from relegation.

Martin Whybrow

NORTH WEST COUNTIES DIVISION ONE

2003/04 was one of the most exciting seasons in the League's history when the Championship was only decided on the final day of the season with Clitheroe beating Nantwich Town at Jackson Avenue in a five goal thriller before a crowd of 480, with Mossley supporters turning up to support Nantwich Town to create a very good atmosphere. It was a pulsating game with Clitheroe leading 2-0 at half-time and looking comfortable. Nantwich came out in the second half determined to make a game of it, drawing level and looking the stronger of the two teams but Clitheroe grabbed the winner in the final five minutes leaving a disappointed Mossley in the runners-up position.

Throughout the season three clubs - Clitheroe, Mossley and Woodley Sports - dominated the top of the table with first place changing hands frequently. Due to the restructure, Clitheroe, Mossley, Woodley Sports and Warrington Town are being promoted to the Northern Premier League First Division. Champions Clitheroe, who so often have seen their league form suffer due to the success they have had in the FA Vase, this year exited the cup competitions early allowing them to concentrate solely on the League, going one better than last season. This is the second time that Clitheroe have won the Championship, the previous time being 1985.

Runners-up Mossley have always been strong contenders for honours but amazingly have never won the domestic league title and, on several occasions last term, dropped points to teams at the foot of the table. Fleetwood Town finished in third place but

their ground had not achieved the required ground grading criteria for entry into the Northern Premier League.

Fourth placed Woodley Sports led the division until the closing weeks of the season when they fell victim to a series of injuries and a slight loss of form. Woodley Sports won the Cheshire Senior Cup against Witton Albion, becoming the first North West Counties team to achieve this honour.

Fifth placed Warrington Town had a remarkable second half of the season, their performances taking them from the foot of the table in December to fourth place thanks to an unbeaten league run of 15 games. They won their last game of the season 1-0 at Bacup Borough to leapfrog over Newcastle Town into that fifth place.

Spare a thought for Newcastle Town though, who missed out on promotion. They had a stuttering start to the season but never fulfilled their potential to reach the top of the League. They also missed out in the Challenge Cup giving one of their worst performances of the season in the Final against Bacup Borough.

Two clubs, Curzon Ashton and Skelmersdale United, are currently in the process of building new grounds - Skelmersdale's is due for the coming season and Curzon Ashton's for season 2005/06. Nantwich Town have obtained planning permission for a new sports complex and are in the process of finalising the details prior to work commencing, they also hope to be ready for season 2005/06.

Alsager Town finishing a creditable eighth place in their second season in the top flight, they were up at the top for most of the season but dropped off in the last two months. Stone Dominoes also had an excellent season in their first year in the league, they are hoping to return to their spiritual home of Springbank Stadium when their new floodlights are installed.

Bacup Borough, champions of Division Two the season prior, fell by the wayside in the league after a good start. However, they won the League Challenge Cup convincingly 3-0 against Newcastle Town at Haig Avenue, Southport. Congleton Town continue to improve their ground facilities and will be pushing hard for promotion in 2004/05.

Salford City also fell by the wayside after a good start to the season and Trafford must be extremely disappointed with their League position of 16th after being relegated the previous season from the Northern League.

St Helens Town finished a disappointing 19th in the table and are hoping that their off field problems are behind them as they look to the future with Joe Paladino in charge.

Squires Gate finished third from bottom but have a new man, Ged Starkey, at the helm for his first full season. The bottom two clubs Abbey Hey and Atherton Collieries have both escaped relegation due to there being four clubs promoted. Coming into the First Division next season will be Second Division champions Colne along with Maine Road, Formby and Great Harwood Town whose main objective will be to remain there for the following season.

Geoff Wilkinson

WESSEX LEAGUE

The 2003/04 Wessex League season belonged to Winchester City. Not only did they win the FA Vase and, in Andrew Forbes, possess the hottest marksman in English football (78 goals in all competitions), they also won the Wessex League title by nine points, beating Wimborne Town into second place. The figures are no doubt worth repeating - 35 wins, three draws and two defeats speak for themselves, but these are stats that are made even more impressive when you take into account the massive 151 goals they scored in the process.

If the other teams in the Wessex League were in any doubt as to Winchester's title winning potential, then

they were given a swift wake up call as City won their opening six games, scoring 27 goals in the process. Despite their winning run being brought to an end at home against Wimborne (a 2-1 home defeat), City were still left three points clear at the top of the table with AFC Newbury (managed by former Portsmouth favourite Guy Whittingham), Gosport Borough and 2002 champions Andover making up the chasing pack.

For the clubs just behind the leaders it must have been like sitting in a Mini trying to overtake a Ferrari as City responded to their first defeat by winning the next nine games at an average of nearly five and a half goals per game. You would be forgiven for thinking that this sort of form would have seen City storming away with the league. However, as the season entered Christmas, it was Wimborne who were setting the pace. The Magpies had gone the first 21 games of the season unbeaten (winning 18 of those), which gave them a seven-point cushion going into the festive period. However, slip-ups against Lymington & New Milton, Whitchurch and Fareham in the New Year let Winchester back in the hunt and, when City defeated Wimborne in the top-of-the-table clash on 17th April, Winchester had opened up a three point lead at the top. Wimborne only had one game left to play so, due to their vastly superior goal difference, City all but clinched the title. That still didn't stop them winning their next two games and, although the season ended on a sour note with a last day defeat at home to Lymington & New Milton, it brought to an end a dominating season for Neil Hards' men - something that was summed up by Gosport Borough boss Mick Marsh after his side were dealt a 6-1 hammering in January - 'When they play like that, you just can't compete.'

The chasing pack were all there or thereabouts for much of the campaign and were in fine goalscoring fettle. However, it was a ferocious pace set by the top two as third placed Gosport ended the season 16 points adrift of the champions. Lymington & New Milton and AFC Newbury made up the rest of the top five with Andover, despite their 100 goals, back in sixth.

It was all a bit tougher to call at the other end of the table, although it didn't always look like being so. At Christmas, Downton and Whitchuch were well adrift at the bottom, only managing three wins between them all season and both with extremely leaky defences (Whitchurch conceding 74 in 22 and Downton 67 in 21). However, they both turned things around in the New Year and really made a fight of it. The real success story was Downton who picked up some vital wins during the run-in and, despite ending the season with the third worst defensive record in the league, they managed to push themselves up to 19th place in the table. On the other hand, Whitchurch's revival was all in vain, as they still finished the season two points adrift at the bottom, despite accumulating double the amount of points in the second half of the season as they had done in the first. Bournemouth and Blackfield & Langley made up the rest of the bottom three, with the latter's failings evident in the fact that they only managed to pick up seven points between Christmas and the end of the season. BAT Sports, also in the bottom three at Christmas, enjoyed a decent second half to the season (the highlight of which was a 2-1 win over Winchester in February) that saw them push themselves up to 15th. Portland, Moneyfields and Alton Town all did enough to ensure that they didn't get sucked into the battle at the bottom.

No teams were promoted from the Wessex League as Winchester failed to get their ground up to scratch in time, but Blackfield & Langley and Whitchurch's demotion means Hamworthy United and Vosper Thorneycroft will be the new kids on the block this season.

Wimborne's disappointment at losing out on the title wasn't made any easier when Winchester rubbed salt into the wound by signing two of their best players in the close season with midfielder Mark Smith and centre-half Darren Powell joining the champions. Winchester also snatched Fareham Town's top scorer Jamie Musselwhite, a move that angered Fareham boss John Gittens. With Musselwhite teaming up with Forbes (whose proposed move to AFC Bournemouth looks to have fallen through), who'd bet against City beating that 151-goal tally this time around - defenders beware!

Joe Bush

Four Nations

2004 saw the Four Nations Tournament switch to four of Scotland's picturesque Highland League grounds. It was in this setting that England's hopes of retaining the title they won in Wales last year were dashed. Wales recovered from taking the wooden spoon on home soil last time around by repeating their 2002 Championship, but all of the sides gave a good account of themselves. There were some positives for England, despite being dogged by injuries and withdrawals in the run-up to the competition, as a number of players made an impressive impact and they saved the best for last by beating Scotland 3-1 despite playing virtually half the game with ten men.

Princess Royal Park, Banff, the home of Deveronvale, and very much the jewel in the crown of Highland grounds, was the venue as 319 watched England versus the Republic of Ireland. When Steve Guinan's tap in put the Three Lions ahead after six minutes, everything seemed on course to retain the title. However, it was not to be a repeat of last season's 4-0 win as John Flood brought the Irish, who consisted exclusively of under-21 Eircom League players, level from close range. They impressed with their quality of play, and stunned England with a double burst just after the hour, as Eamon Zayed tapped in from ten yards after 61 minutes and, moments later, John Russell's powerful strike made it three. However, there was a thrilling finale, as Glen Southam, just on as a substitute, set up Guinan for a stunning 20 yarder, but Ireland held their lead so that England began with a defeat.

Paul Fairclough, the England National Game manager, said: 'I'm disappointed to have lost, but overall the best team won'. He added that his side should have taken their first half chances. His jubilant opposite number, Paddy Devlin, the Bray Wanderers manager, commented that, 'We only had this squad together last Sunday, and you have to admire what they have done against a good side'. The other game that night, a 0-0 draw between Scotland and Wales at Kynoch Park, Keith, attracted 700, and meant that Ireland were in pole position after one match.

Keith, the starting point of Colin Hendry's illustrious career, was also the place where 240 watched England hoping to get their challenge back on track, as they made four changes from the Irish defeat. This was a very tight encounter, in contrast to the Irish game, though Liam Hatch was denied in the first half by Tony Roberts, the Dagenham & Redbridge keeper, one of a number of Conference players in the Welsh line-up. Guinan went tantalisingly close to his third goal of the tournament when his 30 yarder clattered against the woodwork, but it was Wales' Graham Evans who broke the deadlock in the 52nd minute when Damon Searle's long free-kick was backheeled into his path by Ben Davies. England failed to breach their opponents' formidable rearguard and they added a second when substitute Carl Owens clipped in from six yards, leaving Paul Fairclough to comment: 'They

were stronger than us, and more committed and aggressive - they deserved to win'. Wales manager, Andy Beattie, also in charge of Dr Martens Merthyr Tydfil and the Welsh Womens team, observed: 'It was a tight game - all of these games are like derbies. I thought we shaded both halves, but we needed the goals'. Ironically, England's 2-0 win last year against Wales had been played at Merthyr's Penydarren Park.

Meanwhile, at Bellslea Park, Fraserburgh, in front of an impressive 1,171, Scotland moved into title contention as Michael Stephen and Ian Murray gave them a 2-0 win over the Irish, who were down to ten men in the twelfth minute when Robbie Doyle was sent off.

With one game left, Wales, Scotland and Ireland were all in with a chance to win the competition, whilst England had to beat Scotland 3-0, and hope that Wales won, to avoid the wooden spoon. On a bright and sunny Sunday, the staggered kick-offs saw Wales play Ireland at Inverurie, and a scoreless first half ensued. Hugh Davey volleyed the Irish ahead just into the second half, but Wales roared back as Graham Evans headed the Welsh level, Chris Todd put them in front on 71 minutes and a Chris Giles double wrapped things up. It meant that the title was theirs unless Scotland overturned their superior goal difference by beating England 4-0. 2,200 returned to Banff to see whether it was possible. An early goal was crucial to the Scottish aim, and it came as Andy Tretton brought down Stuart McKay; Michael Stephen converted the resultant penalty. McKay then went very close to a second as he missed a 21st minute tap in, and this was to prove the turning point. Guinan notched his third goal of the week when he converted a 25th minute spot-kick after a handball in the area, and an electric spell saw Southam put the Three Lions ahead with a well-struck 15 yarder three minutes later, with Hatch's fierce angled drive providing a third on the half-hour. However, Scotland went close again as Barrie Stephen's powerful strike cannoned off the woodwork, and they seemed to have a chance when Southam was dismissed just a few minutes into the second period, but excellent defending by England kept the score at 3-1.

That meant they pushed Ireland into bottom spot, and Scotland had to be content with second place. Paul Fairclough said afterwards: 'That performance had been something we had been building towards all week. You have seen one of the most professional performances at this level - the way they worked together when down to ten men and restored our pride by holding on to the win'. A disappointed Jim Sinclair, the Scotland coach, observed, 'There was little in the tank and little spark. If we'd have scored the second, it would have been a different result'.

So what of the tournament overall? The Scotland game against England attracted the largest crowd in Four Nations history, and their other two fixtures had very healthy attendances as well, although the figures for the non-Scotland games were modest. It will have increased the profile of the Highland League, in which most of the Scottish players appear, and was well organised throughout, with the good weather helping. The local media really rallied round the competition, compared with previous years, and the Scottish FA and Highland League can be content with a job well done. From an English perspective, it was a little disappointing, but the win against Scotland was undoubtedly something to savour and there were good performances from the likes of Hatch and Southam, and a stirring swansong from Guinan, who signed for Division Three Cheltenham Town just before the competition started. A very enjoyable week, all in all, and this supporter can't wait for Cork in 2005.

Gerard Butler

PyramidFootball Special Reports

2004-05

Grounds to Visit

Stalybridge Celtic

Surrounded by the beautiful rolling Pennines, just nine miles north west of Manchester lies Bower Fold, home of Stalybridge Celtic FC. The quaint town of Stalybridge seems a million miles away from the hustle and bustle of the big city and, indeed, there isn't an office block in sight. If a picturesque stadium, friendly, laid back match atmosphere and guaranteed entertainment on the pitch sounds like your ideal afternoon, then a visit to Bower Fold should be high on your agenda this season.

The actual journey to Stalybridge, from all areas of the country, is not always a pleasant and enjoyable experience, particularly in winter. The wonderful scenery is somewhat offset by narrow roads and sharp bends. Coupled with heavy traffic, it does not make for the easiest of drives.

The main route to Stalybridge from the south or east of England is via the sometimes treacherous Woodhead Pass. This snake-like road weaves and cuts its way through the Pennines and in winter is frequently closed. Many motorists take this route as a short cut to Manchester as opposed to using the M62. However, the inevitable bottleneck that occurs once you arrive at Mottram-in-Longdendale, makes one wonder why so many people believe that this is a better option.

Stalybridge is approximately five miles further north than Mottram and, if you are lucky, the congestion can be avoided. The ground is situated on Mottram Road (A6018), and is approximately one and a half miles past the Roe Cross Inn on the left hand side. The stadium is small and is set back off the road, almost below it in fact, with a large dominating hill as its backdrop.

If you can cope with the traffic jams, then the ground and surrounding area is worth the effort. The over-looking hill above the new 'Lord Tom Pendry Stand' provides a fantastic setting for the ground. With the lush greenery of many large trees immediately behind the stand and then the heather-covered summit further back, it is quite breath-taking. You are drawn towards it and can spend more time watching that than the game itself. It gives a whole new meaning to the term 'grass banks' so infamous amongst non-league grounds.

The team finished fourth in the Unibond Premier Division two seasons ago and most supporters expected the club to be major contenders for promotion, once again, last season. Things didn't go to plan though, and a place in the Conference North this season is all that can be awaited. They are a very ambitious club and, on the many occasions I have attended to report on games, the belief that this team will be back in the Conference is most definitely there. Indeed, there is no reason why this cannot come to fruition; a good nucleus of players is in place and, with a couple of new additions to give that cutting edge, it could happen sooner rather than later.

The fans are passionate too and, although some may go along simply because they can't get tickets to watch City or United, that doesn't mean that they are not behind the team. It is not uncommon to see dozens of Manchester City or United fans in attendance, with one eye on the game but both ears on the radio.

Clubs like Stalybridge symbolise what non-league football is all about. This club is at the heart of the community and it brings people together, purely for the love of the game. It isn't the prettiest football you will ever see and there are no big names on show here. But a good atmosphere and fantastic surroundings make for a thoroughly enjoyable day out.

Mike Jarvis

Lancaster City

If the three buzzwords in property are location, location, location, Lancaster City's home ground is a prime piece of real estate. Situated close to the city centre, their historic Giant Axe ground lies in the shadow of the imposing tenth century castle and the ancient Priory Church.

The ground is named after the shape of the piece of land in which it lies (visible from a bird's eye view). Bordered by Long Marsh Lane to the north, West Lane to the south and west, and the West Coast Main Line to the east, the land bears the shape of exactly that - a giant axe head.

The name has long provided fodder for newspaper headline writers, with a whole host of clubs 'chopped down to size' by the Dolly Blues over the years. As yet, the dream cup tie against Nottingham Forest (that all Lancaster fans want to see) has not materialised.

Organised sport has been played on the site since 1870 when Lancaster Rugby club was formed. The club disbanded around the turn of the century, and when Lancaster Town Football Club were formed in 1905 they chose the ground for their home fixtures.

Despite the club's chequered history - they disbanded briefly in 1911 before reforming - their association with the Giant Axe is unbroken. However, the ground is also very well known in Rugby League circles thanks to Lancaster Rugby's status as one of the first organised clubs. Its historical importance to the game led to its inclusion on a limited edition Rugby League version of the board game Monopoly in 2003 - surely a unique accolade among non-league football grounds.

Lancaster Rugby was reformed in 2003 and last season they shared the Giant Axe with Lancaster City, providing a further boost to efforts to improve facilities at the ground.

Current capacity at the ground is a little over 3,000 with seating for 313 in the main stand. In the 1930s, shortly before the club marked Lancaster's new City status with a change of name, crowds averaged 4,000-5,000, with the record crowd of 7,500 cramming in to see an FA Cup tie against Carlisle United in 1936.

As well as those supporters inside the ground, many others get to see at least some of the action when the Dolly Blues play at home. Views from the castle tour are impressive, while there is also slightly more restricted viewing for those in the castle keep - still used by HM Prison Service.

The West Coast Main Line skirts the ground immediately north of Lancaster station, with a busy flow of Anglo-Scottish express passenger and coal trains also boosting spectator numbers, if only briefly. Rail is the recommended method of getting to Lancaster's home games. A side effect of being situated in an area which was developed long before the car was dreamt of is that parking is very limited but, with the station less than five minutes away, many visiting fans take that option. Another advantage is that this will allow visitors to sample some of Lancaster's fine array of pubs. At the ground itself is the club's large social club, the Dolly Blue Tavern. Other facilities at the ground suffered after a fire destroyed the main stand in 1976. The club was plunged into financial difficulty as a result, hampering efforts to reinvest in the ground, and it is only recently that long awaited improvements have taken place.

Ian Parker

Hassocks

Sussex is blessed with a number of attractive venues but, on a bright afternoon or summer's evening, The Beacon - the home of Hassocks FC since 1992 - is undeniably one of the most picturesque grounds in the Sussex County League, located near the small village of Clayton and overlooked by two windmills - 'Jack & Jill' - two well-known Sussex landmarks. 'Jill' has been completely restored and is open to the public. On occasions, visibility for evening games can be affected by a mist that has a tendency to develop.

Although Hassocks have lived in the shadow of their more successful neighbours, Burgess Hill Town, the club has in many ways shown itself to be a model non-league club in the way it has progressed up the Pyramid and developed its facilities, whilst retaining a strict amateur ethos. That Corinthian spirit is epitomised by the fact that Hassocks not only topped the Division's Fair Play League once again last season, but that The Robins were also credited as one of the most sporting clubs nationally. Add to that the club's highest ever finish in the table - seventh - and one gets the impression of a club in good health that, unusually these days, lives very much within its means.

Hassocks relocated to their own premises at The Beacon from the local recreation ground at Adastra Park in 1992, and the intervening years have witnessed considerable development of the facilities by its members, including extensive work to the drainage. Floodlights were erected in 1995 as a consequence of fund-raising and the generosity of the late Matthew Harding, a local resident and Vice-Chairman of Chelsea FC, whose sons still play for the club.

In the summer of 2002, a 230 capacity seated stand was erected on the far side of the pitch as part of the club's centenary celebrations, along with new dug-outs on the near side. Despite the developments, great care has been taken to maintain harmony with the rural surroundings. There must have been a temptation to install bright red seating in the main stand for example (the club colours), but this was rejected in favour of green. Likewise, the floodlight pylons are a similar colour, whilst white picket gates between the stand and pitch are a nice touch.

The only blot on the landscape is the presence of three large telecommunications pylons behind the goal at the railway end of the ground, although these do provide all-important revenue for the club. There is planning permission for further covered accommodation at that end of the ground but, with gates averaging just over a hundred, there appears little immediate necessity.

However, an impressive new two-storey clubhouse and changing room development at the opposite end of the pitch is very much on the agenda. The cost of the new development is estimated at approaching £500,000 and is obviously a long-term project. Nevertheless, the club has a sound business plan in place and it is hoped that the new building will be in place in time for the 2006/07 season.

In the meantime, however, spectators will have to make do with the current clubhouse, which could best be described as 'cosy', and is unusual in that it is set below pitch level, thereby providing a 'worms' eye' view of the action. An overhang provides further cover, and the building also houses the dressing rooms. However, this will be demolished once the new clubhouse is complete, allowing the club to increase car parking provision to over 200 spaces.

The ground is readily accessible by road from the A23, although if travelling by rail, be prepared for a 15-20 minute walk from Hassocks station. The spirit that pervades The Beacon, and the way that Hassocks have gone about their business, draws comparison with one of its erstwhile rivals in the County League, Eastbourne Borough (neé Langney Sports). Who knows, one day they may even emulate their Sussex rivals' impressive rise up the Pyramid?

David Baukham

Arundel

One of my favourite grounds among the many lovely ones that grace the county of Sussex is that of Arundel FC. It has an attractive rural location and one of the finest backdrops of any ground in the country, with Arundel Castle on the hillside above. The town itself, more famous for hosting cricket, is also delightful, so it is well worth lingering, perhaps for the day or weekend, sampling some fine Sussex ale, and enjoying the sights.

I attended a friendly two pre-seasons ago when the county side entertained Brighton. Mill Road looked particularly fine with a full house (1000+) on a warm July evening. The home side had their moments; Brighton, Sven-like, fielded separate elevens in each half, including most of their first team squad, and came out 5-1 winners.

The ground itself does not consist of too many structures, having to normally accommodate a small fraction of that evening's crowd. As such, Arundel's home is not somewhere to come if you want comfort (but when has following non-league football ever been about this?). The old 'main' stand is pretty basic, with a few chairs, but the roof is adorned with the club's name and it is behind this that the castle stands; you could almost imagine the local duke and duchess looking down from the ramparts on the peasants playing their games. The main stand includes two small dug-outs, with additional chairs for the over-spill from the benches.

The clubhouse is small, behind one goal and, er, that is more or less it, apart from one additional area of covering. There is a fairly large car park but also plenty of parking along the leafy Mill Road. The area around the ground is flat pasture, as it lies slightly outside the town, and the River Arun is nearby. Balls can end up in the surrounding water-filled ditches, and the pitch itself is susceptible to flooding.

The thud of footballs is accompanied by the mooing of cows and, unless the weather is bad - in which case shelter is at a premium - there can be few more relaxing venues to watch a game of football.

Martin Whybrow

Northwood

Judging by its name - Chestnut Avenue - on a visit to Northwood Football Club's ground, you'd expect to find yourself in the middle of the countryside, and that's almost what you get, with a peculiar twist.

Situated on the fringes of West London's suburbia, when I first visited the ground it felt as though I'd arrived at a footballing amphitheatre. The ground is set in a valley with huge fir trees hanging over the western terracing giving a year-round Christmas feel.

At the northern end, looking down upon the pitch from on high, is residential accommodation. It's not known whether the housing provides many home fans but the dwellings to the eastern side, again above the playing surface, provide the odd non-paying supporter, so it's said.

On the other side is a cemetery. Steve Watts, the Scottish boxer known for being a victim of the ring, is a long-term tenant in a beautiful graveyard. For the non-aficionados of the pugilistic arts, Watts died after a Southern area welterweight fight with Rocky Kelly in Fulham in 1986, suffering from brain damage.

The land is Council owned and the club recently signed a 25-year extension of the current lease. Originally, it was a motor-cross track, the legacy being a six-foot drop from the cemetery to the fir tree ends. To rectify the problem, and enable entry into the Ryman League in 1992, earth from a demolished local cinema was used to level the pitch, although a barely visible incline was maintained to aid drainage.

With a capacity of over 3,000 including 320 covered seats, the 'Woods' stadium has attained 'Grade A' standard. This means that promotion to Conference South is not ruled out, the only qualifying requirement being to add 180 seats within three years.

Three floodlights line each side of the pitch and have been the source of some late nights at Chestnut Avenue. In one match against Ford United, the lights literally went out eight times. A lengthy delay resulted each time, as 15 minutes are needed for the bulbs to cool down before an attempt can be made to turn them back on. On the bright side (no pun intended), a match has never been abandoned due to floodlight failure.

The match billed as the greatest in Northwood's history was one of the first played on the newly re-laid pitch in late 1991. Braintree were the opponents in the FA Vase and the game was stopped when the referee was injured and replaced, and the visitors would not accept Steve Williams, the Northwood club secretary, acting as a linesman. It was 4-2 late in the game but the Woods pulled level to take the match into an extra period. Despite having a player sent off and being behind 6-5, Northwood rallied for a 7-6 victory, the final goal coming from the penalty spot. Torrential rain pelted the players throughout the contest and a 3pm kick-off continued until past 7 o'clock. The unlucky losers suffered an injury to their goalkeeper in the additional half hour and two players needed hospital treatment after it was all over.

All in all, it's a very friendly club which is actively involved in and supported by the community. Never was this better demonstrated than the construction of the North stand by supporters, supervised by Harry Currie, a builder by trade and long-term fan. In a sense, community involvement is not optional - a public right of way runs through the ground.

Chestnut Avenue is easy to get to - the Metropolitan line runs nearby - and the future looks bright for the team under the respected tutelage of Mick Harvey, recruited in the Summer to replace Tony Choules - otherwise known as the 'miracle worker' - who has moved on to Hendon.

But beware. If you go down to the Woods on a misty evening, don't be surprised to see the 'silver lady' floating over the pitch, nodding one into the top corner and retiring into the allotment behind the south stand. You have been warned. In case you're interested, I hear there are still plots available.

Steve Hawdon

Meet Lee Boylan

Lee Boylan, the scorer of 43, 48 and 57 goals for Canvey Island in the Ryman Premier League in the last three seasons, arrived in a personalised BMW 330 D Sport. Rumours of the prosperity of Jeff King, the Canvey owner, manager and benefactor who pays the wages were, it appeared, not without substance.

Happily married to a girl from Watford with two young boys, a part-time coaching job and a supportive father, life looks rosy for the Ryman League Player of the Year. But it has not always been so.

As a teenage prodigy, Boylan almost went to the former FA Centre of Excellence at Lillieshall - that's how highly regarded he was. England's loss was the Republic of Ireland's gain, as shortly after being disappointed, he received a call from across the sea and went on to play in three under-18 European Championships and was selected for the under-20 World Cup in Malaysia.

The Harry Redknapp era saw Boylan at West Ham but he couldn't quite make the break-through. However, he did benefit from the tutelage of Ian Wright. The England striker would make time at the end of a training session for some one on one coaching. 'Don't be scared to shoot' was the Wright message which Boylan has taken to heart. 'If you hit it right, it doesn't matter where you are. If you're outside the box, the keeper's not expecting it, so he won't be ready for it.'

Off Boylan went to Sweden to join Trolleberg of the Premier League, but something was not right, something he was unaware of. It started with gastro-enteritis and developed into full-blown Crones disease, a condition where the stomach's intestines become rigid, preventing food passing through and the immune system attacks the bowel. Unfortunately, as is the male habit, Boylan's initial choice was to grin and bear it. Soon, that decision was taken out of his hands.

He was out of football for 16 months and the pain was so excruciating, at one point he didn't even talk to his parents for a month - and they had not fallen out. Steroids - non-performance enhancing ones which soften the intestines of the stomach - were the answer, medication Boylan will remain on for the rest of his life. With a letter in his back-pocket from the FA clearing him to play, it was time to get back to football.

Plain sailing it was not. At Hayes another problem would hamper progress - 'compartment syndrome' which caused Boylan to have rock solid calves after around 15 minutes of running and to lose feeling in his feet. At Canvey the turnaround really began to take shape. In his first season, Boylan was not a fixture in the starting line-up until December, but still banged in 43 goals. Both the team and Boylan prospered culminating in last season's 103 points, promotion to the Conference and an appearance at Villa Park in the FA Trophy Final, in which surprise, surprise Boylan scored, in a heart-breaking 3-2 defeat against Hednesford Town, the winner coming three minutes from time.

The phone-call from Paul Fairclough asking Boylan to join this summer's National Game XI squad - the non-league equivalent of England - on their US tour, was proof his life had turned full circle. As manager of Stevenage, Fairclough gave Boylan a trial shortly after recovering from illness and said he didn't think Boylan was good enough. Now, even in the newspapers, Fairclough has admitted his error. Boylan went on to appear as a second-half substitute in a 0-0 draw in Charleston.

For the record, the official reason for Boylan being able to play for England after representing the Republic of Ireland at professional level was that he had not played for Non-League Ireland. As things stand in the era of international mobility, he is also free to play for England at full international level, if it ever comes to that.

Gary Lineker is a player Boylan admires and has studied in some depth. 'He works the edge of the box from side to side. That's the only area I work. If I'm forward and running everywhere, I'm not going to be in the box when the ball's there'. Boylan added, 'If you watch his videos he doesn't move from outside the 18 yard box. Most of his goals were not long distance - just finishing off rebounds and cut-backs.'

Boylan has an intelligent footballing brain which he keenly employs in the opening exchanges of each match to analyse the opposing defender. 'When I go on the pitch, I'll look at him for the first five minutes, try to judge the qualities he has. If he's kicking more with his right foot, I'll try to work on his left foot,' he said. 'In the first five or ten minutes I try to get the ball behind him, see if he's fast. If he's slow, you know you can turn him, if he's fast you know you need it more to feet and try and move him around to get him tired.'

The secret to his game lies in movement. 'Being small, I can't rely on balls pumped up to me. You can't be standing there because you get easily marked. If I'm moving around, players have got to watch where I'm going.

'I find it quite easy when I have big players on me because I feel quite sharp around the box,' he added. 'If I just take them one way or the other, then obviously I can get a yard on them. Movement is a big asset to my game which I try to work on regularly.'

It also explains his nickname: 'They call me biz, busy I think because they say I'm always moving around, trying to get into things. It's stuck for a while. When I was at West Ham, I was called buzz. I remember it being quoted in the FA Youth Cup Final - 'nickname buzz'. It's like the flea that no one can swat. It's quite a good compliment for me, always moving around and it's gone from buzz to biz.'

Like most footballers, Boylan has a whole host of superstitions: 'When I'm in the changing room, I have to sit at the same peg, wear the same belt on my trousers, the same shoes. If I've got new boots, nobody else can wear them before I wear them. A lot of people say can I try them on, I say no.'

And it does not end there: 'If I've scored the game before, I don't change my boots. I have a fair few pairs,' he added. 'I wear socks underneath my football socks, so I wear the same socks and same briefs. If I wore a vest the game before, I'll wear a vest under my top. If I don't score I'll change it. I've been doing this all my life.'

Ambition still burns strongly in Boylan's heart. 'I'd like to play in the Premiership. That's my dream. I'd also like to get a full international cap with England or Ireland,' he continued. 'I've got about 44 caps for Ireland and it was just a great experience. They make you feel really special. You go away, they treat you right. You get the crowd cheering at the national anthem. I want more of that.'

A goal target has already been set for the 2004/05 campaign: 'I look at what the leading goal-scorer got last season (Daryl Clare with 30 goals for promoted Chester City) and then try to beat that. I know if I play well, I can do it, depending on injuries. I want to get 30.'

At 25, Boylan's best years are still ahead and he admits being selected for Non-League England changed his perspective: 'It makes me think people out there who have judged me when I was ill are now looking and say, I might have made a mistake. It opened my eyes again, made me feel overwhelmed.'

Steve Howdon

Derby Days

Derby rivalries are an important part of the experience of the football fan, whether it be the intensity and bitter rivalry of an Old Firm game or the legendary good humour of a Liverpool v Everton encounter. These are the games that fans look forward to and are often the yardstick for judging a season.

At the non-league level, season 2003/04 provided some remarkable derby games. Prominent among the derbies most looked forward to prior to the start of the season was the 'Battle of Shropshire' encounter between demoted football league outfit Shrewsbury Town and their county neighbours Telford United.

The teams had not met in league action since the end of the Second World War, when Telford were known as Wellington Town and both clubs played in the Birmingham and District League. Apart from their reacquaintance in the league engagements, after such a long absence, fate also conspired to pair the teams together in the FA Trophy Quarter-Finals.

However, the games between the teams were not exactly classics. The first clash came at Shrewsbury's Gay Meadow where 6,738 witnessed a scoreless draw. Telford returned to the Meadow to hold their hosts to a draw in the Trophy thus forcing a replay.

The two towns, some 15 miles apart, could not be more different. Historic Shrewsbury with its Abbey, popularised in the Cadfael books and TV series, standing close to the venerable Gay Meadow stadium which in turn borders the River Severn, providing a home to a club with a footballing pedigree and support base of note. On the other hand, the brash new town of Telford with its newly rebuilt Bucks Head stadium.

Unfortunately for Telford, its proximity to Birmingham and the Black Country means that the growth of the population has not seen a real sense of identity with the town's team develop. It has proved easy for relocating football fans to still travel to maintain their traditional allegiances while even Telford's ambitious plans and investment in playing staff failed to stimulate the sort of interest that the club's efforts deserved.

Shrewsbury's first visit of the season to the Bucks Head for the Trophy replay saw their fans pack the uncovered terrace along the side of the ground as well as filling the Frank Nagington stand behind one of the goals. Security concerns prevented Telford from offering tickets for sale on the night and the game was heavily policed with the county's police helicopter hovering above the stadium and riot police employed as the Oddfellows Arms in Wellington High Street had its windows smashed and its curtains set on fire during disturbances before the game.

On the field, the Bucks had more fizz as they dumped Town out of the competition with a 2-1 victory. The following month Shrewsbury visited in the league and once more suffered defeat as they went down to the only goal of the game.

While Telford had the better of things on the pitch, it was the Shrews who had the last laugh in a memorable season for both clubs, for vastly different reasons. With United going bust, the matches between the clubs during the season looked at one stage as if they would be the derby's swansong. Luckily Telford ultimately survived as AFC Telford United, but there can be few rivalries where, after years of separation, the teams were reunited in league action, only for the end of the season to see the teams separated by three divisions!

If the Shropshire derby largely failed to ignite on the pitch, the same could not be said about the Dr Martens League derby games between Weymouth and Dorchester Town, played on the traditional derby day dates of Boxing Day and New Year's Day.

Weymouth fan Elizabeth Bell noted that the Terras' traditional rivalry was with Yeovil Town but that there was a growing rivalry in recent years with nearer neighbours Dorchester and she understandably termed Weymouth's remarkable 8-0 victory on Boxing Day as 'a wonderful Christmas present'.

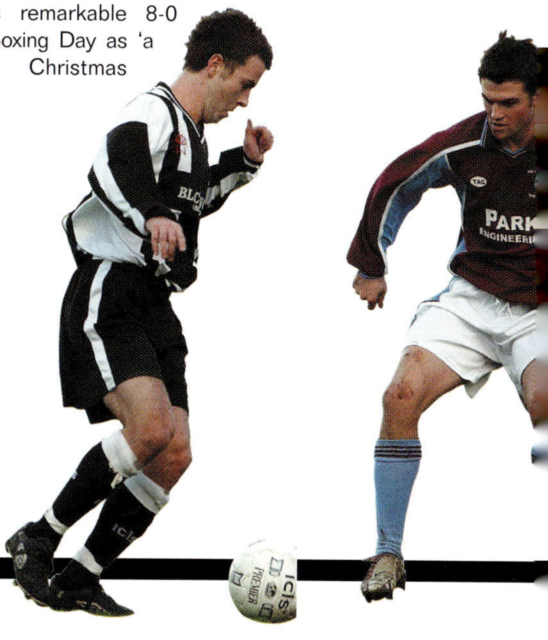

Player-manager Steve Claridge, and Lee Phillips both notched hat-tricks in the rout while the Magpies' disaster was compounded with the dismissal of Jamie Brown as passions spilled over.

A crowd of 3,734 had witnessed the Boxing Day massacre and an even larger crowd, 4,116 gathered for the second holiday installment days later, a massive increase on Dorchester's average home attendance of 500, as the Magpies looked for revenge.

The fans were rewarded with a full-blooded derby game where Dorchester regained some pride by holding the Terras to a two-all draw in an incident packed game which included a penalty awarded, and converted, by each team.

Dorchester's spot kick brought the teams level at 2-2 with six minutes to go and there was still time as the clock ran down for Magpies bad-boy, Jamie Brown, to once more see red with a lunge on Claridge which provoked a mass scrum between the players resulting in Brown's second dismissal in the derby in a matter of days while, for his part in the confrontation, Claridge was similarly ordered to take an early bath.

Also involved in Dr Martens Premier League action over the Christmas period were two clubs narrowly separated by the A5 and by a single league point as third placed Hinckley United played host to fourth placed Nuneaton Borough.

Hinckley had not met their more illustrious neighbours in a league game since season 1963/64 and were seeking vengeance for their defeat in the initial league encounter between the clubs in August when Borough triumphed in front of 1,901 fans by two goals to nil.

It was actually the first home league game against Nuneaton for Hinckley United, the club having been formed in 1997 by the amalgamation of Hinckley Athletic and Hinckley Town. The Boxing Day encounter would also most likely be the last derby between the clubs at the Middlefield Lane venue, with United planning a move into a new purpose-built stadium for next season.

The old ground was filled with a crowd of 2,013 despite admission prices being raised by £1 to cover the costs of extra stewarding. Fortunately, the extra stewards were not kept busy and the action remained where it belongs, on the pitch.

Nuneaton went into half-time with a one goal advantage from a Gez Murphy strike. Hinckley emerged reinvigorated after the break but, despite applying pressure, could not find a way through the Borough defence. Then with a minute of normal time remaining, the Knitters defended a corner and launched a swift counter attack, sweeping into the Borough half and climaxing with Chris Smith ghosting in at the far post to grab a late equaliser.

Hinckley United's example of two clubs from the same town merging in recent years to create a stronger force

was mirrored by the finalists in this year's FA Vase where winners Winchester City merged with Winchester Castle in 2001 thus providing the financial and administrative impetus to stimulate progression. Beaten Vase finalists AFC Sudbury were formed five years ago from the merger of Sudbury Wanderers and Sudbury Town and have also enjoyed an extremely successful period after amalgamation. However, successful as such moves can appear to be, it is difficult for long-term fans of a club to reconcile themselves with following a new entity.

In Eastbourne, a town of some 89,000 residents according to 2001 census figures, the populace has the choice of following either Eastbourne Borough, Eastbourne United or Eastbourne Town.

The main support in the town is at present garnered by Eastbourne Borough, who average around 600 fans for their home games. Borough fan Tony Hylands stated that rivalry with United and Town was considerable when the clubs played in the same league but has since lessened. In season 2003/04, therefore, Borough's biggest derby game was against eventual Dr Martens League Premier champions Crawley Town.

Eastbourne United commented that they saw Town as their biggest rivals and that games between the two sides could attract up to 400 spectators, a considerable increase on United's average attendance of 80.

The situation in Eastbourne has certain parallels with Inverness, a town of 66,000 people, which also boasted three football teams in Scottish Non-League football until the merger of Inverness Caledonian and Inverness Thistle.

The new club of course had the incentive of improving their case for joining the Scottish Football League, which they subsequently did and in season 2003/04 won promotion to the Scottish Premiership.

Such success though can be a bit of a mixed blessing. While the two merged clubs relinquished their individual identities, the Inverness club who were left behind, Clachnacuddin, on the other hand, have shown that going it alone is still viable as they were crowned last season's Highland League champions. There is much to be said for Clachnacuddin's stance as the Lilywhites will be the only club playing in Inverness next season as Caley Thistle once more test their fans' dedication as they are forced to play their SPL home fixtures in Aberdeen.

It raises the question of what price is acceptable for 'progress' in a fluctuating environment such as football. When on-field progress stalls, it is often the local rivalry of comparison with other clubs that maintains interest; mergers, by their nature, reduce the number of potential local derbies and deprive fans of the rivalries that are the lifeblood of the game.

Steve Greenfield

From Premiership

The ever-growing profile of non-league football has attracted many former Premier League players in recent seasons. Whether it be ageing players enjoying an Indian Summer to their careers or keen young coaches looking to cut their managerial teeth, the non-league scene has certainly attracted some big names.

A Liverpool quartet of Nigel Clough, Mark Wright, Steve Harkness and Mike Marsh have all enjoyed successful times in the non-league game, with Marsh winning promotions as a player with Kidderminster and Accrington, Clough as a manager with Burton and, most recently, Wright with Chester.

Former Arsenal FA Cup winner, Christopher Wreh, had a successful if short spell with Bishops Stortford, with fellow former-Gunner Ian Selley proving to be an important cog in Woking's midfield. Not to be out-done, Arsenal's North London rivals Tottenham can also spot some of their former regulars in the non-league ranks with Dean Austin, Andy Sinton, Justin Edinburgh and most notably Chris Waddle all getting involved at the games' grass roots levels. The list goes on. Alan Kimble, Alan Devonshire, Leroy Rosenior, Mark Ward, Shaun Teale, Peter Fear, Martin Allen, Fitzroy Simpson, Steve Claridge, Lionel Perez and, notably this close season, Dean Holdsworth, are just a few former top-flight pros seeing the value and attraction of playing or managing at non-league level. Pyramid Football looks at just a handful of these men who are giving something back to the heart of the game.

Mark Atkins

Atkins spent his formative playing years at Blackburn Rovers (making 257 appearances in a seven year spell, scoring 35 goals). He won promotion to the Premier League in 1992 followed by the Premier League title in 1995, before joining Wolverhampton Wanderers. Once he left Molyneux, he headed back to his home town of Doncaster and played for York City before joining up with his old friend Ian Snodin at his home town club, where he got his first taster of non-league football. Once he left Doncaster Rovers he spent several months at Hull City before he enjoyed a two-year spell at Shrewsbury Town.

He was then contacted by Harrogate Town manager Jon Reed, who he had known since he was a 14 year-old at Hatfield Main over 20 years ago. Atkins has enjoyed a good first season for the Yorkshire club, helping them to an impressive top five finish, barely two seasons after they won promotion from the First Division.

'There's clearly a big difference between full-time football and the non-league' said Atkins. 'In the non-league you get different people working in different jobs all week and then they have to come and play a game at weekends. I think this leads to more inconsistent performances at non-league level.' Speaking of his time with Doncaster, Atkins continued: 'I knew what to expect from the Conference. It's a league that's getting better and better. It's really Division Four. There are better players coming down to the Conference all the time and I think the teams that do well in the Conference can easily finish mid-table in the Third Division and, in the case of Doncaster and Yeovil last season, even higher.

'With more and more foreigners in the top levels of the game, pros will continue to come down to play in the non-league. The simple fact is that players want to keep playing for as long as they can so the number of former Premier League players playing at non-league level will almost certainly increase.' Atkins was also very positive on the restructuring for the non-league game: 'I think it's a good idea. Putting three divisions into two gives players the opportunity to play against the best teams in other divisions. It's got to be good for progression.'

Former Clubs: Scunthorpe United, Blackburn Rovers, Wolverhampton Wanderers, York City, Doncaster Rovers, Hull City, Shrewsbury Town

Honours:
Promotion to Premier League: Blackburn Rovers
Premier League Championship: Blackburn Rovers

Nigel Clough

Few players in this day and age stay at the same club for too long, and the days of the 'one club man' are definitely numbered. Although Burton Albion manager Nigel Clough played for more than one top-flight club in his career, he will best be remembered for wearing the red of Nottingham Forest, the club his father Brian took to the pinnacle of Europe in the 1970s and early 1980s. A City Ground legend, Clough also had spells at Liverpool and Manchester City in a distinguished playing career. It was on leaving Maine Road in 1998 that Clough applied for the vacant manager's position at

non-league side Burton Albion. Since then, Clough, along with former Forest team-mate Gary Crosby, have guided the club to the Unibond Premier Division title in 2002 and they have established the Brewers in the Nationwide Conference. It is an experience that Clough has obviously enjoyed on a personal level: 'The first thing you notice about the non-league scene is that people aren't money orientated', said Clough. 'So many people are working on a voluntary basis. No-one is holding out for a big pay day and everyone is so much more welcoming which makes for a refreshing change from all the segregation you find at the top level.'

In addition, Clough spoke highly of the players at non-league level: 'Clearly the standard of football compared to the top level is quite a bit removed, but it is surprising how many players look after themselves. Even though they are working full-time, most still manage to get down the gym three times a week. As far as they're concerned, they are professionals. In addition, whereas professional players have five to six weeks off in the summer, amateur or semi-pro players still have jobs to go to, so their routine continues as normal. Therefore, they actually end up coming back for the start of the season in pretty good shape.

'The standard of football at non-league level has definitely improved. The amount of foreigners that have come into the game at the top level has created a knock-on effect. Therefore, you have got players playing in the Unibond League that would be in the Third Division a few years ago. And young players are being given less time to impress at bigger clubs before they are released. With the increase in standard, people are investing more and more in non-league football. The Conference is the Fourth Division really and there will probably be about 16-18 full-time clubs next season.'

On the non-league's re-structuring Clough said: 'It seems sensible. Geography is such an issue at our level. When we were in the Dr Martens Premier, we found ourselves travelling down to places like Crawley for a midweek game and getting there 15 minutes before kick off. That is one of the main reasons we moved to the Unibond League.'

Former Clubs: Nottingham Forest, Liverpool, Manchester City

Honours:
Football League Cup (twice): Nottingham Forest

International Caps:
14

Steve Claridge

You could think of many words to describe bustling and busy center forward Steve Claridge, but shrewd manager might not, necessarily, be two of them. However, he answered the call of home town club Weymouth to become their new player-manager in June 2003 after an approach by chairman and friend Ian Ridley. 'Ian came to me and offered me the job with decent money and good opportunities but, not least, it was close to where I was from,' Claridge said.

38 year-old Claridge led the Terras to a commendable second place in the Dr Martens Premier Division in his first season at the helm, narrowly missing out on a place in the Nationwide Conference. Not a bad effort for a man in his first full season in management. He had left the club 16 years previous for a glittering career in the football league: 'The club were in the top level of non-league football when I left in 1988 so, from Weymouth's point of view, things had changed for the worse. However, I was pleasantly surprised by the standard of football at this level, although you do get people who are out to make a name for themselves, and you do get some appalling referees'.

Claridge continued: 'I think the further down the football pyramid you go, the less difference there is between the divisions. Obviously, the gulf in class between the Premiership and Division One is huge but, the lower you go, the more you find recently promoted clubs doing well. The foreign players in the Premiership have squeezed out players who would have still been playing at that level up until about five years ago. The same applies for each division but this does lead to a higher standard of football.'

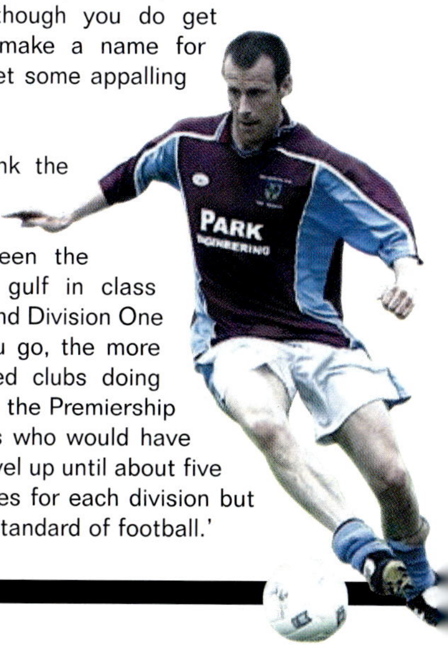

Weymouth's missed opportunity for promotion was clearly something that still disappointed Claridge as he was clearly pleased with the changes made to the non-league's structure: 'I don't think it is fair that you finish second in the league and don't get a shot at promotion - although, I would say that because I'm biased! However, it doesn't happen in any other division. In some divisions of the Football League, you can finish seventh and still have a chance of going up.' The Conference South (where Weymouth will play their football this season) has two promotion places up for grabs, with the top team gaining an automatic place with the four teams below that entering into a series of Play-Offs.

Former Clubs:
Fareham Town, Bournemouth, Weymouth, Crystal Palace, Aldershot Town, Cambridge United, Luton Town, Cambridge City, Birmingham City, Leicester City, Portsmouth (loan), Wolverhampton Wanderers, Portsmouth, Millwall

Honours:

Football League Cup:	Leicester City
First Division Play-Offs:	Leicester City
Third Division championship:	Cambridge United
Second Division championship:	Cambridge United, Birmingham City

Justin Edinburgh

Justin Edinburgh, the former Tottenham Hotspur full back, is one of the more recent arrivals in the non-league game (following a career at the top level). Edinburgh was appointed as the new boss at Billericay Town last May after expressing a wish to get into management. He explains: 'I had been retired from the professional game for about a year and was coaching at the Spurs Academy. I wanted to coach at senior level and Billericay were my local team so, when the manager's position became vacant, I met with the chairman and he offered me the job. I was familiar with the club as I have visited on many occasions. We had friendlies with Billericay when I was at Spurs and I have old friends from the professional game who have also played there.'

Despite, clearly, having his finger on the non-league pulse, Edinburgh's new charges had a tough season - finishing third from bottom in the Ryman Premier Division.

Edinburgh, however, was still upbeat about the standard of football despite highlighting the obvious differences between the levels of football: 'With players coming straight from work to training, it is important not to expect too much fitness wise. I think that maybe there were things that I could do that others couldn't. However, it is a good standard at this level and there are some good players. Professional players are training every day and you have to be fit, quick and strong these days but, having said that, there are a few players that I have seen who could make the step up to Football League level.'

Despite the large influx of foreigners in the Premiership, Edinburgh does not envisage a mass increase of former top flight players coming into the non-league, 'Anybody who has been playing in the Premiership won't, for financial reasons, need to drop down into the lower leagues. I think the big money spending at the top level is slowing down and I think that clubs in Divisions Two and Three are starting to look at the non-league for players again.'

In contrast to some of the other managers we spoke to, Edinburgh was not too complimentary of the restructuring shake-up (a view that is mirrored by many people involved with Ryman League clubs). 'I don't really see what's behind it. It's not saving us any expenditure, infact it's costing us more than before with us having to travel to places like Dover and Eastleigh - therefore, it's not doing what it set out to do. It's a complete non-starter for me.'

Former Clubs:
Southend United, Tottenham Hotspur, Portsmouth

Honours:

FA Cup:	Tottenham Hotspur
Football League Cup:	Tottenham Hotspur

Whatever their views, the impact of these types of players getting involved at Non-League level can only be positive. It has created increased interest and excitement, especially for those clubs involved, and has helped to increase the awareness of the game at grass roots level. We thank them for talking to us and we wish them luck for the coming season.

Nationwide Conference

Club Pages

Accrington Stanley

Address: Interlink Express Stadium, Livingstone Road, Accrington, Lancashire, BB5 5BX
Tel: 01254 356950
Website: www.accringtonstanley.co.uk
Email: info@accringtonstanley.co.uk
Officials: Chairman: Eric Whalley
Secretary: Phil Terry
Manager: John Coleman

Directions

From the M65: Leave at J7, taking the Clayton-Le-Moors turn-off from the roundabout. Turn right at the first set of traffic lights opposite Clayton Business Park, following the A678. Go over the canal bridge to the next set of lights. Turn right again, over the motorway, towards Accrington on the A680. After half a mile, turn left down Livingstone Road, which is 50 yards past the Crown Hotel on the left.
From M66: At the end of the motorway, follow the A56 until the Rising Bridge roundabout. Take the first turning, the A680 towards Accrington, for around three miles. After passing the police and fire stations on the left, follow the ring road dual carriageway around the town centre. At the fourth set of traffic lights, opposite the Castle pub, turn right to rejoin the A680. Follow this up the hill for a mile. Livingstone Road is 400 yards past Accrington Victoria Hospital on the right.
By train: Accrington is served mainly by Preston. Exit the station and go down the hill (Kings Street) which bends to the right and then to the left. At the big roundabout go past the Peugeot dealer (Milnshaw Way). At the top of Milnshaw Way join Whalley Road. Follow this road up past the hospital, through the traffic lights, to a mini-roundabout. The next left after the roundabout is Livingstone Road.

A pleasant ground where improvements have done wonders. This is a typical non-league venue where, in my experience, the hospitality is always good. Wherever you choose to view the action, you are close to the pitch making banter with officials and players a regular event. The ground holds a total of 4,000 spectators with covering along each side of the pitch. There is covered seating for 700, although this is soon to be increased upon completion of the new stand currently under construction. The ground is also a short drive from the M65 and M66 motorways with ample parking at the ground and in surrounding streets. AP

Review

After gaining promotion back to the Conference, Stanley were looking simply for a season of consolidation. Thus, they perhaps exceeded expectations - after pushing for a Play-Off spot, they settled for an impressive tenth place and qualification for the LDV Vans Trophy. Their Conference debut commenced with an unlucky 2-1 defeat at Aldershot, before the Stanley fans were treated to a 4-1 home win over Leigh the following week. The team took time to settle, but took to life in the Conference and remained on the fringes of the Play-Offs. They performed well at home - including a 2-0 win in November over then-leaders, Hereford United - but just couldn't get results away from home.
The FA Cup saw the visit of Huddersfield Town in the First Round. The game was televised on BBC, and Stanley defended well before sealing an unlikely 1-0 win with a last minute Andy Gouck goal. They then disposed of Bournemouth on penalties, before bowing out in a Third Round replay at Colchester.
However, a dreadful away record (no away league victory from the start of 2004) woke them from that dream, although their home record kept them as high as seventh, prior to four successive defeats between late March and April. Fans won't have been too disappointed: tenth place and the FA Cup Third Round represented a great return for them.
Stanley can hope to take further strides forward this year, having switched to full-time during the Summer. Manager John Coleman believes this will help his players' fitness. With six players having left during late April because of the transition, a number of new signings were needed to boost the depleted squad, who will need time to gel. And they will need to improve that away record: Stanley won fewer away games (two) than any other side. MP

The Reds

Aldershot Town

Address: Recreation Ground, High Street, Aldershot, Hampshire, GU11 ITW

Tel: 01252 320211

Website: www.theshots.co.uk

Officials: Chairman: Karl Prentice
Secretary: Simon Pullen
Manager: Terry Brown

The Recreation Ground

Directions

From the M3: From J4 take the A331 towards Aldershot. Exit at Aldershot and take the A323 towards the town centre.
From the M25: From J10, take the A3 towards Guildford. At Guildford, turn off onto the A31 (Hog's Back) leading to Farnham (the exit is on the crest of a hill just past a BP garage). Take the A331 towards Camberley and turn off at Aldershot (the first exit). Head towards the town centre.
From both these routes, follow the A323 and, once past Manor Park (on the left), continue on under the bridge. The Recreation Ground is on the right.
By train: Aldershot station is less than ten minutes walk from the ground and is served by mainline trains on the London Waterloo to Alton line.

It looks like a Football League venue, and it almost was once more. The Recreation Ground remains an intimidating venue, particularly with the larger crowds now attracted, and the roof over the East Bank is well capable of carrying the sound, creating a real atmosphere. It is very handy for both town centre and the station, with a public car park just by the ground, but still retains a rural feel as it is surrounded by trees, particularly at the High Street end, which retains a flat terrace. Segregation is normally applied, in one of two ways depending on the travelling support, with a mixture of terracing and seating provided. GB

Review

2003/04 was a superb season for the Shots, as they followed up their Ryman League Championship success in 2002/03 by being within touching distance of a place back in the Football League, narrowly missing out on a place after an agonising Play-Off defeat. Their success for much of the season was down to the number of players able to score goals, as new signings Tim Sills contributed 21 goals alongside Roscoe D'Sane's 27, but midfielders such as Adam Miller and Jon Challinor also weighed in with more than their fair share.
After their classic opening 2-1 win over Accrington Stanley (also enjoying their first season back in the Conference), the Shots won four of their next five games, establishing themselves in the Play-Off zone, where they would remain for much of the season. Even when they lost a little around the turn of the year, their ability to bounce back was crucial, as they went unbeaten at home in any competition until 20th December.
In the FA Cup, they reached the Second Round proper before being narrowly edged out by Football League side Colchester, but in the Trophy they reached the Semi-Finals before a surprise aggregate loss to Hednesford Town denied them a final berth. However, they were destined to make one final, as Lee Charles provided the vital equaliser which earned them a 1-1 draw against Tamworth on the final day of the season and the point they needed for a place in the Play-Offs. Whilst their defence had been fairly generous throughout the campaign, they managed to keep free-scoring Hereford to an aggregate 1-1 draw in the Semi-Final before beating them on penalties. It was a fantastic result against the Bulls who had beaten the Shots twice over the course of the season. That earned them a place in the Final at the Britannia Stadium - Stoke, and when Aaron McLean nudged them ahead in the first half, the fairytale return to the League seemed complete, but the Shrews levelled and proceeded to win on penalties. GB

The Shots

Barnet

Address: Underhill Stadium, Westcombe Drive, Barnet, Hertfordshire, EN5 2BE

Tel: 020 8441 6932

Website: www.barnetfc.com

Email: info@barnet.com

Officials: Chairman: Tony Kleanthous
Secretary: Andrew Adie
Manager: Paul Fairclough

Review

Undoubtedly it was a memorable season for the Hertfordshire Bees as, under the permanent charge of Martin Allen, they got off to a flyer, with only one defeat in their first twelve, and 13 from 15 points in September, which provided a key platform for their Play-Off qualification. Giuliano Grazioli proved the signing of the season on a free from Bristol Rovers, as he was the key figure in the excellent form of this Autumn run. They were strong defensively, and whilst there was the odd disappointment, such as losing to Brentford, the club Allen would abruptly leave for, after being 2-0 up in the LDV Trophy, they looked in good shape.

There was a wobble at the end of the year with a heavy loss to Yeovil in the FA Cup, but the new year saw an eleven match unbeaten run start. However, then came the nasty surprise when, after a run of three draws, Allen unexpectedly took over at Division Two strugglers Brentford. His assistant, Adrian Whitbread, took temporary charge before joining him, as the side recorded a scoreless draw at home to Chester City.

Paul Fairclough then took temporary charge. However, the Play-Offs seemed to be slipping away as the goals dried up, and March saw a seemingly terminal home loss to Shrewsbury. Their chances, though, were suddenly reignited, in a stirring climax to the season, as they came from behind to beat Burton with a last gasp winner, and were back in the top five, earning their spot in the knock-out by drawing at Northwich and beating Leigh RMI. They were paired with Shrewsbury, and beat the Shrews 2-1 in the first leg courtesy of a winner deep into stoppage time, but Town squeezed through on penalties after squaring the tie at 2-2. GB

Directions

If you are coming to Barnet from anywhere outside the M25, leave the M25 at Junction 23. If you are coming from the east, take the first turning off the roundabout, which is the A1081. Follow this for about two miles until you come to a set of traffic lights. This is the junction with the A1000. Follow the road to the right, Barnet High Street. At the next set of lights, Barnet church will be on your right. Carry on down the hill, past High Barnet underground station. The ground is on your right. There is also a car park near the tube station.

If you are coming from the A406 (North Circular) turn off at the A1000 towards North Finchley. Follow it through Finchley, then Whetstone. One and a half miles from Whetstone, you will come to a set of lights with Barnet Odeon on your left. Park in the slip road or turn right at the lights (Station Road) and park here.

By train: Nearest stations are High Barnet tube (Northern Line) or New Barnet overground, the latter via Kings Cross or Finsbury Park stations (trains for Welwyn Garden City). At New Barnet station turn left at the top of the steps and then right, out of the exit. The ground is behind the Old Red Lion pub.

Underhill: the name is synonymous with the most pronounced slope in senior football. It is a neat and tidy suburban ground tucked in on three sides by rows of semi-detached houses and a cricket ground on the fourth side. There is a really scenic view of the countryside over the small collection of seats in the South Stand, but this only highlights the problems the club faces with expansion of this location on Green Belt land. The main stand gives a good view of proceedings, the smaller family stand alongside it less so, but the covered terrace on the far side carries acoustics well for the noisy Bees' hard-core support, as well as for any travelling fans, who are segregated. It is one of the easier locations to reach by car, only a couple of miles from the M25, and a short walk from the local underground station, High Barnet. GB

The Bees

Burton Albion

Address: Eton Park, Princess Way, Burton-on-Trent, Staffordshire, DE14 2RU

Tel: 01283 565938

Website: www.burtonalbionfc.co.uk

Email: bafc@burtonalbionfc.co.uk

Officials: Chairman: Ben Robinson
Secretary: Tony Kirkland
Manager: Nigel Clough

Eton Park

Directions

From A38: Exit at the first turning for Burton (North). Continue along Derby Road (A5121), past the Pirelli factory on the right. At the first roundabout turn right into Princess Way. The ground is 100 yards on the left.
From M1: Exit at J22 (for Coalville, Ashby, Burton) and stay on the A511 for approximately 17 miles, past Coalville, Ashby-De-La-Zouch, Woodville and Midway. When you enter Burton, move into the right hand lane at the bottom of Ashby Road (A511), going straight through the lights and across the Trent bridge. Staying in the right hand lane, go over both sets of lights at the end of the bridge, into Horninglow Street, straight on again at the next lights (by the Magistrates Courts), then turn right at the lights under the Brewery fly-over, into Hawkins Lane. Go through the industrial estate, across a mini-roundabout, over the railway. At the next roundabout go straight over into Princess Way.
By train: Burton station is half a mile west of the town centre. Trains run regularly from Derby and Nottingham to the north, Birmingham to the south. It is a good 25 minute walk. Out of the station turn left, then next right into Derby Street. Keep going on this road one and a half miles. Go straight across the first roundabout by the Derby Turn pub (left), then immediately left at the next roundabout into Princess Way.

A neat ground set in the peaceful town of Burton. This was good enough for the club when in the feeder leagues but now that they have establish themselves in the Conference, space could become an issue if attendances continue to rise. The ground is equipped with a large social club and car park. I feel that the ground is one of the best in non-league football but work may well need to be done should the club look to meet Football League standards. Travelling to the ground can be confusing so take a good look on a map before you set off. AP

Review

After managing to stay in the Conference in their first season, Burton Albion were hoping to improve on their 16th position with manager Nigel Clough bringing in several new signings to strengthen his squad. Two players were former Hereford United captain Ian Wright and Morecambe striker Robbie Talbot for £7,000.
Burton started the season well with a win on the opening day. Wright scored the winner in the 90th minute to give his new side a 2-1 victory at Gravesend & Northfleet. However, their first home game of the season wasn't such a success as they fell to a 1-0 defeat against one of the teams who were relegated from the League the previous season - Shrewsbury Town.
The FA Cup was to prove a success for Burton Albion and they got off to a flying start in the Fourth Qualifying Round when Buxton visited Eton Park. Aaron Webster scored two (one being a penalty), Talbot netted one, and Dale Anderson grabbed himself a hat-trick, giving the Brewers a convincing win. The First Round proper saw Burton face a tough tie away at Torquay, who were going well in the Third Division. An own goal helped Burton on their way but it was Talbot who was the hero as he scored the winner to send Burton through. However, their luck ran out in the Second Round as Hartlepool came to visit Eton Park in December. This turned out to be a big game and was shown live on BBC One. One of the reasons of course was that Nigel Clough could have pulled off a shock in the cup, and knock out the team his father, Brian, managed many years ago. Unfortunately for Albion, a single goal by Joel Porter was enough to see Hartlepool through.
Despite losing their last three league games of the season, Burton secured a 14th place finish with three points more than their first season in the Conference, giving Nigel Clough some food for thought on how to continue the club's steady improvement. AP

The Brewers

Canvey Island

Address: Park Lane, Canvey Island, Essex SS8 7PX
Tel: 01268 682991
Website: www.canveyislandfc.com
Officials: Chairman: Keith Johnson
Secretary: Wayne Purser
Manager: Jeff King

Review

Canvey went into last season knowing it would really have to be now or never if they were to get out of the Ryman Premier after being pipped to the title for the last three years.

They made an indifferent start, beating Basingstoke, then losing to Bishops Stortford. However, the Gulls then proceeded to go on a four match unbeaten run until a 1-0 defeat at Hendon, who would be amongst the chasing pack for much of the season.

This 1-0 defeat seemed to shake up the team, and they went unbeaten until the middle of March with some astounding performances along the way, including a 6-1 demolition of Kingstonian and a 5-1 destruction of Bishops Stortford. They seemed to have the confidence they had lacked in previous seasons, and to have too much for any team in the league. However, when promotion was assured with a 2-1 win on Good Friday at Thurrock, you could almost sense the relief.

With all the focus on the league it would be easy to forget the FA Trophy. Canvey went into this competition knowing that they had a good chance of recovering the trophy they won three years ago. After disposing of Windsor & Eton, they then had a tough looking visit from Farnborough. However, they put the Conference side to the sword, gaining a resounding 6-0 victory. Canvey held firm for the next two rounds as many fans were starting to think about Villa Park. Telford came out of the hat for the two-legged Semi-Final and 350 fans made the trip to cheer the Gulls on. They returned home none the wiser, as a 0-0 draw set up an intriguing Second Leg. This was much more exciting than the first, with the Essex side eventually winning through 4-3 on penalties. So to Villa Park where, this time, Canvey would be favourites against their Dr Martens League opponents Hednesford. Unfortunately for the Gulls, this didn't work to their advantage and a 3-2 reverse left Jeff King's men having the slight feeling of what could have been as a unique double slipped through their fingers. The FA Cup brought yet more excitement to this small Essex island with a big draw in the First Round proper against local rivals, Southend United. A 1-1 draw set up a replay with a full capacity at Park Lane. Canvey were expecting to shock their rivals and this they did, taking the lead twice only to lose 3-2 with a last minute goal to break the Gulls' hearts. In reality, perhaps it was a blessing in disguise as this allowed them to focus on winning promotion. Overall, it was a brilliant season for Canvey and they can now look forward to long trips to Carlisle and York in the Conference this season. SW

Directions

Pyramid Football reporters have found this ground particularly hard to find. Several have set out and never been seen again. Enter Canvey via the A130 Canvey Way. This will bring you to a roundabout at Waterside Farm. Take the second exit (B1014) for the town centre into Somnes Avenue. The ground is signposted from here. After about a mile take the second exit at a small roundabout, still Somnes Avenue. After a further half mile is a mini-roundabout. Take the first exit into Climmen Road, which then becomes Dovervelt Road (rugby club on the left). After half a mile you come to another roundabout. Take the second exit into Mitchells Avenue (cricket club on your left). There is a T-junction with the High Street 50 yards on, with a Murco garage on the right. Turn left and follow the road for half a mile, pass the Admiral Jellicoe pub. Continue on, past the Transport Museum on the right. Park Lane is 50 yards further on.

Located right at the far end of the Island, tucked inside the sea wall. Suggestions of a move elsewhere mean Park Lane, which has seen the rise from Essex Senior League to Conference National, could be in its last few seasons. Still a relatively modest ground, but the deep open terracing behind the goal nearest the entrance is a recent addition, and there is plenty of covered seating and standing available along the sides of the pitch. Car parking is plentiful outside the ground, but if you're coming by train, a connecting bus is necessary from Benfleet, and can be a little sparse in the evenings. GB

The Gulls

Carlisle United

Address: Warwick Road, Carlisle, Cumbria, CA1 ILL
Tel: 01228 526 237
Website: www.carlisleunited.premiumtv.co.uk
Email: admin@carlisleunited.co.uk
Officials: Chairman: John Courtenay
Secretary: Sarah McKnight
Manager: Paul Simpson

Directions

Exit the M6 at Junction 43 and take the first turn off at the roundabout - it will be signposted for Carlisle City Centre. Follow the road through two sets of traffic lights. After you go through the second set, the ground will come into view on the right-hand side - just continue on this road until you arrive at the stadium. Parking is plentiful around Brunton Park and there is a large car park situated behind the away end which is ideal for travelling fans.

By train: Take the Virginline to Carlisle Station. Once you have arrived, head out of the station and head in a straight line - you will see a bar called 'Bar-Lo-Go' as soon as you exit the station. When you go past the bar you will now be at the top of Warwick Road. Carry on going without turning off and the ground is approximately a mile down Warwick Road on the left hand side.

Brunton Park is the biggest Non-League venue ever, with over 8,000 seats in an overall capacity of some 20,000. Most of those seats are in the huge modern East Stand, where visitors were accommodated; the older stand opposite is still looking good for its age and the large paddock in front continues to be popular with Blues fans who prefer to stand. The Warwick Road end is the ground's best-known feature, with its multi-span roof making for an excellent atmosphere. Carlisle have been relegated with the highest average attendance of any team and their followers are more passionate than most. CF

Brunton Park

Review

The name 'Carlisle United' is synonymous with escapism. Everyone remembers goalkeeper Jimmy Glass scoring that vital goal to pull off one in a long line of Carlisle's brand of footballing Harry Houdini-acts. Every season United seemed to be relegation favourites and every season they defied the odds. But with the season opening with five straight defeats, it was looking like another heart attack-rendering season for Carlisle fans. They did win at the seventh attempt, beating Rochdale 3-2 - but even then they almost squandered a 3-0 lead. With just one point from the next fourteen, Carlisle were truly rock bottom. When they lost 2-1 to leaders Oxford on 13th December, Carlisle had picked up just five points from 21 games.

Being 16 points adrift at the foot of the table was a desperate position. The Cumbrians looked like bowing out of the Third Division, and the pundits looked like getting it right about Carlisle on this occasion. The side then picked up only their second win of the season, in a 2-0 success over Torquay; six days later, they won on Boxing Day at Bury, 3-1. With the following 1-1 draw with Darlington, Carlisle had picked up more points in the last three games of December than they had in the previous 21. A win over Boston cut the safety-gap to nine points, but the mini-turnaround was hit by two defeats in their next three.

Carlisle's form went from strength to strength, as the side lost just four times in 15 games. It was a tight affair at the foot of the table - York's poor form had dragged them into the relegation scrap, one of five sides now in danger. With three games left, Carlisle won at in-form Mansfield 3-2 - and moved off the bottom of the table for the first time all season. They needed wins in their final games - but a 1-1 draw with Cheltenham, in front of a bumper home crowd, meant Carlisle were relegated. The club were four points adrift of Scunthorpe with a game to go - a game away to champions Doncaster, which the already-relegated Cumbrians lost 1-0. United's good form in the second half of the season was simply a case of too little, too late; this was one escape act they couldn't quite pull off.

If they can retain all of their fighting spirit, they could secure an immediate Football League return. Carlisle are the football equivalent of Forrest Gump's box of chocolates - you never know what you're going to get. MP

The Cumbrians

Crawley Town

Address: Broadfield Stadium, Brighton Road, Crawley, Sussex, RH11 9RX

Tel: 01293 410000

Website: www.crawley-town-fc.co.uk

Email: info@crawley-town-fc.co.uk

Officials: Chairman: Jo Gomm
Secretary: Dave Haining
Manager: Francis Vines

Directions

From the M23, take the A23 signposted to Crawley. At the bottom of the hill, the ground is on the left. Turn left at the roundabout to enter the stadium car park.
By train: From Crawley station, turn left onto Station Way. At the junction with the High Street, turn left over the level crossing into Brighton Road. At the end of Brighton Road, you will see the ground on your right. The ground can be accessed by the subways under the A23. It is a 20 minute walk to the ground.

Rightly rated as one of the top grounds in non-league football, the first-class facilities at the Broadfield Stadium put many league clubs to shame. Opened by the then Sports Minister, Tony Banks, in readiness for the 1997/98 season, the £5 million council-owned project replaced long-time home Town Mead as the club looked to capitalise on the passion for their local side. With a 4,996 capacity, an imposing main stand provides the focal point for 1,100 seated supporters and excellent views are guaranteed from most, if not all corners of the ground. A good sized clubhouse comes with a spacious bar and pleasant surroundings. CL

Broadfield Stadium

Review

Crawley Town finally managed to fulfil their potential last season when they clinched the Dr Martens Premier Division title, and with it, promotion to the Nationwide Conference. In each of the last three seasons, Town had looked menacing at the season's outset in August and September, but, in each case, they froze in the cold winter months and their title challenge tapered off leaving them with finishes of eleventh, fourth and seventh respectively.
However, the 2003/04 campaign followed a reverse pattern for Crawley. A sluggish start saw Francis Vines' men win only two of their opening seven games as Steve Claridge's Weymouth set the pace early on. However, as the Terras started to drop points, Crawley began to pick more up as the Sussex side began to hit some form. A 1-0 win over Weymouth on the first Saturday of 2004 saw Crawley move to within three points of the league leaders with a game in hand. Crawley continued their consistent form with Charlie MacDonald up front proving a real handful for opposition defences, at one point scoring nine goals in eight games during March and April. However, it was Weymouth's dip in form that really swayed the title Crawley's way and, by the time that Town completed the double over the Terras on 6th March, Crawley had the bit firmly between their teeth. They could even afford to lose their final two home games of the season against Hinckley and Newport and still finish an impressive twelve points clear at the top of the table. As much of a roaring success as their league campaign undoubtedly was, Crawley didn't have much to shout about in the cup competitions. However, they did blast their way through to the First Round of the FA Cup disposing of lower league sides Harlow Town, Croydon Athletic and Cirencester (scoring 14 goals in the process), before losing to Conference side Telford. The FA Trophy was even less profitable after Town lost a Third Round replay to Dagenham & Redbridge after extra-time. However, few Crawley fans will lose sleep over their lack of cup success after they won the championship (which promised to be a close run thing early in the campaign) by such a canter. JB

The Newtowners

Dagenham & Redbridge

Address: The Glyn Hopkin Stadium, Victoria Road, Dagenham, Essex, RM10 7XL

Tel: 020 8592 1549/7194

Website: www.daggers.co.uk

Officials: President: Harry Hammond,
Chairman: David Andrews
Manager: John Still

The Glyn Hopkin Stadium

Directions

From the North: From the M25 take the M11 (J27). Proceed towards London and follow the signs for the A406. Continue on the A406 and follow signs for the North Circular, Docklands. After the Barking/East Ham turn off, take the left hand lane and follow signs for Dagenham.
From the West: As you approach Dagenham on the A13 there is a leisure complex on the left. Stay in the left lane and follow the signs to the A1306 for Dagenham. Do not continue on the A13. Go straight on at the next two sets of lights and turn left before McDonald's (don't be tempted). Proceed about one mile down this road (Ballards Road) to the Bull roundabout and turn left. Pass Dagenham East tube station on the left and Victoria Road is 400 yards further on.
From the East: If coming from the Southend/Dartford crossing direction, follow signs to Dagenham/Central London on the A13. Proceed along this road and you will see signs for the Ferry Lane Industrial Estate. From the left hand lane, take the next slip road, signposted Elm Park/Dagenham East and turn right at the roundabout. Go straight over the next roundabout. Turn left at the next set of lights onto a dual carriageway. Turn right past McDonald's. You are in Ballards Road (see above).
By Tube: Take the District Line to Dagenham East. Turn left out of the station. Ballards Road is 400 yards on the left, the ground is a further 100 yards down.

There will be many a Pyramid Football reporter who will be secretly pleased that Dagenham, once again, failed to win promotion last season. Not that we wish the team any ill will, far from it. It is just we would have missed out on the Daggers' now legendary hospitality towards the press. It used to be just a cup of tea and a doughnut (still more than you get at most grounds) but is now a full half-time buffet. This is all part of the impressive new main stand which was funded by the Daggers' FA Cup runs of recent years, and which dwarfs the rest of the terraced ground which is hemmed in by houses. JB

Review

After three successful years in the Conference, fans would have been forgiven for expecting more of the same this time around. Boss Garry Hill had led the club to second, third and fifth place finishes in the Conference. They only lost out on a league place in 2001-02 due to goal difference. This time around, they showed their class by thrashing Barnet and Forest Green 5-2 in August, but also lost to relegation threatened Leigh RMI and Tamworth. It was a bad-tempered draw at home to Telford in September that could be cited as the catalyst for their poor form. Hill was alleged to have made racial comments to Telford's Fitzroy Simpson. Mark Stein and Mark Smith both refused to play for Hill and never played for the club again. Stein had been club top scorer for the previous two seasons, and it was a sad way for him to end his successful Daggers career.
By the start of December, Dagenham had won eight, drawn five and lost nine - hardly the form of promotion contenders. Their inconsistency was typified by their first two games of the New Year: after losing 2-1 to fifth-placed Aldershot, they put five past third placed Shrewsbury two days later. February then saw matches against the top two sides. Their 2-1 defeat at leaders Chester was expected; the result at home to Hereford less so. In front of Sky TV cameras, Dagenham completely capitulated and lost 9-0. They followed this with five games unbeaten but four of these were draws and Hill announced he was leaving at the end of the season. But Hill left earlier than expected, resigning after a 4-0 home defeat versus mid-table Gravesend on 3rd April.
The Daggers eventually limped into thirteenth place, not even qualifying for the LDV Vans Trophy. They were 16 points from the last available Play-Off place; for a club of Dagenham's ambition and size, this was a serious failure. One of the team's most obvious failures during 2003-04 was their shocking inconsistency: only twice throughout the season did they string together successive victories. The Hill era had brought much success but he decided to move on; despite the results this season, he will be remembered fondly at the club. His replacement, John Still, is a serious coup for the club and perhaps he is the man to finish the job Hill started and lead Dagenham into the football league. MP

The Daggers

Exeter City

Address: St James's Park, Exeter, EX4 6PX

Tel: 01392 254 073

Website: www.exetercityfc.co.uk

Email: enquiries@exetercityfc.co.uk

Officials: Chairman: Ian Huxham
Secretary: Stuart Brailey
Manager: Eamonn Dolan

St James's Park

Directions

From the North: M5 until J30. Follow signs to the city centre along Sidmouth Road to Heavitree Road. At the roundabout, take the fourth exit, Western Way and, at the next roundabout, the second exit into Old Tiverton Road, then next left into St James's Road.
From the South: Take the A30 (signposted to Exeter) into Heavitree Road, then as above.
By train: Exeter St Davids is two miles from the ground. Take the 'N' bus from the station to the High Street. Then walk up Sidwell Street to the ground and take a right into St James's Road.
Alternatively, Exeter Central: On leaving the station, walk down Queen Street into the High Street and continue into Sidwell Street until you approach Old Tiverton Road.

A strange mixture of the past and the future as far as the stands are concerned. One big old construction, a mini away terrace behind one of the goals (troublesome if it rains) and one big open section of terracing coupled with a modern all seater with boxes along one side of the pitch. The transport links are ample and it is reachable via a walk through several tight streets - look for the floodlights to guide your way. They seem to have put their financial problems behind them and, if the passion of the 2,500 or so faithful keeps up, then St James's could be playing host to League football again before too long. Also, an excellent programme. HM

Review

When you lose your opening pre-season friendly to Exmouth Town, you don't expect to bring the curtain down on the year with a mouth-watering game against former world champions Brazil. Mind you, over the years, Grecians fans have learnt to expect the unexpected.
The Brazilian Samba Kings swaggered into town to complete Exeter City's centenary season celebrations, rounding off a year that many fans didn't think the club would survive. New manager, Eamonn Dolan, quickly established an economical squad, with an intelligent blend of youth and experience, whilst injecting a real sense of self belief into the club that had been seriously lacking in previous campaigns. Unfortunately though, an opening day stalemate with Halifax Town and an away-day defeat to Telford United proved that life in the Conference would be far from easy.
A few days later, however, victory at Margate set the Grecians on their way and triggered an unbeaten league home record stretching to 20th December. Victories against promotion chasing Chester City, Barnet and Aldershot Town made the Conference sit up and take notice as City rocketed up the table. However, the club's crippling debts refused to go away and the threat of a twelve point deduction due to the Grecians' entry into a CVA (Corporate Voluntary Agreement) coupled with an oversubscribed treatment table, threatened to spoil the promotion party. The Grecians found themselves in yet more hot water when the Inland Revenue demanded City pay-off their debt to the Taxman.
To add insult to a growing injury list, Nationwide Conference chiefs complained that Grenada midfielder Dwane Lee had been illegally signed during the Devon club's transfer embargo and thus threatened to dock all the points City had gained in matches featuring the ex-Yeading man. Potentially, this could turn the battle for promotion into a relegation dogfight. Nevertheless, the Grecians continued their Houdini act, escaping punishment whilst turning the heat up on their rivals.
So to the final day of the season. A City victory coupled with Aldershot or Barnet's failure to win, would propel Exeter into the Play-Offs. Expectations were high as 8,000 fans packed into St James's Park in a sea of red and white. Sadly, after a rollercoaster of a season, the promotion bandwagon was derailed on the final bend as both City's enemies kept their promotion bids on track. DS

The Grecians

Farnborough Town

Address: Cherrywood Road, Farnborough, Hampshire, GU14 8UD

Tel: 01252 541469

Website: www.farnboroughtownfc.com

Officials: Chairman: Tony Theo
Secretary: Vince Williams
Manager: Dean Austin

Review

Hopes were high at Cherrywood Road, as former Leyton Orient manager, Tommy Taylor, took control at the Hampshire club. However, what always looked as though it would be a difficult season began even worse than their supporters feared, as Town opened the season with a 14 match winless run, with only a handful of battling draws to their name.

Taylor left in the Autumn, and in the run up to Christmas, the defence tightened up, with home results featuring notable wins against Northwich, Farnborough and Woking, as well as a highly impressive 2-0 success at Barnet. Following their impressive showings in Cup and Trophy in the previous campaign, the boot was on the other foot, as Weston-super-Mare handed them a home reverse in the FA Cup, and they were thrashed at Canvey Island in the Trophy. The turn of the year still saw some good results, chiefly the 4-0 success at Aldershot Town, and a decent showing against fellow strugglers. It meant that they comfortably secured the third from bottom spot which would be sufficient for survival with a few matches to spare. GB

Directions

From M3: Leave at J4 and take the A331 for Farnham. After a few hundred yards, exit at the second slip road, for A325 Farnborough. Turn right at the roundabout and cross over the dual carriageway.

From South: Take the A31, Guildford to Farnham road, and turn north onto the A331 dual carriageway, heading towards the M3. Go past the Farnborough exit and leave the A331 at the Frimley exit and turn left at the top of the slip road.

From both the above, pass the Farnborough Gate shopping centre on your left and, at the next roundabout, turn left onto the A325. At the next set of lights, take the right filter into Prospect Avenue. At the end of this road, turn right into Cherrywood Road. The ground is half a mile on the right.

By train: The nearest stations are Frimley (nearest but not good connections), Farnborough Main and Farnborough North. Farnborough Main has frequent services from Waterloo and Southampton. From the station turn right onto Union Street. After half a mile turn right into Prospect Road, go under the railway and follow this road over two mini-roundabouts and a full one into Cherrywood Road. The ground is half a mile beyond the third roundabout. Farnborough North has hourly semi-fast services from Reading and Guildford.

Cherrywood Road is a modern venue, of a similar vintage to the surrounding houses in a purely residential setting. Not of Football League standard, it is one of the more basic grounds at this level, but can comfortably deal with the current level of crowds attracted. There are two seated stands on either side of the pitch, with a covered terrace behind one goal, and the other end being open. There is a large car park, and it is not far off the M3, but if you are coming by train, wear your walking shoes, and look for Cove's ground on the left along the way. GB

Cherrywood Road

The Boro

Forest Green Rovers

Address: The Lawn, Nymphsfield Road, Forest Green, Nailsworth, Gloucester, GL6 0ET

Tel: 01453 834860

Website: www.fgrfc.co.uk

Email: forestgreenroversfc@hotmail.com

Officials: Chairman: Ken Boulton
Secretary: Colin Peake
Caretaker Manager: Tim Harris

The Lawn

Directions

From the North (M5): Leave at J13 (Stroud A419). Follow the A419 to Stroud then, on meeting the A46, follow signs for Bath, Nailsworth (A46). In the centre of Nailsworth there is one mini-roundabout, turn right here into Spring Hill. Go up the hill and continue along this road, which becomes Nympsfield Road. The ground is on the left.
From the South (M5): Leave at J14. Follow the B4509 towards Wotton-under-Edge, turning left onto the B4058. Follow this road through Wotton, then follow signs for Nailsworth. On meeting the A4135, turn right then left shortly afterwards, remaining on B4058. On reaching Nailsworth, turn left at the mini-roundabout in the centre of the town, go up Spring Hill, then follow directions as above.
From the East (M4): Leave at Junction 18 and follow the A46 directly to Nailsworth and, at the mini-roundabout, turn left up Spring Hill, then follow the directions as above.
By train: The nearest station is Stroud. It is definitely a taxi or bus ride (there is a taxi office opposite the station). The number 93 bus, run by Stagecoach Stroud Valleys, runs from Stroud bus station every 30 minutes (five minutes walk from the railway station, through the Merrywalks shopping centre) to Nailsworth and Forest Green.

Is there a more remote ground in the higher reaches of the non-league game? The continued prosperity of this village team is testimony to a loyal local support. The fans don't exactly come down from the hillsides, leaving their flocks behind, but you get the picture. The ground is neat and compact, with a seated stand down one side and terracing elsewhere. MW

Review

The friendly club from Gloucestershire once again achieved safety fairly comfortably, although not without some upheaval along the way. They got off to their all-too-common shaky start, which did however feature an important 2-1 success at Leigh RMI. They were scoring plenty of goals at this point, but their loose defence was restricting their points return.
There was a particularly disappointing result just after Christmas as Hereford United handed them a 7-1 home reverse, and against a need for financial tightness, particularly given their fall at the first hurdle in the FA Cup against Aldershot, Colin Addison parted company with the club. Assistant Tim Harris took over as caretaker, and led his side to an excellent 2-1 victory over title favourites Chester City. As a result, he was handed the managerial reins to the end of the season, ten days later. Rovers' defence tightened up, and the results improved as they moved up the table. Although Dover knocked them out of the FA Trophy, Alex Meechan's return from a spell at Dagenham was a welcome boost to morale. However, despite this, Forest Green had a poor run in. Rovers lost four of their final five league games (again shipping a hat-full of goals in the process) ensuring that they would finish the season merely hovering above the drop zone in 18th. One plus point from Rovers' season was the prolific form of the evergreen Neil Grayson. The veteran striker enjoyed something of an Indian Summer to his career in 2003/04 as his return of 14 league and cup goals made him the club's top scorer. GB

Rovers

Gravesend & Northfleet

Address: Stonebridge Road, Northfleet, Kent DA11 9GN
Tel: 01474 533796
Website: www.gnfc.co.uk
Email: webmaster@gnfc.co.uk
Officials: Chairman: Brian Kilcullan
Secretary: Rory Edwards
Manager: Andy Ford

Stonebridge Road

Directions

From the M25 take the A2 coastbound. Take the second exit (B262) and turn left at the top of the slip-road. Cross the first roundabout into Springhead Road. Follow the road across one roundabout until you reach a T-Junction. Turn left into Northfleet High Street. Follow the High Street until you come to the top of Stonebridge Hill. Go down the hill and the ground is at the bottom on the right. The car park is at the far end of the ground.

By train: The nearest station is Northfleet which is only about 200 yards from the ground. As you leave the station head more or less straight ahead until you reach the main road. Turn left and walk down the hill and the ground is on your right.

Alternatively, you can go to Gravesend station and catch a bus to the ground. Come out of the station on the town side and turn right. There are bus stops just by the station. A 480 bus will drop you outside the ground (about a 10 to 15 minute journey).

Stonebridge Road is one of those fine, old-fashioned non-league grounds - cavernous, a little run down, but impressive when filled. Its survival is no doubt in part because of its location - hardly the most salubrious of sites, surrounded by grotty North Kent industry. There are large, covered terraces on two sides, and an open terrace at the other end. There is also a seated stand down one side. The locals can be caustic, with opponents likely to be on the receiving end of North Kent wit (if that is not a contradiction in terms). A small but reasonably friendly bar is worth seeking out. MW

Review

In 2002-03, the Fleet had had a number of nervy moments in their debut Conference season and only made their position safe on the last day of the season, finishing just two points above the drop zone. The club's fans were probably expecting much of the same after an appalling run of results in the opening games. After losing their first four league games, they were briefly lifted by a narrow win at Farnborough - only to lose their next two. A run of five games unbeaten followed this, but three of these were draws and they were hovering just above the relegation zone. Then a great run of results in the FA Cup seemed to instill some confidence in the players.

Their FA Cup journey began with a tough game at Play-Off favourites Exeter City. After earning a goalless draw at St James', they overcame them 6-5 on penalties in the replay. Their reward was an even tougher prospect: playing away at Conference leaders, Chester City. After scoring through a Justin Skinner penalty, they defended well to earn a home tie against Second Division Notts County. Prior to the visit of the league side, Fleet won just once in five games - a convincing win at Tamworth but not quite enough to make up for one point in three home games. Nevertheless, 2,998 turned up for the big cup game. Fleet looked like holding on for a replay after losing a first-half lead, but a last minute goal sent County through. Fleet's league form suffered and it was only two precious victories over Kent neighbours Margate that kept them in 16th place.

Two signings during February seemed to be the turning point in Fleet's hitherto unspectacular season. Manny Omoyinmi, once of West Ham, arrived on loan from Oxford, while Roy Essendoh signed for £4,000 from Bishops Stortford. Omoyinmi scored two goals for the club in his loan spell, helping to secure four vital points. Essendoh meanwhile grabbed some crucial goals early in his Fleet career, scoring all the goals in wins over Exeter and Forest Green. That win over Forest Green was the start of a run of twelve games unbeaten for Gravesend; the highlight was a 6-0 thrashing of Play-Off challenging Morecambe. That sequence of results ensured that, rather than having to fight for their safety on the final day of the season, they had already secured a top twelve finish and thus a place in the LDV Vans trophy. All looks bright for the club next season, and they will look to Essendoh to continue his impressive scoring rate of ten goals in just 14 games. MP

The Fleet

Halifax Town

Address: The Shay Stadium, Halifax, West Yorkshire, HX1 2YS

Tel: 01422 341 222

Website: www.halifaxafc.co.uk

Email: theshay@halifaxafc.co.uk

Officials: Chairman: David Cairns
Secretary: Richard Groves
Manager: Chris Wilder

The Shay Stadium

Directions

By road from Rochdale: Travel towards Littleborough and then join the A58. On approaching Ripponden, follow the signs for Halifax, continuing on the A58. Travel through Kebroyd into Sowerby Bridge, at all time following signs for Halifax. Within approximately two miles of Halifax (at King Cross), follow signs for The Shay.

From all other directions: Travel towards the M62 (usually from the A1 or M1). Follow the signs for Leeds until Halifax is signposted. Leave at either Junction 24 (Halifax) or Junction 25 (Brighouse), whichever appears first (this will depend on your direction of travel). On leaving the motorway, follow signs for Halifax. The Shay is signposted from all major routes into Halifax. If all else fails, head for Eureka Children's Museum (which is extensively signposted) and follow signs for the Shay from there.

By train: Halifax station is centrally located on the Caldervale Line, which stretches from Blackpool, on the West Coast, to York. It is either a five minute walk (clearly signposted) or a ride on the tram service. Turn left out of the train station and head towards The Shay Hotel. An alley to the right of the pub leads past the North Stand turnstiles (home fans only) and the changing rooms to the away terracing.

The Shay is a traditional four stand, square stadium that is also shared with the local rugby team. The atmosphere on a match day ebbs and flows - electric with every home team goal and yet a delicate silence when heads are hung in defeat. Fans are kept on their toes in the standing areas of the North and South stands whereas those in the Skircoat Stand can enjoy the comfort of a blue plastic seat. Half-time refreshments are comparable with most other grounds of the same calibre, as are the public conveniences. Car parking facilities are available to the rear of the stadium and surrounding areas closer to the town centre. RK

Review

Fans of Halifax Town will certainly look back on the 2003/04 season with a sense of relief after what was a very disappointing campaign. A football league side until two years ago, Halifax Town's first season in the Conference ended with them finishing in eighth place in the table, just missing out on a Play-Off place. Therefore hopes were understandably high for a promotion push going into the 2003/04 campaign.

Any feelings of optimism looked to be well founded in the opening month of the season as the Shaymen went the first four matches unbeaten. However, three straight defeats in the middle of September curtailed their positive start and was just a small indication of the slump that would hit the club later in the campaign.

Halifax found consistency a problem throughout the winter months and, as such, never really pushed out of mid-table. However, the lack of a Play-Off push was the least of the Shaymen's problems as they entered the run in. An incredible ten successive league defeats from 8th February to the 3rd April saw Town plummet towards the foot of the table and the pre-season promotion aspirations paled into insignificance as the club were sucked into a tense relegation battle.

Ultimately, two wins and a draw from their final four games proved enough to keep the Shaymen's heads above water as they finished fourth from bottom, four points above the drop zone. In the event, Telford's demise and Margate's demotion would have saved Halifax from the drop regardless, but that does not detract from what was a highly sub-standard campaign for the Yorkshire side. JB

The Shaymen

Hereford United

Address: Edgar Street, Hereford, HR4 9JU
Tel: 01432 276666
Website: www.herefordunited.co.uk
Officials: Chairman/Manager: Graham Turner
Secretary: Joan Fennessy

Edgar Street

Directions

From the North: Follow the A49 into Hereford and then signs straight to Edgar Street.
From the East: Take the A465 or A438 into Hereford, then follow signs for Leominster straight to Edgar Street.
From the South: Take the A49 or A45 to the town centre, then follow signs for Leominster straight to Edgar Street.
From the West: Take the A438 into the town centre, then follow signs for Leominster straight to Edgar Street.
By train: Exit the station and turn right into Commercial Road. At a T-junction turn right into Newmarket Street and then, at the roundabout, turn right into Edgar Street. The ground is on the right hand side just past Blackfriars Street.

Edgar Street benefits from a unique character and charm. At each end are covered terraces, which include flat semi-circular areas before the terracing begins to climb, the legacy of a long-gone athletics track. Behind the home, or Meadow end, of the ground, there is a large public car park (pay and display). Along Edgar Street itself is the narrow Len Weston Stand, which crams an upper storey of seats over the terracing that stands in its lea, making the most of the limited space alongside the main road. Away supporters are granted half of this side of the ground. There has been talk of the Bulls leaving for pastures new, but personally I hope that they remain at a ground that has so much tradition and history tied to it. SG

Review

The Bulls' impressive 91 point haul from their Conference season would have been enough to take the title in all but one of the previous four campaigns. However, the imperious form of Mark Wright's Chester City beat Graham Turner's men into second place, where they had to endure heartbreak via the Play-Offs.
United were certainly riding high on the crest of an optimistic wave in the opening weeks of the season. They were living up to their tag of one of the pre-season title favourites as they won seven out of their first eight games, scoring 25 goals in the process. It wasn't until 19th September that the Bulls tasted defeat (a 4-1 reverse at Burton), and, indeed, they only lost seven games all season.
Despite this, Chester had forged their way ahead by the turn of the year and the Bulls seemed to always be just one step behind the Cheshire outfit for the remainder of the title race. The departure of the talismanic Paul Parry to Cardiff City in January did little to help Hereford's cause. However, heads refused to drop as the rest of the squad stuck to the task in hand and won many admirers as their attacking blend of football yielded some impressive wins over the course of the season.
A 9-0 demolition of Dagenham & Redbridge on 27th February signalled a run of eleven straight wins for the Bulls, culminating in a 2-1 win over Chester at Edgar Street on the final day. City's 1-0 win over Scarborough the week before meant that they had already sewn up the title by the time they travelled to Hereford, but the Bulls certainly proved their point to the champions and ensured that Chester's winning margin at the top was just a solitary point.
With eleven successive wins behind them, Hereford were without doubt the form team, and were justifiably the favourites, going into the Play-Offs. Hereford had done the league double over their Semi-Final opponents, Aldershot, and had won 2-1 at the Recreation Ground earlier that month. However, this time around, the Shots proved a tougher proposition, and there was little to choose between the sides as both legs ended in a stalemate - leaving the aggregate score locked at 1-1. The lottery of a penalty competition went the Shots' way as Terry Brown's men triumphed 4-2 and denied Hereford, who had finished 21 points above them in the league, a place in the Final.
There was little solace to be found in the cup competitions either. A bright start in the FA Trophy (following a 6-1 defeat of Harrow Borough) meant little as the Bulls then lost to a late goal at Exeter in Round Three.
Considering they were top of the Conference at the time, the Bulls were also expected to cause Barry Fry's Second Division outfit, Peterborough United, problems when they were paired together in the First Round of the FA Cup. However, the Posh proved too much for United as they ran out 2-0 winners in what was, all in all, a disappointing season for Hereford, and one that promised much but, ultimately, delivered little. JB

The Bulls

Leigh RMI

Address: Hilton Park, Kirkhall Lane, Leigh WN7 1RN
Tel: 01942 743743
Website: www.leighrmi.com
Officials: Chairman: Bill Taylor
Secretary: Alan Robinson
Manager: Phil Starbuck

Hilton Park

Directions

From M6 North: Leave at J23. Head towards Manchester on the A580. Take the A579 for Bolton and Pennington Flash. Continue until you see an Asda store on the left. Turn right at the traffic lights, then right again into Glebe Street. Take the next right into Chadwick Street and the ground is straight ahead.
From M6 South: Leave the M6 at J22 and take the A572 (Winwick Lane) towards Leigh. Then take the A580 towards Manchester, then left onto the A579 signposted Bolton and Pennington Flash, then as above.
M1, M62, M60 (anti-clockwise): Leave the M60 at J14 for the A580 towards Liverpool. Take the A579 signposted Bolton and Pennington Flash, then as above.
By train: From Manchester, transfer to Bolton or Atherton stations. Atherton is the nearest of the two to Leigh. The bus (582) travels between Bolton and Leigh passing through Atherton. Bolton station is approximately nine miles from Leigh. Atherton station is four miles or so from Leigh. The nearest bus stop to the ground on the 582 service is the one after Kirkhall Lane, Leigh.

The stands are typical of a northern rugby league ground, quite uncomfortable seats, draughty, steel columns blocking the view, and the roof (made of corrugated steel) is very noisy. Despite the regular low attendance (compared to the rest of the Conference), the fans are brilliant, and the food is good. Car parking is plentiful because Leigh only get on average 400 per home game. MB

Review

It's fair to say that, other than their reprieve following Margate's demotion to Conference South, high spots were few and far between for the Railwaymen. However, one of them was undoubtedly the form of David McNiven, signed at the start of the season, and contributing an astounding 27 goals of the 46 scored by the team. He got off to a good start by bagging a double in the season's opening 2-1 win against Dagenham but, following a 1-0 win at Northwich, the club went ten games without a win including defeat in the FA Cup at Accrington Stanley. During this sequence, a 4-1 defeat at home to Barnet saw Mark Patterson make way for joint caretakers, Phil Starbuck and Steve Redmond.
Leigh ended the winless sequence with their result of the season as Carl Barrowclough's 85th minute goal provided a 1-0 win at Hereford, but they would endure another six matches before a 2-1 win at Dagenham on the 13th December. By Christmas, McNiven had chalked up 15 goals, but by New Year's Day, the two games against Chester had produced an 11-2 aggregate win for the league champions. Another bright spot appeared with a surprisingly comfortable 3-1 success over Morecambe on 24th January but, two weeks later, they seemed condemned to the bottom three after losing 4-3 at Tamworth although, ironically, Margate, the club who would save them, were handed a 4-2 defeat at the end of February. This ushered in a nightmare close to the campaign, as the last ten games saw eight games lost, one draw and a solitary win (against Northwich). GB

The Railwaymen

Morecambe

Address: Christie Park, Lancaster Road, Morecambe, Lancashire LA4 5TJ

Tel: 01524 411797

Website: www.morecambefc.com

Officials: Chairman: Peter McGuigan
Secretary: Neil Marsdin
Manager: Jim Harvey

Christie Park

Directions

Leave the M6 at J34 and follow signs for Lancaster along Caton Road. Continue until a set of traffic lights. Follow the signs for Morecambe. On Morecambe Road, having admired the castle on the hill to your left, you will pass Riversway House on the right. At the roundabout, go over to another roundabout, with McDonald's on the left. Carry straight on until another roundabout with five junctions. Take the second junction, Lancaster Road. Christie Park is on your left. The car park is just after the ground.
By train: Nearest stations are Lancaster and Morecambe. If the former, turn left into Morecambe Road. Carry on along this road and then into Lancaster Road. The ground is on the left. From Morecambe station, turn right into Central Drive and then bear right into Euston Road. This heads into Lancaster Road and the ground is on the right.

Christie Park is a modernised and compact ground which comfortably meets Football League standards; it is situated in a residential area on one of the principal roads into the seaside town. There is covered terracing at both ends, which is well capable of generating an atmosphere. The sizeable car park contains a club shop selling a range of goods. The elevated main stand offers a decent view of proceedings, and it is a fair walk from the station and seafront. MP

Review

The Shrimps suffered the agony of a Play-Off Semi-Final defeat in 2002-03 after finishing as runners-up, and would have hoped to go one better this term. Under the steady guidance of Jim Harvey, and with a talented squad including Stewart Drummond and Danny Carlton, they had every chance of challenging at the top end of the table. The first seven games of the season yielded four wins and three defeats as they struggled to gain any sort of momentum, and they were looking far from runners-up material. Four games undefeated kept them in touch at the top but early October defeats at the hands of Exeter and Scarborough put Morecambe's promotion credentials in serious disarray.
Worse was to follow as they picked up just two points from their next five games, leaving them languishing in mid-table. It was results they needed, and they put points over performance to end their run with successive 2-1 wins over Stevenage and Forest Green. The fans were then rewarded with an early Christmas present when they witnessed a fantastic 4-0 win over Tamworth in early December. The following week would have left the fans far less impressed, as unfancied Woking cruised to a 4-1 win. The club looked a shadow of the previous season's team as they struggled for any form of consistency; the club were in ninth at the turn of the year and the Play-Offs seemed to be a dim light at the end of a very long tunnel for Morecambe.
February clearly illustrated the club's continuing inconsistency: impressive wins over Northwich (3-0) and at Farnborough (4-2) were followed by a 3-1 defeat at home to Barnet and a 6-0 thrashing against a Gravesend side struggling to break the shackles of mid-table. Those successive wins had allowed Morecambe to briefly reacquaint themselves with the Play-Offs when they moved up to fifth. A win over Scarborough was followed by two defeats that left Morecambe with it all to do as the season reached an end. Four successive wins, including a 4-0 win over Forest Green that saw Wayne Curtis hit a hat-trick, left them with an outside chance of reaching the Play-Offs; however, drawing the last two games meant they finished in seventh, three points off the Play-Offs, and they were left reeling after failing to build on an impressive previous season. A sterner defence and a bit of consistency will be needed this season if the Shrimps want to go swimming with the league's big boys. MP

The Shrimps

Northwich Victoria

Address: (Temporary Address) Leftwich House, Queen Street, Cheshire, CW9 5JN

Tel: 01606 41450

Website: nvfc.co.uk

Officials: Chairman: Dave Stone
Secretary: Derek Nuttall
Manager: Steve Burr

GMB Stadium

Directions

From M6, J19: Follow the A556 towards Northwich for approximately three miles. Turn right onto the A559 towards Lostock (just as the road becomes a dual carriageway). Turn right at the traffic lights immediately before the Slow and Easy pub. Turn left at the crossroads by the Black Greyhound pub (signposted). Follow the road through the industrial estate for about half a mile. Turn left immediately after crossing the canal bridge (signposted). You are now at Wincham Park.

By train: From the station, head past the Lion and Railway pub towards the town centre for 150 yards, until you reach a roundabout. Cross over Chester Way to your right, and take the next right turn into New Warrington Road passing the Mill House pub on your right. Follow the road for about half a mile until you reach Chapel Street on your right (signposted). Wincham Park is a further quarter of a mile along this road (signposted).

The Vics intend to continue their ground-share at the well-appointed Wincham Park until November. It is an isolated venue, surrounded almost exclusively by countryside, situated in a small village a few miles outside Northwich itself, which is fine for car users but not for those who have come by train. Once you are there, it is a modern ground with a main stand along one side of the pitch offering good views with covered terracing behind both goals as well. Nearby, spectators can see Northwich's new ground taking shape in the background. MP

Review

Even the most pessimistic of Northwich fans could not have predicted the dire season that they were forced to endure. As the only team to have played in the Conference every season since its 1979 formation, they were confident of remaining in the division after comfortable mid-table finishes in the previous two seasons. Preparations were hit though by Jimmy Quinn leaving for Shrewsbury; Steve Davis came in to take over. Davis looked to strengthen his forward line, and signed proven goalscorer Chris Ward along with burly Chris Thompson. Northwich started off well enough, gaining two draws and a win, over Tamworth, in their first three games. The Vics then lost seven of their next eight games (including tame 1-0 home defeats against Leigh RMI and Dagenham), and Davis duly resigned.

Alvin McDonald arrived from Vauxhall Motors, and things looked good as the Vics came from behind twice to gain a 3-3 draw with Accrington. Alas, normal service was resumed the following week as Hereford gave them a 5-1 thrashing at Wincham Park. McDonald couldn't steady the ship, despite the arrival of several new players including ex-Everton trainee, Nicky Young. The club's second manager of the season lasted a total of eleven games, comprising eight defeats, two draws and a battling win at Telford. The team showed plenty of character but unfortunately McDonald couldn't find the goal-scorer that Northwich desperately needed. He was sacked in mid-December, and said: 'I feel hard done by; to be judged on eleven games is an absolute joke'.

Ex-Aston Villa defender, Shaun Teale, arrived as replacement, with the club still rooted in last place, and he lost his opening four games. A home draw against high-flying Aldershot gave some hope, but his first victory - and the Vics' third of the season - didn't come until 13th March, at Burton Albion. Teale left after the club's penultimate game, when they completed the double over Telford with a 1-0 win. He had been told that his contract was not being renewed, so left after telling chairman Dave Stone that there was 'no point in me going to Gravesend'. On-loan Shrewsbury defender, Greg Rioch, 28, took charge for the 2-2 draw at Gravesend. This was the game in which the Vics thought they were bidding farewell to the Conference. However, 28th May brought an unexpected reprieve. Telford went into liquidation, and thus had relegation forced upon them, allowing Northwich to stay up. The Vics can count themselves extremely lucky, and they can't afford another season like this one as they look to move into their new stadium in 2005/06 as a Conference side. MP

The Vics

Scarborough

Address: McCain Stadium, Seamer Road, Scarborough, North Yorkshire, YO12 4HF

Tel: 01723 375094

Website: Website: www.scarboroughfc.com

Officials: Chairman: Malcolm Reynolds
Secretary: Kevin Philliskirk
Manager: Nick Henry

Review

The 2003/04 season will live long in the memory of all Scarborough fans, as their FA Cup run saw them come so close to toppling the mighty Chelsea. It wasn't enough to claim the league scalps of Doncaster Rovers, Port Vale and Southend but to push Chelsea all the way too left the entire country in awe of their feat. Manager, Russell Slade, watched as his reputation visibly grew in the weeks surrounding the game and the town was placed firmly on the map. The Non-League game has barely had so much publicity, with weeks of hype surrounding the north-east club. Even a rather famous daily newspaper got in on the act by sponsoring the Seadogs in their efforts. With hundreds of members of the press in attendance (myself included), and countless sponsorship deals, the club's financial status received a welcome boost too.

As a result, their league form never really got started and they stuttered along, finishing a rather ordinary 15th. Slade could have been forgiven this as his paper thin squad were never threatened by relegation, but nor did his side ever challenge the front runners.

Despite signing a new contract days after the Chelsea game, and the team finding a decent run of form in the remaining few games of the campaign, Slade has now moved on to pastures new. An offer from Grimsby Town proved too tempting for him, as he desperately wants to prove himself at a higher level and who, after all, can blame him? His record at Scarborough is phenomenal, saving the club from relegation in his first season, and then just being pipped to the Play-Offs in his second. This season saw the club shine in the FA Cup and finish in a respectable position in the Conference.

Nick Henry (Slade's assistant and former player) now has the job of picking up the team and getting them ready for another bite at the promotion cherry. MJ

Directions

The McCain Stadium is situated on the main A64 York - Scarborough Road about one and a half miles south of the town centre. It is opposite Currys and Borough Tyres on the left as you drive into the town. If approaching Scarborough from the North (Teesside) or the South (Bridlington, Hull), follow signs for York A64 once you enter Scarborough.

By train: On leaving Scarborough station, turn into Westborough. Carry on along this road and then turn left into Seamer Road. The McCain Stadium is down this road on the right hand side just after Barry's Lane, just over a mile from the station.

The Seadogs are intending to move southwards soon, so the days of the pleasantly sited McCain Stadium on Seamer Road seem numbered. The 'Theatre of Chips' is a neat and tidy stadium with a small main stand; a pair of modern all seater stands dating from Football League days offer excellent views of the action behind each goal. Covered terracing on the far side completes the picture, as the ground overlooks a cluster of housing as well as a hillside. It is quite a longish walk from the town centre, but enjoyable on a good day, and is well connected to the road network, although nearby parking is at a premium. Always a friendly club, the McCain is well worth a visit before the North Yorkshire side move on. MP

The Seadogs

Stevenage Borough

Address: Broadhall Way, Stevenage, Herts, SG2 8RH
Tel: 01438 223223
Website: www.stevenageborofc.com
Email: rogera@stevenageborofc.com
Officials: Chairman: Phil Wallace
Secretary: Roger Austin
Manager: Graham Westley

Directions

Approach Stevenage on the A1(M). Take the Stevenage South (A602) exit off the A1(M), and the ground is on the right at the second roundabout. A large car park is opposite.
By train: The ground is roughly one mile from Stevenage station. Take the footbridge into the town centre past the Gordon Craig Theatre. The number four bus will take you to the ground. There is also a taxi rank at the station if you're feeling lazy or lost.

Broadhall Way is one of the better grounds in the Conference - it has been developed in readiness to host Third Division football should the need arise. The addition of an all seater stand at one end ensures away supporters are afforded equal luxury. That the ground hosts reserve team fixtures for Tottenham is a testament to the facilities and surroundings. On my first visit to Stevenage Borough, I waited 15 minutes for a number four bus which then took ages to wind its way round numerous housing estates before delivering me to the ground. On my way home I tried walking back along the main road towards Stevenage station. That took just ten minutes. TW

Review

Hopes must have been high at Stevenage going into the 2003/04 season. After a poor start the season prior, the club had appointed Graham Westley as their new boss. Their fortunes soon turned around after his arrival, and eight wins in the final eleven games saw the club finish twelfth.
An eighth place finish last season was an improvement but Borough fans may be forgiven for being a little disappointed as the club finished six points shy of the Conference Play-Offs (something that seemed a realistic target at the start of the campaign).
Despite going the first five games unbeaten, a lack of consistency always seemed to plague Westley's men throughout the campaign. This was never more clearly highlighted than when the club celebrated a December victory over champions elect Chester City, only to then lose the next three games (two of them at home). Three wins in the final four games pushed Borough up to eighth place but, in truth, they were well out of the Play-Off picture before their final day victory over Forest Green.
Borough did have something to cheer in the FA Cup as they fought their way to the First Round proper and a home tie with Stockport County. Dino Maamria grabbed the headlines as his brace was enough for Borough to secure a 2-1 win and a place in Round Two.
Once more they found Football League opposition lying in wait, this time in the form of Swansea City. However, Borough were just edged out on the day as Lee Trundle (who would make something of a name for himself later in the competition) netted the deciding goal in a 2-1 win for the Welsh side. JB

The Boro

Tamworth

Address: The Lamb Ground, Kettlebrook, Tamworth, Staffs, B77 1AA

Tel: 01827 65798

Website: www.thelambs.co.uk

Officials: Chairman: Bob Andrews
Secretary: Brian Whithouse
Manager: Mark Cooper

The Lamb Ground

Review

After a difficult first Conference season for Tamworth, the Staffordshire side ultimately survived to fight another day. They were hardly title favourites going into the campaign, but not many would have predicted such a tough first season for a side who swept aside all before them in the Dr Martens Premier Division the year before, not to mention storming to their first FA Trophy Final.

The fixtures computer may have been a little nicer to Tamworth as they came away empty handed from their opening two games against Hereford and Chester, hardly the kindest of starts to a first ever Conference campaign.

Early on, it was obvious that the Lambs were staring down the barrel of a relegation battle and were in danger of slipping back through the relegation trap-door after just one season. The departure of Scott Rickards, such an influential figure in their FA Trophy run twelve months previous, to Kidderminster, did not help Tamworth's plight.

Their league form was frustrating as they struggled to gain any consistency, but it would come down to results against the fellow struggling sides that would decide their fate. Wins over Northwich, Farnborough and Forest Green were priceless, but safety was ultimately ensured against Leigh RMI when they came from behind no less than three times before Paul Barnes snatched a last-gasp goal to seal a 4-3 win.

Safety was ensured well before the last day trip to Aldershot but, so too, was the future of manager, Darron Gee. He was quoted as saying he would 'seriously consider' an offer that would benefit him elsewhere. But, ultimately, he felt that he had taken the club as far as he could with the limited resources at his disposal and quit to spend more time with the family.

Leading talisman and skipper, Mark Cooper, the heartbeat of the Lambs side, was named as Gee's replacement soon after but the Lambs are predicted to struggle again this season. CF

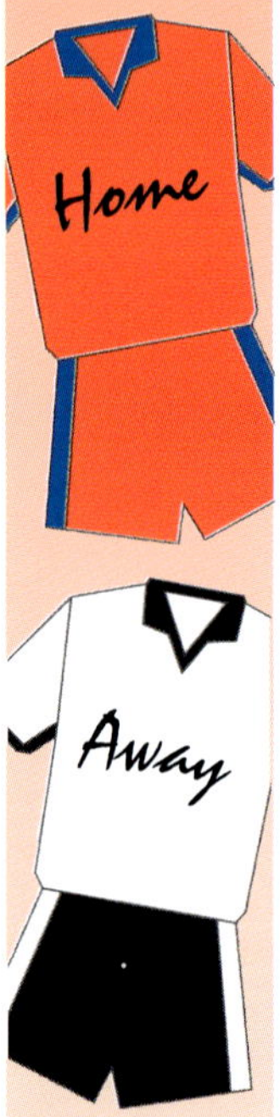

Directions

From the South East/North East: Leave the M42 at J10. Turn south towards Tamworth on the A5. At the junction for Bitterscote, leave the A5. At the roundabout, take the third exit towards Tamworth Castle. At the roundabout, take the fourth exit. Continue with the Snowdome on your right to a roundabout. Take the second exit (direction Nottingham), first exit at the next roundabout (Amington, Glascote), second exit at the next (Glascote B5000). At the final roundabout, take the second exit, Kettlebrook Road. The Lamb is the first right.

From the South West/North West: Approach Tamworth on the A5 from Cannock/Brownhills. Take the turning signposted A51 Tamworth. At the bottom of the slip road, at a T-junction, turn left. At the roundabout, take the third exit for Tamworth Castle, then as above.

By train: Tamworth is on two main lines: Euston to the north-west and Scotland; Penzance to Newcastle, via Birmingham New Street. Leave the station along the approach road to the roundabout. Turn left and cross the road leading under the railway bridge. Walk along Offa Drive to a roundabout. Turn left and cross the river with the railway viaduct on your left and follow the footpath to the left into Amington Road. Cross over before the viaduct and continue along the path, keeping the viaduct on your left. When you reach the roadside railings, turn right towards the Snowdome. At the end of the railings, turn left and cross the road. Once across the road, turn left along the footpath. The entrance to The Lamb is 50 yards ahead on the right.

The Lamb Ground has terrace behind each goal, one end uncovered. One side is the seated stand which you can enter for an extra fee. Down the other side lies the low covered standing area, in the centre of which lies the 'Shed', where the most vocal Lambs fans watch the game. It is not an area for the faint-hearted because of the general noise and commitment of its occupants during a game. HL

The Lambs

Woking

Address: Kingfield Stadium, Kingfield, Woking, Surrey, GU22 9AA

Tel: 01483 772470

Website: www.wokingfc.co.uk

Officials: Chairman: Chris Ingram
Secretary: David Seward
Manager: Glenn Cockerill

Review

Woking kicked off the 2003/04 campaign with an away trip to promotion favourites Morecambe, where Woking were narrowly beaten 2-1. However, Woking managed to finish the first month of the new season in a strong fifth position, with wins over Scarborough, Exeter City and Leigh RMI.

Despite this, the club soon hit a sticky patch as Woking didn't win in the whole of October and wouldn't claim three points until November 11th. November also saw Chris Sharpling recapture some old form, when he managed to score four goals in two games, which saw the drubbing of Northwich Victoria and Tamworth.

December saw Woking handed a home tie against Jan Molby's Kidderminster in the FA Cup Second Round. However, the third division side's class shone through and they ran out 3-0 winners. In the league, Woking managed to push their way up to seventh. However, they were dealt two bitter blows when striker Chris Sharpling sustained a cruciate injury in training and Ian Selley was ruled out for three months with a knee injury. January saw Woking still pushing for the last Play-Off place and, despite defeat against Kettering Town in the FA Trophy Second Round, their league form remained solid after they defeated title chasing Hereford United at Edgar Street.

However, only one win and two draws in March seemingly ended Woking's Play-Off chances. The only win came to bottom of the league Northwich Victoria where Murray, Ferguson and newly signed Luke Cornwall scored to seal a 3-0 win.

The last month of the 2003/04 season saw the biggest crowd of the campaign, when over 4,000 people crammed into Kingfield to see Woking v Aldershot Town. In an action packed match, it was a last minute goal from Cornwall that gave Woking a point in a thrilling 2-2 draw. Woking signed off at Kingfield with an impressive 3-1 win over debt-ridden Telford United.

The last match of the season was away to Halifax Town where goals from Ian Selley and Amos Foyewa gave Woking a useful point in a 2-2 draw. This draw meant Woking finished a reasonable ninth, nine points away from the last Play-Off place. MF

Directions

From the M25, come off at Chertsey J11. At the top of the slip road, turn right and follow signs for A320 Woking. Keep on the left. At the roundabout, turn left onto the A320. At the first roundabout (Harvester on the left), go straight on. Cross a couple of roundabouts. At the third (Six Crossroads), take the third exit into Woking (still the A320). At the next roundabout, take the second exit. After the second set of lights, the road splits into more lanes, but stay on this road. After the next lights, move into the right hand lane just after the bridge. Pass the police station then the Litten Tree pub. Keep to the right past the pub. At the next sharp bend to the right, turn left into Claremont Avenue. At the end, turn left and you are at the ground. Street parking or at the leisure centre opposite.

By train: Woking station is in the town centre, a mile and a half from the ground. Come out of the station by platform four and bear right. Cross over in front of the court and then bear right again and carry on past the court and police station. Cross Hill View Road then carry straight on down Constitution Hill (with the Litten Tree on your right). About 100 yards down on the left is a gate leading into Woking Park. Turn in here then take the first path off to the right. Walk past the swimming pool into the car park and keep going straight out of the leisure centre and park, cross the road and there is Kingfield.

Kingfield is in a particularly attractive part of the Surrey town, and the 20 minute walk through Woking Park from the town centre and station comes highly recommended. Once inside, the ground is one of the most distinctive in the Conference, dominated by the mid-1990s Westfield all-seater stand behind one goal offering unobstructed views. There are two rustic seated stands on one side facing open terracing on the other, and covered terracing behind the goal completes the picture. One of the best programme shops at this level awaits behind the pair of stands. There is plenty of parking at the adjacent Woking Pool across the road from the ground. MF

York City

Address: Bootham Crescent, York, North Yorkshire, YO30 7AQ

Tel: 01904 624447

Website: www.yorkcityfc.com

Officials: Chairman: Steve Beck
Chief Executive: Keith Usher
Player-Manager: Chris Brass

Directions

From the South: Exit A64 at the York (North) A1237 Harrogate sign onto the A1237. Go over three roundabouts and over the River Ouse, to a fourth roundabout. Here, turn right onto the A19 Shipton Road. At the lights go straight on (signposted City Centre). Turn left by the Burton Stone pub into Burton Stone Lane. You'll see the ground on your right.
From the North (A19): At the roundabout junction with the A1237, go straight onto Shipton Road. Then, as for the South.
By train: Turn left out of the station into Station Road, past the Royal York Hotel. Take the first left. At the end of the road, in front of Esplanade car park follow the road round to the left, passing the Royal Mail depot. Just before the railway bridge, turn right along pathway and take the footbridge over the river. Take the path between railway and Marygate car park. At end of car park turn left through underpass and right into Bootham Terrace. At Main Road turn left, then take the second right into Bootham Crescent, leading directly to the ground.

Whilst a bitterly disappointing season saw the Minstermen freefall into the Conference, the sizeable crumb of comfort was the news that they will stay at their attractive Bootham Crescent ground 'for the forseeable future', when it had looked ear-marked for housing development. Hemmed in by terraced houses, it is fairly close to the City Centre. The neat and compact ground has seated stands on either side of the pitch, covered terracing behind one goal, and an open terrace at the other. There is a club shop, as well as a programme shop by the entrance, and the trip to the Minster City is very much one to look forward to. GB

Review

Few expected to see the club around for the 2003/04 season because the previous season it had seemed as though York City FC would not survive. The Minstermen were in danger of administration, and fans thought they were watching their team for the last time. But the Supporters' Trust stepped in - and thus the club were saved. 27 year-old Chris Brass was appointed player-manager, and the club finished 2002/03 in tenth. With a youthful manager behind the team, they made the best possible start to the 2003/04 season by winning their first four games to go top of the table. They then lost three in a row but were still sixth. Inconsistency then became York's byword as they struggled for a string of positive results. But despite this, City looked safe - after 20 games they hadn't once dropped out of the top ten.
York's record of either winning or losing games was turned on its head in mid-October as the team embarked on a run of four consecutive draws. Then followed the club's exit from the FA Cup to Barnsley, which wasn't quite the setback many may have expected it to be. The club responded by beating eventual champions, Doncaster, at Bootham Crescent, with Darren Dunning scoring the winner from the penalty spot. Three draws and a defeat followed that win, with promotion-chasing Swansea and Torquay both being held. York got back on track with three wins in the next four with the two Lees, Nogan and Bullock, continuing their scoring form. But York fans please look away now - this is where it starts to go horribly wrong.
The 17th January defeat to Northampton was the start of an awful run. The consecutive defeats to Northampton and Huddersfield were expected, but the 0-0 draw with Southend that followed was as good as it got. York went on a dire run that saw them plummet down the table, with confidence draining with each demoralising defeat. They did look relatively safe in 16th with nine games still to go. But they picked up just two points from those nine, with relegation confirmed in the penultimate game. A club record 20 games without a win had the worst possible consequences. The final day 0-0 draw with Swansea was to prove their swansong, as City waved goodbye to the Football League after 75 years. The shock stems from the fact that few fans saw it coming after such a decent start. York's season will no doubt be used as an example by future Third Division managers wanting to ward off complacency. MP

The Minstermen

Conference South

Club Pages

Basingstoke Town

Address: The Camrose Ground, Western Way, Basingstoke, Hampshire, RG22 6EZ

Tel: 01256 325063 / 327575

Website: www.btfc.co.uk

Email: mike@btfc.co.uk

Officials: Chairman: David Knight
Secretary: Richard Trodd
Manager: Ernie Howe

The Camrose Ground

Directions

From M3: Leave at Junction 7 (A30) and follow the dual carriageway to the mini-roundabout and travel straight on. Go up to a large roundabout and take the second exit into Western Way. The ground car park is around 50 yards on the right.
From M4: Leave at Junction 11 (A33). Take the dual carriageway to a small roundabout. Go over and carry on for about eight miles, over three mini-roundabouts and then dual carriageway to a large roundabout. Take the third exit and follow the dual carriageway (under the railway bridge) and up to the next roundabout. Take the first exit. Go up to the large (ringroad) roundabout and take the second exit (signposted M3) onto the dual carriageway ring road (stay right) and carry on up to the next roundabout. Take the third exit (A30) and follow the dual carriageway onto the next roundabout and go straight across (A30). At the next roundabout take the first exit (A30) (as you drive up the carriageway you'll see the ground and Main Stand on the right). At the next roundabout take the fifth exit into Western Way and the ground car park is 50 yards on the right.
By train: Basingstoke railway station is about a 30 minute walk so best to take a taxi.

Basingstoke rarely attract attendances over 500 which is a shame as they are a good standard club with a good ground and facilities, they present a match well and you are always assured of a good view from wherever you are standing.
Food is of a high standard and reasonably priced. There is a large bar located behind the entrance and it is spacious enough to accommodate most away fans unless there is a big FA Cup tie on. Parking is easy in the large car park and, if you can't get in here, there is always a retail park just across the road where you can park (and if you are still feeling hungry there is a large McDonald's). Overall, this is a lovely ground full of character and probably one of the best surfaces outside the Conference. SW

Review

There was little to shout about during Basingstoke Town's Ryman Premier Division season, but it was a campaign that ultimately ended in smiles for the Hampshire outfit. They were thrown in at the proverbial deep end as Town opened their season with a 3-1 defeat at pre-season title favourites Canvey Island and there was no respite as, three days later, they lost 4-1 to Hendon (also fancied to do well) at the Camrose Stadium. They finally got off the mark at home to Ford, but it was a season in which Basingstoke never really got out of first gear as they found consistency difficult to come by.
Early exits from the two main cup competitions, to lower league opposition, didn't help matters, although Craig McAllister was showing that he had lost none of his goal scoring touch as his 22 goals for the season earned him a summer move to Stevenage Borough.
A finish of 13th or above would see Stoke claim a place in the new Conference South but a disappointing end to the league campaign saw a 2-0 reverse at Kingstonian and then a final day drubbing at home to Sutton United, condemning Stoke to 14th. However, victory over Ryman Division One South champions Lewes, in a Play-Off, would mean that Stoke would still be in with a chance of a Conference South berth. It all began well for Town who, with home advantage, took the lead in the 26th minute. However, Lewes were on the crest of a wave as they arrived at the Camrose having just lifted the Division One South title. Danny Davis equalised, and then two second half goals swung the momentum Lewes' way. Davis scored his second and Lewes' fourth with eight minutes left to seal an emphatic win.
However, a mere five days later, Hendon, who finished fourth, took the decision to decline their invitation to join the Conference South, which meant that Basingstoke (having finished in 14th) could take their place after all. JB

Stoke

Bishops Stortford

Address: Woodside Park, Dunmow Road, Bishops Stortford, Herts, CM23 5GZ

Tel: 01279 306456

Website: www.stortfordfc.co.uk

Officials: Chairman: John Goodwin
Secretary: Ian Kettridge
Manager: Martin Hayes

Review

Following the previous season's stirring second half in which the Bishops moved from relegation trouble to a mid-table berth, hopes were high for 2003/04. These hopes seemed well founded when the home campaign opened with a 2-0 success over Championship favourites Canvey Island, and a 5-2 win at Hendon. However, these two stunning results were interspersed with a series of draws and defeats. New defensive duo Aaron Barnett and Grant Cooper provided a welcome additional source of goals throughout the season, but poor form in September had the side in trouble. Fortunately, though, things started to pick up after the Bishops defeated Sutton 6-4 after an FA Cup replay. October brought three straight wins versus Billericay, Bedford and Northwood, as well as a thrilling 3-2 FA Cup win against Maidstone United as a last gasp goal by Glen Southam, yet again player of the season, prevented extra-time for the ten man hosts. The cup run was the decisive feature of the Autumn, as a home win over Gloucester City led Stortford into the First Round proper and a heavy defeat at Mansfield. An important 1-0 win at Aylesbury halted the league slide, and a formidable run of home form led the team into the Conference South, as they went unbeaten at home between mid-December and mid-April. With goals flying in from everywhere, they surged up the table, securing promotion well before the last day. The Bishops snared the Herts Charity Cup as well, with a 4-1 win against Cheshunt, and all in all, it was a very satisfying season. GB

Directions

From the M25: Take the M11 towards Cambridge. Exit at J8. At the roundabout take the second exit, then the first exit at the next. After about 400 yards take the first right into the industrial estate and follow the road round to the right. The ground and car park are straight ahead.
From the A10: Take the Bishops Stortford A120 exit. Follow signs for Bishops Stortford. At the roundabout on the outskirts of the town, ignore signs into the town centre and continue around the bypass (A120 still) following M11 signs. Go straight over at the next roundabout (Bishops Stortford, right) and up the hill. At the next roundabout take the last exit, into Dunmow Road, then the first right. Proceed into the industrial park, then as above.
By train: Bishops Stortford is on the Liverpool Street to Cambridge line. The ground is a 20 minute walk from the station, but there is a taxi rank outside. If energetic, on leaving the station walk ahead and bear right, up the slope. Turn right, crossing the railway and proceed to a T-junction. Turn left (London Road) and walk towards the traffic lights, then turn right into Dunmow Road. Pass the Red Cow pub on your right then a row of shops on your left, and carry on over at two roundabouts. The next left turn is for Woodside Industrial Park. Turn here and follow the road round to the right. Go straight on and the ground is ahead.

Woodside Park is a modern purpose-built ground dating only from the late 1990s, right on the edge of the Stansted Airport complex. There is covered terracing behind the goals, as well as a club shop, with the high quality main stand backing onto the clubhouse, and providing a very good view of the match. There is ample parking in the surrounding industrial estate, but train travellers need to be prepared for an uphill walk from the station, although a good ground awaits at the end of the trek. GB

The Bishops

Bognor Regis Town

Address: Nyewood Lane, Bognor Regis, West Sussex, PO21 2TY

Tel: 01243 822325

Website: www.therocks.co.uk

Officials: Chairman: T Martin
Secretary: Peter Helsby
Manager: Jack Pearce

Directions

From Chichester take the A259 into Bognor. Go through North Bersted and stay on the A259. Once in Bognor look out for Hawthorne Road on the right. Turn here and keep straight on until Nyewood Lane and turn left into it. The ground is on the right, the entrance is about 300 yards on.
From London: Take the A251 into Bognor town centre. Turn right at the second roundabout into A259 Chichester Road. Follow this road until you come to Hawthorne Road on the left, then as above.
By train: Turn right out of the station across the lights and down Linden Road to a roundabout. Turn left into Victoria Road. Turn down into Sylvan Road then right into Nyewood Lane and the ground is on the left.

Nyewood Lane, for over 80 years the club's home, is fairly close to the seafront, railway station and pubs. So, if you wanted to make a day of it, you could take in the beach before the game, hit the local hostelries afterwards and still be in time for the last train home. The Rocks were one of the best supported clubs in the Ryman First Division over the last couple of years (even more so during their promotion campaign of 2002/03), and that loyal support continued as the club entered into the Premier Division last season. Three sides of the ground are covered and the main stand houses the dressing rooms and boardroom, holding around 200 people. JB

Review

Bognor Regis returned a solid performance in their first Ryman Premier Division season, and secured a place in the Conference South with a tenth place finish, barely a year after securing promotion from Division One South. Bognor fans were expecting a good season after an unbeaten run in pre-season friendlies, but they got off to a mixed start as their 4-1 win on the opening day against Braintree was followed up with a defeat at Sutton before winning away at Northwood. However, they then started to get the feel for the Premier Division as they won comprehensively at home against Billericay Town, Harrow and Hayes.
The cup competitions didn't hold any glory for Bognor as they crashed out of the FA Cup in the Second Qualifying Round after a 4-0 defeat at the hands of Havant & Waterlooville and then failed to get past the Second Round of the FA Trophy after being beaten on a trip to Weston-super-Mare.
Bognor's form fluctuated throughout the season - a fact that is clearly highlighted when you view a ten day period during the spring. On the last day in March, Grays Athletic soundly beat the Rocks 6-0. However, on 10th February Bognor saw their best home result of the season (6-1) against Thurrock who eventually finished third at the end of the season. Despite suffering a heavy 8-0 final day defeat at the hands of Bedford, the Rocks had long since secured their top 13 berth. AP

The Rocks

Cambridge City

Address: City Ground, Milton Road, Cambridge, CB4 1UY

Tel: 01223 357973

Website: www.cambridgecityfc.com

Email: info@cambridgecityfc.com

Officials: Chairman: Arthur Eastman
Secretary: Andy Dewey
Manager: Gary Roberts

City Ground

Directions

From the North: From the A14, follow the signs for Cambridge A1307. This will take you down Huntingdon Road. At a major junction with a Texaco garage on your left, turn left and follow the road through the lights and into Victoria Road (A1134). At the bottom of this road is a large roundabout with a large shop on it (Staples). Keep left and go past the Portland Arms pub. Carry on for 100 yards and the entrance to the ground is on the left.

From the South: Leave the M11 at J13. At the top of the slip road, turn right towards Cambridge on the A1303 Madingley Road. Continue until a mini-roundabout. Take the first exit into Northampton Street then across the lights into Chesterton Lane. This brings you onto the Staples roundabout (see above).

By train: The station is two and a half miles from the ground. There is a taxi rank outside the station as well as bus stops. Bus service Citi 1 runs between the station and Milton Road every ten minutes (take Citi 1 destination Arbury; for the return journey take Citi 1 destination Fulbourn).

A very neat and compact town centre ground which is concealed by an office block built on the club's former ground, and it boasts extensive car parking. You can take in the sights of Cambridge on your arrival as it is a pleasant walk through the parks from the town centre and station. Milton Road's key feature is the impressive elevated main stand, which, to their credit, City didn't charge extra to sit in when I last visited. The fact that the ground is hemmed in by terraced houses makes for a really good atmosphere when there is a big crowd particularly when fans congregate under the covered terracing on the far side. GB

Review

Despite an inconsistent season result wise, Cambridge City still managed to finish eighth and book their place in the Conference South for the 2003/04 season. They certainly ended the season with a flourish as they signed off their home campaign with an epic 6-4 victory over Tiverton, and then followed that up with a 2-0 win over Worcester City on the final day of the season.

The season started with City looking strong at home, but with poor away form after two early defeats on the road. Form continued to fluctuate as City then beat Bath City only to suffer their first defeat at home, against Welling United at the end of August. Despite the evident peaks and troughs of the club's league season, the main aim would have been to secure a Conference South place - and this they did with some comfort.

The club's inconsistent form was carried over into the FA competitions as well, with the club getting through to the Fourth Qualifying Round of the FA Cup with home wins over Ilkeston and Lowestoft, only to get knocked out after a 3-2 defeat against Ford.

A 3-2 result would also end Cambridge's FA Trophy aspirations in a First Round replay against Worthing. After drawing 0-0 the previous Saturday, Cambridge couldn't beat the Ryman side in extra-time and a Sam Francis goal on 100 minutes was enough to put Worthing through to the next round.

If it was any consolation, Cambridge did produce a double figure scoreline in a cup. The Cambridgeshire Invitation Cup (CIC) saw Cambridge City play host to little known Waterbeach on an October evening at the City Ground and cruelly disposed of their opponents in style with a 12-0 thrashing. If morale needed a boost the players surely got one with this result. Danny Bloomfield had the night of his life scoring half of the dozen goals. AP

The Lilywhites

Carshalton Athletic

Address: War Memorial Sports Ground, Colston Avenue, Carshalton, Surrey SM3 2PW

Tel: 020 8642 8658

Website: www.carshaltonathletic.org

Email: admin@carshaltonathletic.org

Officials: Chairman: Steve Friend
Secretary: Vic Thompson
Manager: Billy Smith

Review

Seventh place seemed a highly creditable result for the side tipped by many to be relegated. However, under the guidance of former manager, Billy Smith, the Robins maintained a strong championship challenge until Christmas, as they got off to a flyer by winning seven of their first ten games to occupy top spot. They did less well in the FA Cup, in which they nudged past Essex Senior League Enfield Town 1-0 before a heavy defeat at Hornchurch. However, Nic McDonnell was a shrewd signing from St Albans City as his goals helped keep the results coming.

However, home results, previously the Surrey club's bedrock, started to trail off and when they lost 2-0 at home to Canvey Island, hopes of the title began to recede. There was the bitter disappointment of the 6-0 thumping in the first local derby at Sutton for a few seasons, but the team bounced back after their wobble at the turn of the year, and won their last three games to comfortably take a Conference South berth which they would have been very pleased with at the start of the campaign. Hopes of silverware disappeared quite quickly, though, as Sutton edged them out of the Surrey Cup, and Harlow Town had a shock 1-0 win at Colston Avenue in the Bryco Cup. GB

Directions

From the M25: Take exit 8 on the A217, passing Lower Kingswood, Kingswood, Burgh Heath and Banstead. Continue until the roundabout, before the sign to Sutton. Bear left still on the A217 and continue until you reach the Rose Hill roundabout (approximately two miles). Take the fourth exit into Wrythe Lane and continue for a mile or so. Turn right into Colston Avenue just before the railway bridge. The ground is 100 to 150 yards away on the right. A private road leads to the stadium and car park.

From London: Take the A23 at the Elephant & Castle or the Oval. Continue along the Brixton Road, A23 through Brixton, up Brixton Hill, through Streatham Hill, Streatham High Road. At the traffic lights (junction St. Leonard's Church) cross into Mitcham Lane (A216). Continue along here and bear left at traffic lights at Figgs Marsh, London Road (A217), through Mitcham on the Bishopsford Road A217, until reaching the Rose Hill roundabout, then as a above.

By train: The nearest station is Carshalton, 200 yards from ground.

Although the planned rebuilding of Colston Avenue is apparently shelved for now, the ground still boasts a substantial terrace on the far side, and the main stand offers a decent view from the opposite side, with the extra option of covered terracing behind one goal which seems especially close to the action. However, the scars of the arson attack of a few seasons ago are still visible, as portakabins remain. Tucked behind a row of attractive houses in pleasant Surrey suburbia, it is one of the more convenient grounds to access by public transport, as the mainline station is a short wander away. GB

War Memorial Sports Ground

The Robins

Dorchester Town

Address: The Avenue Stadium, Weymouth Avenue, Dorchester, DT1 2RY

Tel: 01305 262451

Website: www.dorchestertownfc.co.uk

Officials: Chairman: E C G Belt
Secretary: D R Martin
Manager: Mark Morris

The Avenue Stadium

Review

Dorchester had a disappointing season in the Dr Martens Premier Division finishing just 17th out of 22 and, as a result, missed out on an automatic qualification place to the Conference South. After a mixed pre-season, which started and ended in losses, Dorchester started the season with a draw at the Avenue Stadium against Hinckley United.

The first two months of the season didn't produce many good results if you were a Magpies fan and, with only three wins to their name before going into the FA Cup Second Qualifying Round, it didn't come as much of a surprise when they lost 4-1 to Weston-super-Mare.

However, the real low point of the season came on Boxing Day when Town were put to the sword in their derby against Weymouth, as the Terras romped to an 8-0 win. Some pride was regained on New Year's Day as the Magpies held the Terras to a draw in the return match, but that was to signal the start of a slump for Dorchester. From the end of January to the end of March, Dorchester managed just one win in ten matches and slumped into the relegation zone. However, when it was needed the most, Dorchester recorded six straight wins which lifted them up the league and into a Play-Off position.

Dorchester had to visit Bath City in their first Play-Off match and, despite going down 1-0 after ten minutes, Dorchester came back with goals by former West Ham and Blackburn player Matty Holmes, Justin Keeler and Matt Groves which gave the visitors a 3-1 lead until Steve Tweedle got one back for the home side. However, this was Dorchester's day and Jamie Brown scored a final goal to give his side a 4-2 win. A final Play-Off game against Tiverton Town was played at the neutral venue of Saint James's Park in Exeter and it was Holmes who was the hero scoring a goal after just two minutes. Paul Wood then made it 2-0 in the first half before Tiverton Town got one back through Nathan Rudge in the second. However, the goal wasn't enough and it spurred the first team coach Holmes into scoring his second goal of the game, which ended 3-1 and secured promotion. AP

Directions

From the M3/M27: At J1, the M27 becomes the A31. Remain on this road for 25 miles or so, until Bere Regis roundabout. Take the A35 Tolpuddle Bypass to Dorchester. After the dual carriageway section go over the Kingston Maurward roundabout. Turn right at the next roundabout and right again into the Tesco complex. At the roundabout inside the complex, turn right again past the entrance to the petrol station and take the left hand fork to the parking area.

From the M5: Take J23, and then the A39 towards Glastonbury. At Street, take the B3151 through Somerton to Ilchester and then the A37 into Yeovil. Continue through Yeovil on the A37 for Dorchester. On the approach to Dorchester, follow signs for Park and Ride, turning right onto the bypass. At the next roundabout take the second exit and continue to the next roundabout. The ground is in front of you.

By train from Bristol: At Dorchester West station exit from the platform adjacent to Do-It-All. Walk down the hill past Swinton Insurance to the traffic lights. Turn right at the lights, and continue with the market area to your left. At the next set of traffic lights turn right across the railway bridge. The ground is about five minutes further on the left, just after Tesco.

By train from London: At Dorchester South station, exit through the ticket office. Follow the station approach road to the end (next to the Station Masters pub). Take a left to the traffic lights. At the lights, continue straight across the railway bridge. The ground is about five minutes down the road on your left.

It is hard to think of a modern non-league stadium with quite the attributes of Avenue Stadium. The ground was part of a deal which included the construction of the neighbouring supermarket. This is not hard to spot, as they have been built in the same style. This might sound a bit naff but, in fact, it is a thoughtful and tasteful construction. The ground is spacious and fully enclosed, with plenty of seating in the main stand but also lots of terracing. Extremely accessible by car; not too long a walk from the stations; and loads of parking due to the supermarket. Derbies against Weymouth tend to attract the biggest crowds with both clubs renewing acquaintances of late. With an excellent programme and friendly welcome, this is one of my favourite grounds. MW

The Magpies

Eastbourne Borough

Address: Langney Sports Club, Priory Lane, Langney, Eastbourne, East Sussex, BN23 7QH

Tel: 01323 743561

Website: www.eastbourneboroughfc.co.uk

Officials: Chairman: Len Smith
Secretary: Myra Stephens
Manager: Garry Wilson

Langney Sports Club

Directions

From the North: Approach on the A22 London to Eastbourne Road or the M23/A23 Brighton Road and then eastwards towards Polegate.
From the East: Take the A259 from Hastings and, at the roundabout at Pevensey, take the second exit. Pass through Pevensey and turn left at the Swan fish & chip shop in Westham. Take the first roundabout exit into Priory Lane.
From the West: Take the A27 from Brighton to Polegate. On leaving Polegate turn right for Stone Cross (at the beginning of the Pevensey by-pass). Continue to the village centre and turn right at the crossroads with the Red Lion pub on the right. Continue for 600 metres (Lion Hill and Friday Street, after the railway bridge) to a double roundabout. Take the first exit on each roundabout into Hide Hollow (B2191). Take the third exit at the next roundabout into Priory Road.
By train: The nearest stations are Pevensey and Westham (a 30 minute walk) or Eastbourne (taxi or bus on routes 3/3A, and 10/10A).

The facilities at Priory Lane have been continually improved with the ground now recognised as one of the finest in Sussex, and the only one to be covered on all four sides. This is just as well, as when the wind blows across the Pevensey Marshes, Priory Lane is not a place for the faint-hearted, or unwitting opponents.
Ground developments have continued with an extension to the main stand doubling its capacity and including a new lounge, a further two executive boxes, and disabled access. The covered terracing behind the far goal (The River End) has also been extended from the Chris Cooper Stand, round to the main stand. New floodlights and toilet facilities were opened during the 2003/04 season.
Far from being a sleepy retirement haven, Borough are one of the better supported clubs at their level of the pyramid, and the atmosphere at Priory Lane is usually very lively. The large well-appointed clubhouse is just outside the main turnstiles, and serves real ale. DB

Review

Mindful of the alarming tendency for newly promoted clubs to come straight back down again, Eastbourne Borough approached their inaugural season in the Dr Martens Premier Division with the simple aim of not finishing in the bottom four and thereby making the Play-Offs.
As was widely predicted, the Division was extremely tight throughout the season, and Borough moved up and down the table with great regularity over its duration. The team struggled to find its form at Priory Lane until the turn of the year but fortunately proved itself capable of grinding out results on the road, thanks to some rather uncompromising defensive tactics that won little favour with opposition supporters. Despite a goal difference that meant qualification was not certain until the final day of the season, Borough did in fact record nine clean sheets in the league, and on only three occasions did they concede more than two goals. In front of goal, there was again a heavy reliance on the previous season's top scorer, Scott Ramsay. He rose to the challenge, with 28 goals from 50 appearances.
Only one club in the Division completed a league 'double' over Wilson's side, and the high point of the season came when Weymouth were beaten at Priory Lane in February. In the cups, Welling United proved a thorn in the side in both the League Cup and FA Trophy. The First Round Proper of the FA Cup continues to elude Borough but they came close, after taking Stevenage Borough to a replay in the Fourth Qualifying Round.
Following the pattern of previous years, Priory Lane continued to be developed. October saw the unveiling of new floodlights and a four figure crowd for the visit of Sussex rivals Crawley Town, whilst additional toilet facilities and a new boardroom were also fully operational.
A place in Conference South was achieved on the last day of the season with a nail-biting draw at Newport County, although results elsewhere meant that Borough could have lost and still qualified. In preparation for the new season, boss Garry Wilson has snapped up Richard Brady, who led the goalscoring charts at Fisher Athletic last season, as a striking partner for Ramsay. DB

Grays Athletic

Address: The Recreation Ground, Bridge Road, Grays, Essex, RM17 6BZ

Tel: 01375 377753

Website: www.graysathletic.co.uk

Officials: Chairman: Frank Harris
Secretary: Jeff Saxton
Player-Manager: Mark Stimson

The Recreation Ground

Review

The 2003/04 season once again held a great deal of optimism for Grays Athletic fans and, with the club turning full-time and players such as Carl Leaburn, Jason Dozzell and Roy Essandoh gracing the Recreation Ground in recent seasons, who could blame them?
However, the Grays faithful know only too well how quickly a season can turn sour. Athletic were tipped for a title challenge in 2002/03, only to limp home in a disappointing 19th. 2003/04 was different for the Essex club. Although Canvey Island quickly turned the championship into a one horse race, Athletic saw a marked improvement on the previous seasons' shortcomings as they eventually finished a creditable sixth (thus claiming a place in the Conference South) as they only lost nine games all season (the second lowest in the league behind Canvey).
They were quick to make their mark as they came away from their road trip to Braintree with a 5-0 win in their second game of the season. Despite this, it was a stuttering start, perhaps not helped by the club's progress in the FA Cup. They comfortably defeated St Albans and Hendon before clashing with Conference side Margate over two epic games (which both ended 3-3) before finally winning the replay on penalties. A First Round proper tie against Aldershot was their reward, although this was to prove a bridge too far as two goals by Roscoe D'Sane proved enough as the Shots came from behind to win.
Athletic continued to blow hot and cold as the season entered December, making an early exit from the FA Trophy and failing to make any serious impact in the league. However, a 1-1 draw with leaders Canvey on 10th February seemed to give the team a little self belief as they then went the final eight games of the season unbeaten, culminating in a 4-0 win over Hayes on the final day that cemented their top six place. Progress is clearly being made. JB

Directions

From Junction 30 of the M25, take the A13 towards Southend. At the Grays exit follow the signs to the town centre. On entering the one-way system, keep left, then continue up the hill for about half a mile. Turn right into Bridge Road. The ground is on your right.
By train: Grays is on the London-Tilbury-Southend line, from Fenchurch Street. The ground is about seven minutes walk from the station. Come out of Grays station, turn right, then right again into Clarence Road. You can enter the ground via Bradbourne Road on your right. Alternatively (including access to the bar), keep going along Clarence Road, turn right into Bridge Road, and the main entrance is on your right.

Grays have bucked the trend of moving to out of town grounds by announcing the construction of a new all seater stand, which will dramatically increase the seating capacity at the Recreation Ground. Relatively central and surrounded by terraced houses, there is a cavernous clubhouse behind one goal, a long main stand with terracing and seating along one side, with the remainder of the ground open. Partly cut into a hillside, the ground boasts a large programme shop and its location means that the town centre and station are convenient, even if car parking isn't. GB

The Blues

Havant & Waterlooville

Address: West Leigh Park, Martin Road, West Leigh, Havant, Hampshire, PO9 5TH

Tel: 02392 787822

Website: www.havantandwaterlooville.net

Email: hawks@pinwig.net

Officials: Chairman: Derek Pope
Secretary: Trevor Brock
Manager: Dave Leworthy

West Leigh Park

Directions

From the North: Approach from the A3/A3M. Leave the A3M at the junction for Horndean. Take the first exit at the roundabout onto the B2149 signposted Havant. Go straight over the roundabout, also signposted Havant, and follow the B2149 for a couple of miles. Go straight over two mini-roundabouts, still following signs for Havant. After two and a half miles, turn left into Bartons Road and then take the first right into Martin Road.

From the East or West: Leave the A27 at Junction One signposted Havant/Hayling Island. Follow signs for Havant/Rowlands Castle. Go over the first set of lights then over the second set to the roundabout. Go over the roundabout into Petersfield Road. At the second set of traffic lights, take the right hand lane and turn right onto Bartons Road and then first right onto Martin Road.

By train: Leave the station by the north exit (the side that doesn't have the main ticket office). Walk up Leigh Road, directly ahead of you. The road comes to a dead end by a junction onto a dual carriageway. Cross the road and walk along the right hand side of the dual carriageway (this has a pavement, so not as dangerous as it sounds). Continue up to the next set of traffic lights and, looking right, you should see a dead end road and the ground's floodlights. Turn into the road and the ground is 100 yards on the left.

Westleigh Park has benefitted from extensive upgrading since the merger of the two clubs, and a modern cantilever stand seating 560 is the jewel in the crown of the ground. There is also plenty of covered terracing behind each goal, and the parking is extensive, as well as the stadium being well connected to one of the major roads of the area. The site is fairly compact giving the impression of a neat and high-quality stadium. GB

Review

The Hawks started last season on the road where they managed an opening day draw against Worcester City despite taking the lead on 15 minutes thanks to a Chukki Eribenne goal on his debut for the club. Havant & Waterlooville then recorded their first win of the season the following Monday as they played host to Dorchester City at West Leigh Park.

Through the months of November to January, Havant & Waterlooville went on a run of eight games without a win and, apart from three draws, the winter months were bleak for the Hampshire club. This period also saw the club go out of the FA Trophy at the first attempt as they failed to beat Folkestone Invicta in a replay after a disappointing 2-2 draw at their home ground. The Hawks went two goals up in the first half thanks to a brace by striker James Taylor but it was Folkestone who turned the game around scoring two goals in the second half. They took the game back to the South Kent coast where an extra-time goal by Adam Flanagan was enough to put Invicta into the Third Round.

Back in the league, Havant left it late to qualify for the Conference South after a strong end to their season. A win against Newport County put the club into twelfth place ahead of Moor Green and Merthyr Tydfil, with all three clubs having one game to play. The final day saw Havant lose to Moor Green. This meant Moor Green finished a point behind them so it all went down to the result between Chelmsford City and Merthyr Tydfil. Chelmsford had home advantage and they made it count as they won convincingly 3-1. This meant that both Havant & Waterlooville and Moor Green secured a top 13 berth while Merthyr had to settle for a place in the Play-Offs. AP

The Hawks

Hayes

Address: Townfield House, Church Road, Hayes, Middlesex UB3 2LE

Tel: 020 8573 2075

Website: www.hayesfc.co.uk

Email: saint@hayesfc.co.uk

Officials: Chairman: Derek Goodall
Secretary: John Bond
Manager: Willy Wordsworth

Church Road

Directions

Leave the M25 at J16 and head west on the A40(M) towards London. Pass over one large junction (Denham Roundabout) and under another (Swakeleys Roundabout). Take the next slip road (Hillingdon). At the traffic lights, turn right into Long Lane (A437). At the lights at the end, turn left onto the Uxbridge Road (A4020). Hayes is about two miles away. Look for the Adam & Eve pub and shops on the left. Turn right into Church Road opposite. The ground is on the right.
Alternatively, leave the M4 at Junction 3, and head north onto the A312. Cross the first large roundabout onto the Hayes bypass, then take the A4020 Uxbridge Road westbound. After crossing three sets of traffic lights, turn left into Church Road (opposite the Adam & Eve pub).
By train: Hayes & Harlington is the nearest station, served by trains from London Paddington and Reading. Turn right out of the station and walk through the shopping area to the end of the pedestrianised area. Turn left into Botwell Lane. Just after the swimming pool, turn right at the roundabout into Church Road, and the ground is on the left.
By tube/bus: Frequent service to Uxbridge on the Bakerloo Line, then a 207 bus to the Adam & Eve.

One of London's more characterful stadia, Church Road has a distinctive main stand and a covered terrace on the far side, but a large part of the ground is open to the elements. An impending relocation is apparently due. Prior to this, the ground, which is surrounded by housing, although has a large car park, is well worth a visit. The 'Townfield House' is the clubhouse and, fairly unusually, is not attached to the ground, instead being sited on the road outside. It is about a mile from the station, but connecting buses operate for the less energetic, and both the tea bar and club shop come highly recommended, the latter especially for programme collectors. GB

Review

The Missioners' imposing defensive record for much of the Autumn had the West London side harbouring realistic aspirations of the Ryman Championship, with hopes possibly hinging on their performances against Canvey Island. In the event, by the time they played the Essex side, they had dropped off the pace, as a protracted mid-season goal drought converted the narrow wins into a long winless run, with the more pessimistic of supporters even suggesting that automatic qualification for Conference South could be in doubt.
Ultimately, a strong March, featuring six wins from seven, repaired much of the damage, and Peter Holsgrove became the first Missioner to score four times in a game since 1992, in a 4-3 success at Northwood. Whilst Conference South was reached, Hayes, normally very strong in the knock out competitions, disappointed this time around, as they were knocked out of the FA Cup, Trophy and Middlesex Senior Cup by Boreham Wood, Arlesey and Uxbridge respectively, all sides from Ryman One North. GB

The Missioners

Hornchurch

Address: The Stadium, Bridge Avenue, Upminster, Essex, RM14 2LX

Tel: 01708 220 080

Website: www.urchins.org

Officials: Chairman: Gary Calder
Secretary: Brian Eagling
Manager: Garry Hill

Directions

Hornchurch Stadium is in Upminster, just north of the Dartford crossing. Take the M25 J29 onto the A127 towards London. Come off at the next major turn off (for Upminster) and turn left into Hall Lane. Follow this for about a mile and a half, passing Upminster station on your left, until a major crossroads with traffic lights. Turn right into St Mary's Lane. Continue down the hill and take the second left (Bridge Avenue). The ground is on the right.

By train: Nearest station is Upminster, on the London Fenchurch Street-Southend/Shoeburyness line. Turn left out of the station and follow the directions above.

By tube: Upminster Bridge station (District Line) is also close to the ground. Turn right out of the station, walk under the railway bridge and take the second right turning into Bridge Avenue.

Bridge Avenue is quite a modest, though neat, venue and despite featuring a running track, a pet hate of many non-league fans, the views from the seated stand on one side and the covered terrace on the other remain of a high quality. The original clubhouse has been converted into a well-appointed restaurant. Normally there is no accommodation behind the goals, but temporary seating was fitted here to good effect for the high profile FA Cup ties against Darlington and Tranmere. It is in an unlikely residential setting, but is very convenient for the local District Line station at Upminster Bridge, if a little harder to park. GB

Review

2003/04 was possibly the most eventful season in the Urchins' history, as the ambitious club, who moved to full-time, recorded (by a long way) their best ever FA Cup performance as well as comfortably qualifying for Conference South and making the FA Trophy Quarter-Finals. On the eve of the season, manager Mick Marsden, who had overseen their rise from a modest Ryman Division Three club, parted company with the club as former Aldershot manager George Borg came in. Though they lost their first two matches, they won six of their next eight to surge up the table and they also began their FA Cup campaign with a win over Billericay at the end of September. However, it was October which really set the tone for their season as they failed to concede a goal in any of the six matches played, including the 5-0 win against Carshalton and the 1-0 win against Paulton Rovers in the FA Cup which put them into the competition proper for the first time ever. This ushered in one of the best ever months in the club's history as they started a Trophy run with a win at Wingate & Finchley before the superb 2-0 FA Cup dispatch of League Division Three strugglers Darlington, a game they always looked in control of. They were firmly in the top four of the league, setting up an eagerly awaited clash with leaders Canvey Island. That game ended scoreless but the real disappointment came in the Cup as their run ended in early December in a controversial home reverse to Tranmere Rovers. The new year saw growing momentum in the Trophy as Aylesbury were beaten in the Third Round and, though league results slipped slightly, games in hand meant Conference South qualification was all but assured.

Still to concede a goal in the competition, Hornchurch lifting the Trophy seemed very possible particularly after the Urchins claimed the notable scalp of Stevenage in the Fourth Round. Less than two weeks later, Burton Albion were accounted for in Round Five. Seemingly, they had done the hard work when they were handed a trip to struggling Dr Martens side Hednesford in the Quarter-Finals but, in a rare disappointing moment of an otherwise enjoyable season, the eventual winners dispatched them 3-1. GB

The Urchins

Lewes

Address: The Dripping Pan, Mountfield Road, Lewes, East Sussex, BN7 1BH

Tel: 01273 472100

Website: www.lewesfc.com

Officials: Chairman: Terry Parris
Secretary: Laurie Pilbeam
Manager: Steven King

The Dripping Pan

Directions

The ground is at the very start of Mountfield Road, directly behind the station. If you enter Lewes via the A27 turn-off, be prepared to follow the one-way system patiently around in a circle to get to where you need to be.

By train: Lewes is served by trains that run regularly out of London Victoria and London Bridge. The journey is approximately one hour. The ground is a two minute walk from Lewes station. Turn left out of the station and then left into Mountfield Road. The ground is 100 yards on the right.

Don't be put off by the less than flattering name, the Dripping Pan is well worth a visit. Its character stems from the fact that it is formed from a natural bowl, with grassy slopes on each side. You enter at one end, behind one goal, and look down on the pitch, with steps leading down. A fine, new covered stand now resides next to the quirky three storey clubhouse. The other main structure is a long wooden stand, perched on the bank, running most of the length of the pitch. Character by the bucket-load. MW

Review

Lewes made a fantastic finish to a season in which honours appeared to be drifting away from them. However, such a thrilling and nail-biting climax seemed unlikely back in August as an opening sequence of eight wins and a draw meant they surged to the top of the table. However, there was disappointment in the FA Cup as they were surprisingly eliminated at Lowestoft Town. The FA Trophy began with a win at Dunstable Town, and though their first league defeat of the season came in a single goal reverse at Walton, it was a mere blip, as they bounced back with another string of cup wins. This included a commanding victory against Ryman Premier Division strugglers Northwood, and when Cinderford were seen off in a replay, a mouth-watering home tie with Weymouth awaited. However, their second league loss of the campaign, at Staines, proved harder to come back from, as some shock defeats ensued with Banstead, struggling in mid-table, giving them a 6-1 thumping. A run of poor defensive showings (which would be reflected in a high goals conceded total of 61 at the end of the season), contributed to the 8-5 home reverse against Weymouth in the Trophy and a series of other league defeats. Whilst they were picking up enough points to stay in the top two, the chasing pack were gaining ground on them. A 2-1 loss at home to Windsor in mid-March looked to have handed the visitors the title, particularly when Lewes lost three of the next four, but a similar wobble by the Stag Meadow outfit gave them a lifeline. This they grabbed decisively by winning four out of the next five to take the title before the end of the season. That gave them a place in the Play-Offs and a possible promotion. Lewes nudged out Division One North champions Yeading in their first game before a stunning 4-1 win at Basingstoke put them in the final pair of games for a place in Conference South. This they took with a 1-0 win over Kingstonian to cap a wonderful season for the Sussex club. GB

The Rooks

Maidenhead United

Address: York Road, Maidenhead, Berkshire, SL6 1SF

Tel: 01628 624739

Website: www.maidenheadunitedfc.co.uk

Email: webmaster@maidenheadunited.co.uk

Officials: Chairman: Roger Coombs
Secretary: Ken Chandler
Manager: John Dreyer

York Road

Directions

The ground is close to both the M4 and M40. Exit at Junction 8/9 of the M4 and follow signs for Maidenhead town centre. Go under the railway bridge and follow the one-way system round to the first roundabout. Take the fourth exit and then take a left at the cinema along Broadway. Go down the hill and the second road on the right is the car park. York Road is a short walk across the road. By train: York Road is a short walk from Maidenhead train station. Cross the one-way system and walk to the end of Bell Street.

York Road feels a little bit like a Sunday league ground, which is a shame as they are a club with a long and prestigious history and perhaps deserve a better place to display their wares.

It has a strange feel as cars park alongside the pitch and there were no advertising boards on my visit, so the word 'rustic' definitely applies here. Support is low for a club in this league and, given that the ground is located in the town, there really is no excuse with regards to travel. An annoying feature of York Road is that, on my visit, the tannoy announcer went on talking throughout the whole game and did not stop. A redeeming feature is that the fans are generally friendly and helpful. SW

Review

Although there were some nervous moments before Maidenhead United secured promotion to the Conference South by taking twelfth spot on the last day, such mid-table respectability seemed a world away as a nightmare start to John Dreyer's first job in management brought a paltry return of three points from their first seven games, as they sat at the bottom of the table. In fairness, it was understandable that a side with so many new faces would take time to gel, with so many of the previous season's players following former chief Alan Devonshire to Hampton & Richmond. When they did gel, however, the effect was stunning, as they recorded three straight wins against struggling Harrow, Braintree and St Albans and, most impressively, Sutton. However, the month ended disappointingly with defeat in their first FA Cup game against perennial cup strugglers, Dover. However, they were, by then, in mid-table, establishing themselves as a side that were hard to beat, whilst posing more of a threat up front through the veteran Phil Gray. An epic Trophy adventure began with a win over Swindon Supermarine, at the second attempt and, though league results began to tail off at the turn of the year, their run went on with an excellent 1-0 win at Histon. The push for a best ever Trophy run gained real momentum when Wealdstone were humbled 5-1. By now, league-wise, they were firmly established as one of the 'possibles' for promotion, never far away from the top 13, but lacking the consistency to establish themselves within it. However, there was no doubt what the most enjoyable game of the season, for Magpies fans, came when they visited Halifax Town in the Trophy and flew away with a 2-0 win and a place in the Quarter-Finals. After their elimination by Canvey Island in the last eight, results tended to vary in the league, but they picked up enough points to stay in contention for promotion and, after some nail biting moments, they achieved it by beating basement side Aylesbury 4-2 on the last day. GB

The Magpies

Margate

Address: (Groundsharing with Ashford Town)
The Homelands, Ashford Road,
Kingsnorth, Ashford, Kent, TN26 1NJ

Tel: 01843 221769

Website: www.margatefc.com

Officials: Chairman: Jim Parmenter
Secretary: Ken Tomlinson
Manager: Chris Kinnear

The Homelands

Directions

Leave the M20 at Junction 10 and follow the signs for International Station and Brenzett which will take you onto a dual carriageway. Follow this road straight over the first roundabout, there is a McDonald's drive through and a Travel Inn on your right. At the next roundabout, take the first exit, signposted Kingsnorth. At the next roundabout go straight over (Tescos on your left). Follow this road for approximately two miles. Go through Kingsnorth and past the Cricket Ground on your left. The Homelands is 300 yards on the left.

By train: The nearest station is Ashford International. From here, it is about a four mile taxi ride to the Homelands. There are no buses.

Ashford Town's Homelands ground is actually situated several miles south of Ashford, in the village of Kingsnorth. The ground is approached by a rough track, which in addition isn't particularly well signposted and first time visitors are just as likely to end up at the nine hole Homelands golf course next door as at the football ground. The principal feature of the ground is the large, and undeniably impressive, grandstand housing around 500 seats. The large bar area within is a good refuge from the elements (which can get rather windswept), with large windows overlooking the pitch. If you are able to secure one of the comfy chairs and watch the game from here on a miserable afternoon in November, grab the opportunity with both hands! DB

Review

The Gate have acquitted themselves well in the Conference since their 2001/02 promotion, surprising many with their two seasons in the Division. This season was to be no different, with the fans realistically expecting nothing more than another steady season. Another season of ground-sharing was perhaps what was preventing them from taking significant strides forward. Indeed their early home form was disastrous, as they crumbled to five defeats in their first five 'home' games at Dover's Hoverspeed Stadium.

They did receive a boost with the loan signing of the talented ex-West Ham striker Manny Omoyinmi, and he guided them to their first home win as they defeated Northwich 3-1. Although Margate were comfortable in mid-table, their points total always left them at the mercy of the teams directly below. They sunk as low as 18th after losing both games with Kent-neighbours Gravesend around the turn of the year, but four wins in their next five home games would have left their loyal fans happy and gave the side some breathing space.

The signing of Rocky Baptiste in February brought some power to the front-line, and he got off to a great start with five goals in his first six games. This helped the club achieve a strong late season run. The Kent side finished in 16th and, as a result of this mid-table finish, all looked well at the club. However, the development plan at their Hartsdown Park ground had degenerated into a farce and a refusal by the FA to allow another season ground sharing meant Margate were demoted to the Conference South. It was a bitter blow after a long, hard but ultimately successful season, although if the club can keep hold of some of their more talented players, they can soon reclaim the Conference place if the Hartsdown rebuild can now be completed. MP

The Blues

Newport County

Address: Newport Stadium, Langland Way,
Newport, South Wales, NP19 4PT

Tel: 01633 662262

Website: www.newport-county.co.uk

Email: hq.newportcounty@virgin.net

Officials: Chairman: Wallace Brown
Secretary: Mike Everett
Manager: Peter Nicholas

Newport Stadium

Review

Newport County have been regular finishers in the top ten of the Dr Martens League in recent years, and 2003/04 was no different as the Exiles snatched seventh place and promotion to the Conference South. The Welsh side would surely have been doing themselves a disservice had they not finished above that coveted 13th place, after never finishing lower than tenth since they were promoted to the Dr Martens League in 1999.

However, County's start was an inauspicious one as they bumped along through August and September failing to register a win in their first ten games. Newport finally broke their duck on 17th September when two goals from Jeff Eckhardt helped them to a 4-1 win at Hinckley.

It was a case of wins being a little bit like London buses, as County then collected maximum points from their next two league games (thus pulling them away from the bottom) as well as claiming the scalp of title hopefuls Weymouth in the FA Cup. Despite suffering a surprise defeat in the next round, after an astonishing 6-3 defeat against Mangotsfield, County maintained their improved league form throughout much of the season (despite Garry Shepherd's departure to fellow Welsh outfit Merthyr in March), as they climbed out of the basement and established themselves in the top half of the table.

Their bad start meant that County never threatened the front runners at the top of the league but, three wins in the final five games, meant that the club were safe in the knowledge that a place in the Conference South had been secured. One of the other highlights of the Exiles' season came on 31st March when they took on a Manchester United XI in a friendly, as nearly 4,500 fans packed into Newport Stadium. JB

Directions

From the Severn Bridge: On the M4, leave at Junction 24 and take the first exit at the roundabout (A455, signposted for Newport Stadium). Go left at the next roundabout, straight over the next two roundabouts, then first left into Langland Way and left again into the Stadium's car park.

By train: Either a taxi from the station or make a five minute walk to the bus station. For the latter, walk straight into town from the station (via underpass), turn left at the end of the street, keep straight and pass between the Principality Building Society and Vodafone (Skinner Street). Then turn into Upper Dock Street, with the bus station to the left. Take either the number 9 or number 16 bus (approximately a 15 minute bus ride).

The modern Newport Stadium is situated amidst an industrial estate outside the town centre and the club is adding more facilities all the time. The main part of the stadium is a big stand which houses the changing rooms, bar and a well-stocked club shop. This is a club on the up and the stadium reflects this, with terracing now also on the side of the ground opposite the main stand. The home crowd get worked up by the beating of a drum from the sidelines and their own mini-band. Newport could easily reach the Conference Premier and beyond in the coming years and the ground reflects this. RM

The Exiles

Redbridge

Address: Oakside Stadium Road,
Barkingside, Ilford, Essex

Tel: 020 8550 3611

Website: www.redbridgefc.com

Email: webmaster@redbridgefc.com

Officials: Chairman: Jimmy Chapman
Secretary: Alan Wetherall
Manager: Craig Edwards

Oakside Stadium

Directions

From North Circular Road (A406), M11, A12, Blackwall Tunnel: Take the A12 from Redbridge Roundabout to Gants Hill Cross (roundabout) and take the second exit, the A123 Cranbrook Road. At the traffic lights after Tesco, turn right into Tanners Lane, then third left into Craven Gardens, and finally first right into Carlton Drive. Go straight on into Station Road, over the railway bridge (on the left as the road splits) and the ground is the first right.
From A12 East: Take first right after Newbury Park Station (traffic lights at McDonald's) into Horn Road. After three quarters of a mile, turn right into Craven Gardens and then first right into Carlton Drive, then as above.
By tube: Take the Central Line to Barkingside station, leave the station and turn right, then turn right again into Station Road. The ground is over the railway bridge, first right.

Probably one of the more basic grounds at this level, but this would be to understate the success of upgrading it from the Essex Senior League standard of former sole occupants, Barkingside. The main stand, and covered terracing on the far side, benefits greatly from being very close to the pitch, with the club shop, clubhouse and tea bar tucked in by the entrance. Though part of an Essex suburb, the Oakside Stadium has a distinctly rural feel, surrounded as it is by trees, and it is one of the most conveniently located grounds in the London area, backing onto Barkingside's Central Line station. GB

Review

Ford built impressively from the previous season's 'Great Escape', despite an average start to the season. They staged an unforgettable run to the First Round of the FA Cup, not their first time there of course. This time around, Didcot Town, Worthing and Cambridge City were defeated to earn a trip to Division Two Play-Off chasers Port Vale. Mervyn Abraham gave the league side the lead in the Potteries, but Alex Fiddes rescued a draw for Ford. Glenn Poole, who had another impressive season, earned extra-time in the Essex replay, but Vale squeezed through.
Ford's league form suffered slightly after that heartbreaking defeat, but they recovered with some impressive results, such as a 3-0 win at Kettering Town, which meant, along with their consistent displays at home, that they were always in contention for an automatic spot in Conference South.
In the event it came down to a three way chase for two spots, and United claimed the point they needed with a draw at Harrow. Soon after they announced their intention to rename themselves Redbridge in a bid to attract the extra support their efforts deserve. GB

The Motormen

St. Albans City

Address: Clarence Park, Clarence Road, St Albans, Herts, AL1 4PL
Tel: 01727 866819
Website: www.sacfc.co.uk
Officials: Chairman: John Gibson
Secretary: Steve Eames
Manager: Steve Castle

Clarence Park

Directions

From M25 J21A follow signs to St Albans from the slip road. At the Noke Hotel roundabout, bear left through Chiswell Green towards St Albans, over the mini-roundabout and up to the King Harry pub. Bear right then left over two mini-roundabouts and follow into the town centre up Hollywell Hill. At the far end of the centre (St Peters Street), turn right at the roundabout into Hatfield Road. Go over one mini-roundabout, left at the second lights into Clarence Road, ground is on the left.
By train: A ten minute walk from St Albans City Thameslink station. Turn left out of the station then right into Hatfield Road, then left at the traffic lights (the Crown pub will be on the right) into Clarence Road. The ground is on the left.

This is widely acknowledged as one of the most attractive grounds at this level, in a corner of the public Clarence Park, although now fully fenced off from it. The wooden stand which extends along one side of the pitch and incorporates the clubhouse is the ground's main feature, as other covered accommodation is restricted to a small shelter on the far side, as the rest of the terracing is open; nice in summer, not so much in winter. Very central, and a few minutes walk from both the city centre and main railway station, it is surrounded by trees, despite the felling of the oak that used to stand in the centre of one of the terraces a few seasons back. GB

Review

A comment on the Saints' lively season? 'It turned out well in the end!' There were high hopes of a Championship challenge again, after the previous season, and some high calibre signings, but this failed to materialise, and poor form saw the departure of Steve Cook in October. Steve Castle took over the reins as caretaker, and then permanently, only to see his side lose 9-1 at Grays Athletic.
Results did not improve as the Hertfordshire outfit continued to flirt with the bottom four at times. Players came and went at frequent intervals as the manager tried to find the elusive winning formula. However, Castle recruited former Leyton Orient team mate, Steve Watts, and the experienced forward proved a pivotal figure as his goals enabled City to clear the bottom four and earn a Play-Off spot. What followed was a pair of the most thrilling Play-Off games ever seen at any level. In the first, City trailed at half-time and were down to ten men at Heybridge, before coming back to lead 2-1 deep into stoppage time. Swifts forced extra-time, but with penalties looming, Adam Parker earned a 4-3 win with the very last kick, and a trip to Bedford. Town led 3-1 at the break, but City astoundingly won the game 5-4 to end the most thrilling of journeys to Conference South. GB

The Saints

Sutton United

Address: Borough Sports Ground, Gander Green Lane, Sutton, Surrey, SM1 2EY
Tel: 020 8644 5120
Website: www.btinternet.com/sutton.united
Officials: Chairman: Bruce Elliot
Secretary: Graham Starns
Manager: John Rains

Borough Sports Ground

Review

In the final analysis, it was the proverbial 'season of two halves' for the Gander Green Lane side, as sustained poor form through the Autumn gave way to a storming run post-January as they took second place on the last day, as their young side really came of age. They made their usual solid start in the opening month, and sat among the early challengers before a dramatic loss of form saw only one win in nine, and the end of their interest in the FA Cup as they lost on penalties in a replay at Bishops Stortford. A key element of their problem was a worrying downturn in home league form, which stretched to ten without a win. Although some impressive results were being recorded on the road, they had still slipped into mid-table. There was the comfort of Trophy progress as a rare home win saw them beat Bedford Town 2-0. However, the turning point came just after Christmas, and it was a real present for the Sutton faithful as it centered on the 6-0 defeat of local rivals Carshalton. Though the early weeks of 2004 saw United leave the Bryco Cup and FA Trophy in successive weeks, mid-January heralded the beginning of a run of eight games featuring six wins and two draws as they shot up the table. They sounded a loud warning of their potential by winning at runaway leaders Canvey Island, and they then staged a winning run with a difference. The win at Canvey signalled a six game winning streak, with the club scoring three or more goals on each occasion. The excellent young players at the club were beginning to attract attention, and indeed, Nick Bailey and Jon Nurse were snapped up by Conference clubs at the end of the season. The last ten games brought nine wins and a draw as they clinched second place on the last day and, along with a Surrey Senior Cup Final appearance, it became a season to remember. GB

Directions

If travelling anti-clockwise from the M25, take J10, A3 (for Esher and Kingston). Follow this to Tolworth. The slip road off the dual carriageway is signposted to Sutton A240. At the top of the slip road is a large roundabout. Take the right hand exit to Sutton. Follow the A24 for a couple of miles. At the Organ Inn junction, turn left onto the A24 towards London. Remain on this road for two miles, going straight over the North Cheam crossroads. Shortly after this, with St Anthony's Hospital on the left, turn right into Gander Green Lane. Follow this over the lights at the junction of the A217 (Goose and Granite pub). The ground is on the left.
If travelling clockwise from the M25, take J8, A217 (for Sutton). Follow the A217 for six miles. At the Belmont roundabout bear left and follow the A217 (signposted London). Do not take the road to Sutton. Follow this road until you reach a fire station on the right. Take the right hand lane and turn into Gander Green Lane.
From Croydon A232, follow signs to Cheam A232 round the Sutton one-way system. At the Sutton Cricket Club turn right. The ground is just past West Sutton railway station on the right.
By train: West Sutton station is next to the ground. It is served by Thameslink trains via Wimbledon or Sutton.
By bus: The 413 'hoppa' service runs past the ground down Gander Green Lane. The bus will stop on request and leaves Sutton town centre from outside the main post office. The 80 route from Hackbridge to Belmont runs down Collingwood Road. The ground can be reached through Collingwood Rec.

Gander Green Lane comes across as quite a spacious ground, and is one of the more distinctive at this level. The curved Collingwood End open terrace dates from when there was a track around the pitch, but there is covered terracing on two of the remaining sides with an extensive main stand backing onto the clubhouse to complete the picture. It is a pleasant 10-15 minute stroll from the Town Centre, and West Sutton station almost backs onto the ground, with the car park being reasonably large as well. GB

The U's

Thurrock

Address: Thurrock Hotel, Ship Lane, Grays, Essex, RM15 4HB

Tel: 01708 865492

Website: www.thurrockfc.co.uk

Email: alanreynolds@thurrockfc.co.uk

Officials: Chairman: Grant Beglen
Secretary: Norman Posner
Manager: Colin McBride

Ship Lane

Directions

Extremely accessible from the horrible M25. Take the motorway to junction 30 and leave at the second exit. Go over the first roundabout and take the fifth exit at the next roundabout (Ship Lane). The ground is on the right (next to the Thurrock Hotel).
From the South: Take the M25 to junction 30 and take the third exit at the next roundabout (Ship Lane), then as above.

A fairly new ground that has one main stand and the rest terracing which means that plenty of fans can be accommodated. This came in useful when they played Luton Town last season. Its location on the edge of the M25 means the noise of cars drones throughout the whole match. They get around 500-600 regular fans which for this level is good. The rivalry with Grays still remains strong and the two are bitter foes. Food is of a good standard and the bar has easy access during the game. If it is going to be cold when you visit, wrap up as this has to be one of the coldest grounds in non-league football. Overall a very pleasant ground to visit unless your club is a fierce rival. SW

Review

'A change is as good as a rest' is certainly an appropriate adage for Thurrock. In their first season under their new identity (after their name change from Purfleet last June), the Essex side had a super season, as their final placing of third was their highest since winning promotion to the Ryman Premier Division in 1994.
They took a while to find their feet, but when they did, the results were spectacular. Their 3-0 win over Harrow Borough on 7th October triggered a 14 game unbeaten league run (that would stretch until 3rd February), and wins over Buckingham, Bromley and Dagenham also saw them in the hat for the First Round proper of the FA Cup. Once there, they managed to take Division Two side Luton Town to a replay, before an Adrian Forbes hat-trick gave the Football League side a 3-1 win in the return game.
Sutton ended Thurrock's unbeaten league run only for Bognor to hand them a 6-1 demolition the following week. However, this proved to be a minor blip as they then won five of the next seven, which included a 5-0 win over Aylesbury and a 4-1 victory at Maidenhead.
Despite a few more hiccups against the likes of Kettering and Canvey, Thurrock's run-in was generally smooth, and three wins from their final three games (including a 6-0 drubbing of Northwood) ensured that they finished third, just above Hendon and Hornchurch. Thurrock also boasted one of the league's most prolific goalscorers as Tresor Kandol's 32-goal haul meant that he was second only to Lee Boylan in the Ryman League's hot-shot stakes. JB

The Fleet

Welling United

Address: Park View Road Ground, Welling, Kent DA16 1SY

Tel: 020 8301 1196

Website: www.wellingunited.co.uk

Email: wpc@wellingunited.co.uk

Officials: Chairman: Paul Websdale
Secretary: Barrie Hobbins
Manager: Paul Parker

Park View Road

Directions

From anywhere other than Kent, take the M25 Junction 2. At the roundabout, take the A2 towards Central London. Leave the A2 at the third exit (Danson Interchange, signposted A221 to Bexleyheath and Sidcup). Turn right (second exit) at the roundabout at the end of the slip road, and then right (third exit) at the next roundabout. Go under the A2 bridge and up the slope to another roundabout. Take the second exit and follow the road (Danson Road) to the traffic lights at the end. Turn left at the lights onto Park View Road. The ground is on the left. There is plenty of street parking available.
By train: The nearest station is Welling (services from Victoria, Charing Cross, Waterloo East and London Bridge). From the station, go down the slope to the road at the bottom. Turn left and go to the end of the road. Turn left onto Bellegrove Road. This becomes Welling High Street and then Park View Road. The ground is on the right just after the Guy, Earl of Warwick pub; it is a 15-20 minute walk. Buses 89 and B16 run past the ground from the station.

One of the more extensive London area grounds, it is unusually sited edgeways onto a suburban Kent high street, occasionally meaning passing buses are vulnerable to wayward goal attempts. Park View Road has always struck me as being one of the more characterful grounds in London, the main stand offers a decent view, and in an innovative arrangement, a new seater stand has been constructed, along with a separate clubhouse, by Erith & Belvedere, who now permanently share the ground. Open terracing completes the picture at both ends and, though parking is tricky, the ground is well connected for the A2, as well as by bus and train. GB

Review

It was another inconsistent season for the Wings but, in a remarkably tight division, they ultimately fulfilled their aim of a Conference South berth, with one game left, as they won 2-1 at Hednesford. Their final placing was ninth, three points clear of 14th, in a league in which nothing could be taken for granted until the points were on the board. At the start of the season, new manager Paul Parker made the switch from Chelmsford City, bringing a number of new players with him, but United seemed to suffer badly with injuries. They made a slow start in the first few games, but their first win, almost unavoidably at Chelmsford, was the first of four consecutive victories which pushed them up the table. However, it was to be a season of 'boom and bust' as a long winless spell ensued into November, but yet again, they surged back with six wins and an impressive draw at Crawley, as a spell of defensive meanness gained results. As such, it was this sequence which effectively earned their promotion, as another downturn came in, but the scintillating 6-1 win over Dorchester had the more optimistic supporters dreaming of a late run for the title, as they were yet to play Weymouth, home or away, and still needed to entertain Crawley. However, they slipped up against weaker opposition, which was even more frustrating when they were able to demonstrate their true potential with a win at Weymouth. A very poor run-in had them sweating on the elevation, but they made it in the end. In the national knock-outs, there was an early exit to Dover in the Trophy, but more progress in the FA Cup, as wins over Slough and Folkestone saw them miss out on a place in the competition proper through a 1-0 home loss to Weston-super-Mare. GB

The Wings

Weston-super-Mare

Address: Woodspring Park, Winterstoke Road, Weston-super-Mare, BS23 2YG

Tel: 01934 621618

Website: web.ukonline.co.uk/westonsupermareafc/

Officials: Chairman: Paul Bliss
Secretary: Stuart Marshall
Manager: Frank Gregan

Woodspring Park

Review

After only achieving promotion to the Dr Martens Premier Division in 2003, the emphasis for Weston-super-Mare's first season in the Southern League's top flight must have been on survival. However, not only did they survive, their tenth placed finish also secured them a place in the newly formed Conference South.

They had an indifferent start, winning two and losing two during August. This spasmodic form continued throughout much of 2003 as the Seagulls hovered just above the bottom four as the season approached Christmas. However, if the Weston players were suffering from a lack of concentration in the league, then it was with good reason. The club were enjoying a fabulous FA Cup run through the winter as they dispatched Dorchester, Chesham, Welling and Conference side Farnborough on route to the Second Round proper (the furthest the club had ever been). Only a trip to Sixfields, and a tie against Third Division Northampton, stood in their way of place in the Third Round and a chance to land a money-spinning tie with one of the Premiership heavyweights. However, it wasn't to be, as two goals by Marc Richards helped the Cobblers to a 4-1 win. Weston could only look on as Northampton secured a plum tie with Manchester United in Round Four via a replay win over Rotherham.

Left to concentrate on the league, Weston's form continued to stutter as the season approached 2004. However, starting with a 3-2 win over Merthyr at Woodspring on New Year's Day, the Seagulls began to edge up the table after winning the next three home games. They would go on to reach the Fourth Round of the FA Trophy before losing 4-2 against Telford but, by now, it was that important 13th spot in the league that was the target. The Seagulls put together a four game unbeaten run going into the final day and, despite suffering a 2-1 defeat at home against champions Crawley, they had still massed enough points to secure tenth place. GB

Directions

From M5. Exit at J21 and take the A370 towards Weston-super-Mare. Follow the dual carriageway to the fourth roundabout (Pizza Hut and McDonald's on the left). Take the first left at this roundabout. At the next roundabout turn right into the club car park.

From South: Leave the M5 at J22 and follow signs for Weston for roughly seven miles. Turn right at the first roundabout, near Weston General Hospital. At the next roundabout turn left into Winterstoke Road. Follow this until the next roundabout and turn left into the ground.

By train: From Weston-super-Mare station turn right and follow the footpath along the dual carriageway over the railway bridge and past the shopping complex. The ground is on the right, the walk is 20 minutes or so.

By coach/bus: National Express coaches call into Weston-super-Mare coach terminal several times a day. The terminal is a 20 minute walk from the ground. Walk out towards the dual carriageway so you are facing Tesco, then turn left towards the station, then as above.

Woodspring Park is easily accessible from the M5, although fans may soon find themselves travelling three quarters of a mile up the road to the Westlands Sports & Social Club if the proposed ground move goes through. Parking is plentiful and free and there is even a shopping complex over the ground. Most of the ground is open terracing apart from the west stand which contains 250 seats. The main stand is behind one goal and can house around 1,000 supporters. The club shop is unusual as it is an old railway carriage. JB

The Seagulls

Weymouth

Address: The Wessex Stadium, Radipole Lane, Weymouth, Dorset, DT4 9XJ

Tel: 01305 785558

Website: www.theterras.co.uk

Officials: Chairman: Ian Ridley
Secretary: Lizz Bell
Manager: Steve Claridge

The Wessex Stadium

Directions

Enter Weymouth from the Dorchester direction on the A354. When you reach the first roundabout (about two miles into Weymouth), turn right (third exit), following the signs for the Town Centre. At the next roundabout, turn right (third exit), following the signs for 'Football Ground' and 'Bridport'. After about a mile, you should reach the Wessex Stadium. Turn right at the roundabout and left into the car park and the entrance to the ground.

By train: Weymouth Station is situated in Kings Street, two miles from the Wessex Stadium. There is an hourly service to and from London Waterloo via Southampton run by South West Trains and a more infrequent service to/from Bristol Temple Meads - via Westbury and Yeovil run by Wessex Trains. A matchday Football Special Bus departs from the Seafront at the Kings Statue (Bus Stop K7) at about 2pm on Saturdays and 6.45pm on Tuesdays. This goes via Town Bridge to the ground.

The Wessex Stadium is a traditional large old ground on the outskirts of the Dorset coastal town. There is plenty of seating in the large main stand, with terracing on the other three sides, with a fair amount of cover. There is loads of room for expansion, with not a lot in the vicinity. A large car park means plenty of parking but its narrow entrance can cause queues getting out. MW

Review

The Terras pulled off a major coup before the start of the season as they unveiled Steve Claridge as their new manager. He returned to the club he left back in 1989, after scoring goals regularly for the likes of Millwall, Birmingham and Leicester. It was a real confidence-booster and Weymouth were immediately established as the favourites for promotion. That meant a lot of added pressure, and it showed as they drew five of the first ten games. They did win the other five, however, and a 2-0 win over Weston-super-Mare put them on top but they seemed to get a nose-bleed from those heady heights as they lost two consecutive home games and drew at Worcester. They then got that winning feeling again, as two straight away wins sent them back to the top after a five-game absence. Those two wins were followed by a 14-point haul from the next six games. The highlight of that run was an 8-0 demolition of Dorchester on Boxing Day, with both Claridge and Lee Phillips netting hat-tricks. They drew 2-2 with the same team in their next game, which set them up on a decent run of form for the visit of Crawley, their biggest threat to the leadership. Home advantage counted for nothing as Crawley snatched a 1-0 win, but it was not enough to topple the Terras at the top. They did win their next two games but finally lost pole position following a 1-0 defeat to Cambridge. The club then pulled off another transfer coup, signing the highly rated Robbie Pethick from Brighton. He helped them to two 3-0 wins over Moor Green and Dover, which allowed them to briefly reclaim the top spot in what was a see-saw season. However, they then played the return match with Crawley, who won 2-1 to leapfrog Weymouth yet again in the fight for league supremacy.
That defeat to Crawley gave the Sussex side the advantage and they held that edge in the title race. Claridge faced the first major test of his limited managerial career. Turning a side that finished 17th in the previous season into serious contenders was in itself a significant achievement; but after holding the lead for ten games, they knew they could win the league. However, the pressure on Claridge's team told, and their season ended with indifferent form. Just four wins in the last twelve games after the defeat to Crawley eventually left them twelve points behind. Crawley's brilliant second half of the season left the Terras having to settle for second best - but Claridge's team undoubtedly showed they have the potential and the ability to go one better in 2004/05. MP

The Terras

Conference North

Club Pages

Alfreton Town

Address: The Town Ground, North Street, Alfreton, Derbyshire, DE55 7JT

Tel: 01773 835 121 / 830 277

Website: www.alfretontownfc.com

Officials: Chairman: Wayne Bradley
Secretary: Tom Hill
Manager: David Lloyd

The Town Ground

Review

Alfreton Town had a very strong 2003/04 season finishing fourth in the Unibond Premier Division after winning promotion the previous season, and they will be regarded as contenders for the first championship in the Conference Alliance North.

The Reds made steady progress in the league with a solid defence who kept 16 clean sheets and they had capable goal scorers to give them the vital three points when they were needed. Mick Goddard and Mark Godber netted the bulk of the goals for the team, scoring 28 goals between them in the league and adding a further six in cup competitions.

The Reds were the early season pacesetters as they won seven of the first eight games of the season. However, defeats at inopportune moments saw the Reds fall back down the field and, while they were always in the upper reaches of the league table, they were always playing catch up with the main protagonists in the title race, Droylsden and Hucknall Town.

The biggest win of the season came in late September when Ashton United were the visitors to the Town Ground. With goals from Tony Hemmings, Emeka Nwadike, two from Chris Bettney and a final nail in the coffin by Godber on 86 minutes, a 5-0 demolition was complete.

The end of the season could have seen Alfreton jump to third place after a 2-0 win over Barrow who finished third. However a final day loss at Blyth Spartans kept them two points behind the top three, but a full 17 behind champions Hucknall.

The club suffered a surprise 1-0 defeat at the hands of Gedling Town in the FA Cup Second Qualifying Round but they did notched up two impressive wins in the FA Trophy before succumbing to Telford in Round Three. AP

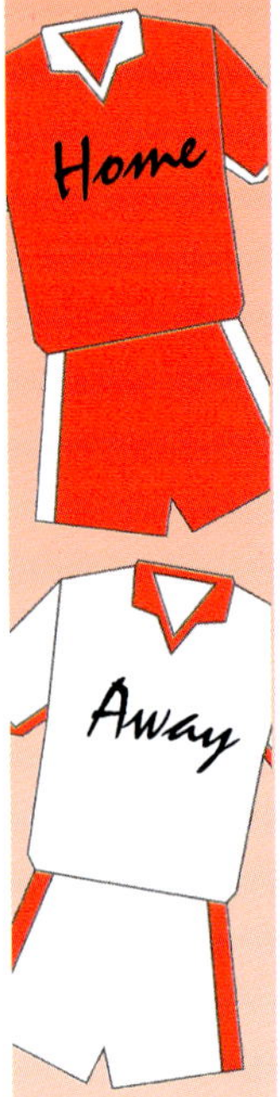

Directions

From the M1: Exit at J28 onto the A38 towards Derby. Follow this for two miles and then take the slip road onto the B600. Turn right at a main road towards the town centre and, after half a mile (immediately after the church on the left), turn left into North Street. The ground is 150 yards on the right.

By train: On leaving the station approach, turn right into Mansfield Road and up the hill towards the town centre. Take the second turn left into Prospect Street (post office on the left, chip shop on the right). Continue to the end of Prospect Street then cross Nottingham Road. Facing you is a Catholic church. North Street runs down the right-hand side of the church. The ground is 150 yards down this road on the right, set well back. Walking time from the station is around 15 minutes.

North Street neatly sums up the advantages and disadvantages of having a ground in the centre of the community. Grounds that began life when cars were much rarer are now choked by space needed to accommodate the travelling fan. Alfreton's ground is one such, nestling behind a housing estate for which there is only one way in and out. Even with relatively small crowds, a police presence is needed to direct the traffic. Parking a little bit away is well worth it. The ground itself is an interesting mix, as the club have some recently acquired seating behind one goal and covered seating down one side.

The club have recently added a concrete terrace, new entrances at both ends of the ground (doubling the number of turnstiles), and the installation of new floodlights. HL

The Reds

Altrincham

Address: Moss Lane, Altrincham, Cheshire, WA15 8AP

Tel: 0161 928 1045

Website: www.altrinchamfc.com

Email: jlaidlar@luso.u-net.com

Officials: Chairman: Geoff Goodwin
Secretary/Manager: Graham Heathcote

Moss Lane

Directions

From the South: Leave the M6 at Junction 19 and follow the A556 to the M56 signposted Manchester Airport. Turn off at J6 for Hale Barns. Pass through Hale Barns. Go straight on at the traffic lights and then take the third right (Westminster Road) and continue for half a mile or so to Moss Lane. The ground is on the right.
From the North: Leave the M60 at Stretford and head south towards Altrincham on the A56 for about four miles. Follow the signs to Altrincham town centre, taking a left turn after about three miles onto the B5164 (Barrington Road). Pass the Old Mill pub on the left, and Moss Lane is the first left. However, Moss Lane is one-way here so carry on south for a quarter of a mile, past Altrincham Post Office (on the right), and turn left at the next set of traffic lights into Lloyd Street. After crossing the railway bridge, with Tesco on the left, turn first left (Manor Road) and proceed to the second set of traffic lights, where you turn right into Moss Lane.
By train/bus/tram: From Manchester Piccadilly or Victoria railway stations, or Piccadilly Gardens bus station, take the Metrolink tram service to Altrincham (it takes roughly half an hour). Metros run every 6 to 12 minutes. Buy your ticket from the platform machines before boarding. Travel to Altrincham station on the bus station (Interchange) side (this is to the right with your back to the Manchester direction). Turn immediately left after the booking office and proceed through the bus station and up the narrow inclined footpath to the junction with Moss Lane bridge. Turn left, over the railway bridge, and then walk straight on, past Tesco (on the right) and the Bridge Inn (on the left) for approximately eight minutes. The ground is on the left. Buses (16/41/263/264) run from Manchester Piccadilly bus station to Altrincham Interchange (immediately outside the Metrolink station).

Altrincham's Conference standard ground sometimes has a warm atmosphere and, with decent terracing and a good main stand, the town has a ground worthy of its football club. They also have a nice bar situated under the stand, while travelling to the ground is fairly easy. AP

Review

Altrincham finished twelfth in the league and qualified for the Conference Alliance North with the improvement of two places from the previous season. Altrincham were off to another sluggish start and drew seven out of their first ten games. The trend continued until half the season was over as the Robins would eventually finish with 15 draws to their name.
A good goal difference at the end of the season of +14 showed the others in the middle of the table that they were worthy of their place in the Conference North. All of the clubs below the qualifying mark had a minus goal tally. The turn around for Altrincham came against Whitby Town at the start of January where a 4-0 victory secured the points, which lifted them to twelfth from which they went on to achieve their highest position of the season of eighth during the month of March. Top goal scorer Ian Craney bagged two on the day with youngster Steve Lunt and second top scorer Marcus Hallows scoring one each to finish the scoring before the hour.
The finishing position wasn't totally secured until the final few games of the season when a string of three wins made them safe. Luckily two of the victories came over Whitby Town and Runcorn who were also challenging for a place. A single goal by Barry Shuttleworth in a final day win against Runcorn saw Altrincham secure their top 13 finish.
There was disappointment for the club in the FA Cup when they were knocked out by fellow Unibond League side Lancaster City in the Second Qualifying Round. However, they did make a few waves in the FA Trophy as they battled their way to the Fifth Round before they lost to a late goal at Conference side Shrewsbury. AP

The Robins

Ashton United

Address: Surrey Street, Hurst Cross, Ashton-u-Lyne, OL6 8DY

Tel: 0161 3301511

Website: www.aufc4.freeserve.co.uk

Officials: Chairman: Tony Ryan
Secretary: John North
Manager: Gerry Quinn

Directions

From the M62 junction 20, take the A627M to Oldham, keep in the right hand two lanes. After two miles take the slip road on the left, signposted Ashton. At the roundabout, take the second left still for Ashton. This is the A627. At the next roundabout, take the third left (still signposted Ashton and still the A627). Keep to the left lane. Take the first slip road about 400 yards for Ashton-under-Lyne. At the next roundabout take the second left (Ashton-u-Lyne). At the roundabout take the third left signposted Stalybridge/Park Road (the B6194). Follow this for three and a half miles. Pass the Welcome pub on your left, then the Red House on the right, and then the monumental stone cross about 15ft high on the right at a set of traffic lights. Turn right at these lights and the ground is on the right.
By train: Ashton-under-Lyne station is just under a mile from the ground. Exit the station in Henrietta Road and turn left into Canterbury Street. This leads into Union Road and then Kings Road. Surrey Street is at the end of Kings Road, on the left.

This is a nice little ground. The main stand offers a good view and the food and clubhouse are a credit to the club. Finding the ground is a little tricky if you miss the turn off but keep your eyes open and it should be easy enough. With a little tidying up the ground will look really special and should attract more supporters into watch games more often. AP

Review

The word 'inconsistent' sums up Ashton's season to a tee. The Robins were never quite able to avoid the shackles of mid-table; not getting the results to push towards the top half but, at the same time, were never in relegation trouble. The season started off with dire 2-0 defeats to Blyth Spartans and Bradford Park Avenue. Narrow home wins over Lancaster (2-1) and Marine (4-3) steadied the ship, before falling 2-0 to in-form Hucknall. The side occasionally showed glimpses of their ability, with Steve Smith and Phil Denney immediately establishing themselves as the key men. The opening 20 games brought eight wins, ten losses and two draws; and only a side as inconsistent as Ashton could follow a 3-2 defeat at home to basement club Wakefield & Emley with a 2-1 victory at title-challenging Droylsden.
The New Year started with wins over Vauxhall and Frickley, and a 1-1 draw with Droylsden. Then followed two home defeats, including a 6-1 humbling against Hucknall. Ashton's response was four wins on the trot, that pushed the Robins up the table. Three of those wins came away from home, and it was games at Hurst Cross that proved a problem for Ashton for much of the season. However, a top 13 place and subsequent elevation to the new Conference North was seemingly likely although far from assured. Results remained inconsistent, as the side didn't achieve successive wins after that four-game run. They vitally needed a win at home to Harrogate on the last day and, despite taking the lead, they lost 4-3 - handing 13th place to Runcorn by a mere two points.
The Harrogate defeat was a cruel blow for the Robins, and they had just three days to pick themselves up before the Play-Offs began. They were drawn at home against Unibond Division One winners Hyde United and, despite going a goal down inside 20 minutes, they put their poor home form behind them to win 2-1 in extra-time. They had home advantage again for the Semi-Final tie with Bradford Park Avenue. Ashton went behind inside 20 minutes but, despite equalising, they eventually lost the tie 2-1. The Robins' season ended on an even sourer note as they lost the Manchester Premier Cup - the competition they had won for the previous three years - to Droylsden. Yet, after all the heartache and disappointments, an unexpected reprieve arrived in late June. Telford's demotion allowed Ashton to fill the subsequent gap left in the Conference North. Thus they achieved their initial target of promotion, but the circumstances in which they did it will leave a somewhat hollow feeling. MP

The Robins

Barrow

Address: Holker Street, Wilkie Road, Barrow In Furness, LA14 5UW

Tel: 01229 820346

Website: www.barrowfc.com

Email: info@barrowfc.com

Officials: Chairman: Brian Keen
Secretary: Neil McDonald
Manager: Lee Turnbull

Holker Street

Directions

The ground is located next to Asda, MFI and Furniture World, on the way into the town centre. Follow the main A590 road into Barrow, passing the industrial units on the way in. Pass over the railway line, with Brady's Road Haulage and warehouses on your left, the fire station on your right. The ground is on your left.
By train: From Barrow station, come out of the approach road and turn right into Holker Street. You can see the floodlights from there.

Situated right by the Asda supermarket in Barrow, Holker Street is one of the easiest grounds to find in the Conference North this season. With a huge main stand with seating and another with terracing opposite, the ground can easily hold the attendances it sees on regular occasions. The food and the club shop are also good value with the bar, looking over the rest of the ground from behind one of the goals, offering a decent beverage as well. AP

Review

Barrow would have been one of the first names on people's lists of Unibond league title challengers. A second-placed finish in 2002-03, and a total of seven signings in August, meant that Barrow were well poised for embarking on a title bid. Two wins in the first eight games, but also just one defeat, showed that the league was more competitive than the Bluebirds first realised. New signings Gavin Knight and Michael Oliver showed good promise as a strike partnership, but scoring goals wasn't a problem: they just couldn't stop conceding. A 3-0 win over Ashton in mid-September seemed to give the side confidence, and they embarked on a seven game unbeaten run which propelled them up to third in the table.
The side began to struggle after throwing away a lead in a 2-1 defeat to Harrogate in late October. There were also too many draws, and they were seemingly unable to keep a clean sheet. The difficult period subsided in December as the Bluebirds won four successive games (including 3-0 and 4-3 wins over Lancaster), but they were a disappointing fifth in the table. They were still within reasonable distance of the top teams, but needed to embark on a run to get within touching distance. A number of wins in February - which saw them score twelve in three games - pushed them up to third. Droylsden had a fight on their hands for that second place.
An FA announcement in early March gave unexpected and fresh impetus to Barrow's season: Since leaders (and probable champions) Hucknall hadn't applied for promotion, the second placed team would be promoted. The Bluebirds were third and were the only side in the top five with a ground of Conference standard. But while the news should have inspired Barrow, their response to the FA's announcement was to lose successive games to Vauxhall and Harrogate. They did beat Droylsden and inflicted a rare defeat on Hucknall, but took one point from two games with Whitby. The announcement had made no real difference to performances as they continued to produce inconsistent results. They were still in with a chance mathematically until a 2-1 home defeat to Alfreton in their penultimate game, as they conceded a goal deep into injury time. Their Unibond League President's Cup win over Workington was of little consolation after losing out on a potential Conference place. MP

The Bluebirds

Bradford Park Avenue

Address: Horsfall Stadium, Cemetery Road, Bradford, BD6 2NG

Tel: 01274 604578

Website: www.bpafc.com

Email: bpa@bpafc.com

Officials: Chairman: Frank Thornton
Secretary: Bob Robinson
Manager: Carl Shutt

Horsfall Stadium

Directions

Take the M62 to Junction 26, then the M606 to the end. At the roundabout, take the A6036 (signposted Halifax) and pass the Odsal Stadium on the left. At the next roundabout, take the third exit (A6036, Halifax) and, after one mile, turn left down Cemetery Road (by the Kings Head pub). The ground is on the left.
By bus: From Bradford, take the 681, 682, 685 from Interchange or outside Jacob's Well pub at 10 and 40 minutes past the hour. Journey time ten minutes. From Halifax, take the 508, 681, 682. Journey time 15 mins. Get off at Cemetery Road/King's Head pub. From Leeds, it is the 508 via Stanningley and Dudley Hill.

Bradford PA have the same problem as clubs such as Grantham and Gateshead: an athletics track. There is also only one stand where supporters can sit, but this isn't a reason not to visit the stadium. You usually have to park on the street as they don't have a car park for supporters but there is plenty outside by the cemetery. AP

Review

A season that started off okay for Avenue worsened as it progressed, and yet ended with the best possible result. A Conference North place looked achievable in the early exchanges, especially after a solid seventh place in 2002/03. But as the season unravelled, the club were spiralling dangerously towards the pits of the Unibond League. The problem was home games: poor old Avenue fans had to wait until 1st November before they won a game at the Horsfall Stadium, when they beat Vauxhall 6-2. They then had to wait until the 31st March until the next home win. However, they were more than capable of performing away from home, and a 4-2 win at Spennymoor saw talented striker Stephen Oleksewcyz finally find his scoring boots. After ten games, Avenue were tenth and looking good for a Conference North place.
A 3-2 defeat at home to Stalybridge - in which Oleksewcyz scored twice - saw the club begin to free-fall towards the bottom three. Within four games they had gone from tenth to twentieth, and the side were barely keeping their heads above the relegation waters.
They then found themselves submerged after the New Year, after they seemed incapable of finding the net. Their away form had been keeping them out of the relegation zone but three straight away defeats - without scoring themselves - meant they looked doomed. Manager Trevor Storton went in March, and in came Carl Shutt who instantly steadied the ship. He lifted them out of the relegation zone and navigated them to the safety of 17th.
Fans were probably just happy to have seen their side steer clear of relegation let alone make the Conference North Play-Offs. In fact, Avenue excelled themselves: they won all three games. Spennymoor (at home), Ashton (away) and Burscough (home) were all disposed of as Avenue won promotion. In the process, they narrowed the gap on their neighbours, Bradford City, to four levels. What a paradoxical season it was: Avenue looked like narrowly avoiding relegation and yet won promotion; and the ground on which the club won two of 22 league games was the scene for two Play-Off triumphs. Maybe that can spur the club on to perform at the Horsfall this season in a difficult looking division. MP

Avenue

Droylsden

Address: Butchers Arms Ground, Market Street, Droylsden, Manchester, M43 7AW

Tel: 0161 370 1426

Website: www.droylsdenfc.co.uk

Email: webmaster@droylsdenfc.co.uk

Officials: Chairman/Manager: David Pace
Secretary: Alan Slater

Butchers Arms Ground

Directions

From the M60: Leave at Junction 23 (Ashton-under-Lyne) take the A635 towards Manchester. After a retail park on the left, including the ubiquitous McDonald's, turn right at lights onto the A662 (signposted Droylsden). Continue along the A662 to the traffic lights at the junction with Market Street. Turn right into Market Street, across the mini-roundabout and the ground is on the left.

By train: The nearest stations are Ashton-under-Lyne, two and a half miles from Droylsden; Manchester Piccadilly; and Manchester Victoria (the latter two are four and a half miles from the ground).

By bus: Both Manchester train stations are a few minutes walk from Piccadilly bus station. From here you can catch bus numbers 231-235 to the corner of Medlock Street/Market Street and the ground is a two minute walk away. Both routes take roughly 20/25 minutes. The bus station in Ashton-under-Lyne is a few minutes away from the train station. From there you can catch the 232, 233, 169 and 168 buses to the corner of Medlock Street/Market Street. Or take the 216, 236 or 237, and alight at the corner of Manchester Road/Market Street. Both routes take 10/15 minutes.

The outside of the Bloods' den looks impressive with the nicely built main stand and the good sized clubhouse, but the rest of the ground needs improving. The areas behind the goals are reputedly having a revamp and it will no doubt do the club good. It is a nice ground right by the market and there is a friendly pub just outside by the car park. Good directions are needed, for this ground can be tricky to find. AP

Review

2003/04 was a fantastic season for the Bloods: runners-up in the league and winning three trophies. The Manchester club provided plenty of entertainment and exceeded all expectations. The season started on an inconsistent note, and the side looked particularly shaky in a 4-1 home defeat to Altrincham. But they were boosted by the September signing of young Chester City striker, Danny Bryne, who scored in each of his first five games. Droylsden took 13 points from those games as they moved into fourth place. Then their title credentials faced the biggest test, as they faced the top two sides in the space of a week. They passed the test with flying colours, with a 4-4 draw at Harrogate followed by a convincing 3-1 win over leaders Hucknall.

Three successive wins later, and the Bloods were top of the league. This is where they remained after another four wins - including an incredible 5-4 triumph over Radcliffe Borough. However, Hucknall had a number of games in hand, and put a run together to topple Droylsden. The Bloods stayed top for six games, before spending the rest of the season playing catch-up. March saw Barrow closing in on second spot, which would have sealed their promotion after the decisions by Hucknall and Droylsden not to apply for promotion. Barrow entertained Droylsden in late March and won 2-1. But Bryne - who finished the season with 21 league goals - and new-boy Steve Brodie scored the goals that eventually secured second place in late April.

Droylsden were far and away the league's top scorers, scoring an incredible 96 goals and failing to score just twice. Their defensive record was what ultimately cost them the title, conceding 64 to Hucknall's 38. They did put one over on the league winners by beating them in two cup finals, winning the Unibond League Challenge Cup 4-1 on aggregate and winning 1-0 in the Peter Swailes Memorial Shield. They made it a hat-trick of cup wins by defeating Ashton United 2-1 in the Manchester Premier Cup final. With that, and with the knowledge that the Butchers Arms will soon be of Conference standard, the Bloods will be fired up to mount another title challenge in 2004/05. MP

The Bloods

Gainsborough Trinity

Address: Northolme, Gainsborough, Lincolnshire, DN21 2QW

Tel: 01427 615625

Website: www.gainsboroughtrinity.com

Officials: Chairman: Pat Lobley
Secretary: Frank Nicolson
Manager: Paul Mitchell

Review

Gainsborough Trinity had a successful season finishing tenth in the Unibond Premier Division with a plus 18 goal difference and the away win record for the season. The result of the season came at Spennymoor's Brewery Field ground. Gareth Grant scored two within the first half hour to give Trinity a 2-0 half time lead. Chris Hurst scored a third on 49 minutes before Grant completed his hat-trick just four minutes later. Chris Timmins then rounded off the scoring with two goals in as many minutes on 72 and 73 and the game ended in a 6-0 victory.
Gainsborough's place in the Conference Alliance North wasn't secured until the final three games of the season as Trinity ended with a flourish, picking up all nine points. Luke Staton and Gareth Grant got the goals that secured the 2-0 win against Wakefield & Emley before they came from behind to secure a 2-1 win over Worksop. Mark Haran was unfortunate to score an own-goal before Grant netted to give them the three points and secure their place in the Conference North.
On the final day of the season Gainsborough finished an impressive double over Spennymoor beating them 3-1. Ben Jones, Hurst and Lee Ellington scored the goals after Steve Preen gave the visitors the lead in the first half.
Trinity also reached the First Round proper of the FA Cup following a replay victory over Farsley Celtic. However, Trinity were overrun during a relentless second half onslaught by opponents, Brentford, as the London side romped to a 7-1 win to end Trinity's cup adventure. There was no such excitement in the FA Trophy as Gainsborough suffered an early exit at the hands of Unibond First Division outfit Guiseley. AP

Directions

From the North: Enter Gainsborough on the A159. The ground is approximately half a mile on the left.
From the South: Enter the town on the A156. Turn right into Ashcroft Road just under the second railway bridge, opposite the Edlington building. Follow this road over the traffic lights, and continue through the town, towards Scunthorpe. The ground is on the right.
From the East: Enter Gainsborough on the A631. At the bottom of the hill, turn right and follow as from south.
From the West: Enter Gainsborough on the A631 across the Trent Bridge. Go over the first set of traffic lights and turn left at the second set, just past the Jet Station. Follow as from South.
By train: Nearest station is Lea Road. Directions are as from the South.

The clubhouse is the main attraction (apart from the football of course) to The Northolme as it provides a good atmosphere and decent seating before and after the match. The food available inside the ground is also an asset to the club and I recommend the burgers. The main stand, which also provides the seating, is small, but standing throughout the match offers the best views. AP

The Northolme

The Blues

Harrogate Town

Address: Wetherby Road, Harrogate, North Yorkshire, HG2 7SA

Tel: 01423 880675

Website: www.harrogatetownafc.co.uk

Email: supine@ntlworld.com

Officials: Chairman: Bill Fotherby
Secretary: John Harrison
Manager: John Reed

Review

After finishing sixth in their first season in the Unibond Premier last year, the club's ambitions for this season were simple: a top 13 finish and subsequent promotion to the Conference North. If you ask fans of the club about this season, they will talk of a Jekyll and Hyde season. In the opening months, Town were serious title contenders. On several occasions they had the chance to go top, only for a defeat or draw to hold them back (a last minute defeat at Worksop in November was a prime example). Nevertheless, they were never far off the pace and the fans were becoming increasingly expectant. Earning 13 points from 15 in December and winning both their January games only fuelled the fans' title dreams.

But from February, Town moved worryingly off the pace. The forwards, including the previously prolific Glenn Naylor, were firing blanks - scoring just two goals in five February games. In March, they conceded 14 goals in five games and their solid defence was beginning to look shaky. During these two months they lost seven of ten league games, of which three were home defeats. Their form did pick up towards the end of the season - winning five of seven games in April, including three 4-3 wins over Stalybridge, Blyth Spartans and Ashton. But they eventually finished 18 points off top spot. The main hindrance was their performances against the bigger teams - they won just seven points from a possible 24 against the eventual top four clubs.

If you had offered Town fans the chance of a fifth place finish before the season, they would have snatched it with both hands. Indeed, their league position represents the club's highest ever finish in the football pyramid. However, in the circumstances, fifth place was a disappointment for a side that, for a long while, had title aspirations. Manager John Reed was pleased though: 'For a club of our stature, I think we have over-achieved and had an excellent season to finish fifth.' They have relied heavily on great performances from a core of key players. James Turley was a creative force, finishing club top scorer with 17 goals from midfield. Forward Glenn Naylor scored 15 goals - including four in one game at home to runners-up Droylsden - while Simon Sturdy and Colin Hunter also performed consistently. With some squad strengthening - a defensive midfielder and a pacey front man the main requirements - they could easily see a title challenge this season. MP

Directions

From the South: Leave the A1 at Wetherby and follow the signs for Harrogate. On entering Harrogate pass Sainsbury's and the Yorkshire Show Ground on your right. At the traffic lights, go straight on and the ground is 500 yards on your right.
From the North: Leave the A1 onto the A59 for Knaresborough and Harrogate. At the first roundabout take the A658 Harrogate bypass. Stay on this road until you reach the roundabout for Wetherby (A661). Turn right for Harrogate and then as above.
By train: Starbeck station is just under a mile from the ground. Exit the station and turn right into the High Street. Continue along this road as it leads into Knaresborough Road. Turn left at the hospital sign along Lancaster Park Road to the end. The ground is on the left.

A quiet, compact and complete venue with an ice cream seller on my last visit to the ground. Wetherby Road could not be easier to find, although parking is a little tricky. Tasty food and a good clubhouse complement the ground nicely and the main stand is also in good nick. AP

The Town

Hinckley United

Address: Middlefield Lane, Hinckley, Leics, LE10 0RB

Tel: 01455 613553

Website: www.hinckleyunitedfc.co.uk

Officials: Chairman: Kevin Downes
Secretary: Ray Baggott
Manager: Dean Thomas

Directions

From the M69: Leave at J1 and head north on the A5 (towards Nuneaton). At the first roundabout (Dodwells Bridge), take the second exit (for Earl Shilton A47). At the third roundabout turn right into Stoke Road and then first left into Tudor Road. Continue down Tudor Road until a crossroads. Turn left here into Middlefield Lane. The ground is 100 yards on the left.

By train: There are services by Central Trains from Leicester, Nuneaton and Birmingham. From the station car park, cross the road and head past the Railway Hotel, along Station Road, up the hill towards the town centre. Cross Market Place into the Borough then into King Street, past the Union pub, and into Lower Bond Street. Carry on up the hill leading into Upper Bond Street. At the next crossroads, turn left into Middlefield Lane. The ground is at the bottom of the hill.

Hinckley United's current home has limited seating and the overall feel of a ground which its occupiers have outgrown due to their impressive on-the-pitch exploits of recent years. There is a small pocket of 350 seats available, with the rest of the 2,661 capacity for standing. Inside the main gates are food kiosks on match days and a club shop run by the supporters' club.

The ground is located just off the A447, at the end of a dead-end road which gives it the feel of an oversized back garden rather than a football stadium. However Middlefield Lane has hosted its final full season of football as Hinckley plan to move to their new 4,000 capacity Leicester Road stadium in November 2004. RC

Review

Hinckley prepared for the 2003/04 season with their sights on a top 13 finish to secure a place in the restructured Conference North. While most fans believed this was certainly attainable, few would have envisaged the season that lay before them.

Hinckley started brightly, taking seven points from the opening three games. Justin Jenkins looked strong and quick up front and the Hinckley rearguard conceded only once. A tricky trio of fixtures foiled a prospective Hinckley charge for top spot as they crashed to successive defeats at the hands of early pace-setters Weymouth, local rivals Nuneaton Borough, and Worcester City.

Hinckley brought in striker Matt Lewis on loan in a bid to ease their increasing injury worries. The move paid immediate dividends as debutant Lewis hit a brace in a 2-0 win over Eastbourne Borough. As Steve Claridge had done with Weymouth, another former local hero came back to haunt United in their next fixture, as ex-Wolves striker Don Goodman's goal earned Stafford Rangers a point after Hinckley had taken the lead.

A solid October (five points, three games) was followed by a surge in form which saw United move up to second. A string of excellent displays from the likes of Leon Jackson, Justin Jenkins and Dave Sadler saw Hinckley take nine points out of nine.

2004 kicked off in disappointing style as a 1-1 draw with Grantham began a run which saw just eight points from eleven games. Goal scoring seemed the problem as United chalked up a host of blanks, losing by the odd goal on numerous occasions. Highlights of the penultimate month of the season included the impressive Jamie Lenton scoring at both ends in a 1-1 draw with Merthyr Tydfil and a Dave Sadler double rescuing a point in a 2-2 draw against Havant & Waterlooville. However, the highlight of the month was the 3-0 demolition of Crawley Town. Another Sadler brace and a Lenton set piece meant that Hinckley did the double over the eventual champions and produced one of the performances of the season. A 0-0 stalemate with Chippenham rounded the season off with United sitting proudly in sixth place.

So a successful season which saw rising stars in the likes of top scorer Justin Jenkins and teenage sensation Matt Lewis, as well as strong seasons from the likes of Jamie Lenton and Leon Jackson. RC

Middlefield Lane

The Knitters

Hucknall Town

Address: Watnall Road, Hucknall, Notts, NG15 6EX

Tel: 0115 9561264

Website: www.hucknalltownfc.co.uk

Officials: Chairman: Brian Holmes
Secretary: Brian Scothern
Director of Football: Ernie Moss

Watnall Road

Directions

Exit the M1 at J27 and take the first left, the A611. Go straight over at the two roundabouts, keeping to the right-hand lane after the second one, in the lane marked for Hucknall. Go through the traffic lights and onto the dual carriageway to the next roundabout. Turn right. Go straight on at the next roundabout and, after half a mile, turn right at the roundabout. The ground is on your right.

By train: There is a rail link between Nottingham and Hucknall, the 'Robin Hood Line'. There is a half hourly service on a Saturday. It takes about 40 minutes to walk from the station to the ground. Leave the station and walk up Station Road to the traffic lights (cinema/bingo club on far corner). Turn right to the next lights, then left and this is Watnall Road. Keep walking to the first roundabout and the ground is on the right.

Being denied access to the Conference because of the standard of the ground might make you think it isn't a good ground when in fact it is very nice, just small. With development behind one goal and down one side it would look complete and give them that chance to progress - both the club and Watnall Road deserves the improvements. AP

Review

What a superb season it was for Hucknall Town, under new manager Steve Burr. His shrewd signings - including striker Danny Bacon - instilled hope into the side. Winning six of their opening seven games, including a 4-0 thrashing of Southport, set them on their way. Two defeats (away to Lancaster and at home to basement club Wakefield) saw the leadership temporarily pass to Alfreton Town. Their biggest game was the visit of title rivals Harrogate - which Hucknall won 1-0. They followed this with four victories in their next five games, including taking a 3-0 revenge against Wakefield, before losing in a top-of-the-table clash at Droylsden. They again responded to defeat with a fine run, this time beating Barrow, Runcorn and Blyth Spartans. They regained top spot in the New Year, with a hard-fought 2-1 win at Runcorn.

That game at Runcorn was the start of an eight match winning run that made them clear favourites for the title. They avenged earlier defeats with a 3-0 win over Lancaster and 2-0 win over Gainsborough, and they won away at Harrogate with a brace from Danny Bacon. Bacon and striker Garry Ricketts were fighting over the position of club top scorer, with the pair scoring the goals to take them into top spot. March saw a massive fixture pile-up, which would see Town play ten games throughout the month. They won seven of their March games, with one defeat at Barrow not enough to deter them as they maintained a twelve point lead over Droylsden. They finally confirmed the title, that had seemed inevitable, with a convincing 3-0 win at Worksop Town.

They took their foot off the pedal after the title was confirmed, and ended the season on a low by losing three cup finals. They lost 4-1 (on aggregate) in the two-legged Unibond League Cup to Droylsden; 2-1 to Eastwood Town in the Notts Senior Cup; and 1-0 to Droylsden again in the Peter Swailes Memorial Shield. This won't have dampened what was an excellent season, as Steve Burr's team won the league by nine points. The scoring exploits of Bacon (19 goals) and Ricketts (22 goals) will be needed next season as Hucknall look to lift the title for a second successive year. However, there is a new face at the helm this year after Steve Burr's departure to Northwich Victoria. His replacement is Ernie Moss, joining the club after a successful season at Matlock Town. MP

Kettering Town

Address: Rockingham Road, Kettering, Northants NN16 9AW

Tel: 01536 483028

Website: www.ketteringtownfc.co.uk

Email: info@ketteringtownfc.co.uk

Officials: Chairman: Peter Mallinger
Secretary: Graham Starmer
Manager: Kevin Wilson

Directions

From any direction, you need to be on the A14 Kettering bypass. From the south, leave the M1 at Junction 15, taking the A45 past Northampton, then the A43 towards Kettering. Turn left onto the A14 Kettering bypass. North of the town turn right onto the A6003. Follow this towards the town centre. The ground is on the left after about half a mile. From the North, come off the M1/M6 at Junction 19, and onto the A14 towards Kettering, then as above.
By train: Kettering station is on the line from St Pancras. The ground is a 20 minute walk from the station. At the end of Station Road, cross over into the High Street, right up Market Street, then left onto the A6003 Rockingham Road. This goes past the ground.

Rockingham Road is a very imposing venue featuring an impressive cantilever main stand which dominates the ground, situated as it is in a leafy northern suburb of the Northamptonshire town, on one of the main roads into it. There is covered terracing along the whole far side of the ground, and open terracing behind both ends. The car park is quite cramped, particularly as part of it is given over to the club shop and a children's activity centre, and it is quite a lengthy walk from the town's railway station. GB

Review

Kettering Town's home form again made life difficult for the club and defeat by Boreham Wood in the Fourth Qualifying Round of the FA Cup put manager Dominic Genovese under pressure. Genovese's days were numbered and, on Boxing Day, former Northampton Town manager Kevin Wilson was appointed. Changes to the team were made and the club obtained some success in the FA Trophy by beating Woking 3-2 at Kingfield Road after a 0-0 draw at Rockingham Road. Another good result followed with a draw at Burton Albion. However, after missing a penalty ten minutes from the end, Kettering lost 2-1 after extra-time in the replay.
With Canvey Island running away with the league, all that was left for Kettering was to try to qualify for either of the two newly structured Conference feeder leagues. A top 13 position was the requirement and, at one stage, the club dropped out of that coveted zone. However, Wilson rallied his troops and they came back with a storming finish to the end of the season. An unbeaten run of twelve games lifted them up into ninth place and claim a spot in the Conference North.

By Kettering Town FC

The Poppies

Lancaster City

Address: Giant Axe, West Road, Lancaster, Lancashire, LA1 5PE

Tel: 01524 382238

Website: www.lancastercityfc.com

Email: info@lancastercityfc.com

Officials: Chairman: Ron Moore
Secretary: Mike Sparks
Manager: Phil Wilson

Directions

Head into the centre of Lancaster on the main roads and you will come to the one-way system around the centre. If travelling from the north, you have to go around this until you reach the southern point of the one-way system, then you turn right into King Street at the Revolution Bar (the Alex pub, as was). If travelling from the south, you will reach this anyway. Continue along this road, through the lights at the Market, and to the next set of lights, with Waterstones on your left. Turn left onto Meeting House Lane, then across the railway by the station, and right into Station Road. Follow this road round as it becomes West Road, and the ground and car park are on your right.

By train: Use the exit from platform three of the station, turn right onto Station Road, and follow the road around as it becomes West Road. It is a five minute walk at most.

With Lancaster's castle overlooking the quiet ground in the City, the Giant Axe (named because of the plot of land's shape, visible with a bird's eye view) is actually well hidden away from the busy town centre, which offers a challenging one-way system to visitors. The bar by the main road and the car park for the club has a large floor space for supporters before and after the match while the terracing behind one of the goals gives supporters a good viewpoint in-between. AP

Giant Axe

Review

Lancaster City started off without a win in their first six matches of the 2003/04 season and gained only one point. The opening day of the season saw them draw 1-1 against Vauxhall Motors at the Giant Axe but the Dolly Blues then lost the next five in a row. When a win finally did come at Burscough in September it failed to lift the club off the foot of the table.

Progress was made in the following game as a 3-1 win over eventual champions Hucknall Town lifted their spirits and the club off the bottom. By the end of the season Lancaster had moved up the table to eighth place with 20 wins, nine draws and 15 losses.

Jamie Hughes was the star of the season after signing from Vauxhall Motors in late August and helped to turn the season around. Hughes scored 22 goals in the Unibond League and added another nine in cup competitions.

With the results in the league starting to pick up, the FA Cup gave the supporters an even bigger lift. After beating Altrincham, Chorley and eventual Northern League champions, Dunston Federation Brewery, in the qualifying stages they were given a home draw against Division Three club Cambridge United where they fell to a 2-1 defeat. AP

The Dollies

Moor Green

Address: The Moorlands, Sherwood Road, Hall Green, Birmingham, B28 OEX

Tel: 0121 777 8961

Website: www.moorgreenfc.co.uk

Email: webmaster@moorgreenfc.co.uk

Officials: Chairman: Ian Childs
Secretary: Nigel Collins
Manager: Bob Faulkner

Review

Moor Green were counting themselves fortunate to qualify for the new Conference Northern Division after finishing in border line 13th place in the Dr Martens Premier Division ahead of Merthyr Tydfil by just one point after a final day win against Havant & Waterlooville. The Moors went behind to a James Taylor goal before Peter Faulds became the hero and scored a brace to secure the position in a dramatic final day.

The Birmingham based club got off to a bad start to the season scoring just one goal in five games in August, and that coming on the opening day against Tiverton Town with Daire Doyle giving them the lead before going down 2-1. Moor Green did manage two points with goalless draws before the month of September brought their first win: 2-1 over Stafford Rangers with both goals by Rob Elmes. The rest of the month didn't fare so well and they lost all five league games.

Moor Green picked up in November and embarked on a twelve game unbeaten run in the league which included an impressive 5-0 win against Stafford Rangers with goals scored by five different players: Phil Trainer, Lee Collins, Guy Sanders, Daire Doyle and Jae Martin.

A roller coaster season saw the Moors lose just one of their final eight games (and that against eventual champions Crawley Town) as they just sneaked into the promotion places after that dramatic final day. It was unlikely that the club's cup exploits could live up to the drama of the league campaign. And so it proved as the Moors suffered early exits from both the FA Cup and FA Trophy against Hinckley and Cinderford respectively. However, consolation was found in the form of the Birmingham Senior Cup, which they lifted after a 1-0 win over Wolves in the Final. AP

Directions

From the M42 Junction 4, take the exit signposted Birmingham and follow the A34 Stratford Road for four miles. At the large traffic-lighted roundabout (Robin Hood pub), take the second exit into Robin Hood Lane (dual carriageway). After half a mile, you come to a roundabout. Take the third exit (right) into Highfield Road. After a quarter of a mile, take the second left into Sherwood Road. The ground is 200 yards on the right.
By train: The Moorlands is a half mile from Hall Green train station. Go down Stratford Road, bear left into Highfield Road and then turn right into Sherwood Road.

The Moorlands is in the Hall Green area of Birmingham. This is one of the city's smarter suburbs, a circumstance that has played its part in shaping the ground. The Moorlands' most distinctive features are a fine old stand behind one goal and eight tiny floodlight pylons. Both are the result of planning conditions imposed following protests from the well-heeled neighbours. The stand used to be on the halfway line, but the pitch was turned around so that the lights wouldn't shine into adjacent houses. As a consequence, one goal-end terrace is now a grassed over bank in the car park, while another has been demolished. To compensate, the club built a neat, modern cover behind the re-sited far goal, but the two undeveloped sides of the ground have a strangely naked feel. The lights, meanwhile, have to be cranked up by hand before a game. Even then they are slender enough to sway in any but the mildest breeze. Hall Green station is within walking distance and, for the motorist, nearby Stratford Road leads directly to the M42 with adequate street and on-site parking. However, allow plenty of time as Birmingham's traffic isn't getting any better. SF

The Moorlands

The Moors

Nuneaton Borough

Address: Manor Park, Beaumont Road, Nuneaton, Warwickshire, CV11 5HD

Tel: 02476 385 738

Website: www.nbafc.net

Email: office@nuneatonboro.fsnet.co.uk

Officials: Chairman: Roger Stanford
Secretary: Paul Lewis
Manager: Roger Ashby

Manor Park

Directions

From M6, Coventry and south: From the M6 J3, take the A444 for Nuneaton until a roundabout. Take the second exit (A444 Nuneaton). Go straight ahead at the next roundabout (George Eliot Hospital entrance) until another roundabout next to a school. Branch left here onto College Street and down to traffic lights. On the uphill climb, move into the right hand lane and turn right into Greenmoor Road. At the end of Greenmoor Road, turn right into Croft Road, go over the canal bridge and left into Beaumont Road. The ground is on the left.

From A5, Hinckley and north: Enter the town on the A444, passing Liberty's nightclub on the right. At the Liberty's traffic island, turn left and follow the road until the next roundabout. Go straight ahead, passing Sainsbury's on the left. At the next roundabout, go straight ahead. At the crossroads, turn left into Queens Road. At the end of Queens Road, take the second exit at the mini-roundabout into Beaumont Road.

By train: Exit the station and turn right onto the A47. Carry on along this road, past the fire station. Bear right into Corporation Street until an area called Abbey Green (still on A47). Turn left into Manor Court Road. At the end of this road is the Cock & Bear pub, with the ground directly behind.

Manor Park is a well presented stadium which serves well for a team chasing a return to the Conference. The ground features three covered areas, one of which is home to a small collection of seats, with the rest of the ground standing. Limited parking space is available on the stadium grounds, as are a club shop, food kiosks and, of course, the essential social club which is open for a pre- or post-match drink. Manor Park is located on Manor Road near the banks of the canal and can be easily found by following the A444 into Nuneaton and then following road signs to Manor Park. RC

Review

The start of the 2003/04 season not only saw Borough return to the Dr Martens Premier Division but also saw them lose a host of players in the process including free scoring striker, Mark Quayle. However, hopes of a quick return to the Conference were furthered by Borough's impressive start which saw them unbeaten in their opening eleven games.

However, Borough's championship hopes took a major dent as the season moved into October, with four defeats in eight games. The lack of Quayle's killer instinct up front showed as Borough's usually solid centre back pairing of Neil Moore and Terry Angus faced a torrid time from the likes of Moor Green and Dover Athletic.

Inconsistency proved to be Nuneaton's downfall, and the New Year was welcomed in by more indifferent form. Despite numerous excellent performances, a lack of a sustained run of form and at times a lack of creativity on the attack saw Nuneaton rarely trouble top spot in 2004. Another poor run was ended in emphatic style as the Manor Park faithful saw Gez Murphy and Gary Fitzpatrick rediscover the goal scoring touch and net five goals between them in their next two games, 2-1 and 5-0 wins over Bath City and Grantham Town respectively. This was followed by an unbeaten spell in March, including an inspiring 4-3 victory over fellow promotion hopefuls Weymouth in which a Stuart Whittaker brace and strikes from Murphy and Fitzpatrick saw Borough's slender title aspirations kept alive.

However, three defeats on the bounce saw these hopes disappear in April. A typically inconsistent end to the season, with two wins, a draw and a defeat, saw Nuneaton ultimately forced to settle for fourth spot.

While the title hopes died too early for many Borough fans, a respectable fourth place sees Nuneaton playing their football in the Conference North this season. An impressive season from the likes of fans' player of the year, Neil Moore, and Gary Fitzpatrick will go a long way to instilling confidence that another eventful and ultimately successful season lies ahead. RC

Boro

Redditch United

Address: The Valley Stadium, Bromsgrove Road, Redditch, Worcestershire, B97 4RN

Tel: 0151 510 6000

Website: www.redditchunited.com

Email: info@redditchunited.com

Officials: Chairman: Pat Cremin
Secretary: Kenneth Rae
Player-Manager: Rod Brown

The Valley Stadium

Directions

From the town centre ring road take Access 7 and follow the road round to the left and turn right into Church Road. Then turn right and go straight on through the traffic lights. The ground entrance is 400 yards on the right on the brow of the hill (look for the Hill View Surgery at the top of the drive of the club).
From Bromsgrove M5 & M42: Take the Bromsgrove Highway (dual carriageway) towards Redditch. Take the first exit off and go round the roundabout, take the third exit which goes across the dual carriageway over a bridge. Go round the bend and turn right into Birchfield Road (by a garage), go past the Foxlydiate Hotel (on your right). Proceed along this road and take the first left into Bromsgrove Road (there is a road sign on the right at this junction). Go down Bromsgrove Road for one and a half miles, past the Queen's Head pub on your right. Turn left into the drive at the side of Hill View Surgery and continue down the drive to the ground's entrance.
By train: Nearest station is Redditch. Turn right out of the station and go up the hill to the lights. The ground is 100 yards on the right hand side on the brow of the hill.

The ground entrance is a joint entrance with Hill View Medical Centre - so look out for both as the signposts can be easily missed. The main stand takes up half of one side of the pitch. It contains seating at the front, with executive boxes at one end. The other side of the ground has covered terracing running almost the full length of the pitch, with seats donated from Aston Villa. The snack bar and club kitchen are at the side of the main stand. This is a new addition to the ground and was put in at the same time as the new floodlights. There is ample parking down the steep hill drive way to the club, as well as in the grounds of the club itself.
www.redditchunited.com

Review

Redditch United walked away with the Dr Martens Western Division Championship losing just six games and scoring 45 more goals than they let in. The opening day of the season showed to the league that they were going to take some beating as they defeated Ilkeston Town, who were relegated the previous season from the Dr Martens Premier Division, 6-0. 37 year-old Martin Myers showed age wasn't a concern scoring a hat-trick in the second half with Richard Leadbeater, Lee Ross and Jimmy Quiggan also getting on the score sheet.
No quarter was shown to struggling Atherstone in the next game as Redditch stuck in five without reply (although this result was later regarded as void after Atherstone's departure from the league).
A 14 game unbeaten run from October to January put United firmly in the driving seat and, by the time they suffered defeat at home to second placed Gloucester on the final day of the season, they had already sewn up the championship that they eventually won by five points.
This meant they played the champions of the Eastern Division in the first of two games to see which club went into the Conference Alliance. Kings Lynn had home advantage in the Play-Off game but it wasn't enough to spur them on to victory as Redditch won by a single goal scored by Richard Burgess on 55 minutes in front of a healthy crowd of 2,014.
Redditch then played away for the final Play-Off game against Merthyr Tydfil who finished 14th in the Dr Martens Premier Division, just one point away from automatic promotion. The disappointment must still have been affecting the team and Redditch were run away winners thanks to two goals by top scorer Richard Leadbeater and a goal by Mark Shepherd in-between, giving them a 3-0 victory and a place in the Conference North. AP

The Reds

Runcorn FC Halton

Address: The Halton Stadium, Lowerhouse Lane, Widnes, Cheshire, WA8 7DZ

Tel: 0151 510 6000

Website: www.runcornfchalton.co.uk

Officials: Chairman: Dr David Robertson
Secretary: Chris Henshall
Player-Manager: Chris Lightfoot

The Halton Stadium

Directions

From the North: Take the M6 to Junction 21A, joining M62 Junction 10 towards Liverpool. Leave the motorway at Junction 7 and follow signs towards Widnes. Continue through the first set of traffic lights (near Focus and B&Q), then get in the right hand lane and go through the second set of lights following signs for Liverpool. Continue at the third set of lights, then at the roundabout (near MacDonald's) go straight ahead, then straight ahead again at the third roundabout. The ground is on this road.

From the South: M6 Junction 20, joining M56 Junction 9 towards Chester. Leave the motorway at Junction 12 and follow signs to Widnes. After going over Runcorn Bridge, take the second exit and then the third right off the roundabout. At the second roundabout (near MacDonald's), take the first exit, then go straight ahead at the third roundabout. The stadium is on this road.

By train/bus: From Runcorn East or Runcorn stations, catch any number bus towards Widnes or Liverpool. Alight at Widnes Town Hall, and the stadium is a five minute walk from here. From Widnes station, come out of the main exit and continue up to the main road. Follow this road towards the town centre (past the Crown pub) and the ground is a 15 minute walk.

Halton Stadium (which is also the home of the Widnes Vikings Rugby League team) offers Runcorn a ground where they can progress higher than the Conference North if needs be. Once in Widnes, the ground should be easy to find, as there are signposts; there is also plenty of parking. It is not as nice as the old Canal Street ground which they left just a few years ago but it does the job it has to. AP

Review

Finishing 13th in the Unibond Premier Division for the second season running was, for once, lucky for Runcorn FC Halton as they secured the final automatic place for the Conference North. They also saw luck come their way on the final day of the season because, despite losing 1-0 to Altrincham, they stayed ahead of Ashton by two points thanks to Harrogate who beat Ashton 4-3 at Hurst Cross with a 90th minute winner by James Turley.

Consistency was a problem for Runcorn throughout the season as decent wins on the road against Southport, Marine and Burscough were sandwiched in between disappointing defeats like the 6-0 reverse against Vauxhall in early October.

However, Runcorn had a strong end to the season and finished with a plus goal difference of four after a 3-0 win against Stalybridge Celtic, a 4-1 win over Harrogate Town and a 5-3 success against Wakefield & Emley.

The Linnets narrowly missed out on a place in the First Round of the FA Cup after losing at the Halton Stadium in the Fourth Qualifying Round to a single goal against Bradford Park Avenue who then went on to play Bristol City. Runcorn also fell short of reaching a regional final when they crashed out in the Semi-Final of the Liverpool Senior Cup to the under-19 side of Liverpool, 3-1. Limited success was found in the FA Trophy after they were beaten by Altrincham in Round Three. AP

The Linnets

Southport

Address: Haig Avenue, Southport, Merseyside PR8 6JZ

Tel: 01704 533422

Website: www.southportfc.net

Email: info@southportfc.net

Officials: Chairman: Charles Clapham
Secretary: Ken Hilton
Player-Manager: Liam Watson

Haig Avenue

Directions

From the South: Take the M6 and exit at Junction 26 for the M58. Follow the M58 until Junction 3, and take the A570 past Skelmersdale. Stay on the A570 past Ormskirk, and this will take you into the Kew district of Southport. At the roundabout take the second exit, Scarisbrick New Road. The ground is just past the college on the right (Haig Avenue).

From the North: Exit the M6 at Junction 28, signposted Chorley. Then take the B5248, which runs onto the A59/A565. On reaching Southport, take Preston New Road at the roundabout. Follow this until a set of traffic lights. Go straight across into Cambridge Road. Continue into Southport town centre, proceeding down Chapel Street (one way). Continue straight on until you reach a T-junction (MacDonald's is on the right). Turn left into Eastbank Street and go over a roundabout into Scarisbrick New Road. Turn left into Haig Avenue, and the ground is on your right.

From the East: Take the M62, then the M60. Then join the M61 northbound and exit at Junction 8 signposted Chorley, then as above.

By train: Southport station is one and a half miles from the ground; Meols Cop is the nearest station and is half a mile from the ground. Exit the latter station and turn into Norwood Road. Carry on along this road and then turn right into Haig Avenue. The ground is halfway along this road.

Haig Avenue is on the outskirts of Southport. It has a main seating stand which overlooks the pitch from the dugout side but, for away fans, it is a bit less accommodating as the away stand is uncovered terracing behind one of the goals. At the opposite end, however, the Southport fans that choose not to sit can watch from the covered Jack Carr stand. Parking is not much of a problem. SL

Review

After being relegated from the Football Conference in the previous season after a bitterly disappointing campaign, Southport entered the Unibond Premiership as one of the favourites to lift the title. However, ambitions didn't pan out, despite winning the August award for team of the month. They eventually finished in sixth position, 25 points behind champions Hucknall Town.

In their first month of Unibond football they went unbeaten in four matches, keeping a clean sheet in every match which included a 3-0 win over near neighbours Burscough who had won the FA Trophy the previous season. However, September showed the Sandgrounders that life in a lower division wouldn't be all plain sailing, with successive defeats against Stalybridge Celtic, Hucknall Town and another neighbour in Runcorn FC Halton. Later in the month Worksop Town and Ashton United also picked up three points each from the former Conference club.

Southport didn't go far in the FA Trophy, losing in the Second Round at Altrincham thanks to a single Peter Band goal for the home side. Southport didn't have much luck in the FA Cup either, crashing out in the Second Qualifying Round to Vauxhall Motors 3-1. Thankfully though their league season picked up and a run of eleven matches without defeat, which included nine victories, between February and April lifted them well away from the lower reaches of the table. A place in the Conference North was the reward for Southport's up-and-down season but, in truth, it was a return to the main Nationwide Conference that was the goal, but it is one that will have to wait at least another season. AP

Sandgrounders

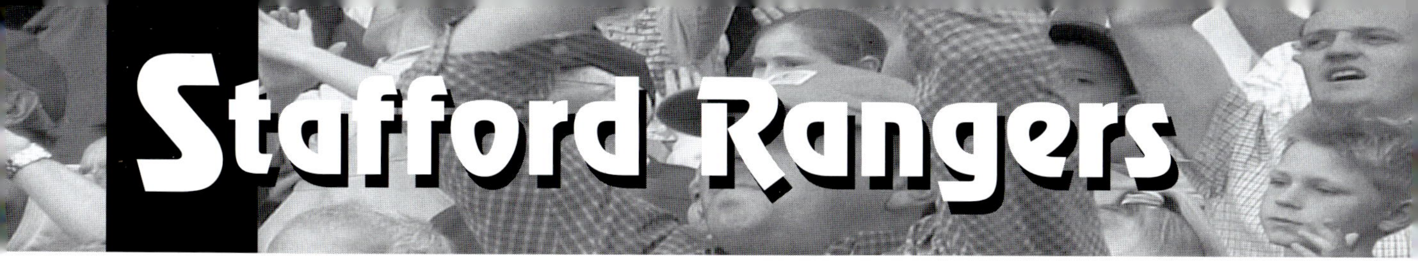

Stafford Rangers

Address: Marston Road, Stafford, Staffordshire, ST16 3BX

Tel: 01785 602430

Website: www.staffordrangers.co.uk

Email: srfcmarstonroad@tiscali.co.uk

Officials: Chairman: Cliff Went
Secretary: Michael Hughes
Manager: Phil Robinson

Marston Road

Review

Rangers enjoyed another successful season in the Dr Martens Premier Division, finishing in third place behind champions, Crawley Town, and Weymouth. This third place followed the runners-up spot the previous season. They also reached the final of the Staffordshire Senior Cup for the second consecutive season. They failed to retain the Cup at Stoke City's Britannia Stadium, losing to Kidsgrove Athletic by the only goal in extra-time.

Manager, Phil Robinson, is insistent on high fitness levels and his policy of encouraging local talent is also a major factor in Rangers' recent successes. This was evident throughout the season and in particular in the FA Trophy Third Round at Scarborough when they shocked many non-league followers by beating the Seadogs away from home, just days before they took on mighty Chelsea in the FA Cup. Unfortunately Rangers fell at the next hurdle losing at home to eventual finalists, Canvey Island.

The third place was sufficient to ensure that Rangers were comfortably into the newly formed Conference One North. They have enjoyed many of their past successes whilst playing in the north and will be meeting many old rivals such as Altrincham, Runcorn, Barrow and Bradford. This league promises to be very competitive.

Ken Hunt - Programme Editor, Stafford Rangers FC

Directions

From the North West: Head for the M6 Junction 14. Take the first exit off the roundabout (for Uttoxeter A518 & A34). At the next roundabout (about half a mile), go over, still heading towards Uttoxeter and RAF Stafford. Take the third exit on the right (the first two are entrances into a housing estate). Follow the road (Common Road) about a mile, around to the left at the bottom of the railway bridge. The ground is on the right.

From the East and North East: From Uttoxeter, head for Stafford on the A518. Travel through Weston, past the Agricultural Showground, and down towards Stafford. Go past Staffordshire Police Depot and turn right at the University roundabout (third exit). Follow this road (Beaconside) for just over a mile and turn left at the second set of traffic lights into Sandon Road. Follow this for about half a mile, then take a right turn at the traffic lights towards Astonfields Industrial Estate (just before the Shell garage). The ground is 200 yards on the left.

From the South: Come off at Junction 14 of the M6 and then follow the directions as if from the North West, taking the second non-motorway exit off the roundabout.

By train: The station is on the main line from London to Manchester but it is a good half-hour walk, so probably a taxi ride.

Marston Road is on the northern fringes of the town. There is adequate parking around the estate but not much at the ground itself or on adjacent terraced streets. This is a big and solid ex-Conference venue, with over 400 seats and plenty of covered terracing. About the only major change in the last 30 years has been the addition of a massive social club extension on top of what used to be an open shale bank behind one goal. This drinking-den alone makes the ground worth a visit. SF

Rangers

Stalybridge Celtic

Address: Bower Fold, Mottram Road, Stalybridge, Cheshire

Tel: 0161 338 2828

Website: www.stalybridgeceltic.com

Email: webmaster@stalybridgeceltic.co.uk

Officials: Chairman: Peter Dennerly
Secretary: John Hall
Manager: Dave Miller

Bower Fold

Directions

From Junction 4 of the M67 take the A57 to Mottram-in-Longendale. At the lights, turn left onto Stalybridge Road. At the mini-roundabout, take the first exit onto Roe Cross Road. Continue up this road, passing the Roe Cross Inn on the right, and then passing through Mottram Cutting (the road is now called Mottram Road). The ground is past the cutting on the left-hand side.

By train/bus: Stalybridge station is on the main Trans-Pennine line between Manchester and Leeds/York. Outside the station is a bus stop and, a little further down the road, on the right, there is one of the town's bus stations. From either point, take the 217, 236 or 237 buses; all three go past Bower Fold, with a bus stop opposite. Journey time is less than 15 minutes.

If energetic, turn right out of the station, under the railway bridge and past a number of shops and pubs, including the White House Inn, opposite the bus station. Continue along this road (Market Street) until Melbourne Street. Turn right here and cross the bridge into the town centre. Go right to the end of Melbourne Street, and turn left at the top by the Weatherspoons pub into Grosvner Street. Turn right, and cross Acres Lane at the crossing to the Pineapple. Turn left and walk up Acres Lane to the lights at the end. Turn right onto Mottram Road. After ten minutes, Bower Fold is on the right.

Bower Fold is another of the Conference North grounds that is of a high standard and will allow Stalybridge Celtic to progress into the higher leagues should the situation arise. With a good main stand, which also holds the dug-outs and changing rooms, it offers a decent view of the match. The clubhouse is nothing special but the programme has a good editor and is always a fine read while you wait for the match to begin. AP

Review

Last season will be best forgotten by all at Stalybridge. They failed to live up to the early season expectations as promotion contenders as their season faded badly, just making it into the Conference North for this season. A lack of consistency in team selection and the ability to self destruct at any given point in a match isn't really a recipe for success. No surprise then to know that they stumbled over the finish line, finishing tenth.

They qualified for the First Round proper of the FA Cup by overcoming Guisborough Town, Gedling and Ossett Town but were knocked out by Barnet 2-0 after a replay. They also reached the Fifth Round of the FA Trophy but Canvey Island put an end to their cup exploits after they lost 4-0.

The season couldn't have finished quick enough for the men at Bower Fold. Their inconsistency is underlined if you look back over the last 15 games of the season. They managed to win seven, lose six and draw two. A mixed bag, I think you'll agree.

On my many previous visits to Bower Fold I have been 'privileged' to watch the team attack their opponents and there has always been a little spark of magic from someone, a 'cutting edge', if you like. Last season, that was lacking, with only a handful of good wins under their belt. For the fans of this special footballing town, that is simply not good enough. The supporters expect more. Hopefully this season they can wipe the slate clean and start all over again to launch an attack on gaining promotion to the Conference proper. MJ

Celtic

Vauxhall Motors

Address: Rivacre Park Stadium, Rivacre Road, Hooton, Ellesmere Port, South Wirrall, CH66 1NJ

Tel: 0151 328 1114

Website: www.vauxhallfc.co.uk

Officials: Chairman: Alan Bartlam

Secretary: Carole Paisley

Manager: Owen Brown

Rivacre Park Stadium

Review

Vauxhall Motors were entering their third year in the Unibond Premier, and had enjoyed second and third place finishes in their previous seasons. They commenced the season by beating Bradford P.A. 6-2 and Blyth Spartans 6-3, but then succumbed to defeats at Marine and Droylsden. Manager Alvin MacDonald's departure to Conference side Northwich at the end of September didn't bode well for the Motormen (although he left the club a parting gift of two successive league wins). New boss, Owen Brown, started his reign with a 6-0 win over Runcorn in early October. But a poor run of form followed, as the Motors went on a 14 game winless streak. This run included some excessive defeats: 6-2 to Bradford P.A, 5-1 to Alfreton and 5-0 at home to Radcliffe Borough. Brown clearly had his work cut out, and the board may have had second thoughts: one 6-0 triumph does not make up for 14 games without a win.

After 24 games, Vauxhall were just one place and one point above the relegation zone. A 3-2 win over Southport on 31st January - the side's first win since 7th October - kept them just above Bradford in 20th. Brown must have heard the board grinding the axe, but they kept faith in him, maybe seeing something in him that the fans didn't. The fans of the club weren't impressed at this stage but then came a superb run of results that shocked the division. Although they lost twice in February (one of those an expected defeat to champions-elect, Hucknall), they won twice and that in itself gave hope to the Motormen. A win at high-flying Barrow and a comprehensive victory over title challengers, Harrogate Town (3-0), gave momentum to Vauxhall's turnaround.

The club's incredible run of form led them to ninth in the table and a Conference North place; not bad for a side that were just five points off the bottom spot at the beginning of February. In their last 20 games, they won twelve, drew five and lost three. They were aided by having the two top scorers in the division in Terry Fearns (35 league goals) and Peter Cumiskey (22 goals). In fact, Fearns may have been disappointed as his immense tally was his lowest in his three seasons at the club! MP

Directions

From the Wallasey Tunnel and the motorway network, take the M53 to Junction 5. Exit the roundabout towards Chester and North Wales. At the first set of traffic lights, turn left into Hooton Green. Follow the road until you reach a T-junction. Turn left. At the next T-junction turn right. Vauxhall Motors Sports & Social Club is on your right.

From the Birkenhead Tunnel, follow the signs for North Wales and Chester A41. At the first roundabout take the second exit (still A41) and follow the road to the next roundabout. At this roundabout, take the second exit, New Ferry Bypass (A41). At the end of the bypass take the second exit (still the A41) and follow the road. At the sixth set of traffic lights, with Appliances Express on the corner, take the road to the left. Follow the road past the Hooton Arms pub. Rivacre Road is on the left. Turn up here, over the M53, and the ground is on your left.

By train: The nearest station is Hooton on the Merseyrail Wirral Line, with services running out of Chester and Liverpool. It is a long walk to the ground from the station so probably best to take a taxi.

By bus: From Birkenhead or Chester, catch the number 1 and alight at Hooton Green. Alternatively, catch any bus that goes to Mill Park Estate and get off at Eastham Library. From Heswall, go through Eastham Village. Unfortunately, all of these options leave you with a fair distance to walk.

Rivacre Park could be something special with new terracing behind one of the goals and a large stand to provide a good number of seats. I doubt they could progress higher than the Conference North although the club shop, food and the bar are all plus points for the ground. AP

Motormen

Worcester City

Address: St George's Lane, Worcester, WR1 1QT

Tel: 0190 523003

Website: www.worcestercityfc.org.uk

Officials: Chairman: Dave Boddy
Secretary: Graham Hill
Manager: John Barton

St George's Lane

Review

Once again, Worcester were dark horses for the Dr Martens Premier Division title in 2003/04 and, once again (as they have done several times in recent years), they fell away after a promising start.

They won five of their opening seven games, with their only reverse coming away at eventual champions Crawley on 30th August. This impressive form saw Worcester sitting pretty at the top of the table. However, they then won only one of their next seven league games (albeit a 7-0 win at home to Bath), and were also knocked out of the FA Cup at the hands of Nuneaton.

League form continued to be a problem and, despite rediscovering the winning formula against Chippenham, they soon fell back into a rut as Newport stuck five past them in the next game. Losses were all too frequent and it soon became apparent that City would not be challenging pacesetters Crawley and Weymouth in the title race.

A quick departure from the FA Trophy didn't aid City's cause, although a nine game unbeaten league run from January to March placed a more respectable slant on Worcester's season as they pushed up the table as high as third during the Easter period. However, a typically indifferent run-in saw Worcester win only one of their final six games, with a 4-3 defeat at Grantham on the final day condemning them to fifth place. Whilst this was a more than respectable final position, Worcester were never really challenging for honours at the top (finishing 21 points behind champions Crawley) a fact that they will no doubt like to rectify in their first season in the Conference North. JB

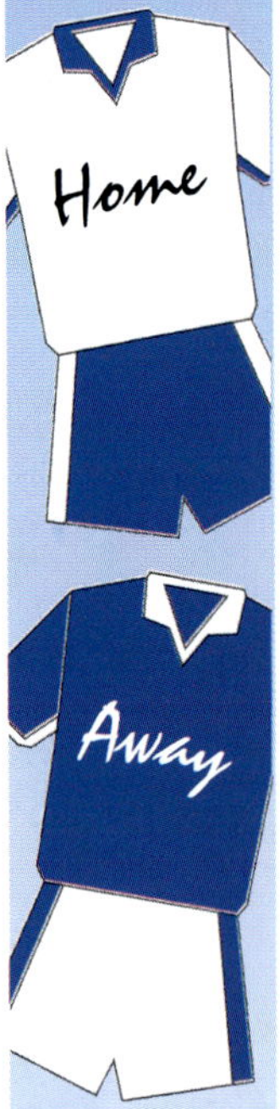

Directions

Take the M40 to its end. Then take the M42 west, towards the M5, and the M5 southbound. Leave the M5 at Junction 6 (Worcester North) and follow the A449 to Worcester to a roundabout. At the roundabout follow A449 signs to Worcester (not Kidderminster). Remain on the A449 into Worcester. Pass through traffic lights at the park after one and a half miles. After 200 metres you pass the Swan pub on the left. Turn left slightly further on, and follow this road to the ground.

By train: Worcester has two stations, Foregate Street and Shrub Hill. There are several routes to Worcester but direct trains leave from Paddington and call at both stations.

The club currently have plans to move to a new purpose-built stadium elsewhere in the city and, should this come to fruition, it would certainly benefit motorists, as there is no associated public car park attached to the St George's Lane site. Furthermore, street parking is extremely limited as, apart from two, the rest of the side streets in the vicinity come complete with double yellow lines.

Inside, the large wooden edifice that is the Main Stand dominates one side. To the left and right are moderate stretches of uncovered terracing, while opposite the Main Stand there is both uncovered and covered terracing.

The club attracts very good gates but the cavernous nature of the ground tends to swallow up the spectators and does not lend itself to the creation of a great atmosphere. Apart from the 'big games', segregation of supporters is not an issue. SG

The City

Worksop Town

Address: Babbage Way, off Sandy Lane, Worksop, Nottinghamshire, S80 1UJ

Tel: 01909 501911

Website: www.worksoptownfc.co.uk

Email: info@worksoptownfc.co.uk

Officials: Chairman: Howard Raymond

Secretary: Keith Ilett

Manager: Ronnie Glavin

Sandy Lane

Review

Newly installed manager, Steve Ludlam, was given the daunting task of leading Worksop Town to the Nationwide Conference in his very first full season in Worksop's hot seat. Having purchased seven experienced players in the close season, the fans were optimistic that 2003/04 could be Worksop's season. However, the team under-achieved and finished the season in seventh place which, although this position gave them Conference North football in the coming season, was not good enough for the Board, who accepted Ludlam's resignation following a disappointing 3-2 defeat at the hands of Frickley Athletic in the Sheffield Senior Cup Final at Hillsborough. The Board then acted immediately in replacing Ludlam with the experienced Ronnie Glavin, formerly of Barnsley and Wakefield & Emley. He now faces a difficult season in consolidating Worksop Town's position in the new set-up, as well as working under financial constraints.

The season started brightly enough after pre-season games had seen the Tigers record seven wins, two draws and just one defeat. This form continued in the league as the team embarked on an impressive twelve match unbeaten run which came to an abrupt halt at the hands of Farsley Celtic in the FA Cup Third Qualifying Round. They were now up to fourth place and were challenging for honours with games in hand over the Premier league's leading contenders.

As is so often the case during the winter months, Worksop were hit by a succession of injuries to key players and their form dipped as a result. Linden Whitehead, who had skippered the side superbly for the past eight seasons, handed the captain's arm-band to Mark Haran as Worksop battled to stay with the leading pack.

Having fallen to eleventh place in the league, Gary Townsend aided the Tigers' fortunes with the only goal against high-flying Droylsden to put Worksop into the next round of the FA Trophy against Guisley who they defeated 2-0. The run ended when Chris Kinnear's Conference side Margate won 2-0, albeit against the run of play. Despite attaining their place in the new Conference North after finishing in seventh place, Worksop's form dipped as the season drew to a close with just two wins coming in their final nine league games. Consolidation must be the aim of new manager Glavin and no doubt the fans will wish him well in his quest. MT

Directions

From M1 North: Take Junction 31, A57 Worksop. After seven miles carry on to the bypass. At the third roundabout turn left (Sandy Lane Estate). The ground is one mile on the left.

From A1 North: Go to the Blyth roundabout and follow Worksop signs into Blyth (A57). Turn right at the fourth set of lights, passing the hospital. Turn left under the bridge, then take an immediate right. The ground is on the right.

By train: Worksop station is half a mile from the ground. Exit into Clarence Road and then turn into Gateford Road. Head south east down Gateford Road and turn right into Sandy Lane. Babbage Way is halfway down Sandy Lane on the right.

Sandy Lane is a tight compact little venue that lends itself well to a good atmosphere for the bigger matches. The terracing behind the goals is good and the food available by the main entrance is of a high standard. The bar is quite small so can become cramped if the attendance is big but the atmosphere more than makes up for this. AP

The Tigers

Southern Premier

Club Pages

Aylesbury United

Address: The Stadium, Buckingham Road, Aylesbury, Bucks, HP20 2AQ

Tel: 01296 436350

Website: www.aylesburyunited.co.uk

Officials: Managing Director: Graham Reed
Secretary: Peter Ash
Manager: Paul Curtis

Buckingham Road

Review

An eventful and ultimately disastrous season for the Ducks saw them finally finish ten points adrift at the bottom of the Ryman Premier Division, with a mere five league wins to their name. The season saw three managers plus two caretaker managers take charge of the club.

It all began with the surprise appointment of the inexperienced Chris Boothe as manager. Despite the signings of high profile players like Karl Ready and Danny Grieves, an opening day victory over Billericay proved to be a false dawn, as the below par Ready and Grieves departed with Boothe only winning one more game while in charge.

He was dismissed after only 13 games, with the club already in the bottom four. Boothe was swiftly replaced by Bedford boss Kevin Wilson - a decision which, while exciting at the time, was to prove costly with hindsight. United hit their best form of the season during Wilson's honeymoon period, going six games unbeaten. However, despite some success in the FA Trophy, Wilson's 16 match reign was again disappointing, with Aylesbury winning just three league games and dropping further into relegation trouble. When Wilson resigned in late December, the club hit rock bottom as accusations and mud-slinging in all directions saw the Ducks' loyal fans baffled and angry.

Even worse was to come as most of the first team squad effectively went on strike following a pay dispute, with caretaker managers Pete Remnant and Simon Lacey forced to play an inexperienced reserve line-up over the festive period.

The final chapter of the season saw former Northampton youth coach Paul Curtis take over the hotseat with a nominal budget and a very young inherited team. Despite the commitment of player of the year Matt Hayward and the brilliance of goalkeepers Kevin Davies and Jack Rashid, Aylesbury finished the season with a run of 25 matches without a win and having failed to score a single home league goal under Curtis.

Leon O'Sullivan - 21CD Programme Editor

Directions

From the M1: Exit at J15a and take the A43 towards Towcester. From there, follow all signs to Buckingham on the A413 and stay on this road until you reach Aylesbury. Once in Aylesbury, go straight over the first roundabout and the ground is the next turning on the left, about 100 yards on.

From the M40: Exit at J9 then take the A41 through Bicester to Aylesbury. Go straight over the first four roundabouts, following signs for the A413 to Buckingham. At the fifth roundabout (by the Shell garage), take the left exit. Go left at the next roundabout and the ground is 100 yards on the right.

From the M25: Exit at J20 and take the A41 for Aylesbury. As you enter Aylesbury, go over the first two roundabouts. At the two mini-roundabouts, go over the first and turn right at the second. Continue over the bridge and the next roundabout, following signs for A413/Buckingham. Go right at the next roundabout and the ground is 100 yards on the right.

By train: Aylesbury is well served from Marylebone via both Amersham and High Wycombe. The walk from the station takes approximately half an hour, so probably best to take a taxi.

The Buckingham Road stadium, approaching its 20th year, boasts one of the best pitches in non-league football and has an impressive main stand, which runs along most of one side. Opposite is the covered Chicken Run terrace, where the vocal home support is situated. One of the end terraces is also covered, although in the rare event of segregation, away supporters are placed at the uncovered Country End. The clubhouse is home to the popular Corner Bar and a large function room. The club can be found easily by car just off the ring road, but it's a long walk from the railway station.

Leon Sullivan - 21CD Programme Editor

The Ducks

Banbury United

Address: The Spencer Stadium, Stadium Approach, Banbury, Oxfordshire, OX16 8TA

Tel: 01295 263354

Website: www.banburyunited.co.uk

Email: admin@banburyunited.co.uk

Officials: Chairman: Paul Saunders
Secretary: B.Worsley
Manager: Kevin Brock

The Spencer Stadium

Directions

Leave the M40 at J11 and head for Banbury. At the first roundabout turn left. At the next roundabout turn right. Carry on until a left turn for the station. Follow this and take the track on the right until you reach stadium.
By train: Take the main exit towards town. At the end of the forecourt, take the track on the left which doubles back towards the station, then as above.

Banbury moved to the Spencer Stadium in 1934. The original changing rooms were old railway coaches, but were removed in 1966 and new changing rooms, a clubhouse and floodlights were put in. A new stand was built in just seven weeks, in time for Banbury's promotion to the Dr Martens in 2001. Banbury are working towards an A grading. Recent work includes a new club shop, infill of the pitch fence and redecoration of the clubhouse. The pitch was plagued in 2000/01 with waterlogging, resulting in many matches being postponed and some matches being played knee deep in mud! A new drainage system was installed in 2001.
www.banburyunited.co.uk

Review

After consolidation within the Dr Martens Eastern during the previous two seasons, the club were expecting more of the same. They had an extra incentive this year, as a top seven finish would see them 'promoted' to the Southern League Premier. Even if the Puritans could match their 2002/03 finish of eighth, they would make the Play-Offs. Their opening to the campaign wasn't what they'd wanted: one goal and three defeats in the first four. An emphatic 3-0 win over Fisher Athletic was the tonic they needed as they embarked on a five game unbeaten run. A couple of defeats against top of the table sides were followed by a six-game unbeaten run. At this stage, they were sixth and on-course for promotion.
Whenever a side does go on an unbeaten run, they soon become the team to beat; opposition lie in wait to seize upon the slightest slip. This became true of Banbury as Eastleigh seized on a great number of slips to demolish them 6-1. This was the start of a dire run that saw one win in the next six, as both Eastleigh and Tonbridge completed the league double over Banbury. With Stamford, Burgess Hill and Bashley all aiming for the top seven and Play-Off places, the Puritans could afford no further slip-ups - they were down to ninth and needed results badly. Home wins over Hastings (1-0) and Bashley (1-0) gave the side a boost, and they leapfrogged Burgess Hill as they humbled them 4-1. Four wins and two draws in the next six still couldn't get them into the promotion places.
As they approached the final three games, they needed at least two wins. They entered their game at lowly Hastings on the back of a 12-game unbeaten run. Facing a demoralised side with little to play for, Banbury missed chances and lost 1-0. To finish seventh, the Puritans needed to win their last two and hope Stamford lost their last two. It went according to plan in the penultimate games as Stamford lost and Banbury beat Folkestone 4-3. However, it all went wrong on the final day: Stamford's win over Burgess meant that Banbury (who lost 2-1 to second-bottom Erith) were consigned to the Play-Off lottery. They faced eighth-placed Western Division side Sutton Coldfield in a home tie. The tie was goalless in normal time; Banbury went behind before equalising within minutes. With penalties looming, Wayne Blossom headed home to seal promotion. So the Southern League Premier beckons for Banbury, and they deserve their place after some memorable performances - not least their nail biting Play-Off triumph. MP

The Puritans

Bath City

Address: Twerton Park, Twerton, Bath, BA2 1DB

Tel: 01225 423087

Website: www.bathcityfc.com

Officials: Chairman: Steve Hall
Secretary: Quentin Edwards
Player-Manager: Gary Owers

Review

In truth 2003/04 was, yet again, another confusing season for the Romans. Once again the former Conference club failed to challenge for a return to the non-league's top flight and, once again, they could only muster a finish in the bottom half of the table. Regular top ten finishes in the late nineties must seem a world away as the new millennium has brought with it lacklustre final placings of 15th, 17th, 14th and 16th respectively.

Last season's 16th was even more of a disappointment as they missed out on an automatic place in the Conference South (with 13th being the cut-off point), and then blew their chance in the Play-Offs, losing 4-2 to Dorchester in their first game.

Wins were fairly hard to come by for much of the season and a run of eleven games without a win leading up to Christmas (which only included two draws) gives you a fair idea of the sort of season City had. Alan Pridham was shown the door in November, with Gary Owers filling the hot-seat.

Despite breaking the winless streak against Tiverton on Boxing Day, Bath fans didn't see a vast improvement in results, and it was the 21st February before they witnessed City's first win on the road as a Scott Partridge hat-trick gave them a 3-0 triumph at Moor Green. Indeed, had it not been for Partridge's fine form during the run-in, then it could have been an even sadder state of affairs for the Romans. His 17 goals in the final 16 games of the season really pulled Bath up by the boot-straps. City won their final four games (due in no small part to Partridge's eight goals, which included two hat-tricks), and this was enough to push Bath clear of the bottom four and into the Play-Offs.

City had even less cause for celebration in the cup competitions as they went out to lower level opposition in both the FA Cup (Thame) and the FA Trophy (Staines). JB

Directions

Take Junction 18 off the M4. Take the third exit off the roundabout and follow the A46 (ten miles) to Bath city centre. Go along Pulteney Road then turn right into Claverton Street and then follow A36 Lower Bristol Road (one and a half miles). Take a left under the railway bridge (signposted Bath City FC) into Twerton High Street and the ground is the second turning on the left.

Alternative Route: Take Junction 19 off the M4 onto M32. Take Junction 3 off M32 and follow signs for Bath (A4). Go through Keynesham (five miles) and Saltford (eight miles) and take the right hand exit off of the dual carriageway onto Lower Bristol Road (A36). Go for one mile right under the railway bridge (signs for Bath City FC) then as above.

For high vehicles (such as coaches), follow the alternative route until the roundabout at Newton St Low, before the dual carriageway, then take the second exit (signposted Combe Down) and follow this road for one mile then turn left (signs for Twerton) and the ground is three quarters of a mile on the right. This avoids a low bridge.

By train: Exit the station onto Dartmouth Avenue and then turn right into Lymore Avenue. Bear right into Shophouse Road and then left onto the High Street. Then follow the directions above. Just over a mile.

Twerton Park is in Twerton, about two and a half miles from the city centre, and whilst still having the feel of a 'real' football ground, it is apparently not as impressive as it once was, even from when Bristol Rovers shared here in the not too distant past, as the terraces don't extend as far back as they once did. However, they do present a match very well and create a big time atmosphere over the PA and with various presentations on match days. The catering is also more than adequate - the bar even serves a special Bath City beer on occasions. Bath still get pretty decent gates and the club is run in the main by a supporters' trust and you can tell that they have an impressive history. There is a car park just outside the stadium to make parking relatively easy. RM

The Romans

Bedford Town

Address: The New Eyrie, Meadow Lane, Cardington, Bedford, Bedfordshire, MK44 3SB

Tel: 01234 838448

Website: www.bedfordeagles.net

Officials: Chairman: David Howell
Secretary: Dave Swallow
Manager: Nicky Plantnauer

The New Eyrie

Review

A season which started with great promise ended in ultimate disappointment as the Eagles failed to make the newly revamped Conference. Back in August, hopes were high, as Kevin Wilson had overseen a surge up the table in the previous campaign. Indeed, it was an encouraging if slightly inconsistent beginning to the 2003/04 season, with Darren Lynch in excellent early form. However, results had already begun to trail off when Wilson surprisingly left for Aylesbury - apparently because ground improvements, which would enable Town to progress, were being affected by an argument with the local council about a roundabout. With some players leaving with him, it was no surprise when a nine match winless run surrounded his departure, and form became so patchy that the 5-2 success against Basingstoke was the sole victory in 18 games, as they slipped into mid-table. Nicky Plautener came in, and Spring saw a scoring streak for Drew Roberts leading to critical wins against St Albans and Braintree. Chris Dillon had made an excellent impression since switching from Hitchin as he scored twice in an impressive win over runners up Sutton, raising hopes of a late burst into the top 13. However, although getting some impressive wins in places, they never had the consistency to bridge the gap, and finished well short. That meant the Play-Offs were the Eagles' only hope. They had a good start as Hitchin were seen off 3-1 in the first game, and it looked good with the same scoreline at the interval against St Albans. However, City won 5-4, condemning their hosts to a continuation of Premier Division football - but this time at a lower level. GB

Directions

From A1: Heading north, take the left hand turn to Bedford (A603) at the Sandy roundabout. Go over a small bridge and, where the road bends to the left, take the right hand turn to Bedford (A603). Remain on this road for five miles and the ground is on the right.
From M1: Heading north, take junction 13 signposted to Bedford (A421). At the roundabout at the end of the slip road, take the Bedford turnoff. Stay on this road for seven miles until the second roundabout.
Take the third exit to Cambridge (A1) and Bedford (A603). At the roundabout, take the fourth exit to Sandy (A603). The ground is half a mile on the left.
By train: The ground is several miles from the station and you can either catch a cab from outside the station or a bus. To reach the bus station, cross the road outside the station and go down Woburn Road. At the junction at the end of Woburn Road turn right into Alexandra Road and then first left. At the end of this road, the bus station is on the right. The 171 and 172 bus goes from the station past the ground and leaves from bay six. Buses leave at 2:10pm or 2:40pm.

An ambitious club who have become increasingly frustrated at the Council's reluctance to allow redevelopment work on their ground. It is a sad fact but most in the town would rather go and watch the rugby team, while some residents haven't even heard of Bedford Town! The New Eyrie is situated on the by-pass, and is easily reachable by car, but otherwise the journey can be a chore, as the ground is situated a long way out of the town. As for the Eyrie itself, it is friendly and welcoming and covered on all four sides, with a mixture of seating and terracing. There is a small clubhouse, where you can get a well deserved pint after the trek from the town. It gets crowded on matchdays but is still worth a visit. CF

The Eagles

Chesham United

Address: Amy Lane, Chesham, Bucks, HP5 1NE
Tel: 01494 783 964
Website: www.cheshamunitedfc.co.uk
Email: website@cheshamunitedfc.co.uk
Officials: Chairman: Phil Morgan
Secretary: David Stanley
Manager: Steve Bateman

Directions

From the M25: From Junction 18, take the A404 to Amersham. Take the A416 signposted to Chesham. You will enter Chesham travelling down Amersham Hill. Take a sharp left at the roundabout at the foot of this hill into Chesham United's ground.
From the A41: Take the junction signposted to Chesham. Continue through Ashley Green and into Chesham. Follow signs to Amersham until you pass two petrol stations which are opposite each other. At the next roundabout take the third exit into Chesham United's ground.
By train: Chesham is part of the London Underground network and is on the Metropolitan Line. Walk out of the station and head towards the High Street. Turn left and follow signs towards Amersham until you pass two petrol stations which are opposite each other. At the next roundabout take the third exit into Chesham United's ground. The walk takes between five and ten minutes.

The Meadow is in a fairly central part of the attractive Buckinghamshire town, with the Chiltern Hills providing an impressive backdrop which can really be appreciated on a sunny day. It is very convenient for the town centre, as well as Underground station, which means it can be reached from the centre of London quite quickly. The main stand is linked to the clubhouse, and both offer good views, and there is an extensive amount of covered terracing also available. A programme shop is located by the turnstiles and is well worth a visit. GB

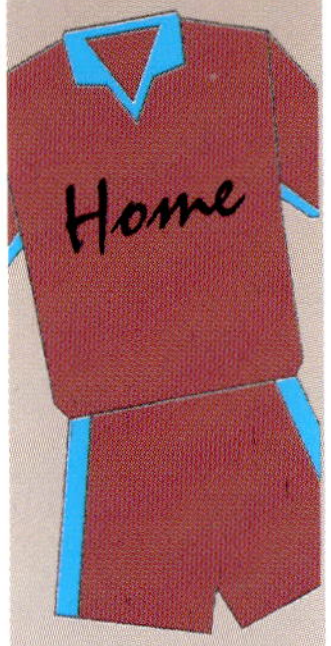

Review

The Generals had something of a rollercoaster ride on their journey to fourth place in the Ryman Division One North, as the popular former player Steve Bateman took charge after switching from Berkhamsted. Their first league game brought a 1-0 reverse at Uxbridge, and a torrid opening sequence brought just two wins from the first eleven - although the inconsistency was baffling, as one of these wins was an 8-2 victory over Wivenhoe and yet they were still among the strugglers in late September. There was solace to be found in the FA Cup as Chalfont St Peter, Yaxley and Abingdon Town were seen off, but the dreams were ended in a home replay by Weston-super-Mare, who went onto the Second Round. In contrast, Worthing knocked them out of the Trophy at the first hurdle. However, the Buckinghamshire side's league form was dramatically transformed by the return of John Lawford who formed an irresistible partnership with Gary Sippetts and, as November came and went, the results improved, at one stage recording eight wins from nine games, including victories at challenging Cheshunt and Leyton. The strong form continued into the new year. Defeats to fellow hopefuls Wingate, Dunstable, Arlesey and Wealdstone in the Spring threatened to blow them off course, but a very strong close to the season saw them collect 20 points from the last 24 on offer to assure promotion. They picked up the Berks and Bucks Senior Cup as well, crushing Bracknell Town 4-1 in the Final. GB

The Generals

Chippenham Town

Address: Hardenhuish Park, Bristol Road, Chippenham, Wiltshire, SN14 6LR

Tel: 01249 650400

Website: www.chippenhamtownfc.co.uk

Officials: Chairman: Malcolm Lyus
Secretary: Chris Blake
Manager: Steve White

Hardenhuish Park

Directions

Leave the M4 at J17 and take the A350 towards Chippenham and Poole. Follow signs for Bath and Trowbridge until you reach a roundabout. Here, turn left onto the A420 and follow signs for town centre/Calne A4. The ground is on this road on the left.

By train: On leaving the station, turn right. Pass a post office depot on the right and carry on walking to the bottom of the hill (Station Hill). Turn right, under the railway arch and, immediately after, enter the subway system by turning left and walking down the ramp. In the subway system you will see two exits on the right. Take the left exit, which comes out by the side of a tall office building. From here you will see a cinema which is located on Marshfield Road. Walk up the road to a small mini-roundabout. Go straight over. Hardenhuish Park is 150 metres on the right. Alternatively, taxis are generally available outside the station.

After more than half a century, Hardenhuish Park has undergone redevelopment work in recent years, a step in the right direction for a club with Conference ambitions. However, the club is looking into the feasibility of moving to a new ground. Until any move, the club are situated about a mile out of town. The ground is easily accessible, although parking is limited. Alternatively it is only a five to ten minute walk from the town centre. The ground itself is of an average standard, with seating available in the main stand (300 seats) or behind one goal. At the other end, there is terracing available for visiting supporters. The food is top notch, and with an average gate around the 800 mark, you can be sure of a vibrant atmosphere as well. CF

Review

Chippenham Town made a rather huge splash after they won promotion to the Dr Martens Premier Division in 2002, as they surprised a few people by finishing fifth in their first season, with the club seemingly moving in the right direction. However, 2003/04 saw the Bluebirds crash down to earth with a bump as they finished second from bottom in the table, thus missing out on a place in the revamped Conference in what was a highly disappointing season.

One win from their opening eleven games set the tone for the rest of the season as they also made swift exits from both the FA Cup and FA Trophy (against Gloucester and Basingstoke respectively). Five straight defeats soon after their FA Cup exit meant there was little for the fans to cheer going into the festive period. Indeed, Tommy Saunders quit the club in November, with Steve White coming in to replace him. Chippenham would not taste victory again until 10th January when they picked up a welcome, but surprising win, at Newport. Three more consecutive wins followed and it looked as though the Blubirds would make make a push for mid-table as they began to rediscover some of their form of the previous season. In fact, the Bluebirds only lost one of their final eight matches (which included a victory at high flying Weymouth). However, by this time the damage had been done and, despite their positive run-in and the fact that the battle at the bottom was very tight, they could not avoid finishing in the bottom four, a point behind Hednesford and two behind Dover and Chelmsford. JB

The Bluebirds

Cirencester Town

Address: Corinium Stadium, Kingshill Lane, Cirencester, Gloucestershire, GL7 1HS

Tel: 01285 654543

Website: www.cirentownfc.com

Email: info@cirecesterfc.com

Officials: Chairman: Steve Abbley
Secretary: Jim Saunders
Manager: Brian Hughes

Corinium Stadium

Directions

From A417 bypass (Cirencester Junction) join Burford Road roundabout and take the Stow exit. At the next set of traffic lights turn right into Hunters Lane. Turn right at the T-junction, and then take the first left into Kings Hill Lane. The ground is 500 yards down on the right hand side. By train: The nearest station is Kemble. The ground is approximately five miles from the station so it is advisable to get a taxi.

With its ten pitches and new facilities, the Corinium Stadium is an enviable Non-League football venue. Having gained planning permission for housing and offices at their former ground at Smiths Field, the club were able to fund the new stadium without borrowing. Overall, the club has invested over £2million in the Corinium Stadium - of which some £684,000 came in grant aid from the Football Foundation. The grant aid was available because of the club's work promoting football amongst young people in the local community. The Corinium Stadium offers a range of brand new facilities. The Barbican Suite, Corinium Sports Bar, Board Room and Gymnasium are all available for a variety of functions.

www.cirentownfc.com

Review

2003/04 was a highly successful season for Ciren as they comfortably clinched a spot in the Southern Premier Division with a third place finish in the Dr Martens Western. Although they never really challenged eventual champions Redditch at the top (eventually finishing eight points behind), last season must still be looked on by Cirencester fans as a roaring success, following their modest 13th the season before. Their accomplishment was undoubtedly based on their fine form at the Corinium Stadium, as Ciren's 13 home wins were more than any other team in the league. Despite this, things got off to a fairly ominous start as Ciren lost their opening four league games (their opening day win over Atherstone was chalked off after the Adders folded). However, the confidence gained from two FA Cup wins carried over into the league as Town then won their next seven games as they began to push themselves up the table.
On the other hand, this period also saw the end of both their cup campaigns as they crashed out of the Trophy after a 6-2 reverse against Redditch, and their bright start to the FA Cup was halted by eventual Premier Division champions Crawley in the Fourth Qualifying Round.
With their focus now on the league, Ciren continued their impressive form and, in fact, would not taste defeat again until 27th January - a run of 15 games stretching back 6th September. Small pockets of defeats, such as three in a row in late March and two at the end of the campaign, meant it was always going to be tough for Ciren to challenge at the top. However, they continued to pick up wins as they beat off the challenge of Halesowen, Rugby and Team Bath to take third place. JB

Dunstable Town

Address: Creasey Park, Brewers Hill Road, Dunstable, Bedfordshire, LU6 1BB

Tel: 01582 667 555

Website: www.dunstabletownfc.co.uk

Email: email@dunstabletownfc.co.uk

Officials: Chairman: Tony Potton
Secretary: Malcolm Aubrey
Joint Managers: Darren Croft & Paul Reeves

Creasey Park

Directions

From the South: When travelling north on the A5 go straight across the double roundabout in the centre of Dunstable. Turn left at the next roundabout into Brewers Hill Road.
From the North: When travelling south on the A5 go through the chalk cutting and over the first set of traffic lights. At the next roundabout turn right into Brewers Hill Road.
From the East: Turn right at the roundabout in the centre of Dunstable. Turn left at the next roundabout into Brewers Hill Road. When in Brewers Hill Road go straight on at the first mini-roundabout and the entrance to Creasey Park Drive is 50 yards on the right.
From the West: When coming into Dunstable go straight across the first roundabout you come to. Then turn left at the mini double roundabout (not the ones in the town centre) into Brewers Hill Road. Follow this road for about three quarters of a mile as it bears to the right. Turn left into Creasey Park Drive about 50 yard before the last mini-roundabout on the road.
By train: The nearest station is Luton on the London St Pancras/Bedford line. The bus station is right next to the train station and the ground is approximately a 15-20 minute bus journey.

Creasey Park is situated to the north part of Dunstable and the ground is close to the A5, with easy links to the M1. A friendly welcome awaits all travelling fans in the clubhouse with its subsidised bar. The buffet is basic but serves good food on matchdays along with the clubhouse. There is adequate room outside the ground to leave your car in a spacious car park. The ground has undergone some redevelopment recently with a new grand stand opening down one side and terracing around the rest of the ground (with one area behind the goal under cover) and now complements an excellent pitch. There are also plans to build a new club shop despite a restrictive financial budget as the club looks to evolve in the community and attract more than their average 100 plus gate. AP

Review

The Spartan South Midlands League title winners of 2002/03 took to their new Ryman League surroundings like a duck to water, as they maintained a steady top six berth throughout the season. Their settled side's progress was helped by the 27 goals of top scorer Grant Carney, who was ably assisted by Thomas Hayes and Jonathan Barnett, with many other players chipping in as well. They made a solid start to the campaign with an opening day win against Wingate and, although they fell at the first FA Cup hurdle against Hampton & Richmond, Town really took off in September by recording four straight wins. However, there was soon an early exit in the Trophy as they found themselves eliminated by Lewes in early October. They bounced back with a 2-2 draw at leaders Cheshunt in the league, as they continued to hold down a place in the top four. Important reverses to Wealdstone, Hemel and Boreham Wood threatened to halt their push, and inconsistency continued into the new year with defeats to Uxbridge and Great Wakering. Dunstable, though, were starting to make a name for themselves as Sutton and Grays were both eliminated from the Bryco Cup in quick succession and, though they relinquished their grasp on the Bedfordshire Senior Cup as Leighton Town beat them 1-0, another 2-2 draw with Cheshunt put new life into their challenge. They took an impressive eight points in crunch matches with Chesham, Hemel, Leyton and Wealdstone, whilst Hayes hit a scoring streak in March and his two goals against Harlow in the Bryco Cup helped put them into the Semis. In the two legged affair Dunstable defeated Hampton 5-2 on aggregate to earn a final date with Thurrock, which is scheduled to be played in early October. Dunstable sealed a well deserved promotion with one game left as they beat Thame 2-1. GB

The Blues

Gloucester City

Address: City Stadium, Meadow Park, Sudmeadow Road, Hempsted, Gloucester, GL2 5HS

Tel: 01452 421400

Website: www.tigerroar.co.uk

Email: Email: neil@tigerroar.co.uk

Officials: Chairman: Colin Gardner
Commercial: Natalie Ward
Manager: Chris Burns

City Stadium

Review

Gloucester City supporters witnessed a dramatic improvement in their team's fortunes in 2003/04 as they eclipsed their humble 14th the season before, by pushing Redditch United hard for the Western Division championship before being beaten into second place.

That finish obviously booked them a place in this season's Dr Martens Premier Division but it didn't always look that cut and dry, as two wins, two draws and two defeats in the Tigers' opening six games gave their start a balanced yet unimpressive look. However, six wins in the next seven games gave an indication of the sort of form that Gloucester would hit later in the season as they began establishing themselves amongst the front-runners. Progress was also being made in the FA Cup as City disposed of Team Bath, Merthyr and Chippenham before being beaten by Bishops Stortford in the Fourth Qualifying Round.

Gloucester continued to chase Redditch at the top and, when a 6-0 drubbing of Shepshed Dynamo triggered an eight game winning run during March and April, the leaders were left looking over their shoulder as the Tigers looked ready to pounce. However, key defeats at inopportune moments in the season meant that Redditch always had the edge over the Tigers. A surprise 5-0 reverse against Taunton on 7th January began a run of only one win in five and, when their eight game winning streak was brought to an end with a 4-2 defeat at Evesham, it left the way clear for Redditch to clinch the title. JB

Directions

From the North: Leave the M5 at J11 and follow A40 signs to Gloucester. At the roundabout turn right onto the dual carriageway following the A40 towards the Forest of Dean, and go straight on at first roundabout. At the second roundabout take the A417 into the City Centre bearing right around the Homebase island and follow signs to the Historic Docks. Take the next right onto Severn Road and then right again onto Llanthony Road/Hempstead Lane past the Colin Campbell pub. The ground is signposted.

From the South: From the M5 J12, following the signs to Gloucester and take the second exit at the first roundabout on to the A38. At the traffic lights go straight ahead following signs for City centre on the A430 (Bristol Road). At the Peel Centre traffic lights, continue to follow signs to City centre. The ground is sign posted from the eighth set of traffic lights from the M5, turn left here into Llanthony Road towards Hempstead, over the swing bridge and follow the road around to the left, past the Colin Campbell pub. The ground is signposted.

Train: The nearest station is Gloucester. The ground is approximately two miles from the station so is it is advisable to get a taxi.

The ground was built in 1986 as part of the deal that saw Westbury Homes build the Swallow Park housing estate on the old stadium in Horton Road. The club purchased the surrounding football pitches from Fieldings in 1995 and renamed the whole area, from Sudmeadow Road to Spinnaker Road, 'Meadow Park', and called the football ground the 'City Stadium'. The capacity is 5,000 with 560 seats, although most standing is under cover. Segregation is in operation for most big games, and visitors have toilets and refreshment bar. Refreshment bars (1-3, depending on size of match) sell the usual fare of hotdogs and burgers, hot and cold drinks. There are two sets of toilets which are in good condition by Non-League standards. The only bar is now upstairs in the clubhouse since the closure of the old sports and social club. It is a little cramped. Beer is Banks's with GL cider - an essential to get a little bit of local flavour.

www.tigerroar.co.uk and www.t-ender.co.uk

The Tigers

Grantham Town

Address: South Kesteven Sports Stadium, Trent Road, Grantham, Lincolnshire, NG31 7XQ

Tel: 01476 402224 / 01476 566370

Website: www.granthamtownfc.co.uk

Email: kevmary@harrowby48.fsnet.co.uk

Officials: Chairman: Barry Palmer
Secretary: Pat Nixon
Manager: Dave Norton

South Kesteven Sports Stadium

Directions

From the North: On approaching Grantham from Nottingham, follow the signs for A1 south. You should reach this junction before you enter Grantham. Take the next junction off the A1 southbound, the A607 for Melton Mowbray. At the bottom of the slip road, take the first exit at the roundabout signposted Earlsfield Industrial Estate. This is Swingbridge Road. At the end of this road, turn left into Trent Road. The stadium is on the right.

From the South: From the A1, take the second exit for Grantham which will be signposted A607 Melton Mowbray. Turn right at the junction towards Grantham and take the next left signposted A1 South Stamford and London. Then as above.

By train: The station is less than one mile from the ground so it is well within walking distance. On exiting the station take a left into Huntingtower Road and then right into Trent Road. The stadium is a few hundred yards down this road on the right.

This is a strange ground as it is actually an athletics arena that is used as a football ground. When I visited it bucketed down with rain for the whole game and, as it was an open terrace, it is not the most pleasant ground to watch football in such conditions. The social club is attached to it and is spacious and comfortable and the fans have a sense of humour even in defeat. It is quite overpriced for this level of football and the running track around the pitch means that atmosphere is rare. A good stadium but unfortunately not for a football team. It is close to the A1 so transport isn't a problem but the town is 20 minutes away so if you want to visit it, you will need to get a bus or enjoy the walk. SW

Review

2003/04 was Grantham's second season in the Dr Martens Premier Division, after winning promotion from the Eastern Division in 2002 but, if fans were hoping that the club were going to build on their position of 16th in their first season, then they were sadly mistaken. The Gingerbreads had a miserable season as they missed out on a place in the restructured Conference, finishing bottom in the Premier Division. Those dark days in late April seemed a world away from a sunny August and a bright and optimistic start as Town went the first eight games of the season unbeaten, which lifted Roger Ashby's men as high as fifth in the table. They were also making headway in the FA Cup as they were one of a handful of Dr Martens League sides to make it through to the First Round Proper. They were paired with Londoners, Leyton Orient, and, despite going in front through a Kevin Wilkin goal after just four minutes, the Gingerbreads couldn't hold on. Orient levelled just past the quarter of an hour mark and, in a controversy filled match, Gary Alexander broke Grantham hearts as he put the Third Division side into Round Two with a last minute winner.

In the league, their form was on the wane after that positive start and, by the time Orient had put paid to their FA Cup run, the Gingerbreads were in the middle of a ten game winless run which had seen them slip down the table.

Three wins just after the turn of the year raised some hopes. However, it proved to be a false dawn as Grantham won only three of their remaining 18 games. Roger Ashby departed in February and made way for Dave Norton, but he couldn't turn things around as Town finished in last place - missing out on a Play-Off spot by four points. JB

The Gingerbreads

Halesowen Town

Address: The Grove, Old Hawne Lane, Halesowen, West Midlands

Tel: 0121 550 2179

Website: www.yeltzland.net

Email: poll@yeltzland.net

Officials: Chairman: Nigel Pitt
Secretary: Stewart Tildesley
Manager: Paul Holleran

The Grove

Directions

Leave the M5 at J3. Follow the A456 to Kidderminster to the first island and turn right. Signposted A459 Dudley. Then turn left on to the A458 Stourbridge.

At the next island take the third turn on the left into Grammer School Lane, then Old Hawne Lane. The ground is about 500 yards on the left.

Public Transport: If you are travelling from anywhere except Buckinghamshire, London, Herefordshire, Worcestershire and Oxfordshire this is a tricky one to get to as you have to walk through Birmingham. If you are lucky and get to Birmingham Snow Hill, leave the station through the main exit and turn right where the bus stops are. To get to the ground you need a 9 or a 109.

If you come into New Street leave the station by the exit marked 'The Pallasades' shopping centre. Leave by the main exit (down the ramp) and turn left down the pedestrianised street. Follow signs for Broad Street and go through the shopping mall. Carry on past the war memorial hall and cross Broad Street. The bus stops are to your right and again you will need the 9 or 109.

Entering the ground via the main entrance and inching past a programme kiosk, catering and a small club shop, leads the fan to a spot above the corner flag. From here the choice is whether to stand on the uncovered stretch of terracing running for the length of the field and stretching away behind the goal at the other end (Stourbridge Road end), or turning immediately right to seek shelter beneath the covered 'Shed' enclosure which stands behind the goal at the Old Hawne Lane end. The dressing rooms are behind the Shed and the players gain entry to the field through this terrace and down to the pitch via a gate set to one side of the goalposts.

To the right of the Shed, the Harry Rudge stand sits wedged narrowly between the pitch and the factories behind, offering a slim wedge of seating for a couple of hundred or so spectators along with a fully enclosed press box. SG

Review

Halesowen Town have endured a topsy-turvy last few seasons in the Dr Martens League. The Yeltz bounced back from relegation from the Premier Division in 2001 by winning the Western Division championship the following year. The yo-yo effect continued, however, as they once again couldn't sustain their Premier Division place as they went back down in 2003.

2003/04 was a campaign which ended on a high for Halesowen as they finished fourth in the Western Division and secured a place in the Premier for this season. This achievement was due in no small part to the Yeltz's impressive home form. Twelve wins, seven draws and only one defeat meant that the Grove was something of a fortress throughout the campaign. As it turned out, this was just as well, as Halesowen had the worst away record of any of the teams that finished in the top seven.

Halesowen got off to a stuttering start, losing their opening match to Clevedon but then responding by hammering Mangotsfield 6-0 the following week. Then a disappointing 4-2 reverse at Swindon Supermarine was followed up with three straight wins, the third of which was a 6-3 drubbing of Bedworth United with Jason Ashby and Leon Mitchell both grabbing hat-tricks. This sort of form left the Yeltz comfortably in the top ten but they were always just off the pace of the leaders.

This form persisted into 2004 as Halesowen exacted revenge on Swindon Supermarine, knocking six past them on 17th January but, just a week later, Evesham United inflicted Town's only defeat at the Grove as they claimed a 2-0 victory to leave the fans continually frustrated.

Their run-in was no more consistent as they finished eleven points behind eventual champions Redditch in fourth. JB

The Yeltz

Hednesford Town

Address: Keys Park, Hednesford Road, Cannock, Staffordshire, WS12 2DX

Tel: 01543 422870

Website: www.hednesfordtownfc.co.uk

Officials: Chairman: Steve Price
Secretary: Rod Hadley
Manager: Chris Brindley

Review

Hednesford Town's 2003/04 campaign could best be summed up as a 'Jekyll and Hyde' season. The Staffordshire side who, up until three years ago, were a Conference club, once again had a disappointing league season as they missed out on a place in the new Conference divisions - finishing third from bottom in the table - a far cry from their third placed finish in their debut Conference season in 1995/96.

However, when people look back on Hednesford's season in years to come, where they finished in the league will be irrelevant. Just as Burscough had done the previous season, the Pitmen brushed aside a poor league campaign and became the second non-Conference club in as many seasons to lift the FA Trophy after a dramatic final against Ryman League champions and odds-on favourites Canvey Island.

They negotiated the early rounds with little fuss disposing of Shepshed, Lancaster, Gresley Rovers and Worthing.

Hednesford continued to avoid Conference opposition, and further wins over Dover and then Hornchurch booked the Pitmen's place in the last four. With opponents Aldershot pushing hard for promotion to the Football League, few people gave Hednesford a prayer over two legs. However, the Shots were stunned in the first game at the Recreation Ground, as goals from Mark Danks and Anthony Maguire gave the Pitmen a 2-0 win. It was always going to be tough for the Shots to overturn the deficit in the return leg and, when Maguire gave Town a tenth minute lead at Keys Park, Hednesford were already heading for the ticket office to book their seats at the Final. Roscoe D'Sane clawed one back for the Shots late on but it was too little too late.

If Hednesford didn't receive many backers prior to the Semi-Final, they received even fewer for the Villa Park Final. Opponents Canvey had won the Ryman Premier Division at a canter and, in Lee Boylan, they possessed one of the most prolific strikers in non-league football. However, the Pitmen silenced all the doubters and wrote themselves into the history books as player-manager Chris Brindley went from villain to hero as he cancelled out his own-goal just after half time and netted a late winner to give his side a dramatic 3-2 win. JB

Directions

From the North and South: Leave the M6 at Junction 11, and follow the A460 to Cannock, to the Longford mini-roundabout. Turn right for Brownhills. Continue along the A5, through the traffic lights and under the railway bridge to Churchbridge Island. Turn left on to the A460 for Rugeley. Pass over five mini-roundabouts and, at the sixth, turn right (third exit) and follow the road to the next island. Continue over (Crosskeys) and, at the next island, turn right and the ground is on your left.

From the East: From the A38 or M42, join the A5 and head towards Brownhills. Pass Little Chef/Burger King (yuk) on your left and, at the next island, take the right exit for Hednesford. Remain on this road until you reach an island (Five Ways) take the second exit (B4154) through Heath Hayes to Crosskeys then as above.

By train: From the south, services to Hednesford run from Birmingham New Street every 40 minutes, to either Stafford or Rugeley Trent Valley. From the north, services run from Stafford every hour, but this can be more sporadic of a weekend. On arriving at Hednesford, walk back over the bridge and follow the road down through the town centre. At the Uxbridge Arms hotel turn right and follow the road over a hill to the Cross Keys hotel. Continue to walk along this road, until you reach the Keys Park roundabout. Turn left here, then right at the roundabout at the top of the hill, to arrive at Keys Park. Walking time is 15 to 20 minutes.

Keys Park is a modern stadium situated in the middle of contemporary housing estates, far from pubs and shops. The facilities at the ground are good and so is the car park that surrounds the stadium, but the ground doesn't quite have the character of an 'organic' stadium such as Edgar Street (Hereford), with all its quirks and foibles.

The stadium is entirely under cover with terracing situated opposite the Main Stand which continues to sweep round behind one goal. The other end of the ground is seated. Keys Park is quite clearly well kept and capable of staging football at a higher level than the Dr Martens League. With the decline of the team's fortunes on the field, security is relaxed and fans swap ends at the end of each half quite happily. SG

The Pitmen

Hemel Hempstead

Address: Vauxhall Road, Adeyfield Road, Hemel Hempstead, HP2 4HW

Tel: 01442 259 777

Website: www.hemeltownfc.com

Email: info@hemeltownfc.com

Officials: Chairman: Dave Boggins
Secretary: Bob Jackson
Manager: Tony Kelly

Vauxhall Road

Directions

From The M1: Leave the motorway at junction 8. At the first roundabout go straight ahead (2nd exit), at the next roundabout straight ahead (2nd exit) keep to right hand lane and turn right at the first available cut through in the central reservation into Leverstock Green Road. At double mini-roundabouts turn left into Vauxhall Road and at the roundabout turn right into the ground.
From the M25 & A41 Hemel Hempstead Bypass:
Leave M25 at junction 20, Kings Langley. Follow the signs for Aylesbury A41. Leave the bypass at the Hemel Hempstead exit and follow to Town Centre, eventually arriving at the famous funny roundabout. From there follow the signs for the M1. At the top of the hill go straight over the roundabout, at the next roundabout straight ahead (2nd exit) then take the third turning on the left into Leverstock Green Road, then as above
By train: The nearest station is Hemel Hempstead on the London Euston/Northampton line (Silverlink Trains) and is approximately one and a half miles from the station. Turn right out of the station and, at the first roundabout, turn left. When you arrive at another roundabout, follow the signs for the M1. Go straight over at the next two roundabouts and then take the third turning on the left - Longlands. The second turning on the right is Vauxhall Road. The ground is down this road on the left hand side.

The most immediate impression one forms of the Vauxhall Ground is that it is very red - no casual visitor attending a match there would be in any doubt which was the home side! A major problem for the club is the perennial vandalism the ground has suffered. In 1992 the original clubhouse was gutted by fire and rebuilt adjacent to what was then the main stand. It was rebuilt once again in 2001 and is now a more substantial building inside the main gate. The new millennium saw two large covered terraces erected at either end of the ground. DB

Review

Hemel Hempstead Town narrowly missed out on promotion in 2002/03 after being beaten into third place in Division One North by Hornchurch and Northwood.
As a result, Tony Kelly's men were expected to challenge for the title in 2003/04 or, at least, achieve a top seven finish that would see them elevated to the Dr Martens Premier Division, as a result of the restructuring shake-up.
As it turned out, one out of two wasn't bad. Hemel were never in contention to challenge for the title as Yeading had the bit between their teeth for much of the campaign - striding to the championship amassing a whopping 103 points, seven more than second placed Leyton and a huge 25 more than Hemel, down in sixth.
Indeed, a top seven finish was never a sure thing for Hemel as they made an indifferent start. They suffered a 7-3 hammering at home to Cheshunt, just three games in, and were dumped out of the FA Cup after a surprise defeat by Enfield in a replay.
They continued to stutter through the winter months as the odd win was sandwiched in between disappointing results, such as a 6-1 league reverse away to Yeading at the end of September, followed by a 4-1 defeat at Folkestone in the FA Trophy just over a month later.
With both cup competitions out of the way, Hemel's league form did begin to pick up as they constructed a seven match unbeaten run going in to December (which included five straight wins).
That revival pushed them up to eighth by Christmas; however, a 5-0 defeat in the return game with Cheshunt on New Year's Day was a dent to their confidence. Indeed, it looked as though Hemel would be pushed hard for a promotion spot, and numbing defeats in the middle of March, to Tilbury (5-1) and away at Chesham (5-2), really put the pressure on. However, Kelly's boys responded and went on a seven game unbeaten run until the end of the season to secure a top seven finish. JB

Hemel

Histon

Address: Bridge Road, Impington, Cambridge
CB4 9PH

Tel: 01223 232301

Website: http://histonfootballclub.tripod.com

Email: stevenwells1@compuserve.com

Officials: Chairman: Gareth Baldwin
Secretary: Lisa Baldwin
Manager: Steve Fallon

Bridge Road

Directions

From Junction 14 of the M11, follow the A14 eastbound. Take the first exit onto the B1049. At the top of the slip road turn left over the traffic lights and past the Holiday Inn on the right. Continue over the bridge and the ground is on the right just before the pedestrian crossing.

By train: The nearest station is Cambridge which is approximately five miles from the ground. Either get a taxi from outside the station or a number 104 bus.

Bridge Road, in Impington, Cambridge, is quite easy to get to from the A14. Parking on match days is never a problem with amble parking on the roads surrounding the ground. As regarding public transport, the local bus service is quite limited and there are no train stations in close proximity to the ground. The 3,250 capacity stadium can seat up to 250 fans in their modern main stand. On-site facilities include an adequate food kiosk and a clubhouse, bar and lounge area. MP

Review

Cambridgeshire club Histon have, over the last few years, been one of the more consistent clubs in the Dr Martens Eastern Division and, as such, were amongst the favourites for the title in 2003/04. As it turned out, the Stutes were one of the three main protagonists in a championship race that saw the balance of power shift several times and, ultimately, went to the wire.

Histon got off to a flyer. They won their opening four matches. Infact, they went the first 18 games of the season unbeaten, with their first loss coming at home against Kings Lynn on New Year's Day. However, despite this undoubtedly impressive run, it was the early season form of Kent side Tonbridge Angels that had everyone talking. They won all but one of their first 17 games and it was they who, unsurprisingly, sat on top of the pile going into 2004, with Kings Lynn in second and Histon in third.

For much of the spring, Tonbridge and Kings Lynn wrestled for the top spot with Histon jostling for position just behind. Despite showing title winning potential, Histon suffered damaging defeats against their title rivals - defeats that would ultimately cost them. The loss to Kings Lynn on New Year's Day was followed up by a 4-3 reverse at Tonbridge in February and, when Kings Lynn completed the double over the Stutes in April, it all but ended Histon's title challenge. However, Steve Fallon's men didn't let their heads drop, and a free-scoring run-in which saw them win three of their last four games (netting 14 goals in the process) ensured that Histon snatched second place from under the noses of Tonbridge on goal difference.

Histon's goal scoring exploits were not just confined to the league. Their first two ties in the FA Cup yielded 13 goals - following a 7-0 win over Yeading and a 6-1 win over Mildenhall Town. The Stutes were clearly enjoying their cup run as they battled their way to the First Round proper before being beaten by Conference side Woking. JB

The Stutes

Hitchin Town

Address: Top Field Stadium, Fishponds Road, Hitchin, Hertfordshire SG5 1NU

Tel: 01462 434483

Website: www.hitchintownfc.co.uk

Officials: Chairman: Terry Barratt
Secretary: Roy Izzard
Manager: Kerry Dixon

Top Field Stadium

Review

Hitchin fans had to endure one of the worst periods in the club's history but still saw their club only just miss out on a place in the Conference South. For the second season running, there was a high expectation at Top Field, with a glut of new signings that gave the club arguably its best side for a decade. Three straight wins sent Hitchin to the top of the table, but September and October were bad months, with an FA Cup exit at Folkestone in the Second Qualifying Round depriving the club of much needed revenue.

Poor commercial activity and the early cup exit meant the club had to rethink, and as a result, a number of players departed. Matt Nolan and Dean Brennan were sold to Peterborough and Stevenage respectively, and following manager Robbie O'Keefe's departure in November, there was a mass exodus. Players like Chris Dillon, Carl Williams, Adam Parker, Craig Rydeheard and James Ayres all left either side of Christmas. The heart was ripped out of the club.

Amidst the turmoil, former Chelsea and England striker, Kerry Dixon, was appointed manager. But 2004 started badly, despite three wins for a reshaped side that included Aylesbury refugees, Josh Sozzo and Paul Covington. Hitchin then failed to win a single game in 13, including eleven defeats - the worst run in the club's history. Surprisingly, Hitchin did win three of their last five league games, including successes at Basingstoke and Bedford. And, on the final day of the season, Hitchin leapfrogged Northwood to finish outside the bottom four. This set up a Play-Off with local rivals Bedford. However, there was to be no repeat of the 2-1 league success, and the home side won 3-1.

Although there was much to complain about during an unsatisfactory season, Hitchin fans look forward to the new challenge of the Southern League in 2004/05.

Neil Jensen - Media Officer Hitchin Town FC

Directions

Leave the A1(M) at Junction 8, for Hitchin and Luton Airport. Take the first exit at the bottom of the slip road onto the A602 to Hitchin. Follow this as far as the edge of the town. At the roundabout, go straight across, under a footbridge (Three Moorhens pub on your right and signposted Luton/Bedford). At the next roundabout, go straight across (for Bedford) and you should be in the left hand lane of the one way system with Safeways about 200 yards ahead on the right. Continue over at the lights and Butts Close green space is on the right. Top Field is on the opposite corner, next roundabout. Turn right and the car park is on the left.

By train: On the Kings Cross to Cambridge or Peterborough line. Top Field is a 20 minute walk from Hitchin station. Turn right out of the station approach road and cross over. Pass B&Q on the left. At the bottom of the hill, go past the Woolpack pub on the left, then a recreation ground also on your left. Turn right at the roundabout, go past the Victoria pub on the right. The ground is at the top of this road.

One of my favourite grounds. It is surrounded by tall trees and boasts two sets of wooden terracing behind the goal and facing the main stand. Apparently, when the lease to the ground was granted in the 19th century, a condition was that there should be no permanent structures erected, hence wooden terracing - a throwback to the good old days. There are five steps on this terracing (some of which has cover). I recall bouncing on it vigorously when the splendidly named Paul Giggle equalised against Swindon Town in an FA Cup tie in the late 70s. I suppose the only danger is from splinters!

The main stand on the Bedford Road side of the ground seats 450 and is also pretty venerable. The most modern feature is the concrete terrace behind the other goal, complete with crush barriers, in contrast to the wooden terraces. I believe it was built after the Canaries' giant killing in the late 90s when Hereford and Bristol Rovers were beaten in successive FA Cup runs. MC

The Canaries

Kings Lynn

Address: The Walks Stadium, Tennyson Road, Kings Lynn, Norfolk, PE30 5PB
Tel: 01553 760060
Website: www.kingslynnfc.co.uk
Email: webmaster@kingslynnfc.co.uk
Officials: Chairman: Colin Nichols
Secretary: Nigel Link
Joint Manager: Darren Bloodworth
Joint Manager: Kevin Boon

The Walks Stadium

Directions

Approaches from the north or the west come out at the A17/A47 roundabout south-west of Kings Lynn. From here follow the by-pass (dual-carriageway) crossing the River Great Ouse. Continue to the first roundabout and then take the first exit into Kings Lynn (sign-posted Town Centre). Go straight on through two sets of traffic lights and over a railway bridge. Once over the bridge, get in the right hand lane at the first opportunity. At the next roundabout turn right (this is the third exit off the roundabout) into Vancouver Avenue. Follow the road for about half a mile, the ground is on the left. There are small car parks at each end of the ground. Failing that, it is on street parking for which there are plenty of streets. Approaches from the south or east result in the A47/A10 roundabout. From here follow the signs to Kings Lynn Town Centre as described above.
By train: Out of the station turn left, enter the park and take the path towards Red Mount Chapel (keeping to the right of the lake). The ground is ahead and off to the left.

The Walks has an impressive capacity of 8,200 - 5,000 of which is under cover and 1,200 seated. However, the stadium is beginning to look a little run down, and in need of some work. The main stand looks particularly dilapidated, with holes in parts in the walls and a rusting roof. As for facilities, there is a clubhouse, a fairly standard club shop and a food kiosk with a minimal selection. There are small car parks at each end of the ground which tend to fill up early - but there is plenty of unrestricted street parking. MP

Review

Expectations were high for the Linnets despite a modest sixth place finish in 2002/03. Despite the Linnets' strong start to the season, Tonbridge's spectacular form saw them run away at the top of the table. The game between the sides in late October was marked, even in those early exchanges, as a title decider. Tonbridge won 2-0 to end Lynn's unbeaten away record. The Angels were 14 points clear but Kings Lynn still had two games in hand - and those games in hand were to prove decisive.
At the start of December, the Linnets suffered a morale-sapping away defeat at lowly Chatham and dropped to third. They had just four days to recover before coming face-to-face with still unbeaten leaders, Tonbridge. Dave Staff gave Kings Lynn the lead, before the Angels equalised. With the scores level at half-time, three second-half goals ensured a convincing win for Kings Lynn. This defeat and off-field financial problems saw the Angels slip and drop points, while the Linnets went on to collect 20 points out of a possible 24. A 4-1 win in February, this time over Banbury, saw the club take top spot for the first time all season. The leadership didn't last long though as they immediately lost 3-1 at struggling Ashford.
Kings Lynn regained top spot in style, with three wins, yet things were too close to call and taking one point from three games saw Lynn back down to third. However, a 1-0 win against Bashley put them top with two games left, and a win over Erith meant Tonbridge would have to win at least 21-0 to win the title. Unsurprisingly, the Angels couldn't reach that target but the Linnets' 2-0 win meant it didn't matter - the Linnets had secured the title.
There was little time for champagne as they faced a Play-Off with Redditch United for a Conference North/South place. Kings Lynn lost the tie 1-0, so the chirruping Linnets ended the season wailing rather then crooning. MP

The Linnets

Merthyr Tydfil

Address: Penydarren Park, Merthyr Tydfil, Mid Glamorgan, CF47 8RF

Tel: 01685 384102

Website: www.themartyrs.com

Officials: Chairman: Wyn Holloway
Secretary: Anthony Hughes
Manager: Andy Beattie

Penydarren Park

Directions

From M5: Leave at J8 and join the M50 for Ross-on-Wye, then the A40 to Abergavenny and then the A465. Follow signs for the town centre. At the mini-roundabout bear right. At the traffic lights turn right, then first right and first right past the church. Penydarren Park is 250 yards at the end of the access road. Limited parking is available at the ground. There is pay-and-display parking facilities available in the town centre which is approximately half a mile away.

From M4: Leave at J32, join the A470 expressway and, on approaching Merthyr, take the exit at the roundabout for the town centre. Turn left at the second roundabout and join the ring-road to the south of the town centre. At the third set of traffic lights bear right and at the next set of traffic lights turn left. Take the first right and then the next right, immediately after the church, then as above.

By train: Penydarren Park is a mile from the station. Exit the station and go into the High Street. This leads into Penydarren Road.

An intriguing ground concealed at the end of a cul-de-sac, it is nonetheless an extensive venue with a large main stand containing a programme shop and good value tea bar as well as a substantial number of seats. The terracing on two of the remaining sides is conspicuously deep, particularly under cover on the far side, and the seats behind one of the goals also enjoy cover which creates a cosy and excellent vantage point for the action. The Strikers clubhouse is detached from the ground itself but is well furnished, and is popular for its town centre location, which is easier to reach on foot than by car. GB

Review

The South Wales outfit finished the 2003/04 season in a fairly disappointing 14th place in the Dr Martens Premier Division table. In any other season it would have been a fairly sub-standard finish. However, a bitter pill was made even harder to swallow as the Martyrs just missed out on a place in the new Conference South, which they would have claimed with a finish in the top 13.

They came into the campaign on a high after having runaway with the Western Division championship the season before, and they certainly carried their momentum over into the opening game in the Premier Division, as goals by Cortex Belle and Gary Thorne gave them a 2-1 win at eventual champions Crawley. However, that excellent opening day victory proved something of a false dawn as Andy Beattie's men wouldn't taste victory again until mid-September.

The Martyrs did suffer from a lack of consistency for much of the season but, despite this, they were still sitting comfortably in the top ten, and on course for a top 13 finish, going into the final month of the season.

Despite there being many different possible outcomes going into the season's final day, Merthyr's task was simple. Due to the fact that Moor Green and Havant & Waterlooville (Merthyr's nearest rivals for promotion) were playing each other, they knew that a win against Chelmsford would guarantee promotion. However, as Moor Green pulled a win out of the bag at home against Havant, it meant that Merthyr's 3-1 defeat away to Chelmsford saw the Moors snatch 13th to leave the Merthyr fans heartbroken.

Despite the disappointment of the final day's dramatics, all was not lost. If Merthyr could defeat Redditch in a one off Play-Off, then they would still achieve a promotion place. However, not even home advantage could help the Martyrs as they were well beaten by a Redditch United side riding high after winning the Western Division championship. Two goals by Richard Leadbeater saw United win 3-0 to pile the misery on Merthyr. JB

The Martyrs

Rugby United

Address: Butlin Road, Rugby, Warks, CV21 3ST

Tel: 01788 866920

Website: www.rugbyunited.co.uk

Email: football@rugbyunited.co.uk

Officials: Chairman: Brian Melvin
Secretary: Doug Wilkins
Manager: Tony Dobson

Review

The 2003/04 season saw Rugby United clinch a place in the Dr Martens Premier after a creditable fifth placed finish in the Western Division. Tony Dobson's men, who had been making steady progress in the Western Division, finishing in twelfth in 2002 and eighth in 2003, hit the ground running as they began the season with three straight wins. There were slight blips early on after defeats against eventual champions Redditch and newly promoted Team Bath but, all in all, Rugby made a solid start as the next three point haul was never far away during the opening months of the season.
Infact, United never really had a lean spell throughout the entire campaign, never going more than three games without a win - they even pushed themselves as high as second place in the table at the half way point in the season (albeit ten points behind leaders Redditch).
However, Rugby carried on steadily picking up points as they eased their way towards a top seven finish. Just two defeats from the club's final ten games, saw them beat Solihull and Team Bath into fifth and comfortably clinch a Dr Martens Premier Division place. Rugby's success was due in no small part to Robert Beard who spearheaded United's attack, finishing the season with 18 goals. JB

Directions

Exit the M6, Junction 1 (or M1, Junction 19), and follow signs towards Rugby (first exit on the roundabout). Then go straight over the next two roundabouts until you come to a main 'Mr Kipling' roundabout. Take the first exit on the roundabout, which follows downhill to a mini-roundabout, where you should carry straight on.
You should come past housing on both sides of the road before a large field. Continue along this road (Boughton Road/Butlers Leap) until you come to its end at a T-junction.
Turn right here, and continue up the hill past the golf course on the left and take the second left turning, which is at a mini-roundabout (Butlin Road). Carry on down here until you come to cemetery gates when you should take a left turn at the top of the road and then a quick right, but the ground will be in view already.
By train: The ground is an easy 15 minute walk away from Rugby Station. From the station walk out towards car parks 1 and 2 and turn left on to Murray Road. When you are opposite car park 2, turn right. Almost immediately, turn left into Abbey Street. Carry on until you come to the end of Abbey Street. Go straight on, up South Street. The first right off South Street is Biart Place. Carry to the end of Biart Place and turn left. Almost immediately on the right is Butlin Road. The ground is at the end of this road.

Developments such as the new 500-seater cantilever stand, recently opened by England international Darius Vassell, and the VS Bar, make Butlin Road a great stadium and always provides a great day out. The ground, unlike many at this level, has covering on all four sides and seating on two sides. The official capacity has been confirmed as 5,375 with approximately 1,500 able to be accommodated under cover and 740 of these can also be seated. The ground is nearly up to Conference standard, and with the completion of new turnstiles and an external wall around the whole ground, it will be very close to being so.
www.rugbyunited.co.uk

Solihull Borough

Address: Damson Park, Damson Parkway, Solihull, West Midlands, B91 2PP

Tel: 0121 705 6770

Website: www.solihullborough-fc.co.uk

Email: webmaster@solihullborough-fc.co.uk

Officials: Chairman: Trevor Stevens

Secretary: Margaret Smith

Manager: Guy Russell

Damson Park

Directions

From M42: Take Junction 6 and head in the direction of Birmingham. Stay on this road until you come to a crossroads with traffic lights and the Forte Posthouse on your right. Turn left at these lights and you will see the ground on your right. Continue along this road (Damson Parkway) until you come to a mini-roundabout. Come back on yourself and take the left hand lane and filter into the ground car park.
By train: The nearest station is Birmingham International. Catch an A6 or 966 bus to the ground.

Damson Park is a new ground and, it has to be said, a little more imaginative than most. The first thing visitors encounter is a truly palatial building holding several bars, the club offices and a full-sized conference centre. This backs onto the ground's seated stand, in which the players' facilities are equally top-drawer. The remainder of Damson Park is neat but relatively undeveloped, although it has been built to allow for future expansion should this prove necessary. Borough are a community club, now reunited with their support base after years away. The number of families attending games and the many tiers of football played here demonstrates that everything in the garden is rosy. CF

Review

When previous manager Paul Holleran departed to take over the reins at Halesowen Town, in March 2004, his assistant and former Boro player Guy Russell was appointed as his replacement at Damson Park.
By then, the Boro were some way off the pace in the championship chase, where they eventually finished some 18 points behind the winners, Redditch United.
Their main strength last season was their solid defence, which conceded just 31 goals, a record only bettered by the title winners. This impressive statistic was further highlighted by the fact that Boro did not concede more than two goals in any league match, home or away, all season.
Conversely, however, goalscoring was a significant problem and it is true to say that they never recovered from the loss of their leading scorer, Andy Corbett, from the previous season, to near neighbours Nuneaton Borough. His departure proved to be crucial in this department. Indeed, the Boro failed to score in no fewer than 16 games during the season.
The Boro's cup dreams were short lived and, by early October, they had been unceremoniously removed from the FA Cup and FA Trophy, by Redditch United and Shepshed Dynamo respectively.
In the league, they did, however achieve a notable scalp with a hard-earned victory away to Redditch.
Despite a mixed bag of results last season, Boro are now elevated to the Southern League Premier Division as a result of their seventh place finish under the new restructuring system.
Manager Russell will, no doubt, be looking to consolidate their position in his first full season in charge and, although there are the inevitable budget constraints, he will be looking to strengthen his squad to achieve this objective. PM

The Boro

Stamford

Address: New Flame Stadium, Kettering Road, Stamford, Lincs

Tel: 01780 763079

Website: www.stamfordafc.s5.com

Email: webmaster@stamfordafc.s5.com

Officials: Chairman: Ken Joynson
Secetary: Jeremy Biggs
Manager: Billy Jeffrey

New Flame Stadium

Directions

From the A1 Southbound carriageway: Leave at the A43 junction. Take a left at the bottom of the slip road. The ground is approximately one mile away on the left.

From the A1 Northbound carriageway: Leave at the Carpenters Lodge roundabout (signposted Burghley House) follow the road for approximately two miles and then turn left (signposted A43 Kettering). The ground is 300 yards on the right.

By train: The nearest station is Stamford. Come out of the station. Head up the small lane on the right that runs parallel to the train tracks. Go up the steps after about 60 yards and turn right at the top. Follow the road around and that brings you to the ground.

The New Flame Stadium was built in 2001. It holds as many as 5,000 fans, with 250 of them seated - these seats are quite low, which allows a better view of games.

At the stadium you will find a decent clubhouse, a standard club shop and a food kiosk. The spacious public house on site overlooks the pitch, although even in the poorest of weather this remains empty during games. The bar area is also extremely well furnished and inviting, although it does get crowded very quickly. As for the stadium, its young age shows as it looks, on the most part, immaculate - although it does look somewhat compact despite its 5,000 capacity. MP

Review

Lincolnshire outfit Stamford were amongst the favourites for the Dr Martens Eastern Division title in 2003/04 after they had finished in an impressive third place the season before. They were certainly quick to signal their intent as they won their opening two games (the second, a fine 4-0 win away at Burnham), to get their campaign off to a perfect start.

However, three key defeats before the turn of the year, against title challengers Kings Lynn (once) and Tonbridge Angels (twice), suggested that the Daniels might not have the capacity to sustain a challenge for the top this time around. Indeed, it was Kings Lynn, Tonbridge and Histon who were setting the pace and Billy Jeffrey's men simply couldn't keep up.

Stamford would eventually finish a full 20 points behind champions Kings Lynn, so they were pretty much out of the title race at a fairly early stage. This left the club to concentrate on second prize - to ensure that they earned themselves a place in the Dr Martens Premier Division for the 2004/05 season. This would be guaranteed with a finish of seventh or higher, with the eighth placed team going into a Play-Off.

A twelve game unbeaten run, after the turn of the year, put Stamford well in contention for a top seven finish. However, an inconsistent run-in meant that Daniels fans were never assured of anything until quite late on in the season. Stamford finally scraped into seventh place, four points ahead of Banbury United but four wins and three defeats from their final seven games kept the fans guessing and saw the Daniels limp across the finish line rather than finish with a flourish.

Stamford had little to cheer in the cup competitions as they were soundly beaten by Kettering in the Second Qualifying Round of the FA Cup and were edged out at the First Round stage of the FA Trophy, 2-0 by Kingstonian. JB

The Daniels

Team Bath

Address: Sports Training Village,
University of Bath,
Claverton Down, Bath, BA2 7AY

Tel: 01225 826656

Website: www.teambath.com

Email: team@bath.ac.uk

Officials: Chairman: Matt Birch
Secretary: Phil Searle
Manager: Ged Roddy

Sports Training Village

Review

Following their much documented FA Cup run the previous season, hopes were understandably high at university side Team Bath as they entered into their debut Dr Martens League season.

Amidst much media coverage, Team Bath had battled their way to the First Round of the FA Cup in the 2002/03 season before they were eventually knocked out by Mansfield Town in front of Match Of The Day cameras. Their efforts had put the club on the pages of all the national newspapers, as it was the furthest a university side had gone in the competition for 128 years. The impetus gained from their cup run spilled over into the league and Team Bath went on to lift the Western League championship trophy by eleven points.

Despite losing the first two games in the Dr Martens Western Division, Team Bath were quick to find their feet at the higher level as they then embarked on a seven game unbeaten run which included impressive wins over Yate Town (3-0) and Cinderford Town (4-0).

Ged Roddy's men went merrily about their business as they firmly established themselves at Dr Martens League level, quashing any thoughts by critics that they might struggle. Team Bath never lost more than two consecutive league games and could even afford to lose three of their last six matches as they finished comfortably in the promotion places for the Dr Martens Premier Division, in sixth.

The club would have been doing well to emulate their FA Cup exploits of the previous year and, indeed, they found it too hard to live up to expectations as they were knocked out at the First Qualifying Round stage after going down 2-0 to Gloucester City in a replay.

The club didn't fare any better in the FA Trophy as they succumbed in the First Round, again after a replay, this time against Halesowen Town. However, these were minor blips in what most fans of Team Bath would consider a highly successful season. JB

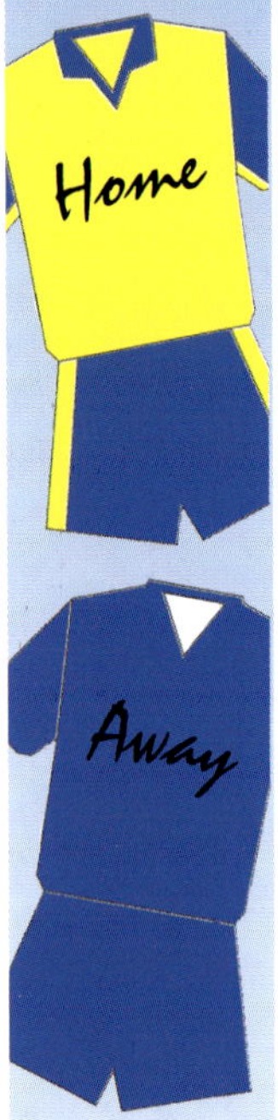

Directions

Leave the M4 at a Junction 18 and then follow the A46 into Bath. Once in Bath follow the signs for the University (about one mile from the city centre). Once on the Campus, follow the signs for Team Bath Football and Sports Training Village.

Train: The nearest station is Bath. The ground is approximately one and a half miles up a very steep hill so, unless you are a keen hiker, it is advisable to get a bus or a taxi. There is a bus service that runs every ten minutes from the bus station just outside the train station. The bus goes straight into the centre of the University Campus and the ground is a two minute walk from there (signposted).

Team Bath's Sports Training Village is quite a strange and unique venue. As part of the university campus, it is not a football ground in its own right. There is an athletics track running around the outside of the pitch and a temporary stand running along one side. There is no bar on the site but the student union bar is on campus and is about a ten minute walk. There is a pay and display car park approximately 400 yards from the ground. There is a cafe in the main complex and a mobile vendor at pitch side.

Tiverton Town

Address: Ladysmead, Bolham Road, Tiverton, Devon, EX16 8SG

Tel: 01884 252397

Website: www.tiverton-town-fc.co.uk

Email: tivvytown@eclipse.co.uk

Officials: Chairman: Dave Wright
Secretary: Tony Floyde
Manager: Martyn Rogers

Directions

Take Junction 27 on the M5. Head towards Tiverton on the A361 for about seven miles. Ignore the first junction for the A396 Tiverton and Bickleigh (Gornhay Cross) and keep going a little further until a large roundabout. Turn left here (A3126) for the town centre and castle. Continue along this road for about 400 yards, passing Tiverton Rugby Club. At a mini-roundabout go straight across (first exit). Ladysmead is on your right. Travel along this road for about 200 yards and turn right just beyond the BP garage on your right. There is car parking at the club.

By train: Tiverton Parkway is seven miles outside of the town. Buses leave the train station 16 minutes to the hour every hour and leave the bus station in Tiverton 15 minutes past the hour every hour. The journey time is 38 minutes. The other option is a taxi from the station.

Ladysmead is a picturesque, small ground near the edge of the Town. There is covered terracing at both ends and along one side. The covered seating runs over half the length of the pitch on the side opposite the clubhouse. The record gate stands at 3,000 for a First Round FA Cup tie against Leyton Orient but the present limit is 2,320. A spacious clubhouse provides two bars with a variety of liquid refreshments, including a guest Real Ale, and normal refreshment facilities are available from two outlets, with the beef pasties highly recommended! JR

Review

The prospect of the 2003/2004 season carried little reason for apprehension for Tiverton Town. Whilst only the most blinkered of fans would consider the Devon side to be serious contenders for the Dr Martens Premier Division, the general feeling around Ladysmead was one of confidence that Tivvy would have little difficulty in qualifying for a place in the new Conference South. After all, a top 13 finish should present only a modicum of difficulty.

Everything appeared to be going to plan when the season got underway with an opening day league victory over Moor Green, followed by an away draw at local rivals Chippenham Town. Then the bubble burst. Three defeats on the trot and some inconsistent and lacklustre performances, culminated in an ignominious defeat at the first hurdle in the FA Cup at the hands of Newport IOW. The writing was on the wall but Tiverton bumbled on, financially unable to strengthen the squad. Those finances were further hit when the FA Trophy was rapidly exited at the hands of Isthmian League side Marlow as Tivvy collapsed in the final six minutes. Nevertheless, Tiverton were still grinding out occasional wins and draws - enough to see them remain apparently safely established in the top half of the table.

The turn of the year saw the Devonians in a strong looking sixth position in the table. For all their inconsistency, the prime target for the season - securing Conference football for 2004/05 - still seemed unthreatened despite the fact that The Yellows had played more games than their nearest rivals.

In their remaining eleven contests Town suffered just four defeats. Unfortunately for their ambitions the remaining seven matches finished all square. It went to the wire, but a final day home defeat by already doomed Hednesford Town saw Tiverton slip to 15th place in the table. But all was not lost. The back door was still open, courtesy of the Play-Off system. Having beaten Chelmsford City in the first game, the season's finale had to be moved to Exeter City's St James's Park (due to a concert at Ladysmead). It was a fine setting for such a game but it was visitors Dorchester Town that responded to the surroundings better and convincingly terminated Tiverton's dreams of making it to the Conference by inflicting a 3-1 defeat on their hosts. JR

Ladysmead

Tivvy

Isthmian Premier

Club Pages

Billericay Town

Address: New Lodge, Blunts Wall Road, Billericay, Essex, CM12 9SA

Tel: 01277 652188

Website: www.billericaytownfc.co.uk

Officials: Chairman: Steve Kent
Secretary: Len Dewson
Manager: Justin Edinburgh

The New Lodge

Directions

From Chelmsford: Take the Galleywood Road, just past St John's Hospital, via Wood Street. Join Stock Road (B1007). Go straight on at the Running Mare pub, through Stock, and straight over the roundabout by the golf course. At the railway bridge, go straight across the roundabout and turn right at the lights into Western Road. Continue over a mini-roundabout, until traffic lights with a parade of shops on the left. Go straight across and take the first right turning, Blunts Wall Road. Half way down is New Lodge.

From M25: Leave at J28 (A12) and take the A1023 through Brentwood. At Shenfield, take the A129 towards Billericay. On entering Billericay, turn right at the first set of traffic lights (near the Esso garage). Blunts Wall Lane is a little way along on the right.

By train: Billericay is on the Liverpool Street/Southend Victoria line. The ground is a 25 minute walk from the station. On leaving the station, turn right into Radford Way. At the top of the road, turn right, crossing the railway line by the footbridge. Turn right again at the bottom of the High Street into Western Road. Walk the full length of Western Road, then cross over at the traffic lights into Tye Common Road. Blunts Wall Road is a little way along on the right.

It is looking more and more likely that Town will stay here now, as plans to move to Basildon appear to have stalled for the moment. The ground is placed right on the outskirts of the Essex town on a narrow country lane, and possesses a strange mixture of stands and buildings which are dominated by the signalbox-esque clubhouse. The ground slopes from side to side. Both sides have seated stands of differing designs and covered terracing is behind both goals. Billericay have a club shop right next to the clubhouse, and programmes are sold from a distinctive wooden shed. Parking is notoriously tight, though, given the setting of the ground, and there is a long walk from the station. GB

Review

At the start of the campaign, Billericay supporters had high expectations due to an impressive pre-season, many new faces in the side, and a new management team of ex-Spurs defender, Justin Edinburgh, and assistant, Andy Polston. However, things failed to materialise as the season got off to the worst possible start. August wasn't too sunny for Billericay as they lost all five games. In truth, Town failed to find any sort of form in the early months.

An improvement in results through December and onwards coincided with a number of new signings, particularly loanees Luke Weaver in goal, Luke Graham in defence and Pat Sappleton. Billericay seemed to have a renewed confidence, which saw them start to win again including the 5-2 annihilation of Hitchin. January saw Billericay continue to pick up points including impressive wins over Heybridge and Basingstoke. In the end though, they failed to pick up points when they mattered against other struggling sides and lost crucial 'six pointers' against Braintree and Harrow. Billericay managed to keep themselves in the Play-Off hunt until their penultimate game, but the bad start to the season proved too difficult to recover from. Despite having nothing to play for in the final game of the season, Billericay still finished in style beating Northwood in a nine goal thriller (5-4) to stop Northwood achieving a Play-Off place.

The player of the season for Billericay was Danny Hockton by a long way. Despite injuries and playing in a side near the bottom, he still managed to score 26 goals. The signings of Pat Sappleton from Farnborough and Luke Weaver from Northampton were crucial as they both performed excellently in Billericay's second half of the season recovery. The season was ultimately a disappointment for Blues fans as Billericay had become an established top half Ryman Premier side. However, credit must be given to the management and players for turning the season around from an almost impossible position to just miss out on the Play-Offs. www.billericaytownfc.29m.com

Braintree Town

Address: Cressing Road, Braintree, Essex CM7 6RD
Tel: 01376 345 617
Website: www.braintreetownfc.co.uk
Email: mail@braintreetownfc.co.uk
Officials: Chairman: Lee Harding
Secretary: T. Woodley
Manager: George Borg

Cressing Road

Directions

Turn into Braintree at the McDonald's roundabout after leaving the Braintree bypass and follow signs for East Braintree Industrial Estate. The ground is approximately three quarters of a mile on the left past the Orange Tree pub.
By train: Braintree is just over an hour's journey from London. A regular service runs from Liverpool Street. On leaving Braintree station, turn into Railway Street and then take a right into Manor Street. Follow this road bearing left into Chapel Hill and then turn right into Clockhouse Way.

This small ground is located in the centre of Braintree which you would think means it is close to the train station. However, this is not the case as the station is a good 30 minutes walk and it is easy to get lost. Once inside the ground, the first thing that hits you is the size of the pitch as, for this level, it is big. The bar is located behind one of the goals and the fans are friendly and always jovial. One really good point about this ground is that if you only have a handful of supporters it is possible to create lots of noise as it is a small compact ground. The catering is average and if you start queuing before half-time you might see the last ten minutes of the match as the service can be painfully slow. SW

Review

It was a season to forget for the Iron, who failed to repeat the previous campaign's escape from relegation and finished second from bottom, a distant eight points short of a Play-Off berth. There were some bright spots though, none more so than at the start of the season, when three straight losses opened the campaign, only to give way to a 2-1 win at Kettering Town, at the time one of the favourites for the title. When this was followed by a 2-0 home success at home to Aylesbury United, hopes were raised that a season of struggle would not ensue, but two points from the next seven games decisively suggested otherwise. The Iron made progress in the FA Cup, winning an exciting game against Aylesbury United, 3-2, and one of their best league results followed, a 1-0 victory against high-flying Thurrock. However, the prospect of a morale-boosting cup run was clinically extinguished by a visiting Eastbourne Borough outfit who won 4-0. Trophy hopes then fell at the first hurdle thanks to yet another home defeat, this time by Harrow. At times, the team would produce a set of results to suggest an improvement, such as the three wins in November against Harrow, Bishops Stortford and Hitchin, but this run wasn't sustained, with Gary Bellamy making way for Dave Culverhouse and Dean Parratt at the helm. A meagre return of two points from eleven games across the turn of the year effectively sealed their fate; Culverhouse resigned in early March. His replacement was Graham Roberts, who had a strong record of turning clubs around in a short time, and the start was encouraging enough as his first game brought a 1-0 win at Billericay to ignite the survival fight. However, the woeful home form which had undermined the whole season reared its ugly head again, and though a superb win at Thurrock completed an unlikely double, the club ended the season with a run of eight straight home reverses. Roberts left soon after the end of the season, having commuted from his business interests in Spain, making way for former Aldershot manager George Borg. GB

The Iron

Chelmsford City

Address: (Ground-sharing with Billericay Town)
New Lodge, Blunts Wall Road,
Billericay, CM12 9SA

Tel: 01277 652 188 (matchdays)

Website: www.chelmsfordcityfc.com

Officials: Chairman: Peter Stroud
Secretary: David Clarke
Manager: Steve Mosely

Review

With the departure of former manager Paul Parker to Welling United, there was a new man at the helm at the start of the 2003/04 season. Steve Mosely, a former City player, was the new man in charge.

Following six victories in eight pre-season friendlies, there was an air of optimism surrounding the club, leading up to the start of their Dr Martens Premier Division campaign. Sadly this optimism proved to be unfounded and it was only by the skin of their teeth that City avoided relegation, on goal difference, on the final day of the season with a 3-1 home win over Merthyr Tydfil, whilst their closest rivals Dover Athletic were being held to a goalless draw.

A narrow defeat in the restructuring Play-Offs, away to Tiverton Town, means that City will now take their place in Step 3 in the new Isthmian Premier Division this season.

Scoring goals was their main problem, with just three goals and no wins in their opening eight matches of the season. With Dale Watkins often operating by himself up front, City were hardly likely to net many goals but with the central defensive partnership of Ian Wiles and Russ Edwards blossoming in the Autumn shades, Steve Mosely's side did develop a dependable look at the back.

An early departure from the FA Cup at the first hurdle, in a replay defeat to Eastbourne Borough, did nothing to lift the gloom enveloping City in their temporary home at Billericay Town. Then, at the end of November, City crashed out of the FA Trophy, also at the first hurdle, losing 4-1 to Ford United.

City struggled particularly at 'home' with just one win at the turn of the year. Their home form only really picked up at the business end of the season when they finally put together a consistent run of results losing just one game in a run of eight matches, a run which, ultimately, proved to be their saviour.

Highlights of the season? Well, perhaps the victories away to Nuneaton Borough and Hinckley United rank highly on the list, coupled with excellent away draws at high-flying Crawley Town and Weymouth Town, the eventual top two in the division. PM

Directions

From Chelmsford: Take the Galleywood Road, just past St John's Hospital, via Wood Street. Join Stock Road (B1007). Go straight on at the Running Mare pub, through Stock, and past the Cock Inn. Go straight over the roundabout by the golf course. When you reach the railway bridge, go straight across the roundabout and turn right at the traffic lights into Western Road. Continue, over a mini-roundabout, until traffic lights with a parade of shops on the left. Go straight across and take the first right turning, Blunts Wall Road. Half way down is New Lodge.

From M25 North: Leave at the junction with the A12 (J28) and take the A1023 through Brentwood. When you get to Shenfield, take the A129 towards Billericay. On entering Billericay, turn right at the first set of traffic lights (near the Esso Garage). Blunts Wall Lane is a little way along on the right.

From A127/M25 South: From J29, take the A127 to Basildon, the junction after the Fortune of War pub. Turn left at the first two roundabouts (Billericay is signposted on both of them) and then go straight over (second exit) at the third. Continue along this road until you enter Billericay. At the first roundabout, take the first exit, go straight over (first exit) at the next roundabout, then left into the one way system at the final roundabout. Go straight over at the first set of lights, then turn left at the next set. Blunts Wall Lane is a little way along on the right.

By train: Billericay is on the Liverpool Street /Southend Victoria Line. The ground is a 25 minute walk from the station. On leaving the station, turn right into Radford Way. At the top of the road, turn right, crossing the railway line by the footbridge. Then turn right again at the bottom of the High Street into Western Road. Walk the full length of Western Road, then cross over at the traffic lights into Tye Common Road. Blunts Wall Lane is a little way along on the right.

Ground-sharing with Billericay is a far from ideal situation but no need to tell this to City's supporters. It might be more acceptable if it was a more attractive ground (no doubt Billericay fans like it). More progress was made last season with regard to the club's intended return to Chelmsford but, with their new home at Melbourne Park still in the proverbial pipeline, it will be back to the New Lodge again this term. MW

New Lodge

The Clarets

Cheshunt

Address: The Cheshunt Stadium,Theobalds Lane, Cheshunt, Herts, EN8 8RU

Tel: 01992 626752

Website: www.cheshuntfc.com

Email: cfcsec@brassett.net

Officials: Chairman: Vince Satori
Secretary: Robert Brassett
Manager: Andrew Leese

The Cheshunt Stadium

Directions

From the M25: Exit at Junction 25 and take the third exit off the first roundabout on the A10. At the next roundabout, take the first exit and go under the railway bridge. Take the first left into Theobalds Lane. If you are travelling north on the A10, there is no entrance to Theobalds Lane as the road is a dual carriageway.
By train: The closest station is Theobalds Grove, which is served by London Liverpool Street and is less than half a mile from the ground. Exit the station and turn left into Theobalds Lane. The ground is down this road on the right hand side, opposite the Cedars Park.
By tube: Take the Victoria line to Seven Sisters in Tottenham then change onto an overground train to Hertford East and get off at Theobalds Grove (takes about 30 minutes) or catch a 279 bus to Waltham Cross (takes an hour roughly) and walk the rest - about 15 minutes.

Theobalds Lane is a new destination for most Premier Division clubs, and is in an unmistakably rural setting surrounded by trees and fields. When constructed, it was envisaged as a multi-sports stadium, and as a consequence both stands are set back from the pitch to allow for a track. The ground has now been upgraded to meet ground standards, and is a brisk ten minute walk from Theobalds Grove station, as well as being well-connected to the road network. GB

Review

Despite surrendering the top two spot that they had occupied for much of the campaign, it was still a record-breaking season for the Ambers, as they reached their highest ever position, with a best ever points tally (91). With virtually the same squad as the previous season, when they won Ryman Division Two, a scintillating start saw them lead the table virtually non-stop from mid-September to January, showing the benefits of a settled side, with nine of the first team regulars having represented the club in 100 or more games. The campaign started with a low key 1-0 win over Tilbury, but a stunning run of five league wins on the road, including a 7-3 success at Hemel, put them on top. Their positive attacking play reaped dividends all season, as the lethal Darrell Cox/Leon Archer partnership contributed 63 goals in a team that scored five or more goals on nine occasions. Whilst they departed both the Trophy and FA Cup after the first match, strong Autumn form had seen them progress in the Bryco Cup, and they stayed top of the league into the new year, before a thrilling penalties win at Yeading dislodged the holders from the Bryco. Just a few days later, Hitchin were dispatched from the Herts Charity Cup, but league results began to slip as Harlow Town beat them for the third time in the season, as they only took a solitary point from four games in the league. However, the Bryco Cup progress continued to intrigue as they won 4-3 at Heybridge Swifts to march on, and they reached the final of the Charity Cup by beating Hemel on their own ground. This had a positive effect on their league matches, as six successive wins restored them to second, only for a shock 2-0 home reverse to Berkhamsted, heralding an inconsistent run-in. Although they reached the Semi Final of the Bryco Cup by winning at Marlow, their championship hopes suffered a hammer blow as they fell to a 2-1 loss at leaders Yeading, and fell back to third. With games now coming thick and fast, Thurrock beat them 2-0 in the First Leg of the Bryco Semi-Final, and though they won 2-1 in Essex, it wasn't enough. Too many draws in the final games held them to third, but despite this, the club's progress from just a few seasons ago is astounding. GB

The Ambers

Dover Athletic

Address: Hoverspeed Stadium, Lewisham Road, River, Dover, Kent, CT17 0JB

Tel: 01304 822373

Website: www.dover-athletic.co.uk

Officials: Chairman: Mick Kemp
Secretary: Judy Yetman
Manager: Richard Langley

Hoverspeed Stadium

Review

Expectations at the Hoverspeed Stadium were high after Clive Walker had guided Dover to third place in 2002/03. He raised expectations even further when, pre-season, he said: 'I think the object has got to be to try to be number one.' And yet a season of such promise began with just two wins in the first ten games. New striker Craig Wilkins had no trouble finding the net, but then neither did Dover's opponents. Dover kept two clean sheets in those opening ten games, as the side sat uncomfortably in eighteenth place. Hovering outside the relegation zone had not been on Athletic's agenda, and they needed a change. After just two wins in the next five games (a total of four wins in 15 for the season) that change arrived as Dover parted company with Walker. Richard Langley took over and he started his reign with a 3-2 win over Nuneaton. But three defeats in his next four games was evidence that the season was going to be a long one.

As the Christmas decorations went up, Dover got into the festive mood. December was a great month for them as they won four games out of four, without conceding a goal. Langley won manager of the month, and he started the New Year with four points in two games. They looked on course for a Conference South place (although this was the minimum requirement for a club that was playing Conference football two seasons ago). The club were hit by the departure of strikers Tommy Tyne and Michael Smissen in February, so brought in unproven Jones Awuah from Division One Gillingham on loan. He played five and scored once but Dover gained five points from those games. This meant that even excessive away defeats to leaders Weymouth (3-0) and Worcester (5-1) couldn't push Dover out of the top 13.

After that defeat to Weymouth, Dover embarked on a dire run that saw them spiral downwards. In their last twelve league games, they won once and scored just five goals. It was a bad time to go on a losing run, but with four games left they were still clinging to thirteenth. Not being promoted to the Conference South would be an absolute disaster, and the Whites needed to raise their game for the season's finale - three home games in the last four gave them some hope. However, they lost 2-1 to Havant and 2-0 to Dorchester in front of their loyal fans and produced two dull 0-0 draws in their last two games. Thus, they finished in a dire 19th place - and even missed out on qualifying for a Conference South Play-Off place. The Isthmian Premier Division will be a bitter pill to swallow for Dover fans after a season of high hopes. MP

Directions

Take the M2/A2 (following the signs for Dover) as far as the Whitfield roundabout. Take the fourth exit, down Whitfield Hill. At the bottom of the hill, turn left at the roundabout and follow this road until the first set of traffic lights. Turn right here, pass under the railway bridge, and the ground is just up the road.

From the M20/A20, either go all the way into Dover and then through the town centre and along London Road until you reach the Crabble traffic lights, or leave the A20 in Folkestone (exit after the tunnel) and travel through Alkham Valley, which will eventually take you past Kearsney Abbey. Turn right into Lower Road just before the railway bridge.

By train: From Kearsney station, turn right under the railway and then first right (Lower Road). Follow this all the way along, past Crabble Corn Mill on your left. At the end, turn right and you will see the ground. It is a long walk from Dover Priory station. Buses go to the ground from Worthington Street (follow the road down to the roundabout at the bottom of Folkestone Road, cross over, turn right and it is the second street on the left).

The ground is in a natural bowl, surrounded on two sides by woodland. There is a low stand of seats down one side, and another seated stand on the other. Spectators viewing from the adjacent standing area are actually below the level of the pitch, which does not command the best of views, particularly if the subs decide to warm up in front of you. There is terracing at either end, where resides Dover's more vocal support. MW

The Whites

Eastleigh

Address: Sparshatts Stadium, Stoneham Lane, Eastleigh, SO50 9HT

Tel: 023 8061 3361

Website: www.eastleighfc.net

Email: eastleighfc@msn.com

Officials: Chairman: Roger Sherwood
Secretary: Derek Brooks
Manager: Paul Doswell

Sparshatts Stadium

Directions

From the M3: Leave the motorway at Junction 13 and turn right onto Leigh Road. Turn right at the lights onto Passfield Avenue. Go past Flemming Park Sports Centre and, at the roundabout, take the second exit. At the next roundabout take the first exit past the Concorde Club. Take the next turning on the right - Stoneham Lane - and the ground is 100 yards on the left.
From M27 Eastbound: Exit the motorway at Junction 5. At the roundabout take the first exit - Stoneham Lane. Go past the rear of the ground on the left and go all the way to the end of the road. At the next roundabout take the third exit and double back. Go past the Concorde Club and take the next turning on the right, Stoneham Lane.
From M27 Westbound: Exit the motorway at Junction 5. At the roundabout take the third exit. Then as for M27.
By train: The nearest station is Eastleigh Central - about a 20 minute walk to the ground. Depart Eastleigh station on to Station Hill. After about half a mile, turn left onto Cheshnut Avenue for just under a mile. At the roundabout take the first exit onto Stoneham Lane and continue for approximately a mile to the ground

Following the granting of planning permission by Eastleigh Borough Council, Eastleigh received funding for their new stand back in February. This new stand will seat 350 spectators and will also house the team and officials' changing facilities, a treatment room, committee room, and catering facilities. The stand should be ready for the start of the 2004/05 season. Eastleigh fans, who have enjoyed their club's rise in recent seasons, will no doubt be looking forward to a few South Coast derbies next season when they play host to Folkestone and Dover. JB

Review

At the start of the 2003/04 season, Eastleigh manager Paul Doswell set out with the objective for his team to gain a second successive promotion. A fourth-placed finish within the Dr Martens Eastern Division secured this. Despite this finish and some exciting passing football along the way, Doswell and the club will look back at this season with some disappointment, after two Semi-Final defeats, and defeat in the FA Cup against VCD Athletic.
The star performers of the season were inspirational skipper Rob Marshall and free-scoring striker Paul Sales. Both were bought just before the start of the season and continually impressed throughout the campaign. The commanding performances and stylish defending of centre-half Marshall, signed from Fleet Town, earned him the Supporters' and Manager's player of the season. Super striker Sales, signed from Bashley for an undisclosed five-figure sum, proved many people wrong. Although none doubted his goal scoring ability, his signing raised eyebrows due to his previous recurring hamstring problems. Yet, after a season of full fitness, the pony-tailed front man scored 29 goals to become the Eastern Division's top goal scorer, as well as earning a place in the Division's team of the year.
There were many highs during the season for Eastleigh, including victories over Conference side Aldershot Town in the Hampshire Senior Cup, and against Dorchester Town and Weymouth in the Dr Martens League Cup. In the league, a double over Folkestone Invicta, and other wins against Tonbridge Angels, Salisbury City and Bashley were also impressive. Another performance of note was the battling 1-1 draw away against Kings Lynn, in front of an intimidating crowd of 944.
Eastleigh also suffered lows during the campaign. Losing away to VCD Athletic in the FA Cup was very disappointing. So too losing in the Semi-Final of the Hampshire Senior Cup, after winning the first leg away at Fareham Town of the Sydenhams Wessex League, partly due to the fact that the winners would face Conference side Farnborough Town, at Southampton's St Mary's stadium in the Final. The Dr Martens League Cup Semi-Final defeat to Crawley Town was also upsetting. Substandard home league defeats to Histon, Stamford, Sittingbourne, Salisbury City, and Ashford Town, were also frustrating.
The other major success for Eastleigh in the 2003/04 season was that the club's future was secured and looks promising. Since the change of stadium name, Eastleigh have gained lots of extra sponsorship money. This has ensured that the re-development of the new stadium can take place. With extra car parking spaces made available, and another stand being erected, the stadium's facilities and capacity have improved. JRI

Folkestone Invicta

Address: Westbourne Stadium, Cheriton Road, Folkestone, Kent CT19 5JU

Tel: 01303 257461

Website: www.folkestoneinvicta.co.uk

Email: info@folkestoneinvicta.co.uk

Officials: Chairman: Bob Dix
Secretary: Alan Hall
Manager: Neil Cugley

Westbourne Stadium

Directions

Leave the M20 motorway at Junction 13 and head south onto the A20 (Cherry Garden Avenue). At the traffic lights, turn left onto the A2034 (Cheriton Road) and pass the Harvey Grammar School. The ground is the next left before the Safeway supermarket, opposite the cemetery. Some car parking is available at the Stripes club.
By train: Disembark at Folkestone West. On leaving the station, follow Station Road right and take a left onto Beachborough Road, then a right onto Cheriton Road. The ground is down this road next to Safeways.

The Westbourne Stadium (re-named last season due to a new sponsorship deal), is easily accessible as the ground sits on the main road and is just a short walk from Folkestone West train station. The friendly 'Stripes Club' tends to all your post - and pre-match drinking needs and there is a more than adequate food kiosk in one corner of the ground. There is a large function hall that is regularly used for entertainment, parties and the odd programme fair. While the away dug-out does not provide the best observation point (as it is tucked towards one of the corners), the rest of the ground provides excellent and close views of the pitch. Even if the football does get too dull, spectators in the stand opposite the dug-outs can watch the lorries rumbling backwards and forwards as the ground sits just beneath the South Downs and the main road link to Dover. This gives the ground quite an enclosed feel which adds to the atmosphere on a busy day. JB

Review

Folkestone started the season suffering from the bitter disappointment of having been relegated from the Dr Martens Premier Division the season before. However, having already been promoted from the Eastern once before, they knew exactly what was expected of them. And they made it look easy early on, as they strolled to victory in their opening three games, with Allan Tait netting four goals in the process. However, two successive 2-1 defeats and a draw later, and Folkestone were already trailing as Tonbridge began to pull away at the top. So, despite getting back on the winning trail with five wins in their next six, Tonbridge were already stamping their authority on the leadership with their breath-taking early season form.
Invicta then drew their next two games in unconvincing performances, which wouldn't have inspired much confidence as they travelled to runaway leaders Tonbridge, who at that time faced a number of off-field problems. Folkestone took full advantage, beating them 2-1 to stake their claim as serious title rivals. Invicta did show glimpses of their ability after this, but were drawing too many games to be in a position to snatch the leadership from under Tonbridge's noses. After their early September 2-1 defeat to Eastleigh, Folkestone went 29 games without defeat - not losing again until 30th March. Their best run came in late February, as they won three successive away games and scored 15 goals in the process. However, this success proved a double edged sword for Invicta as they were dealt a blow amidst that run when the club's and league's top scorer Tait left for Dr Martens Premier league leaders Crawley Town.
Despite going so many games without a defeat, Invicta were still nine points off the top spot in early April, despite only having lost four games out of 35. In the end the club finished in fifth - claiming a promotion place to the Premier - but they had, for a long time, a mathematical chance of winning the league. It was eight games without a win after their unbeaten run, just before their 3-0 final day win over Newport, that was to ultimately prove their downfall. They finished 16 points off of top spot, and to close that gap next year they will need to shore up a defence that leaked too many goals, thus resulting in too many draws. MP

Invicta

Hampton & Richmond

Address: Beveree Stadium, Beaver Close, off Station Road, Hampton, Middx, TW12 2BX

Tel: 0208 979 2456

Website: www.hrbfc.co.uk

Email: hamptonrbfc@aol.com

Officials: Chairman: Graham Wood
Secretary: John Tanswell
Manager: Alan Devonshire

Directions

Exit the M3 at Junction 1 and follow the A308 (signposted Kingston). Take the first left after Kempton Park into Percy Road. Turn right at the level crossing into Station Road, then left into Beaver Close (half mile).

From Twickenham, turn left onto the A311. Pass through Hampton Hill onto Hampton High Street. Turn right at White Hart pub (just before the junction with the A308), right into Station Road and right into Beaver Close.

By train: The ground is within a quarter of a mile of Hampton railway station (Waterloo-Shepperton line, SW Trains, 40 minutes from Waterloo) and is accessible by bus from Kingston, Sunbury, Staines, Richmond. Come out of the station and, if you are on the right side, there is a Chinese takeaway opposite (if there isn't, go over the bridge to the other side of the station). Turn left and the ground is along this road on the left.

One of my personal favourites, the Beveree is one of London's most attractive suburban grounds, hidden at the end of a cul-de-sac and heavily surrounded by trees which create an unmistakably enclosed feel. There is a modern seater stand at the clubhouse end of the stadium which offers excellent elevated views, particularly of action in the nearest goalmouth, and there is covered terracing and seating along part of one side. The rest of the ground is open, which is great on a good day. GB

Review

After the nightmarish 2002/03 season which saw Boro' finish a distant last in the Ryman Premier Division, former Maidenhead manager Alan Devonshire and his flock of ex-Magpies restored the Middlesex side to a solid outfit who comfortably returned to the Premier Division. Though billed as title favourites at the start of the season, too many draws meant they didn't run the top two close, although 89 points was still a superb haul.

Back in August, they made a good start, establishing themselves as a team who were hard to beat, and who were also making progress in the FA Cup, including a satisfying 2-1 victory against local rivals Kingstonian. However, this run, perhaps surprisingly, ended at the hands of Screwfix Western side Paulton Rovers in the Third Qualifying Round. There was a contrasting lack of success in the Trophy as Arlesey Town dispatched them in the first game after a home replay. League results began to trail off slightly in the weeks before Christmas, although there were three straight away victories at the turn of the year, as goals seemed easier to come by on the road. Always looking likely to remain in the top six, they began to close the gap on the top two. However, surprise losses against Bromley and Egham hindered their progress. Costly reverses against Worthing and Dulwich in the last few games meant they had to be content with fifth spot, but the overall impression was of a well-balanced side with 68 of their goals spread amongst four players, with Adrian Allen top scoring with 24. GB

Beveree Stadium

The Beavers

Harrow Borough

Address: Earlsmead, Carlyon Avenue, South Harrow, Middlesex, HA2 8SS

Tel: 020 8864 0933

Website: www.harrowboro.com

Email: inquires@harrowboro.com

Officials: Chairman: Jim Ripley

Secretary: Alan Murray

Manager: David Howell

Directions

From the M25 Junction 16, take the M40 east towards Uxbridge and London. Continue onto the A40, passing Northolt Aerodrome on the left. At the Target Roundabout Junction (A312) turn left towards Northolt. Just after passing Northolt underground station on the left, turn left at the next set of traffic lights, onto Eastcote Lane, becoming Field End Road. Just after passing under a railway bridge, turn right into Somervell Road and then first left into Walton Avenue. Continue straight over at the small roundabout. Earlsmead is the next road on the right.

By train/tube/bus: The ground is near South Harrow (Piccadilly Line), Rayners Lane (Piccadilly and Metropolitan lines) and Northolt (Central Line). From South Harrow station, it is a 20 minute walk, or buses 140 and 114 to within a few minutes walk of the ground (114 is the nearest). The 140 is for Heathrow and Hayes. Leave the bus at Alexandra Avenue. The 114 is direction Ruislip. Leave the bus just after passing Rooks Heath School on the right hand side. It is then a five minute walk to the stadium. Regular buses from Rayners Lane station (H10 direction South Harrow station) run as far as the junction of Eastcote Lane and Carlyon Avenue. From Northolt station, route 282 runs to the end of Somervell Road. Route 140 (direction Harrow) takes you as far as the junction of Alexandra Avenue and Northolt Road.

Earlsmead always seems an unlikely place for a football ground, hemmed in by rows and rows of Metroland semi-detached houses, with the floodlights the only guide from any distance. Once you have reached it, it reveals itself to be a neat and compact venue with the main stand recently renewed, with no posts to block the view of the game. A terrace stretches along the far side, and is very close to the dug-outs, should you want to pick up any tactical hints. Both ends are open, with the clubhouse at one end, and car park at the other, both looking a tad vulnerable to any wayward goal attempts. GB

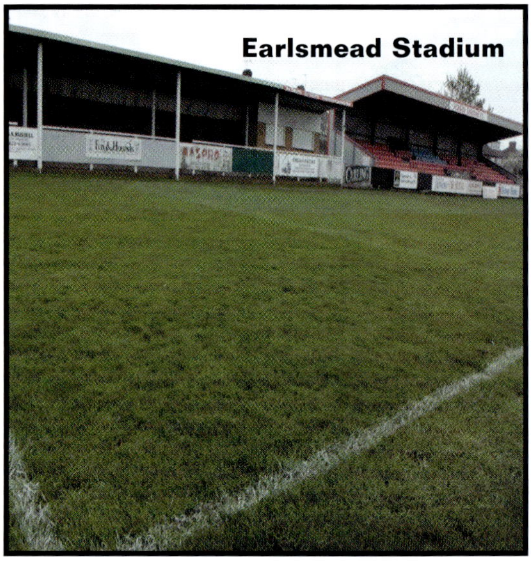
Earlsmead Stadium

Review

Despite their elimination from the Conference South Play-Offs by Kingstonian on penalties, it can still be seen as a relatively successful season, given their very bad start. Poor form in the opening months brought a formation change by then manager, Edwin Stein, and this brought a change in fortune which saw a welcome trio of October wins against Billericay, Bedford and St Albans.

Alongside this, there was progress in the FA Cup, as Flackwell Heath and Newport IOW were both seen off after replays to earn a plum tie against then-Conference leaders, Hereford United, who won 6-1 despite Borough hitting the woodwork in the first minute. League results trailed off in late November, and Stein was replaced by David Howell who tightened up the side's defence considerably, producing a ten match unbeaten spell in the Spring which was instrumental in their Play-Off qualification. There was disappointment in the other competitions, though, as they were edged out of the Middlesex competitions by Southall and Hanwell, and lost in the FA Trophy at the first hurdle as well. GB

The Boro

Hendon

Address: Claremont Road, Brent Cross, London NW2 1AE

Tel: 020 8201 9494

Website: www.hendonfc.net

Officials:
Chairman: Ivor Arbiter
Secretary: Graham Etchell
Manager: Tony Choules

Claremont Road

Directions

From M1: At Junction 1 take the second exit off the roundabout, a minor road called Tilling Road. Travel over three mini-roundabouts before turning right into Claremont Road at the fourth (signposted Hendon Football Club). The stadium is under half a mile away on the left.
By train: Travel to Cricklewood Thameslink station. Turn left out of the station, then left again soon after, into Claremont Road. The stadium is around three quarters of a mile on the right.
By tube: Travel to Brent Cross station (Northern Line). Turn right and then left at the end of the road. Around 100 metres on, cross the A41 using the subway on your right, and follow the alleyway, passing Tesco on the right, and a school. Turn left and then follow Claremont Road to the stadium on the left, a few hundred yards up.

Claremont Road's days are numbered, with a move to Copthall Stadium, a few miles away, scheduled for the early part of the season. Whilst their present venue is good location-wise, it is beginning to show its age, as the once expansive terraces begin to crumble, and the diminutive main stand doesn't offer the best of views. The new ground has an extensive stand, but features a running track. It is situated in Mill Hill, just off the M1, but without buses stopping outside as with their current headquarters. GB

Review

The 2003/04 season will go down as one of the most successful in decades for Hendon, even if all the good work was undone within ten days of the season's conclusion.
An opening day victory over newly-promoted Hornchurch was a good start, and things got even better as a magnificent second 45 minutes brought four goals and three more points at Basingstoke Town. This was followed by a blip in fortunes as a couple of injuries left the attacking options severely limited.
By the start of September the ship had been steadied, and consecutive victories over Ford United and Canvey Island were good signs. At the halfway point, the Greens' record was twelve wins and eight defeats from 23 games, a total 39 points, well over halfway towards the expected top-13 cut-off point.
January did not start particularly well and consecutive 1-0 away defeats left Hendon in eighth place. However, the Dons suddenly turned their form around and a run of 15 consecutive league games without defeat saw Hendon rise to second in the table with only the out-of-sight Canvey Island ahead of them.
The unbeaten run ended at Bishops Stortford on the Saturday before Easter and it was followed by a 2-0 loss at Sutton. A point from the final home game against St Albans meant victory at Kettering would then seal second place. In the end a tired, lacklustre 4-1 defeat meant that although the Greens accrued four more points than in 2002/03 and were five points closer to the champions, they finished a place lower in the table: fourth.
However, all the good work was overshadowed a week after the season ended when the club announced it would not be joining the Conference South set-up, opting instead to remain in the Isthmian League. Three days later, in an unrelated move, manager Dave Anderson left to take over at AFC Wimbledon and he took his entire management staff with him. In early June, former Northwood boss Tony Choules was appointed Hendon boss. DBL

The Dons

Heybridge Swifts

Address: Scraley Road, Heybridge, Maldon, Essex, CM9 8JA

Tel: 01621 852978

Website: www.heybridgeswifts.com

Email: info@heybridgeswifts.com

Officials: Chairman: Mike Springett
Secretary: Liz Creasy
Manager: Keith Martin

Review

A season that began well with the club dreaming of a place in the new Conference South ultimately ended in disappointment with Swifts losing in the Play-Offs after a topsy-turvy season. A change of manager after a poor run in the new year and an influx of new players failed to keep the Swifts' promotion hopes alive.
Danny Barber, John Pollard and Lee Kersey picked up the player of the year awards but a lack of consistency in performance from the side throughout the season was the main reason why Swifts will take their place in the re-vamped Ryman Premier Division in the 2004/05 season.
With a proud cup tradition, Swifts departed both the FA Cup and FA Trophy at the first time of asking to teams ranked lower in the pyramid; but some fine performances on their travels kept Swifts in a solid mid-table position throughout the season, but without seriously threatening for an automatic Conference spot.
Local youngster James Robinson was one high point of the campaign, as he came through from junior football to show he has the capability to make an impact at this level.
Aside from the serious matters, West Ham's Boys of '86 side took on a mixed Swifts team in front of a 1,500 crowd as Swifts continued to build their links with the local community.

Tony Foster - Heybridge Swifts FC

Directions

Exit at Junction 28 of the M25 and take the A12 to Chelmsford for ten miles. Then follow signs to Colchester (A12) and keep going for six miles before taking the A414 signposted Malden. After six and a half miles, you reach a junction for Malden town centre. Take the A414 for Colchester and, in just over a mile, you come to a roundabout. Take the first exit (B1018) and, in under half a mile, you should come to Heybridge. Follow signs for Great Totham (B1022). In just over half a mile turn right into Scraley Road. The ground is a mile further, on the right.
By train: The nearest station is Witham which is approximately six miles from the ground (there are taxis and bus services via Chelmsford and Malden).

A small, but neat and tidy ground situated in the heart of rural Essex. An impressive sight when there were more than two thousand crammed onto the terraces for an FA Cup tie with Bristol City a few of years ago.
Two small seated stands on the touchlines provide a fine vantage point for spectators, while there is a covered terrace behind one goal. At the other end, a friendly and hospitable welcome is guaranteed in the club bar.
A lush green playing surface is the envy of most visiting sides, while a small car park is available, but usually fills quickly on matchdays. Ample street parking can be found in Scraley Road. IL

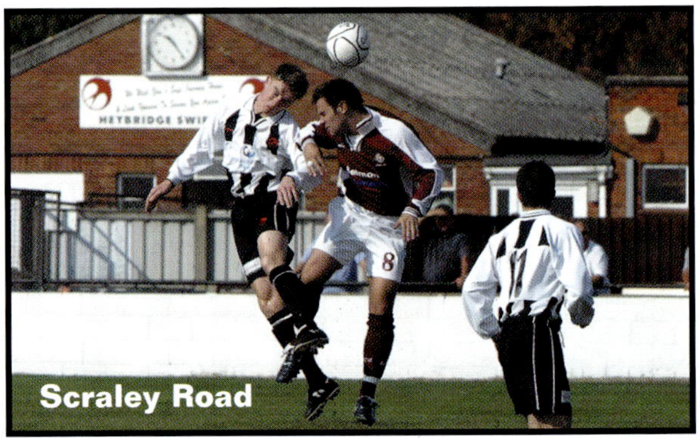

Scraley Road

The Swifts

Kingstonian

Address: Kingsmeadow Stadium, 422A Kingston Road, Kingston-Upon-Thames, Surrey, KT1 3PB

Tel: 020 8547 3335

Website: www.kingstonian.net

Email: ksweb@kingstonian.net

Officials: Chairman: Rajesh Khosla
Secretary: Graham Richards
Manager: Kim Harris

Kingsmeadow Stadium

Directions

If travelling from the M25, exit at Junction 10 (the A3) and head towards London. If travelling from London, head towards the A3. From both these routes, exit the A3 at the New Malden junction and head towards New Malden (left turn if from the M25). Turn left at the next roundabout (The Fountain), onto Kingston Road (A2043). The ground is in Jack Goodchild Way, before you reach the town centre, a few miles along Kingston Road. By train: The nearest station is Norbiton, on the Waterloo-Kingston Line (trains every 15 minutes, Monday to Saturday). The ground is one mile from here. Head towards the main London Road and then turn left into Cambridge Road after the supermarket. The ground is on the right, about a ten minute walk up this road.
By bus: Many buses serve Kingston town centre. The 131 passes the ground (from Kingston town centre).

This is one of my favourite grounds to visit. You can see it was meant for Conference or even league football, which is what makes it such a shame that the team that plays here are languishing in the depths of lower non-league. The food is of a high standard and the bar is connected to the main stand which looks impressive when full. Kingstonian now no longer own it as the lease was bought out by AFC Wimbledon but this doesn't stop the 400-500 fans supporting their team. Hopefully they can get their act together on the pitch and move back into the upper echelons of non-league soon. SW

Review

A traumatic season for the K's, dominated by off-the-field problems, saw them miss out on a Conference South place in the end of season Play-Offs. Their solid defence, compared with the sides around them, meant they didn't slip into trouble. This was just as well as their strike rate of only 40 goals for the season was even less than the bottom two, as they found goals especially hard to come by in the second half of the campaign. However, their start to 2003/04 had been reasonably bright with three of their first away games resulting in wins. Though they were knocked out of the FA Cup by local rivals Hampton & Richmond Borough, their form in the league had been encouraging until October and the start of a lean spell which saw them claim one league victory in nine attempts, although cup victories punctuated this sequence, as their FA Trophy, Surrey Senior Cup and Bryco Cup involvement started with a win in each case. Wins became more and more intermittent as 2003 became 2004, as the likelihood of avoiding the Play-Offs was receding amid a collection of single goal losses and a sustained goal shortage. The Surrey Cup offered some cheer as Egham and Banstead were beaten away from home, but Sutton handed the K's a home defeat to end any hope of silverware. A seven match winless run into April threatened to plunge the K's into the bottom four, but late wins against Billericay and Basingstoke, combined with the points accumulated earlier on, meant that they secured a Play-Off date at Harrow. A 0-0 draw and extra-time ensued, with the K's winning on penalties. However, the hastily arranged game with Lewes on the South Coast saw the Rooks beat the K's 1-0 and thus they missed out on Conference South. GB

The K's

Leyton

Address: Leyton Stadium, 282 Lea Bridge Road, Leyton, E10 7LD

Tel: 020 8539 5405

Website: www.leytonfc.co.uk

Email: enquiries@leytonfc.co.uk

Officials: Chairman: Costa Sophocleous

Secretary: Tony Hampford

Manager: Costa Sophocleous

Leyton Stadium

Directions

From M11: Proceed along the A406 to the first exit (Waterworks Roundabout), then take the first exit into Woodford New Road A406 leading into Lea Bridge Road. Proceed along Lea Bridge Road through four main sets of traffic lights. The ground is 250 yards on the left, next to the Hare and Hounds pub.
From A12: Take the A12 to the Gants Hill Roundabout, then the third exit into Woodford Avenue, A1400. Continue along this road to Charlie Brown's Roundabout. Take the second exit onto the A406 then follow the directions above from the Waterworks Roundabout/Lea Bridge Road.
Car parking is limited at the ground so if the car park is full, park opposite the club beside the B&Q Superstore where there is a small industrial complex.
By train: Leyton is on the Liverpool Street/Chingford Line. Alight at Walthamstow Central. The bus terminal is adjacent to the stadium and a number 48 bus will take you to the ground
By tube: Take a Victoria Line train to Walthamstow Central then as train directions. Alternatively you can take a Central Line train to Leyton. Then, take either a number 58 or 158 bus, alighting at Markethouse Corner. The ground is a short walk west down Lea Bridge Road.

Leyton Stadium has moved into the 21st Century with huge off the pitch renovations. The internal structure has been transformed into one of the most luxurious club facilities in non-league football. On the first floor, accessed by lift, is 'The Digby Suite' where patrons can wine and dine in five star luxury whilst listening to premier cabaret acts. The ground floor offers a futuristic styled cocktail bar, restaurant, modern kitchens and a separate club lounge with additional space for a new office complex, boardroom and entrance to the players' lounge. Leyton is definitely a club going places. JB

Review

It was an excellent season for the Lea Bridge Road club, who achieved their second successive runners up position after promotion from Ryman Division Two in the 2002/03 season, and boasted the best defence in their league. Trevor Paul proved an astute signing from Bishops Stortford and started well with four goals in his first four games as well as a brace to earn an FA Cup replay with Norwich United. Home form proved the bedrock of their early success, and their away form took off as well following the significant 4-2 win at Hemel Hempstead Town. Arlesey and Leatherhead were seen off as the Cup run progressed, and a long unbeaten sequence saw them rise up the table. October saw two memorable performances, a thrilling 4-3 win at Molesey in their first FA Trophy tie, and a comfortable 3-0 win over Ryman Premier Division side Bedford Town in the FA Cup which saw them earn a Fourth Qualifying Round spot, where their hopes were ended with a home defeat by Histon. Shrewd acquisitions such as Leli Bejada, Scott Honeyball and Paul Armstrong kept the league momentum going and, by February, they were in a three way battle for the title, as a crucial 2-1 win over Cheshunt was the start of four wins and two draws from six, as the goals continued to fly in. As the season entered its closing months, Cheshunt faltered, as Leyton became the main challengers to Yeading's top spot. Leyton collected four wins from their last five games, but still couldn't pip Yeading to the championship trophy. GB

The Lillywhites

Northwood

Address: Northwood Park, Chestnut Avenue, Northwood, Middlesex, HA6 1HR

Tel: 01923 827148

Website: www.northwoodfc.com

Email: northwoodfc@freeuk.com

Officials: Chairman: Andy Johnson
Secretary: Steve Williams
Manager: Mick Harvey

Northwood Park

Directions

From the A40 Western Avenue (Hillingdon Circus junction), head north along Long Lane, B466. Stay on this road (it becomes Ickenham Road) past West Ruislip station (on your right at the top of the bridge). At the next roundabout take the second exit, to stay on the B466. At the end of the road turn left into Ruislip High Street (A4180). At the end of the High Street, turn right onto the B466 Eastcote Road. Stay on this road (keep left) when it forks at the second roundabout. When the road forks again, just before Eastcote Village, take the left fork into Joel Street (B472) and head towards Northwood Hills. At the first roundabout after Northwood Hills station (on your right), turn left onto the A404 Pinner Road towards Rickmansworth. Chestnut Avenue is the fourth on your left, the first left turn before the railway bridge.

By tube: The ground is a third of a mile from Northwood Hills station (Metropolitan Line). Turn right out of the station. At the roundabout turn left onto Pinner Road, then left into Chestnut Avenue.

By bus: Numbers 282 and H11 to Northwood Hills.

Chestnut Avenue is a diminutive ground in a corner of a public park, and has gradually developed as the club has progressed from Spartan League and up the Ryman ladder. It is enclosed by trees and is separate from its clubhouse which stands at the end of a long narrow driveway from the road itself. There is open terracing at one end behind which there is a graveyard, with covered terracing on two of the other sides, and a main stand which is quite small for the level but benefits as a result from being so close to the pitch. Though small, it is a homely and friendly venue. GB

Review

It was a baptism of fire for the Woods, at their highest ever status in the game but, despite this, they narrowly failed to clinch a Play-Off place as they finished fourth from bottom. They scored a highly respectable 65 goals, which was more than fifth placed Hornchurch, but the goals against of 95 clearly indicates where the problems lay. Back in August, it took a while for the runaway Division One North champions to establish themselves at the higher level, as they took a solitary point from their first four matches. However, they opened their account on 30th August by beating Hitchin 1-0 and showed they could compete by beating a Bedford Town side, who had made a good start, 3-1. Their third win, against Braintree in late September, marked the start of a trend which saw them win many of their important games to stay just out of trouble, despite not putting any real runs together. However, both Cup and Trophy involvement ended after the first game, with heavy defeats at home to Ridgeons League side AFC Sudbury and at Lewes respectively. A poor spell in November was halted by their first away league success, a priceless 4-1 victory at Billericay, and that was followed soon afterwards by an equally crucial 2-1 win at Aylesbury just before Christmas. Their inconsistency continued into the New Year, though a Play-Off spot still seemed possible. Mark Nicholls was crucial in keeping their hopes alive with 18 goals in 35 games, thus ensuring that the loss of Chris Moore to Dagenham was not felt too harshly. A win over Hitchin, at the start of April, seemed to set them up well for a late dash but, in the event, Woods lost their last four games, allowing Hitchin to take 20th place on the last day. GB

The Wood

Salisbury City

Address: Raymond McEnhill Stadium, Old Sarum, Salisbury, Wiltshire, SP4 6PU

Tel: 01722 326454

Website: www.salisburycity-fc.co.uk

Email: trevor@salisburycity-fc.co.uk

Officials: Joint Directors: Neville Beale/Stuart McGlashan
Secretary: Douglas Ferraro
Manager: Nick Holmes

Raymond McEnhill Stadium

Directions

From the North: Exit the A303 at the Countess Roundabout/Amesbury Junction and go through the town onto the A345. Continue towards Salisbury, past the turn off to Boscombe Down on the left, up the hill and through the traffic lights at High Post (a hotel and nightclub are on the right) and carry on down to the Beehive junction roundabout. There is a large sign here for the ground. Turn left, through the first small roundabout and then left into Partridge Way.
From the South: Travel along the A36 Southampton Road to the College Roundabout (Salisbury College is on the right). Turn right and follow the dual carriageway (Churchill Way) to the next roundabout (St Mark's). Turn slightly to the left at this roundabout, as if going towards Wilton, Bath and Bristol, and you will go downhill towards the Castle Street roundabout. Take the A345 (Castle Road) marked 'Amesbury'. Carry straight on up this road, past Victoria Park until Hudson's Field and Old Sarum on the left. Continue over and down the hill and you will come to a new, large roundabout at the Beehive, then as above.
By train: Salisbury is on the main London/Exeter line. The ground is approximately three miles from the station so it is advisable to get a taxi.

Salisbury moved to their current new ground in 1997 - named the Raymond McEnhill Stadium after the then chairman whose money built the ground. The main feature of the stadium is a large stand situated along the near touchline. There are two seated levels, with the upper tier providing a particularly good view of the action below.
To one side of the stand is a separate covered terraced area, extended around behind the near goal. The remaining two sides of the ground remain undeveloped, with banking behind the far goal, and open fields opposite the main stand - with stiles thoughtfully provided for ball boys to retrieve misplaced (or desperate) clearances. DB

Review

In August 2002, the club achieved a major coup in tempting the legendary former Southampton midfield player and member of the FA Cup winning side of 1976, Nick Holmes, to leave the Florida sunshine for the Wiltshire town, to take over the reins in his first managerial role.
After finishing in a more than creditable fourth place in his first season, and that after having had three points deducted for fielding an ineligible player, it was always going to be difficult for the Whites to match their performance of the previous campaign.
From the start, there was never any doubt that the Whites would be able to consolidate their position in the Dr Martens Eastern Division but there was never quite the necessary consistency in their performances to suggest that they would stand any chance of winning the Championship. Indeed, the Whites finished a distant 17 points behind the eventual winners Kings Lynn but, by virtue of finishing in sixth position, they gained promotion to Step 3 in the new restructuring system and with it a place in the new Isthmian Premier Division.
Undoubtedly, the highlight of the season for the Whites was their exploits in the FA Cup where they reached the First Round only to lose with honour to Sheffield Wednesday, after an FA Cup odyssey, which began in August in the Preliminary Round with a home tie against the quaintly named Odd Down. Indeed, the Second Division side were flattered by the 4-0 scoreline. Heartbreaking though it was, the Whites' performance on the day, and the quality of their football, received glowing praise from the national media.
Certainly, Nick Holmes has built a strong-looking squad, which could well challenge for honours in the new Isthmian Premier Division, with the exciting young goalscoring prospect Matt Tubbs one to watch. Tubbs, who was once a youth team player with AFC Bournemouth and Bolton Wanderers, is likely to trouble many defences and alongside strike partner Adam Wallace will no doubt prove to be a potent attacking force. PM

The Whites

Slough Town

Address: Groundsharing with Windsor & Eton FC: Stag Meadow, St Leonards Road, Windsor, Berkshire, SL4 3DR

Tel: 01753 554 833

Website: www.sloughtownfc.net

Email: feedback@sloughtownfc.net

Officials: Chairman: Martin Deaner
Secretary: Roy Merryweather
Manager: Eddie Denton

Stag Meadow

Directions

From M4: Exit the M4 at Junction 6. Follow the signs for Windsor. Once on the Eton/Windsor Relief Road (A355/A332), continue and go over the river Thames, a fly-over and a roundabout. When you reach a large roundabout with traffic lights, take the third exit into Imperial Road. When you reach a T-junction, turn left into St Leonards Road. The ground is on the right after a quarter of a mile.

From M25: Travelling anti-clockwise, exit at Junction 15 onto the Westbound M4 then follow directions as per M4 above. If clockwise, exit at Junction 13, follow signs to Windsor (A308), eventually reaching a large roundabout. Take the first exit (signposted Ascot/Bracknell), and take the first road on the right (Bolton Road). At the end of Bolton Road, reaching a T-junction with mini-roundabout, turn left into St Leonards Road. The ground entrance is about a mile down this road, opposite the Stag & Hounds pub.

By train: Windsor & Eton Riverside/Windsor & Eton Central: Windsor Riverside: Trains run directly from Clapham Junction and Waterloo. Windsor Central: From Paddington, change at Slough for branchline to Windsor. The Ground is a good half an hour walk from the town centre. There is a frequent bus service from the town centre which stops just outside the ground.

The Stag Meadow is situated on the edge of Windsor's Great Park, which offers a stirring backdrop to events on the pitch, and continues to play host to the area's two main senior sides. It has a fairly small main stand with a reasonable view, but covered terracing stretches along the far side; Slough and Windsor operate separate club shops on their respective match days. The drawback of such a pleasant setting is that parking is awkward, though the motorway is not far away. The walk from the centre of town is lengthy, though amiable. GB

Review

The Rebels overcame the upheaval of the move to groundshare at Windsor & Eton, as a storming finish to the season saw them claim fourth place and a promotion which appeared to have been drifting away from them. Making the switch from Division One North to South, and under the new management of Eddie Denton, they had something of a mixed start, as comfortable wins intermingled with defeats and made a promotion challenge seem unlikely. FA Cup progress brought early wins against East Grinstead Town and Godalming & Guildford but, after Welling defeated them 4-1 in the next round, it raised questions about the Rebels' defence, particularly when the next game saw a 4-0 loss at Hampton. They picked themselves up with only one defeat in the next seven, including a 5-1 hammering of Banstead, but there was disappointment in both the Trophy and Bryco Cup as Bishops Stortford and Cheshunt accounted for them in the first game of each. When Worthing beat them 2-0 in mid-January, promotion looked tricky to achieve, but crucially they bounced back with six straight wins. The Tony Boot-Ian Hodges partnership, a danger all season, really ignited, and they provided 61 of the team's 103 goals by the end of the campaign (the second highest in Division One North). Hodges' 34 got him the Golden Boot by some margin, whilst Boot's 27 saw him in third place. This translated itself into results in devastating fashion as 16 of the last 20 games were won, with two draws, and an incongruous pair of defeats at Corinthian Casuals and Bracknell Town, as most sides struggled to deal with Slough's lethal attack. The Semi-Final of the Berks and Bucks Senior Cup was also reached, but Bracknell proved the bogey side again as they beat them 1-0. GB

The Rebels

Staines Town

Address: Wheatsheaf Park, Wheatsheaf Lane, Staines, Middlesex, TW18 2DP

Tel: 01784 463100

Officials: Chairman: Alan Boon
Secretary: Steve Parsons
Manager: Steve Cordery

Directions

Leave the M25 at Junction 13 and turn east onto the London-bound A30. At the Crooked Billet roundabout, bear left and turn right back across the A30 onto the A308 towards Kingston. At the next roundabout turn right towards Staines and bear right at the mini-roundabout. At the next mini-roundabout turn left into Worple Road. Continue until a T-junction at the Lucan Arms public house. Turn right towards Staines. After about half a mile the road curves left and Wheatsheaf Lane is the next turning on the left. Wheatsheaf Park ground is about 100 yards along on the left, with plenty of parking available.
By train: Come out of Staines station and go straight down Gresham Road. Turn left into Laleham Road and the ground is about half a mile down this road on the right hand side.

Wheatsheaf Lane was impressively rebuilt as Town returned from exile midway through the 2002/03 season, and it now boasts an eye-catching new stand which backs onto the sports centre development now at the site. This stand offers a very good view, and there is plenty of terracing available as well. It is one of the most notable rebuildings of a non-league ground in recent years, all the more remarkable for its presence in an exclusively residential area. The car park is fairly big, though it is quite a long, though not unattractive, walk from the town centre and the station. GB

Review

With new first team manager, Steve Cordery, at the helm at Wheatsheaf Park, the Swans achieved a creditable sixth place in the Ryman Division One South, a big improvement on the previous season when they were languishing in the lower half of the division.
Their season started with an unbeaten run of eight matches - six wins and two draws - which only ended with a narrow 1-0 defeat at Leatherhead on the last day of September. The managerial partnership of Cordery and Craig Maskell, which had been so successful at Aylesbury United, continued to prosper and there were high hopes that the Swans would be challenging for honours.
Interestingly, Ali G (Sacha Baron Cohen), the local celebrity, has publicly declared his infatuation with the town, which has inevitably led to a section of Swans' supporters adopting the name of 'Staines Massive'.
An early exit from the FA Cup, at East Thurrock United, meant that the Swans could concentrate on the league but things turned a little sour in November with a run of three defeats in four matches, when their attack was not firing on all cylinders. However, a fine home win against the eventual league winners, Lewes, in December meant that the Swans started 2004 still in with a chance of the championship.
Cordery, who had taken Aylesbury to the Semi-Finals of the FA Trophy, was looking to repeat that feat with the Swans and when they defeated Premier Division side Bath City in the Third Round they were drawn a plum tie against Halifax Town. Frustratingly, the bad weather in West Yorkshire forced the tie to be postponed on several occasions and when it did eventually take place on a Tuesday night in February the Swans forced a 1-1 draw. With the replay scheduled for just 48 hours later, the Swans were finally ousted from the competition, after an extra-time winner from the Shaymen.
The strain of playing two games in three days inevitably took its toll on the team and it was no real surprise that their form suffered, with a run of four defeats in five games, which ultimately cost them any chance of the championship.
Nevertheless, Cordery can be justifiably proud of his team's efforts and although they are likely to lose the services of their exciting young prospect Kezie Ibe who is being targeted by a number of league clubs, there is good reason for optimism as they take their place in the new Isthmian Premier Division. PM

Wheatsheaf Park

The Swans

Tonbridge Angels

Address: Longmead Stadium, Darenth Avenue, Tonbridge, Kent, TN10 3JW

Tel: 01732 352477

Website: www.tonbridgeafc.co.uk

Email: tonbridgeafc@hotmail.com

Officials: Chairman: Paul Dainty
Commercial Director: Paul Kelly,
Manager: Tony Dolby

Longmead Stadium

Review

A season that promised so much for the Angels ended in disappointment. Boss Alan Walker certainly expected much from his side, as he announced: 'I have told the chairman that if we don't win promotion, I expect to be sacked. But I honestly believe we will - the potential here is awesome.' His comments certainly seemed well founded judging by the form the Angels showed in the early months of the season. They won four out of four in August, three of four in September, and six of six in October - including a 2-0 win over promotion favourites Kings Lynn. The side were playing extremely well, aided by the creative brilliance of Hamid Barr and the goals of teenage striker Brendon Cass. By the end of November, the team had won 16 of their 17 league games and were 14 points clear at the top of the league.

However, there was a cloud on the horizon: they couldn't find a sponsor, and no sponsor would mean no Walker. He agreed at an early December meeting to see through the month without being paid. His first game after this meeting was a trip to Kings Lynn, where his side lost for the first time, suffering a 4-1 thrashing. Then came two seemingly easy home games against Kent neighbours, Folkestone and Chatham, but the Angels lost both. Walker then resigned, leaving Barr and Tony Dolby in charge. Three straight wins in February, including a nail-biting 4-3 success over Histon, kept them on top. Alas, Kings Lynn weren't slowing up, and a 0-0 draw with Eastleigh saw Angels fall off the top spot for the first since September. A home defeat to Sittingbourne the following week saw them fall to third. They squeezed back into top spot with three straight 1-0 wins in March, and they remained top despite successive 2-0 defeats to Newport and Bashley.

It was tight at the top, with five sides still in with a chance of the title, and Angels couldn't afford to slip up. A 2-1 win over Hastings and a 6-0 win at Bashley kept up the pressure, but they slipped and lost 2-0 in their penultimate game at home to Eastleigh. Kings Lynn still had a game in hand, and a win would effectively end Angels' title bid due to their vastly inferior goal difference. Kings Lynn won their game in hand 2-0. Thus Angels finished the season on a fine haul of 88 points, but still came third and so all that hard early season work went to waste. There has perhaps never been a better chance for Tonbridge to have won the title, and they will no doubt look back on an opportunity missed. MP

Directions

The town is reached from most directions via the M25 and A21, but from the south via the A26 or A21. Longmead is at the north-western edge of the town, off the A227. From the M25 Junction 5, take the A21 southwards towards Hastings. After a long downhill run of four miles or so, exit the A21 for the B245 through Hildenborough towards Tonbridge. Three miles later, just past the Langley Hotel, take the (slightly obscured) signposted left turn (Dry Hill Park Road). After another 400 yards, go left at the mini-roundabout (A227 Borough Green and Gravesend). At the next roundabout, by the Pinnacles pub, turn left again and follow Darenth Avenue to the bottom of the hill and the car park.

By train: Tonbridge station is one and a half miles south of the ground and is served by four trains per hour from London Charing Cross. Turn left out of the station and continue through the town centre until the junction where London Road (B245) forks to the left, after 15 minutes or so. Take the right fork (Shipbourne Road) and continue on until the Pinnacles pub. Turn left and go down the hill, with the ground at the bottom.

By bus: Buses leave from the station forecourt every 20 minutes Saturdays and every 30 minutes weekday evenings (219/214 Willow Lea) and stop at the bottom of Darenth Avenue near the ground (ask for one stop after the Pinnacles), but weekday services returning from Longmead after 9.30pm are practically non-existent.

Longmead Stadium has a friendly bar with TV for final scores, a club shop and a food kiosk. The stadium has two identical North and South stands which are covered terracing. The east stand holds just over 200 seats, but the majority of Angels fans stand on the wooden blocks on the opposite side. MP

The Angels

Wealdstone

Address: Sharing with Edgware Town: White Lion Ground, High St Edgware, Middlesex

Tel: 0208 552 3595

Website: http://cometowealdstonefc

Email: office@wealdstonefc.co.uk

Officials: Chairman: Nick Symmons, Secretary: Roger Slater, Manager: Gordon Bartlett

Camrose Avenue - under construction

Directions

Wealdstone are currently ground-sharing with Edgware Town but plan to be in their new ground at the Prince Edward's Playing Fields - Camrose Avenue - by the turn of the year.

Their current home at Edgware is behind the Premier Lodge Hotel (opposite Warwick Wright's car dealership), When they make the move, leave the A5 at junction 4 and follow signs to Edgware. Continue straight on at the lights in Edgware. Continue 600 yards to another set of traffic lights and turn right into Camrose Avenue. Travel along the Avenue for three quarters of a mile, through the width restrictions, and the entrance to Prince Edward's Playing Fields is 100 yards on the right. By tube: The nearest Tube Station is Canon's Park on the Northern Line. On leaving the station cross the road and walk to the left. The pedestrian entrance to Prince Edward's Playing Fields is 100 yards on the left.

The Stones' long-term share with the Wares will come to an end soon with their move to a purpose built new ground about half a mile west. The White Lion ground is earmarked for extensive rebuilding. At present it is hidden behind a budget hotel which replaced the White Lion pub in the 1990s. Probably one of the more basic grounds at this level, the main stand offers an elevated view of proceedings which is highly recommended, and there is a far side covered terrace, but next to no space behind either goal. GB

Review

It was a very exciting season for the Stones, who achieved promotion in dramatic style, as well as enjoying their best ever run in the FA Trophy since winning the competition in 1985. After they slipped off the promotion pace alarmingly in 2002/03, they got off to an encouraging start this time around, winning their first four away games. FA Cup hopes were extinguished in a home reverse to Uxbridge, but October brought a useful FA Trophy win at Leatherhead, soon followed by a 5-0 demolition of East Thurrock United. Their league form, though, continued to be inconsistent but it was their away form that continued to keep them on the fringes of the challengers. November ended brightly with a Trophy win against Premier Division Hitchin Town but their league campaign was undermined by a sequence which saw just two points from nine games between December and March. They exited the FA Trophy and slipped down the league into mid-table. There seemed to be too much ground to make up despite an impressive 3-1 home win against Chesham. However, five straight wins (including a priceless win at Arlesey) changed that. They now found themselves in the top six, but a 2-0 home loss to Hemel in the second to last game seemed to extinguish their hopes, as they dropped out of the top seven. A strange quirk of the fixtures saved them, though, as Hemel met Arlesey on the last day, meaning that Stones could nudge one of them out of the top seven with a win at East Thurrock. They duly obliged, and Wealdstone took seventh on goal difference over Arlesey - the significance of an 8-0 win at Enfield in April clear for all to see. So, to a Play-Off with Dulwich for the last Premier Division spot. The Stones were not to be denied as they clinch a topsy-turvy match in a penalty competition. GB

The Stones

Windsor & Eton

Address: Stag Meadow, St Leonards Road, Windsor, Berkshire, SL4 3DR
Tel: 01753 860656
Website: www.wefc.co.uk
Email: webmaster@wefc.co.uk
Officials: Chairman: Peter Simpson
Secretary: Steve Rowland
Manager: Dennis Greene

Stag Meadow

Directions

From M4: Exit the M4 at Junction 6. Follow the signs for Windsor. Once on the Eton/Windsor Relief Road (A355/A332), continue and go over the river Thames, a fly-over and a roundabout. When you reach a large roundabout with traffic lights, take the third exit into Imperial Road. When you reach a T-junction, turn left into St Leonards Road. The ground is on the right after a quarter of a mile.
From M25: Travelling anti-clockwise, exit at Junction 15 onto the Westbound M4 then follow directions as per M4 above. If clockwise, exit at Junction 13, follow signs to Windsor (A308), eventually reaching a large roundabout. Take the first exit (signposted Ascot/Bracknell), and take the first road on the right (Bolton Road). At the end of Bolton Road, reaching a T-junction with mini-roundabout, turn left into St Leonards Road. The ground entrance is about a mile down this road, opposite the Stag & Hounds pub.
By train: Windsor & Eton Riverside/Windsor & Eton Central: Windsor Riverside: Trains run directly from Clapham Junction and Waterloo. Windsor Central: From Paddington, change at Slough for branchline to Windsor. The Ground is a good half an hour walk from the town centre. There is a frequent bus service from the town centre which stops just outside the ground.

The Stag Meadow is situated on the edge of Windsor's Great Park, which offers a stirring backdrop to events on the pitch, and continues to play host to the area's two main senior sides. It has a fairly small main stand with a reasonable view, but covered terracing stretches along the far side; Slough and Windsor operate separate club shops on their respective match days. The drawback of such a pleasant setting is that parking is awkward, though the motorway is not far away. The walk from the centre of town is lengthy, though amiable. GB

Review

The 2002/03 season marked the Royalists' first in the Ryman Division One South, and they finished in a creditable 13th place. A run of five straight wins saw Windsor shoot up to the top of the table early on. However, a home defeat to Lewes pushed them off the top spot, and they were playing catch-up from then on as Lewes set the pace. They remained in second in the following months, despite not losing a game. Three 0-0 draws in four games reflected the team's relative shortcomings, but they were picking up points and that meant Lewes were looking nervously over their shoulders.
October, November and December came and passed without a defeat. Their good form was finally rewarded with the reclaiming of the leadership. They were showing no signs of letting up: six wins and two draws in their following eight games extended their unbeaten run to 22 games. That run came to an end in abrupt fashion, with a 3-0 defeat to mid-table Ashford Town in late February - their first in over five months.
The club took a sudden dive after the Ashford defeat with one point from the next two games. Three wins in a row, including a 2-1 win at title-rivals Lewes, put them back on track, but they then took just one point from the following four games. A hard-fought win at Horsham gave them a vital three points in their quest for the title, before they faced a Slough side hungry for revenge. The Royalists never stood a chance as they were demolished 4-1 in front of their home fans. As they then fell to a 1-0 defeat to Bromley, Lewes took over at the top and a 4-2 penultimate game win over Egham wasn't enough, and they ended with a goalless draw at Croydon which allowed Worthing to snatch second place. Windsor finished with 91 points, three points behind title-winners Lewes but just two in front of fifth-placed Hampton. They did well in a competitive league, but will have been disappointed to have finished third after leading the table for so long. MP

The Royalists

Worthing

Address: Woodside Road, Worthing, West Sussex, BN14 7HQ

Tel: 01903 239575

Website: www.worthingfc.com

Email: contact@worthingfc.com

Officials: Chairman: Beau Reynolds
Secretary: Paul Damper
Manager: Alan Pook

Woodside Road

Directions

From the North: Turn left onto the A27 at Durrington Cemetery roundabout. Continue until the next roundabout (Warren). Take the town centre exit and continue until the mini-roundabout at the end of the green. Go right along the green, past the fire station on the left, until the next mini-roundabout. Go left into South Fram Road and take the fifth turning on the right (Bulkington Avenue). Woodside Road is the first on the left. Park in Bulkington Road.
From the East: Continue along the A27 until the Warren Roundabout. Then as above.
From the West: Continue along the A27 until Durrington Cemetary Roundabout. Then as above.
By train: Come out of Worthing station, turn right and follow the road to the level crossing. Go over the crossing and take the second turning on the left, Henty Road. The ground is at the end of the road.

Woodside Road is one of Sussex's finest grounds - it boasts a modern 500 capacity all-seater stand which incorporates an enclosed press box, VIP area, fully-functional bar, an office, boardroom, toilet facilities, dressing rooms for the home and away teams and also a comprehensive medical room. Within the Woodside Road complex are two other covered stands, two catering blocks, a club shop and a large function room incorporating the Supporters' Bar which features further catering facilities. The pitch was also relayed in 2003 and it now sports a state-of-the-art irrigation system.
www.worthingfc.com

Review

It was an excellent season for the south coast club under Alan Pook, for whom the signing of Sam Francis from Combined Counties Champions Withdean 2000 proved a masterstroke, as he top scored with 23 goals. An impressive start to the season brought seven league wins from the first nine, to firmly establish themselves amongst the challengers, but the number of clean sheets they were keeping also augered well. In the FA Cup, after a 7-0 thrashing of Ash United and a replay win over Premier Division Heybridge Swifts, their journey was ended by Ford United.
However, it was the Trophy in which they would make a mark, starting their run with a 2-0 victory at Chesham United. At this stage, league progress trailed off slightly, but their good form on the road continued as they beat Cambridge City 3-2 in a replay. They remained hard to beat in the league, but defeats to Hampton and Dulwich seemed to damage their promotion hopes, but a 4-0 Trophy win at Whyteleafe continued to see them at their best in the knockout competitions.
Their reputation as away day specialists (they went unbeaten on the road from December to the end of the season), meant that they were handily placed at the turn of the year. 2004 heralded further success in the Trophy with a comfortable 3-0 win against Taunton Town to put them into the Fourth Round, and hopes were high when the struggling Hednesford Town of the Dr Martens League were brought back to the south coast, only for the Pitmen to go through 2-1. With the team knocked out of the Bryco Cup soon afterwards, that left them with the League and Sussex Senior Cup, and they were destined to be runners-up in both. A stunning last 20 games yielded twelve wins, seven draws, and a solitary defeat to Lewes, who were all but assured the title. In the Sussex Cup, the Woodside Road club made the final, beating Dr Martens Champions Crawley Town to get there, but on the day, a strong Brighton & Hove Albion Reserves beat them 2-0. GB

The Rebels

Yeading

Address: Beaconsfield Road, Hayes, Middlesex, UB4 0SL

Tel: 020 8848 7362

Website: www.yeadingfc.co.uk

Email: yeading@yeadingfc.co.uk

Officials: Chairman: Phillip Spurden
Secretary: Bill Gritt
Manager: Johnson Hippolyte

Beaconsfield Road

Directions

From the M40: Head eastbound towards London. After passing RAF Northolt on the left, the next junction is the Polish War Memorial. Ignore this turning but take the next junction about a mile further on, the Target Roundabout, for Northolt & Harrow. At the top of the slip road, take the fourth exit onto the A312 towards Hayes. At the next roundabout, about a mile and a half on, ignore signs to Yeading (third exit) but take the second exit towards Hayes and Heathrow to stay on the A312 (Hayes Bypass). Carry over the the next roundabout, then take the next exit for Southall and Uxbridge (A4020 Uxbridge Rd). At the top of the slip road take the first exit towards Southall and follow the directions below.

From the M4: Take Junction 3 (Southall & Hayes). Head northbound along the A312 The Parkway (Hayes By-Pass). Go over the first roundabout (Tescos is to the right) and over the flyover. Ignore the next junction (signposted to Hayes) and take the second (signposted Hayes, Uxbridge & Southall). At the end of the sliproad is the Ossie Garvin roundabout. Take the third exit towards Southall and follow the directions below.

For both the above, head eastbound along the Uxbridge Road towards Southall. Get into the far right hand lane and turn right into Springfield Road at the next set of traffic lights (a petrol station and retail development with a Wickes store). Follow the road past Technicolour Sports ground on the right. The road bears left and about 100 yards on is the entrance to the ground.

Train: The nearest station is Hayes & Harlington. The ground is a long way from the station so it is advisable to take a taxi (approximately ten minutes).

The Warren is famous for featuring in the film, 'Bend It Like Beckham' as well as in a recent insurance commercial, but it is still tricky to find, being hidden in an industrial estate. It is a modern venue dating from the Ding's meteoric rise of the 1980s, with a covered terrace behind one of the goals, and a covered stand along around half of one side. The clubhouse is well-appointed and the car park has plenty of space with good road accessibility and frequent buses passing along the nearby Uxbridge Road. GB

Review

Hayes-based Yeading enjoyed an excellent season despite having a fairly unspectacular record in recent seasons. 15th, 14th and 13th were the positions they had finished in the last three years and at that rate they would have won the league by 2014/15. 'The Ding' instead decided that 2003/04 was to be their season, as they won five and drew two of their opening seven games - including a spectacular 7-0 win over Tilbury. A 2-1 defeat to highly-fancied Cheshunt proved a minor set-back as Yeading then took maximum points in their next five games. It was Cheshunt, however, who led the table with Yeading tagging along just behind.

It wasn't until Valentines Day, with a 4-3 win over Berkhamsted, that Yeading re-acquainted their relationship with the top spot. It was their fifth win in a row, after overcoming a 5-0 hammering by Arlesey. A 6-0 thrashing of Barton followed that and they won their next four games by a single goal. But its points that win leagues, and although Cheshunt were in good form, a home defeat to Harlow allowed Yeading to overtake. It was a lead that they never gave up; they lost just three times in their last 20 games. A 2-1 win over Cheshunt on the 20th March made it abundantly clear that Yeading were in no mood to give up their lead. They ended the season with an impressive points tally of 103, and they scored an incredible 112 goals - their prolific strike partnership of Dudley Campbell and Errol Telemague contributed over half of those goals, with 57 between them.

They ended the season with a tough-looking Conference South Play-Off tie with Ryman Division One South winners, Lewes, who had won their league by two points (in contrast, the Ding held a seven point lead over nearest rivals Leyton). On the day, Lewes proved too strong and triumphed 1-0 over a tired-looking Yeading. But for the Ding, one promotion was enough - manager Johnson Hippolyte admitted the season was 'all about getting promotion, and we've done that'. They can take a lot of comfort from the knowledge that they will be playing the likes of Dover and Kingstonian next season rather than (with all due respect) Uxbridge and Barton Rovers. And with their superb strike partnership of ex-Aston Villa and QPR trainee Campbell (37 goals over the season) and Telemague (20 goals), few would bet against Yeading holding their own against their more distinguished opposition. MP

The Ding

Northern Premier

Club Pages

Bamber Bridge

Address: Irongate Ground, Brownedge Road, Bamber Bridge, Preston. PR5 6UX

Tel: 01772 909690 / 01772 909695

Website: www.bamberbridge.supernet.com

Officials: Chairman: Nigel Webster
Secretary: George Halliwell
Manager: Paul Byron

Irongate Ground

Directions

Leave the M6 at Junction 29. Take the A6 (Bamber Bridge bypass) onto London Way. At the first roundabout, take the third exit (Brownedge Road, east) and then take the first right. The ground is on the left at the bottom of the cul-de-sac.
By train: From Bamber Bridge Station. Turn left and walk for half a mile until you reach a set of traffic lights with the Top House pub on your left. Turn into Brownedge Lane which in turn leads on to Brownedge Road. The ground is down this road on the left hand side after about half a mile.
From Preston. Come out of the station and turn left over the bridge. Bear left onto Penworthan Road until you reach the traffic lights at Tardy Gate. Then turn left into Brownedge Road. Go through one set of traffic lights at Four Lane End. Go over the humpback bridge for another 500 yards. At the next roundabout bear right following the sign for Bamber Bridge (second exit). Then take a right by the Bamber Bridge FC sign. After 100 yards turn left by the bridge.

Bamber Bridge's ground has changed dramatically over the last few seasons with a new bar and a new stand stretching the length of one side making it close to Conference standards. The bar is a good size and easily holds both sets of supporters before and after a match. If the club can rebuild the terracing opposite the bar, allowing more space for supporters with the same area covered, the ground would be unrecognisable from what it was five years ago. AP

Review

Bamber Bridge made a good start to the season, losing just one of their opening six games (which included an FA Cup victory over Prescot Cables). Mark Wane and Barry Massey were scoring the bulk of the goals but it wasn't enough to see them progress past the Third Qualifying Round of the FA Cup as they lost 3-0 at Blyth Spartan's Croft Park.
After a slender 1-0 defeat at Marine in the First Round of the FA Trophy, results started to go the oppositions' way as they lost heavily to Hyde United before losing to Matlock Town (two sides who were challenging for the title).
Bamber Bridge's season then became inconsistent with a number of draws and losses thrown in amongst too few wins as the club never really managed to put any sort of run together resulting in a final mid-table position of tenth. However, despite the lack of impetus throughout the campaign, Bamber still finished comfortably in the promotion places as they claimed their place in the Unibond Premier Division.
There was one highlight to the season though, as Bamber Bridge travelled to North Wales to play Colwyn Bay at the start of April. Wane completed a hat-trick before Adam Lucas and Stuart Honor added one each to finish the game and claim the away win record for the season with a 5-0 scoreline. All in all, season 2003/04 didn't produce very many moments to savour for Bamber Bridge followers but, ultimately, they did what was required in order to seal promotion and they can now look forward with renewed optimism to life in the Premier Division in 2004/05. AP

The Bridge

Bishop Auckland

Address: Sharing with Spennymoor Unitcd: Brewery Field, Durham Road, Spennymoor, County Durham

Tel: 01388 773877

Website: www.bishopafc.com

Email: coweyhome@tiscali.co.uk

Officials: Chairman: Terry Jackson
Secretary: Tony Duffy
Manager: Brian Honour

Review

Bishop Auckland played in neighbouring town Shildon for a second and final season hoping to secure a place in the Unibond Premier Division at the end of the season. They just managed that target, finishing 13th in the league and only three points ahead of Ossett Town (who incidentally had a three point deduction imposed for fielding an illeligible player earlier in the season).

With their league season inconsistent with a final tally of 14 wins, 13 draws and 15 losses, the cup competitions provided the season's entertainment for the supporters. Their FA Cup Preliminary Round match against Flixton in August saw a devastating performance from the Bishops. Stuart Irvine scored twice before Ian Chandler and Mark Foster made it 4-0 after just 19 minutes. Chandler scored his second right on half time before Neil Maddison bagged a second half brace. Substitute Steven Manson netted another on 82 minutes. 8-0 was the final score and it equalled Bishop Auckland's best previous performance in the FA Cup - an 8-0 victory over Sunderland Royal Rovers in 1902. Pickering Town were the opposition in the First Qualifying Round, but they weren't such a push-over and came away 1-0 winners. The FA Trophy also sparked a high scoring game but Bishop Auckland found themselves on the wrong side this time as they played Runcorn in the First Round and crashed out 7-0. AP

Directions

From The North & East: Take the A1/A1M southbound and turn off at Junction 61, onto A688 towards Spennymoor. At Bishop Auckland, turn right at small roundabout, and go straight on at Thinford roundabout. Head straight over the mini-roundabout, and take the third exit into Town Centre from the next large roundabout. Go left at the next roundabout and go straight on past Asda on left and over a light controlled pedestrian crossing. Go straight on at the next mini-roundabout and the ground is on the left behind Durham Road.

From the South: Take the A1/A1M northbound and turn off at Junction 59, onto A167 towards Spennymoor. Go past Newton Aycliffe, straight on at the Rushyford roundabout and through Chilton. Go straight on at the mini-roundabout, under the bridges at Ferryhill, turn left onto the A688 at the Thinford roundabout. Then follow the directions from the North.

From the West: Take the M6 northbound, and turn off at Junction 38 onto the A685 towards Brough, through Kirkby Stephen. Turn onto the A66 at Brough and take the A67 toward Barnard Castle. Go over the bridge at the traffic lights, through Barnard Castle market place. Take a left at the next mini-roundabout onto the A688 towards Bishop Auckland and Spennymoor. Stay on the A688 and go past a BP petrol station on the left and Park Head Hotel on the right. Stay on the A688, by-passing Middlestone Moor.

Take a left at the roundabout and follow Town Centre signs. Go past the Peugeot garage on the right and take the third exit at the next roundabout. Bear left over the zebra crossing, opposite the town hall tower, and go past town centre parking. There should be a Co-Op Superstore on the right. Take a left at the mini-roundabout and the ground is left behind Durham Road.

Parking is available on Durham Road. Town centre car parks within a short walk.

By train: The nearest station is Durham mainline station. As Durham is approximately six miles from the ground it is best to get a taxi from outside the station.

After two seasons ground-sharing at Shildon FC, the Bishops have moved to Spennymoor United's Brewery Field ground. The ground at Shildon wasn't very glamorous or homely for Bishop Auckland after leaving their long standing home, Kingsway. Hopefully Spennymoor will provide a better home. The luxury bar suffered extensive fire damage on Christmas Day 2003 and this was a big blow for Spennymoor. The ground itself is better than Kingsway and Shildon, with a small but neat

The Bishops

Blyth Spartans

Address: Croft Park, Blyth, Northumberland, NE24 3JE

Tel: 01670 352 373

Website: www.spartans.freeserve.co.uk

Email: generalmanager@blythspartans.com

Officials: Chairman: Tommy Hedley
Secretary: Joe Hobin
Manager: Paul Baker

Croft Park

Review

Blyth Spartans had their worst season for quite a few years in 2003/04 and if this was a regular season they would have found themselves relegated to the Unibond First Division. However, due to the restructuring, their blushes were spared and they stayed in the same division, which now operates one rung lower on the pyramid.
With ex-Blackburn midfielder Graham Fenton signed from Blackpool, optimism was high at the start of the campaign and they began well with victories over Ashton United, Spennymoor United and Radcliffe Borough in their opening three matches. The highlight was a 5-0 demolition of near neighbours Spennymoor featuring a Fenton hat-trick, with a goal scored by former Spennymoor player Anthony Woodhouse to boot.
However, the early season fireworks didn't last long as they failed to win in the league for the next ten matches before finally beating Altrincham 2-1 with Fenton and Woodhouse again the goalscorers. However, this did not spark a revival and, infact, it had the complete opposite effect. As the season entered February, the Spartans began a run without a win that would span 15 games and include a run of five matches without a goal. The dreadful form was finally brought to an end in what would be the club's penultimate game of the season as they won 1-0 against Alfreton - by which time their fate had already been decided. Spartans finished the season in the bottom three, two points shy of a chance to contest a place in the Conference North via the Unibond Play-Offs.
Blyth did claim some recognition and some pride in the FA Cup as they defeated Bamber Bridge and Halesowen en route to a Fourth Qualifying Round date against Conference title favourites Chester. The Spartans acquitted themselves well - only losing1-0 at Croft Park. The FA Trophy also saw a good run with Blyth reaching the Fourth Round after beating Wakefield & Emley, Stocksbridge Park Steels and Barrow before losing 3-1 against Conference high flyers Aldershot Town. AP

Directions

Join the A189 towards Ashington from the A19 either north or southbound. Take the Cramlington/Blyth exit on the A1061. Turn right at the first roundabout following signs for Blyth. Go straight ahead at two roundabouts and then cross the railway line. Turn left at the next roundabout and straight ahead at a mini-roundabout. Turn right at the next roundabout onto Plessey Road. The ground is visible on the left. Car parking is available in surrounding streets. Croft Park is close to the town centre and can be easily reached by bus from Newcastle.

Vast improvements were made during the close season of 2003 and, on my first visit after this, I thought it lacked its old spirit. However, a visit a couple of months later and it felt right. Blyth have taken care of their supporters' needs with a small separate stand where wheelchair users can sit above the standing crowd for the duration of the match. Croft Park still isn't one of my favourite grounds but, with the improvements, it is not bad. I must also recommend the bar just outside the ground and the food van still offers quality nourishment. AP

The Spartans

Bridlington Town

Address: Queensgate Football Ground, Bridlington, Yorkshire YO16 7LN

Tel: 01262 604 036

Website: www.bridtownafc.freeserve.co.uk

Email: admin@bridtownafc.freeserve.co.uk

Officials: Chairman: Gary Wilkinson, Secretary: Chris Bemrose Manager: Billy Heath

Review

After gaining promotion to the Unibond First Division the previous season, Bridlington were hoping to secure a top 13 place to stay at the same level of the pyramid after the reconstruction. They did this with a creditable eleventh place finish, six points clear of 14th placed Ossett Town.

Their home record was something to be proud of, winning eleven of their 21 home matches. An interesting fact for the superstitious fan is that Bridlington (with the exception of Belper) won all of their home games against teams coming before 'L' in the alphabet and failed to win against teams listed after 'L' - spooky! What made their season all the more exciting for their fans was that they only failed to score in five matches making Town one of the more entertaining sides to watch. Indeed, they notched up some impressive wins at Queensgate with free-scoring victories over Farsley, Kendal, Colwyn Bay and eventual champions Hyde United. There is no doubt that, had Town been a little more durable on their travels, then they may have finished even higher in the table. They lost as many games on the road as they won at home - eleven.

With such a good home record you might be excused for thinking that Bridlington would do well in the major cup competitions if they were drawn at home. That theory was correct as the FA Cup saw wins against Peterlee Newton (although that game was away), and Salford City at home before they drew against Farsley Celtic and lost the away replay.

Bridlington were drawn away in the FA Trophy Preliminary Round to Ilkeston Town but in a month where the club was in good form both at home and away, they went through to the First Round. However, once there they lost at Rossendale United. AP

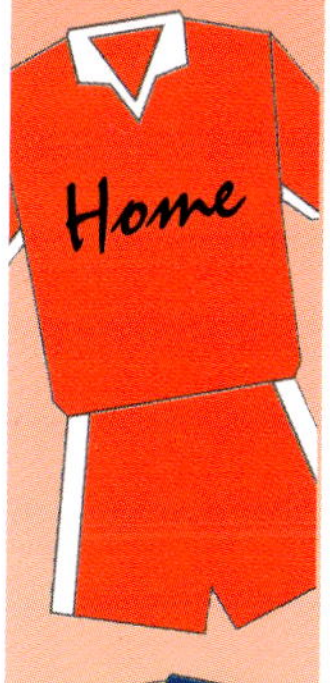

Directions

From the South (Hull, Beeford, Barmston): Approach Bridlington on the A165, passing the golf course on the right and Broadacres pub and Kingsmead Estate on the left. Go straight over the traffic lights to the roundabout by B&Q. Turn right. At the next set of traffic lights, turn left and go over the railway bridge. At the next roundabout, bear left and carry on north up Quay Road. After the traffic lights turn right into Queensgate. The ground 800 yards on the right.

From the South and West (Driffield, Hull, York): Approach Bridlington on the A614. Go straight on at the traffic lights (Hospital on the right) and follow the road round the bend. At the roundabout go across to the mini-roundabout and bear right (second exit). Follow the road around to the right and onto the traffic lights. Go straight on. At the next set of traffic lights (just after Kwik-Fit) turn left into Queensgate.

From the North (Scarborough): Approach Bridlington (Esso garage on right). At the roundabout turn left then at the next mini-roundabout take the second exit. Follow the road around to the right and onto the traffic lights. Go straight on. At the next traffic lights (just after Kwik-Fit) turn left into Queensgate.

By train: Bridlington station is on the main Hull/Scarborough line and is a two minute walk from the ground. Come out of the station and cross Quay Road. Head along the side of Higgs & Barker Garage and follow the road down to the back of the ground.

Bridlington offers a lovely ground, which is bigger on the inside than it looks from the outside. While the bar sits on the south stand and offers a busy place for supporters to drink before and after the game, it needs to increase in size now they are in the Unibond Premiership. The main stand is a good size and there is covered terracing down the other. On a windy and wet day the ground can look miserable and there is little protection from the elements in most parts of it. AP

Burscough

Address: Victoria Park, Bobby Langton Way, Mart Lane, Burscough, Lancs, L40 0SD

Tel: 01704 893237

Website: www.burscoughfc.co.uk

Officials: Chairman: Frank Parr
Secretary: Stan Strickland
Manager: Dave Goulding

Victoria Park

Directions

Take the M6 to J27. Follow the signs for Parbold (A5209). Go down the hill, through Newburgh and into Burscough. Turn right at the mini-roundabout into Junction Lane (signposted Burscough and Martin Mere) to the traffic lights. Turn right onto the A59 and go over the canal bridge into the village. Take the second left into Mart Lane to the ground.
By train: The nearest station is Burscough Bridge (on the Manchester-Wigan-Southport line), a mere five minute walk to the ground. Exit the station and turn into Liverpool Road North. Mart Lane is on the right.

With its incredibly narrow turnstiles where the larger supporter would fail to get through, the inside of Victoria Park is nicely adequate for the club. The bar could be improved as well as the turnstiles but for watching the match the ground is a good place to stand or sit. The terracing around the ground needs some money spent on it to take away the gravel and replace it with tiered steps but the main stand gives a good viewpoint for everyone. AP

Review

After lifting the FA Trophy the previous season, under the management of former Aston Villa favourite Shaun Teale, Burscough surely wouldn't have wanted to give up their silverware without a fight, despite the departure of their influential boss. However, their Third Round opponents Tamworth had a score to settle, as it was they who suffered at the hands of Teale's men in the Villa Park Final earlier in the year, and they were not to be denied their chance of revenge as the holders bowed out. Any hope of another season of cup glory was dashed as the Linnets exited the FA Cup at the Second Qualifying Round stage - losing to Unibond Premier Division title hopefuls Droylsden.
The lack of cup success was the least of Burscough's worries as their league form started to suffer badly following a solid if unspectacular start of a win and a draw in their first two games. Goals stopped going in and an incredible seven games went by before they found the net again after a 1-1 draw with lowly Wakefield & Emley.
Burscough found themselves at the wrong end of the table by the turn of the year as their durability that had seen them ground out much needed results the previous season seemed to desert them. However, Boxing Day brought a belated Christmas present for the supporters with three valuable points gained against Vauxhall Motors.
The second half of the season was more positive as the Linnets managed to push their number of league wins into double figures. This saw Burscough finish the season two places above the drop zone in 19th but, in truth, it was another frustrating season in terms of the league. The club's shortcomings were clear for all to see as their goal haul of 47 was the second lowest in the league - only bottom club Wakefield & Emley returned a lower total. Despite this, the club still had a chance of claiming a place in the Conference North (something that looked highly unlikely at the turn of the year) as they entered into the Unibond League Play-Offs. Their chances of promotion increased still further as the Linnets defeated Marine and Radcliffe Borough on their way to a Final date against Bradford Park Avenue. However, it was more heartbreak for Burscough as they went down 2-0 in extra-time. AP

The Linnets

Farsley Celtic

Address: Throstle Nest, Newlands, Farsley, Leeds LS28 5BE

Tel: 0113 256 1517

Website: www.farsleyceltic.com

Email: celtalk@farsleyceltic.com

Officials: Chairman: Andy Firbank
Secretary: Nick Gill
Manager: Lee Sinnott

Throstle Nest

Directions

The Throstle Nest ground is located between Leeds and Bradford, close to the Leeds Inner Ring Road, and minutes from the Asda/Marks & Spencer shopping complex adjacent to Pudsey Railway Station. Travelling out of Leeds, around the Stanningley Bypass, the Asda/M&S complex appears on the right hand side. At the Green Flag roundabout turn right and then from this main road turn left into New Street (just before Tradex). After approximately 800 yards turn right into Newlands and follow the road to the end, where the club is located.
By train: The nearest station is New Pudsey which is served by the Leeds/Bradford line. From the station it is 100 yards to the main road. Turn right at the end of the main road and then, after a quarter of a mile, turn right again towards Stanningley. Tradex Warehouse will be on your left. Then, take a left into New Street. A quarter of a mile is Newlands. At the end of that road there is a sign for Farsley Celtic. The ground is situated at the very end of Newlands.

The Throstle Nest ground, which has been home to Farsley Celtic since 1948, has seen transformations over the years, and new fencing around the ground has helped to finish it off nicely. The main stand holds around 400-500 people and is newly built to make it a fine place to sit for a match without the obstruction of pillars. Gravel opposite the main stand and behind both goals also improves the overall look of the ground and is much safer for the supporters to stand on during the game. The food is also nice at the ground although you have to watch out for the salt and sugar pots as they both look similar and a friend ended up with sugar all over his food due to a lack of concentration. AP

Review

Farsley Celtic had a strong season in 2003/04 finishing an impressive third in the Unibond First Division behind champions Hyde United and Matlock Town. They finished just two points behind second placed Matlock who, at one stage, were threatening to walk away with the league.
Celtic also finished the season with just eight defeats, the lowest in the division. The club were also the joint second highest scorers in the league, further highlighting what a good season the Yorkshire club had. However, in terms of pushing for the title, it was the number of draws that proved the club's undoing. Seven draws at home and seven away saw Celtic finish the season with 14 stalemates with only Belper Town, who finished 20th, having more.
The highlight of the season for Celtic must have been on the 27th December when they played host to local rivals, Guiseley. The match ended happily for Farsley who saw five goals fly past the Guiseley keeper with only three in reply. This also clinched the December award for Farsley as Unibond First Division Club of the Month.
Where the club found form in the league they could not in cup competitions, losing to Bishop Auckland 4-2 in the FA Trophy Preliminary Round at Shildon's Dean Street after being ahead 2-1 and they also dropped out of the FA Cup at the first attempt to Gainsborough Trinity in a replay - 3-0. AP

The Villagers

Frickley Athletic

Address: Westfield Lane, South Elmsall, Pontefract, West Yorkshire, WF9 2EQ

Tel: 01977 642460

Website: www.pennocks.freeserve.co.uk

Email: steve@frickleyafc.co.uk

Officials: Chairman: Peter Bywater
Secretary: Ruth Simpson
Manager: Phil Sharpe

Westfield Lane

Directions

From the A1, turn off onto the A638 towards Wakefield. At the roundabout, turn left onto the B6474 towards South Elmsall. Turn left at the traffic lights and then turn right at the T-junction to stay on the B6474. Go over the railway and turn right at the bottom of the road and then take an immediate left up Westfield Lane.
By train: The nearest station is South Elmsall, just under half a mile from the ground. Exit the station onto the High Street. Head south west along the High Street, going over Doncaster Road and into Westfield Lane. The ground is half way down this road.

Frickley Athletic's Westfield Lane ground is situated in the former mining village of South Elmsall in West Yorkshire, which is easily accessed from the A1. The ground itself is set back from Westfield Lane against the renowned backdrop of the large 'pit-tip'. The large main stand seats 500 people and there is a covered standing area on the opposite side, with grass banks behind both goals. The cosy clubhouse serves a good pint and is open well before kick-off whilst the food from the mobile catering van is also worth a try. Steve Pennock - Frickley Athletic

Review

Like every side in the Unibond Premier Division, the Blues kicked off the 2003/04 season with hopes of qualifying for the new Conference North and, for the first half of the season, they looked as if they would manage this. However, a dreadful finish to the campaign saw a run of only two wins in 19 League games and a final finishing position of next to bottom. Despite this, it was still an anxious last few games for Frickley as they only finished two points shy of 20th position, which would have seen them enter a Play-Off and at least have a shot at promotion to the Conference North.
The Blues started the season slowly but, just as performances were improving, they suffered an embarrassing 5-1 defeat at Shildon in the FA Cup to go out of the competition in their first game. However, a good run from mid-October to early January saw the Blues move to within a couple of points of the all-important 13th spot, although they suffered a heartbreaking last minute 3-2 defeat at Runcorn FC Halton during this time to bow out of the FA Trophy in the Second Round. The sudden downturn in form came immediately after comprehensively defeating Barrow 4-2 at Westfield Lane on 3rd January, as the Blues embarked on that terrible run.
The one highlight of the season was reaching the Sheffield & Hallamshire Senior Cup Final at Hillsborough when the Blues twice came from behind to defeat rivals Worksop Town 3-2. Leading goalscorer Lee Morris lifted the trophy (the club's eleventh success in the competition), in what was, all in all, a difficult and ultimately disappointing season for the club. Steve Pennock - Frickley Athletic

The Blues

Gateshead

Address: The International Stadium, Neilson Road, Gateshead, Tyne & Wear NE10 0EF

Tel: 0191 478 3883

Website: www.gateshead-fc.com

Email: info@gateshead-fc.com

Officials: Chairman: Mick Harland
Secretary: Phil Chambers
Manager: Derek Bell

The International Stadium

Directions

The stadium is situated a mile or so from Gateshead town centre on the A184 (Park Road) towards Sunderland. Turn left 200 yards past McDonald's into Neilson Road, then right into the Stadium car park (free).

From the south, take the A1(M) past Washington/Birtley services to Junction 65. Take the right hand fork signposted A194 (M) Tyne Tunnel. Proceed to the roundabout at the end of the motorway and turn left onto the A184 signposted Gateshead/Newcastle. The stadium is three miles on the right. Turn right immediately after the Stadium Pub into Neilson Road, then right again into the car park.

By train: Metro service from Newcastle Central Station to Gateshead Stadium Metro Station (ten minutes walk).

By bus: Half-hourly service from Gateshead Metro Interchange or Heworth Metro (service 93/94).

The International Stadium has both its good and bad points but, for most supporters, it is a great stadium to visit. The local council runs the bar. Food prices may not be to supporters' liking but the quality is as good as anywhere. With 4,000 seats to choose from in the main stand you are bound to find a place to sit, although fans would like to have somewhere to stand as well, which is one of the drawbacks. Another is the running track separating the supporters from the players but one plus is that the club could rise a long way without worrying about ground improvements. AP

Review

After the disappointment of relegation from the Unibond Premier Division the previous season, Gateshead rebuilt not just the squad but the club as well, bringing in reserve and intermediate teams for the 2003/04 campaign. After a mixed start to the season, Gateshead found some good form and sat proudly at the top of the league until disaster struck. Four points were deducted after two players who were not registered made appearances. The point gained on the opening day against Leek Town and the three against Chorley were wiped out and, as a result, the Tynesiders slid down the league.

This disappointment knocked the morale of the team and they crashed out of the FA Cup in the Preliminary Round away at Liversedge. Gateshead also failed to go further than Round One of the FA Trophy, falling to Altrincham at the International Stadium in November. After the Christmas period, form hit a low point and the club struggled to stay in the top six of the league. Dropping down to eleventh made the club nervous and thoughts that they might not make the top 13 to stay at the same level of the pyramid for next season saw a switch in management. Director of Football and manager Derek Bell then agreed to allow reserve team manager and younger brother, Alan Bell, take over first team affairs and a top 13 finish was eventually secured before the end of the season. AP

The Tynesiders

Guiseley

Address: Nethermoor, Otley Road, Guiseley, Leeds, LS20 8BT

Tel: 01943 872872

Website: www.guiseleyafc.co.uk

Email: info@guiseleyafc.co.uk

Officials: Chairman: Phillip Rogerson
Secretary: Bruce Speller
Manager: Neil Parsley

Nethermoor

Directions

Via M1 to M62-J28 follow the Leeds Ring Road to the junction with the A65 at Horsforth roundabout. Turn left onto A65 through Rawdon to Guiseley town centre, past Morrisons and straight through the next lights. Nethermoor is a quarter of a mile on the right past the Ford dealership next to the cricket field and opposite the Silver Cross factory. Carry on and take the first right turn after the ground and first right again almost immediately into Ings Crescent for the car park adjacent to a bowling green.
By train: Regular trains run from Leeds and Bradford Forster Square to Guiseley station on the Wharfedale line at about 30 minute intervals. Journey takes 20-25 minutes. Exit into station car park, walk diagonally across towards the path between the hedges to a stone terrace of houses. Walk to end of terrace, turn right into Otley Road and continue for 200 yards. Nethermoor is on the right.

The 3000-capacity Nethermoor has over 425 seats, with opening standing either side of the seated stand. Both goal ends are open standing, while the other touchline is mostly covered terrace. There is a bar inside the ground, where the food kiosk is situated. A club shop is also on site. MP

Review

After finishing 14th in 2002/03, the Leeds-based side were looking to finish a place higher and thus earn 'promotion' to the Northern Premier League. They opened their season with a loss at North Ferriby, before bouncing back with two home wins. A narrow loss at Belper preceded a fine run of six games unbeaten, which saw the team rise as high as third. That run included a 5-1 win at Gateshead, and a 2-2 home draw with Witton Albion which saw full-back Peter Atkinson notch up his 600th game for the club. But Guiseley seemed to get giddy up in the heights of third, and came crashing back down with five straight losses - each one by a single goal. They dropped to fifteenth but all was not lost with so much of the season still to play.
The team got back on track with nine points in the next four games. They were also putting a run together in the Unibond League Cup, beating Premier teams in Wakefield (4-1) and high-flying Harrogate (2-1). This had a bearing on league results as they took four points from the next four games, and they went into 2004 in 14th place. Results needed to be positive from then on: consecutive 2-2 away draws gave them a starting block. From here they sprinted to four straight victories, including a win away at leaders Matlock. This took them up to tenth, but they did their best to undo their good work by embarking on a run that saw just two points emerge from six league games.
Despite that poor run, the side still found themselves in the comfort zone of the top 13, albeit with six games still to play and with a number of teams scrapping to break into the top half of the table. One of those challengers was Ossett, whom Guiseley overcame 2-1 to end that barren run. And the threat of missing out on the Northern Premier provoked Guiseley into an end of season run that brought four wins and two draws in those last six, propelling them to ninth. They achieved what they set out to do, and for that their season cannot be faulted. They will take their place in the newly-structured level three with something to build from - and they will need to do so, with so many strong teams in the division. MP

Hyde United

Address: Ewen Fields, Walker Lane, Hyde, Cheshire SK14 2SB

Tel: 0161 368 1031

Website: www.hydeunited.co.uk

Email: agh@hydeunited.co.uk

Officials: Chairman: Stephen Hartley
Secretary: Tony Beard
Manager: Steve Waywell

Ewen Fields

Directions

Take the M60 junction 24, and then the M67 (towards Sheffield) to junction 3 (Hyde, Dukinfield, Stalybridge). Once on the exit slipway, keep to the right-hand lane heading for Hyde centre. At the traffic lights at the end of the slipway, turn right onto Clarkway. On Clarkway/Reynard Street, at the second set of lights, turn left (Morrisons superstore on the left) onto Mottram Road. At the first set of lights on Mottram Road, turn right onto Lumn Road. After 200 yards, turn left onto Walker Lane. Approximately 50 yards on is Hyde Leisure Pool on the left. The entrance to Ewen Fields is to the right hand side of the leisure pool.
By train: Take the line to Newton - 15 minutes from Manchester Piccadilly. From the station, go down the hill, over the motorway and up to the traffic lights. Turn left and then first right into the ground - approximately a ten minute walk.

There is good terracing and a fine main stand at Hyde. Most of the terracing is covered and the ground can be considered one of the finest in the Unibond Premier going into this season. The only problem is the lighting in the bar which can make it feel dingy and lifeless inside. The food is one of the highlights of any visit though as the burgers are the best in the league, in my opinion, and although you might feel as though they are a little pricey, they are worth every penny. AP

Review

Hyde United fought hard to clinch the Unibond First Division title and eventually did so just ahead of Matlock Town after the pair battled against each other in the table for much of the season only to see both entering the last day on equal points.
After spending money to bring in a new squad after relegation from the Unibond Premier the previous season, Hyde started very poorly. First Division new boys Bridlington were the first to play Hyde and the gap in divisions the previous season didn't show as Hyde fell to a 3-1 defeat. Debutante Neil Tolson scored the first of his 21 league goals, but it wasn't enough.
The Tigers had a bad year in the two major cup competitions going out of the FA Cup in the Third Qualifying Round to Ashton United in a replay and losing to North Ferriby in the FA Trophy Preliminary Round.
However, Hyde United secured the championship after beating Rossendale United 2-1 at Dark Lane with Phil Salt netting a brace in what was an enthralling championship season. Earlier that week Hyde lifted the Chairman's Cup with an aggregate score of 2-0 after Salt scored a single goal in the away leg against Leek Town.
With a league and cup double in the bag, Hyde were hoping to reach the Conference North through the Play-Offs but it all ended in disappointment as they crashed out to Ashton United 2-1. Tolson scored for the newly crowned champions but a goal by Steve Smith took the game to extra-time and Lincoln Adams scored the winner in the additional period to break Hyde hearts. AP

The Tigers

Leek Town

Address: Harrison Park, Macclesfield Road, Leek, Staffs ST13 8LD

Tel: 01538 399278

Website: www.leektown.co.uk

Email: brian@alltheresults.co.uk

Officials: Chairman: Marvin Clarke
Secretary: Christine A Osmond
Manager: Paul Ogden

Harrison Park

Directions

From the North West: M6 junction 18. Take the A54 towards Congleton. Follow signs towards Buxton and turn right at the traffic lights (about four miles past Congleton) towards Leek on the A52. Harrison Park is on the right as you enter Leek, just past the Shell petrol station.

From the North East: M1 junction 30. Take the A619 towards Chesterfield and then Bakewell. Follow the signs to Buxton on the A6 and then Leek on the A53. Stay on this road as you enter Leek, following signs to Macclesfield. Harrison Park is on the left as you leave the town, just after the car dealership.

From West Midlands: On entering the town, go straight across at the first set of traffic lights into St Edwards Street. Then, left again at the T-Junction.

From the East Midlands: M1 junction 24, take the A50 towards Stoke-on-Trent. At Meir, join the A520 towards Leek (just after the 50 mph restriction starts). On entering the town, go over at the first set of traffic lights, then turn left at the T-junction at the top of the hill. Harrison Park is on the left as you leave the town.

By train: The nearest train stations are Stoke-on-Trent, Macclesfield, Buxton/Sheffield and Derby.

A friendly atmosphere awaits you at Leek Town and few supporters would leave unhappy from the ground, unless their team had lost of course, with its good bar, main stand, parking area and terracing. The bar stretches half the length of the east side, with the big main stand, which provides seating and the turnstiles, on the other half. The terracing behind the goals and down one side is covered and it is easy to see why the ground is suitable for Conference standards. AP

Review

Leek Town had a comfortable season in the Unibond First Division and finished in eighth place to secure their place at the same level of the pyramid after the reconstruction. The season started slowly though, with two 0-0 draws and a 1-0 loss in their opening three matches of the season.

A Monday night game at Harrison Park, against Rossendale United, saw Leek collect their first win of the season. Goals by Josh Ford and Jon Hassell sealed a 2-1 victory. The confidence from this win saw the team make it through to the First Qualifying Round of the FA Cup as they beat Lincoln Moorlands 2-1 with eventual top scorer Dave Whittaker grabbing his first and second goals of the season.

Their league form stayed inconsistent with another win, draw and loss before crashing out of the FA Cup against Congleton Town - 1-0 away from home. As league form started to pick up with victories over Stocksbridge, Bridlington and Ossett Town it then came as a shock to go out the FA Trophy in the Preliminary Round as Stocksbridge got their revenge.

As league form started to produce more positive results a disappointment came in April when they lost to Hyde United in the Chairman's Cup Final on an aggregate score of 2-0, losing each leg by one goal. AP

The Blues

Lincoln United

Address: Ashby Avenue, Hartsholme, Lincoln, LN6 ODY

Tel: 01522 696 400

Website: www.lincolnunitedfc.co.uk

Email: webmaster@lincolnunitedfc.co.uk

Officials: Chairman: Robin Taylor
Secretary: Peter Doyle
Manager: John Wilkinson

Directions

Take the A57 via Saxilby. Take the A46 roundabout towards the Birchwood housing estate, travel one mile along Skellingthorpe Road, passing Hartsholme Park. Take the first right after the 30mph sign and it is a further 200 yards to the ground.
By train: Come out of Lincoln station onto the High Street. Turn right onto Dixon Street and then turn left onto Tritton Road. Then turn right onto Skellingthorpe Road and then left onto Ashby Avenue.

Sitting amongst trees, Lincoln United's ground needs a bit of work to make it a better standard. One area behind the goal holds the changing rooms while the bar is situated outside the ground. The bar itself is fairly small and you can feel a little claustrophobic inside but the friendliness of the home supporters more than makes up for it. The ground has a good setting and could easily be made into one of the best grounds in the Unibond Premiership. AP

Review

Following finishes of 16th, 19th and 15th in each of the last three seasons, Lincoln United had an excellent season in 2003/04 as they clinched a fourth place finish in the Unibond First Division. With 20 wins, and a plus 20 goal difference, United fans must have been pleasantly surprised with their side's performances after those several seasons of mid-table stagnation.
Unfortunately for them, they didn't have as much luck in the FA Cup Preliminary Round, going out to Corby Town 2-1 in August. United also lost out in the FA Trophy, after a replay against Workington. After drawing the home match at Ashby Avenue, they then lost 1-0 in the replay the following Tuesday, leaving them with a long drive home.
However, the early exits from the two main cup competitions removed any distractions from what was becoming a very interesting league campaign. Lincoln had their home form to thank for their push up the table, suffering just two defeats at Ashby Avenue against Gateshead in October and Farsley Celtic in March.
The saying 'save the best until last' certainly springs to mind when discussing Lincoln's season after they produced one of the biggest away wins of the season on the final day. United travelled that long distance to Workington once more, as they prepared themselves for revenge after their early FA Trophy exit. Gary Bull started the scoring on 22 minutes before Ian Williams scored the second and Chris Hall added a third before half-time. Jon Hawley added two more in the second half, thanks to two penalty kicks, which completed the rout. AP

United

Marine

Address: Rossett Park, College Road, Crosby, Merseyside, L23 3AS

Tel: 0151 924 4046

Website: www.marinefc.com

Officials: Chairman: Paul Leary
Secretary: John Wildman
Manager: Roly Howard

Rossett Park

Directions

Come off the M57 or M58. These motorways converge at a huge roundabout called Switch Island. Take the A567, with Bootle's ground on your right. At the first set of lights after the ground, continue straight on until you come to a roundabout in Seaforth (one mile from the motorway).Take the third main exit. This takes you to another roundabout at Seaforth Docks (the Freeport). At this island, drive three quarters of the way around it and continue for about half a mile until you reach a set of traffic lights (with the Liver Pub on the left just ahead). At the next set of traffic lights at a crossroads you will see Merchant Taylor's School ahead. Turn left here into College Road and the ground is half a mile on the left. Park in one of the side roads.

By train: The nearest station is Blundellsands & Crosby, just under half a mile from the ground. Exit the station in Agnes Road and turn left into Mersey Road. College Road is on your right.

Rossett Park is still one of my favourite grounds despite it having only three sides to accommodate supporters. The area behind the south goal is packed with the small car park, bar and main stand. While the car park could be bigger, the clubhouse is a good size for the number of supporters who regularly attend matches and the main stand, which provides seating and terracing, is a favourite for supporters. The terracing around the rest of the pitch also has its plus and negative points though. The east side terracing isn't very deep and it can be a struggle to walk down it if there are a lot of fans attending the match. Behind the goal isn't covered like the rest of the ground but it constitutes a good area for supporters during the match. AP

Review

After finishing in a positive mood at the end of the previous season (eleventh in the Unibond Premier Division and lifting the League Cup), the Mariners were hoping to improve on things in 2003/04 targeting a top 13 finish in order to qualify for the Conference North. However, things didn't go to plan for Roly Howard or his players as they finished a poor 16th - ten points behind the qualifying positions.

It was goals galore in their opening fixtures with a 3-1 defeat on the opening day against Spennymoor followed by a 3-3 draw against Altrincham, and then a heavy 4-1 defeat at Harrogate. Marine bagged their first three point haul after a 3-2 win against Vauxhall Motors before they went down to another high scoring defeat, this time at Ashton United - 4-3. To give his team a boost, Steve Whitehall then scored four goals for the Mariners against struggling Burscough at Rossett Park to give the home side a 4-0 victory.

Although results were starting to pick up in the league with goals going in at both ends, the FA Cup ended in disappointment. After beating Rossendale comfortably at Rossett Park, Marine lost, also at home, to Northern League club (and eventual champions) Dunston Fed, 2-1.

Marine did have a good run in the FA Trophy beating Bamber Bridge, Worcester City and Conference side Northwich Victoria to reach the Fourth Round where they faced Stalybridge Celtic at Bower Field. A 1-1 draw saw Marine take Celtic back to Rossett Park the following Tuesday. However, it wasn't to be as Celtic clinched a 1-0 win.

The club's 16th placed finish meant that a Conference North place was still available through the Play-Offs. Marine were paired up at home against Burscough but, despite taking the lead, Burscough won through 3-1 thanks to goals from Ben Kay, Liam Blakeman and Drew Hyland. However, the biggest news at the club came in February when legendary manager Roly Howard announced that the 2004/05 season would be his last after 32 years at the helm. AP

The Mariners

Matlock Town

Address: Causeway Lane, Matlock, Derbyshire DE4 3AR

Tel: 01629 583866

Website: www.matlocktownfc.co.uk

Email: webmaster@matlocktownfc.co.uk

Officials: Chairman: Darrell Holmes
General Secretary: Keith Brown
Managers: Phil Brown & Gareth Williams

Causeway Lane

Directions

From the M1: Leave at junction 28, signposted to Alfreton, Derby (A38) and the Derbyshire Dales. At the roundabout, take the exit marked A38 Derby. Stay on the A38 for about two to three miles then leave at the junction signposted as A615 Matlock. Turn left almost immediately to stay on the A615. After about two miles turn right at the T-junction and then left after about 200 yards, still following signs for A615 Matlock. In another four to five miles the A615 enters Matlock. Matlock's Causeway Lane ground is on the right, opposite the park, about 200 yards after passing Kwik-Fit on the left.

From the A6 South: Coming north on the A6, pass through Matlock Bath and then enter Matlock on Dale Road. Cross the bridge over the River Derwent in the middle of town and then turn right (third exit) at the Crown Square roundabout. Causeway Lane is on the left, opposite the park, about 100 yards after the Ritz Cinema on the left.

From the A6 North: Coming south on the A6, pass through Bakewell and Darley Dale and then into Matlock. After passing the bus station and Somerfields supermarket on the left, go straight on (second exit) at the Crown Square roundabout in the middle of town. Causeway Lane is on the left, opposite the park.

By train: You reach Matlock via Derby Mainline Station. Come out of the station, turn left and go over the bridge (River Derwent) and into Crown Square. You will then come to a pedestrian crossing. Cross the road just before the roundabout and head left. This will bring you onto Causeway Lane (the main A615). The park is on your right and Woolworths on the left. Follow the road around and the ground is on your left on the opposite side of the road to the park (approximately 300 yards from the roundabout).

With the ground overlooked by the town's castle on a hill behind one of the goals, it takes the focus away from the timbered seating and wooden bar. Matlock, like Marine, also have just three sides to their home as the goal, overlooked by the castle, opens out into a cricket pitch. The lack of terracing behind this goal could stop any entry into the Conference should they happen to reach it. Despite this it is a unique and picturesque ground and is well worth a visit. AP

Review

In season 2003/04, Matlock Town were unlucky not to have won the Unibond First Division trophy and gain a place in the Play-Offs for the Conference North, after topping the table for most of the season, only to lose out to Hyde United on the final day, in what was one of the closest title races seen anywhere in the non-league last season.

Matlock were also handed a blow when manager Ernie Moss made a decision to leave the club at the end of the season. Moss said that quitting Causeway Lane was one of the hardest decisions he had had to make in his footballing career.

The season started brightly for the Gladiators, with three wins from three matches against Prescot Cables, Leek Town and Gateshead. However, they then suffered a 5-2 defeat against Lincoln United in the league before crashing out of the FA Cup in the Preliminary Round against Shirebrook Town. The match ended 2-1 with Simon Barraclough scoring a late goal to bring the Gladiators back into the game, but it was too little too late.

After beating Ossett Town 2-0 in the FA Trophy Preliminary Round, Matlock were handed an away tie against Gresley Rovers on the 1st November. A solitary goal in the first half ended the visitors' hopes of Trophy glory.

However, it was the league where Matlock were making waves as a nine game unbeaten run at the end of the season pushed Hyde all the way for the title. However, Town only managed to take two points from their final two games which proved too little as the Tigers beat the Gladiators into second place. During the Summer, Phil Brown and Gareth Williams were named as joint managers to succeed Ernie Moss. AP

The Gladiators

Ossett Town

Address: Ingfield Ground, Prospect Road, Ossett, West Yorks, WF5 9HA

Tel: 01924 272960

Website: www.ossetttown.org.uk

Email: ossetttown@aol.com

Officials: Chairman: Graham Firth
Secretary: Bruce Saul
Manager: Steve Richards

Ingfield Ground

Directions

From M1 Junction 40: Take the A638 signposted Ossett Town Centre. Take the first left off the A638 onto Wakefield Road, then take the sixth left into Dale Street (B6120) to the traffic lights. Turn left at the lights. The ground is in front of you opposite the bus station. The entrance to the ground is just before the Esso petrol station.
By train: The nearest station is Wakefield Westgate. Outside the station is a bus stop. Take a 126 or 127 bus towards Dewsbury. The ground is directly opposite Ossett Bus Station.

Ossett Town is slowly getting better. With a good size bar, which welcomes all, and a new stand being built behind one of the goals, the ground is taking shape. Good terracing is badly needed around the rest of the ground though, and the sheltered areas down both sides need modernising. In Winter the ground takes a lot of weather damage, which is a shame because in the Summer when the pitch is at its best it is a nice ground to visit. AP

Review

Ossett Town had a season which could have been made into a movie. The 2003/04 season was the story of a side who started badly but overcame obstacles and progressed, nearly reaching the top by the end of the campaign, only to be disappointed as they just missed out on glory. Then, in true Hollywood fashion, and after all hope had gone, they get a call saying a team in the higher division has gone out of existence and that they are to be moved up instead.
Town certainly could have been following a film script as something happened after October that made Ossett play for their lives. Sitting at the bottom of the table, they had a second season spurt that lifted them to 14th, just three points behind 13th placed Bishop Auckland. The kick in the teeth for Ossett was the knowledge that they were deducted three points at the start of the season for playing an illeligible player, which would ultimately cost them a top 13 finish.
After losing twelve of their first 14 league matches, socks were pulled up (you can almost hear the 'Rocky' theme tune) and the club only suffered another five reverses in the remaining 28 matches. One factor could have been the new manager. Steve Richards joined the club after leaving Goole Town in October and the change made a positive impact on the squad.
By the time Richards took over, the side were already out of the FA Cup (a result of a First Qualifying Round defeat against rivals Ossett Albion) and the FA Trophy. The biggest achievement was to make that 14th spot, despite the disappointment of only just missing out on a promotion place. However, the story is not without a fairytale ending. With Telford dropping out of the Conference North, Ashton United took their place leaving a gap in the Unibond Premier. With Ossett being the club who finished 14th, it was they who were handed the opportunity to fill that gap - one that they grasped with both hands, of course. AP

Prescot Cables

Address: Valerie Park, Hope Street, Prescot, Merseyside L34 6HD

Tel: 0151 430 0507

Website: www.prescotcablesfc.com

Email: cables@onlinegenie.net

Officials: Chairman: Ted Mercer
Secretary: Doug Lace
Manager: Tommy Lawson

Valerie Park

Directions

From the North: Take the M6 to Junction 26, onto the M58 to Junction 3. Follow the A570 to the junction with A580 (East Lancs Road). Cross the A580 and take the first right (Bleak Hill Road). Follow this to Prescot (two miles). At the traffic lights turn right and then go straight on at the large roundabout (do not follow the route onto the Prescot by-pass) and right at the next lights. After 100 yards turn right at the Hope and Anchor pub into Hope Street. The ground will be in sight at the bottom of road.

From the South: Take the M6 to Junction 21a (M62 junction 10). Follow the M62 towards Liverpool, to junction 7. Follow the A57 to Rainhill and Prescot. Go through the traffic lights at the Fusilier pub. After 100 yards turn right at the Hope and Anchor pub, then as above.

By train: Go to Liverpool Lime Street and then get a connection to Prescot. It is advisable to get a taxi to Prescot Cables FC outside the station as it is a long walk. Taxi fare approximately £2.50.

The main attraction of Prescot Cables is the huge main stand, which has plenty of seating and the bar area underneath. The bar is a good size for all supporters to meet and chat, and the food isn't that bad either. There is a good covered area behind one of the goals while the opposite end isn't developed yet along with the other side stretching opposite the main stand. There is a good disabled area for supporters also down the side of the main stand and behind one goal. AP

Review

Prescot Cables' first season in the Unibond League ended very well with a final position of twelfth, which basically meant that they weren't going to drop down a level of the pyramid after the reconstruction. Despite a shaky start at home against eventual runners-up, Matlock Town, Cables were quick to find their feet, and a first win was not far away.

The following Wednesday saw the newcomers travel to Kidsgrove Athletic where they came away with a 1-0 victory thanks to a Mike O'Donnell goal. A single goal by Carl Rendell gave Cables their first home win the following Saturday, against Lincoln United - once again 1-0. The season appeared to be progressing well with a further win against Colwyn Bay with a goal apiece by Rendell and Ben Obong.

However, by the end of August, Cables had exited the FA Cup at the first attempt after they went out against Bamber Bridge in the Preliminary Round. Despite beating Belper Town 2-1 in the Preliminary Round of the FA Trophy, their run in that was also soon to end. In the First Round they managed to take Premier Division Alfreton Town to a replay following a 0-0 draw. However, Town (who were riding high in the Premier Division at this stage in the season) proved to be too strong for them and they fell to a 4-1 defeat after being three goals down by half-time.

However, all in all, most Cables fans will look back on the season with a smile. After all, it was only their first season in the Unibond League (after lifting the North West Counties League title in 2002/03) and, as well as establishing themselves in the higher level, they managed to clinch a place in the Premier Division which definitely would have been the main target at the season's outset. AP

The Tigers

Radcliffe Borough

Address: Stainton Park, Pilkington Road, Radcliffe, Lancs, M26 3PE

Tel: 0161 724 5937 / 0161 724 8346

Website: www.radcliffeborough.com

Email: info@radcliffeborough.com

Officials: Chairman: Bernard Manning Jnr
Secretary: Graham Fielding
Manager: Kevin Glendon

Stainton Park

Directions

Radcliffe is ten minutes' drive between Bury and Bolton and only 20 minutes from Manchester. Leave the M60 at Junction 17 (Whitefield). Head towards Whitefield but keep left. Take a left at McDonald's and Aldi just after the first set of lights. Carry on through two sets of lights until a mini-roundabout, with a Chinese restaurant opposite. Turn left and head down the hill. Continue through the town centre and turn right at the sixth set of lights (a used car garage on your left). Carry on up the hill, turning left at the Queen Victoria pub. Carry on until the second mini-roundabout. Stainton Park is just on your right.

By tram: Metrolink runs from Manchester Piccadilly or Victoria. Join the Metrolink towards Bury. Radcliffe is the next to last stop. From here you are 10-15 minutes walk away. Proceed through the car park and go left, slightly uphill, to the traffic lights. Turn right and proceed to the next lights. Go right, again uphill (Ainsworth Rd), until you reach the Queen Victoria pub. Go left here past Red Bank (large playing fields). Stainton Park is at the far end, just to your right (400 metres).

Another ground with an impressive slope, with the bulk of Stainton Park's seating behind the top goal. Not too difficult to find and with ample parking, a trip to Radcliffe once more gives the opportunity to visit an outstanding bar and pleasant surroundings. The support, while generally quiet during the match, can be rousing when the team is on top.

The home supporters' regular haunt is, as ever, behind the visiting goalkeeper, and they have been known to enter into entertaining banter with the opposition custodian on more than one occasion (what more would you expect from a club whose honourary President is one Bernard Manning?). As with many grounds, Stainton Park is in a residential area, with the neighbours' greenhouses coming under threat from wild clearances over the low walls, but this does not detract from what is always a pleasant journey. AP

Review

Radcliffe Borough had a tough first season in the Unibond Premiership and only just managed to reach the Play-Offs for the Conference North after finishing a disappointing 20th.

Borough were riding high on a success story after clinching a place in the Premier Division the previous year after a penalty shootout win over Chorley in a Play-Off. However, they were brought down to earth with a bump as just twelve wins, six draws and 26 defeats saw Radcliffe at the wrong end of the table for most of the season, with a defence that leaked a whopping 99 goals. On the plus side Radcliffe did score 74 goals, which helped their goal difference and, if their defence had been a little stronger, then they would certainly have been higher in the league as their goals for total was higher than some top ten sides (and it was certainly by far the highest goal haul out of the sides in the bottom half). This goal scoring form was due, in large part, to the exploits of frontman Jody Banim. The striker was seemingly scoring for fun in the early months of the season, and actually went on a run which saw him find the net for a record 14 consecutive games. However, such form attracted the attention of the non-league pond's bigger fish and Conference side Shrewsbury managed to lure Banim to Gay Meadow in December for a five figure sum.

Radcliffe had some luck in the FA Cup but were knocked out in the Third Qualifying Round away to Buxton 2-1 after beating Oldham Town by the same scoreline the round before. However, the FA Trophy was far less fruitful as Radcliffe suffered another heavy defeat in the First Round when they lost 5-1 against Frickley Athletic.

Overall, a defence that managed just five clean sheets all season was always going to struggle and, despite beating Whitby Town in an epic opening Play-Off tie (8-7 on penalties following a 2-2 draw), Burscough ultimately had the upper hand when the two sides met on 1st May. The Linnets won through 2-0 to end any hopes that Radcliffe had of a second successive promotion. AP

The Boro

Spennymoor United

Address: Brewery Field, Durham Road, Spennymoor, County Durham

Tel: 01388 814100

Website: www.spennymoorunited.fsnet.co.uk

Officials: Chairman: J.B. Hindmarch
Secretary: B. Boughen
Manager: Tony Lee

Review

Spennymoor United had a mixed start to the season when, after they won their first game against Marine 3-1 thanks to a goal by Anthony Shandran and two by Danny Brunskill, they lost 5-0 against Blyth Spartans just three days later. It was this somewhat inconsistent form that saw the Moors finish in a fairly lacklustre 18th place. Infact, the season saw Spennymoor blowing more cold than hot after they lost ten more games than they won.

However, the biggest disaster for Spennymoor came off the pitch as the club faced a nightmare Christmas. The Moors lost their clubhouse after it was burnt to the ground in a Christmas Day blaze that would, ultimately, cost the club up to £2,000 per week.

After the fire, their season took a while to get back on track as they lost to Whitby Town, Harrogate Town and Droylsden before climbing up the league again after a win against Runcorn. The season ended with mixed emotions as, despite the lowly 18th place finish, the side could look foward to the Unibond Play-Offs. However, any optimism was squashed as the club crashed out against eventual winners Bradford Park Avenue.

The FA Cup also saw no luck for the Moors as they were dumped out against Warrington Town 2-0 at Brewery Field in the Second Qualifying Round. The FA Trophy saw a better performance, beating Workington 3-0 in the First Round, before going out to Stafford Rangers. AP

Directions

From the North and East: Take the A1/A1M southbound and turn off at J61, onto the A688 towards Spennymoor. At Bishop Auckland, turn right at the mini-roundabout, and go straight on at the Thinford roundabout. Head over the mini-roundabout and at the next large roundabout take the third exit into the town centre. Go left at the next roundabout, past Asda then over another mini-roundabout and the ground is on the left behind Durham Road.

From the South: Exit the A1/A1M at J59, onto the A167 towards Spennymoor. Go past Newton Aycliffe, straight on at the Rushyford roundabout and through Chilton. Go straight on at the mini-roundabout, under the bridges at Ferryhill, and then left onto the A688 at the Thinford roundabout. Then as above.

From the West: Turn off the M6 at J38 onto the A685 towards Brough, through Kirkby Stephen. Turn onto the A66 at Brough and take the A67 towards Barnard Castle. Go over the bridge at the traffic lights, through Barnard Castle market place. Turn left at the next mini-roundabout onto the A688 towards Bishop Auckland and Spennymoor. Stay on the A688, by-passing Middlestone Moor. Take a left at the roundabout and follow town centre signs. Go past the garage on the right and take the third exit at the next roundabout. Bear left opposite the town hall tower, and go past town centre parking. Take a left at the mini-roundabout and the ground is on the left. Parking is available on Durham Road. Town centre car parks are also within a short walk.

By train: The nearest station is Durham City. However, the ground is around five to six miles from the station and it is therefore advisable to get a taxi.

After the shock of losing their bar on Christmas Day 2003, Spennymoor's Brewery Field ground has changed. They still have the main stand though, which holds enough for all supporters that visit the ground. However, without the nice bar by the entrance of the ground, which looked out at the pitch from behind one of the goals, the Moors have lost a good source of income. AP

Brewery Field

The Moors

Wakefield & Emley

Address: Emley Welfare Sports Ground, Emley, Huddersfield, West Yorkshire, WF1 5HT

Tel: 01924 840087 / 848398

Website: www.emleyafc.free-online.co.uk

Email: emleyafc@hotmail.com

Officials: Chairman: Peter Matthews
Secretary: Alan Hirst
Manager: Paul David

Emley Welfare Sports Ground

Review

It was a tough season for Wakefield & Emley as they slumped to the bottom of the Unibond Premier Division, failing to gather any momentum in their season - hard to take for a side that were challenging for the title just three years ago. With just eight wins and six draws the club sat ten points adrift at the bottom with a minus 54 goal difference.

A bad season for Wakefield & Emley was not made any easier with manager Ronnie Glavin's departure in June of last year. The man who had so nearly brought the club the league title in 2001 was lured away to a coaching job at Barnsley. Ian Banks was named as his replacement, but the season was barely two months old before he also exited the club, following a defeat against Blyth Spartans.

The FA Cup didn't give the club any sort of respite either after the Pewits were knocked out in the Third Qualifying Round to Hinckley United - 2-0 at Belle Vue. They didn't fare any better in the FA Trophy in what was turning into a disastrous season.

With only two wins in their last ten league fixtures (which also produced eight defeats), the club and the supporters will be hoping to start the season much better than they ended the last one. One statistic that they will want to address is their obvious lack of goals. Wakefield & Emley drew a blank in no fewer than 18 league games last season, higher than any other club in the Unibond League. Perhaps under new boss Paul David they can put this right. AP

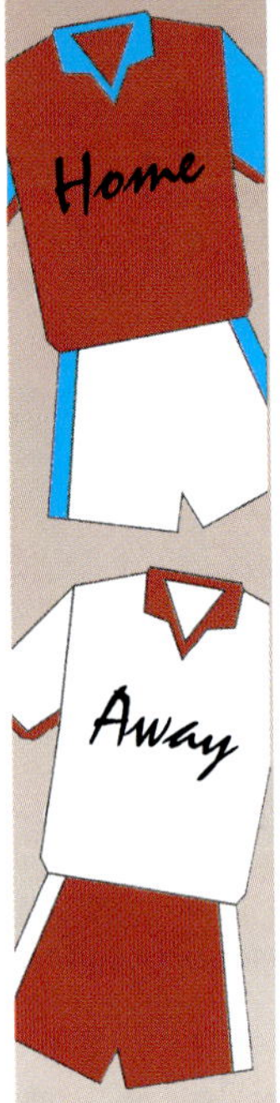

Directions

These are for Belle Vue, where Wakefield & Emley now play the bulk of their matches. From the M1: Exit at Junction 39 and follow signs for Wakefield (A636). Carry on over three roundabouts towards the city centre. At the fourth roundabout (Sainsbury's on the right) turn right and follow signs for A638 Doncaster. Follow that road through two sets of traffic lights and, at the third, turn right onto Doncaster Road (look out for brown signs for Wakefield Trinity Wildcats). Stay in the left lane and the ground is one mile on the right. The entrance is via Superbowl 2000.

From the M62: Take junction 31 and then follow the A655 towards Wakefield. Turn right and join the A638. Go under the railway bridge and head straight on and the ground is on the left. Entrance is via Superbowl 2000.

Belle Vue may not be as nice as Emley's old ground but it does have its plus points. For starters, it is an easy ground to find, as there are directions to the Wakefield Wildcats, the Rugby League team who share the ground. Wakefield & Emley can also move up divisions without having to worry about ground gradings because of the huge stand with good seating plus terraces surrounding the pitch, apart from one end, which holds the clubhouse and a smaller area to view the match. AP

The Pewits

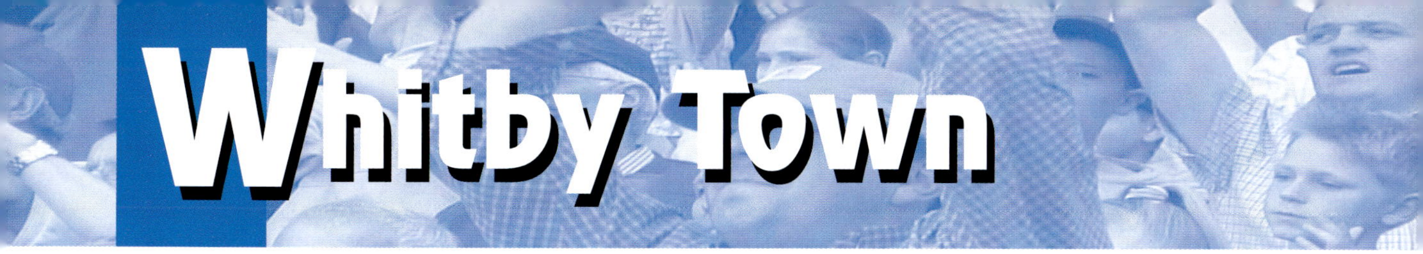

Whitby Town

Address: Turnbull Ground, Upgang Lane, Whitby, North Yorkshire, YO21 3HZ

Tel: 01947 604847

Website: www.wtfc.freeserve.co.uk

Email: wtfc@hotmail.com

Officials: Chairman: Graham Manser
Secretary: Mike Green
Manager: Harry A Dunn

The Turnbull Ground

Directions

From the West: From the A1 in North Yorkshire follow the A64 towards Scarborough. After passing York, pass through Malton via the bypass. Follow this until the A169. Take this, through Pickering, until (after 20 miles of moorland) reaching Sleights. Go through Sleights up a large hill to a new roundabout. Turn right and then first left to Whitby. Follow this road until you come to a garage and turn left opposite the Spar shop (signposted Sandsend). Follow this road to another T-junction with the A174. Turn right, and follow the road for about a mile and the ground is on the left.

From the North: From the A171 from Middlesbrough go all the way to the junction with the A169 Pickering Road. Pass this junction and take the next left. Follow this road until you come to a garage and Spar shop, then as above.

From the South: From Scarborough take the A171 towards Whitby. Follow this to Whitby and eventually you go over a high level bridge, then traffic lights and down a hill. At the bottom, turn left up another hill (Chubb Hill). At the roundabout at the top, take the second exit and follow this road for a mile or so and the ground is on the right.

By train: Whitby station is only half a mile from Upgang Lane. Exit and head into St Hilda's Terrace. Follow this until it bears right into Upgang Lane.

The Turnbull Ground may not be a tourist attraction for visitors arriving for a day at the seaside but it complements the town nicely. It is fairly easy to find if following directions but if you reach the beach you have gone too far. The bar at the Turnbull Ground has a cosy feel about it but it lacks an atmosphere. Depending on when you are travelling to Whitby, you may want to think about the day-trippers who could hold you up on the roads leading to the east coast. AP

Review

Whitby Town had another mixed season, both at home and on their travels, with inconsistency spoiling what could have been a good season. For most of the season, Whitby stayed in the top 13, which would have seen the club qualify for the Conference North. However, they would ultimately slip to a rather more modest final position of 15th.

Manager Harry Dunn didn't have much money to strengthen his squad because of the fund for a new main stand and this may have been a contributing factor to how the season panned out. Whitby did get off to a good start, however, beating newly promoted Radcliffe Borough with a last minute penalty scored by Craig Veart to give his side a 1-0 win. However, it was somehow ironic that the side with whom Whitby started the season, also brought it to an end. Radcliffe were to get their revenge for their opening day defeat at the end of the season in the Unibond League Play-Offs. With a chance of a place in the Conference North at stake, the two sides traded blows as the lead changed hands. With the game locked at 2-2 after extra-time, it was Radcliffe who held their nerve better in the penalty shootout, going through to the next round, winning 8-7.

The FA Trophy was a disappointment as they lost to Bradford Park Avenue in a Second Round replay 1-0. However, Whitby were to gain a bit of extra funds with an FA Cup run. After beating Winsford United 3-0 in the Second Qualifying Round they faced replays against Warrington and Bromsgrove Rovers before facing a tough tie in the First Round Proper. Whitby couldn't stand up to the challenge of a strong Hartlepool United side playing on their home turf. Town made the short journey home after a 4-0 defeat. AP

The Seasiders

Witton Albion

Address: GMB Stadium, Wincham Park, Chapel Street, Wincham, Northwich, Cheshire, CW9 6DA

Tel: 01606 43008

Website: www.wittonalbion.co.uk

Email: wittonalbionfc@aol.com

Officials: Chairman: Mike Worthington
Secretary: Phillip Chadwick
Manager: John Davison

GMB Stadium

Directions

From M6, J19: Follow the A556 towards Northwich for three miles. Turn right onto the A559 towards Lostock (just as the road becomes a dual carriageway). Turn right at the traffic lights immediately before the Slow and Easy pub. Turn left at the crossroads by the Black Greyhound pub (signposted). Follow the road through the industrial estate for about half a mile. Turn left immediately after crossing the canal bridge. You are now at Wincham Park.
From M56, J10: Follow the A559 (Northwich Road) towards Northwich for six miles. Turn right at the crossroads by the Black Greyhound pub, then as above.
By train: From the station head past the Lion and Railway pub towards the town centre for 150 yards to a roundabout. Cross over Chester Way to your right, and take the next right turn into New Warrington Road passing the Mill House pub on the right. Follow the road for about half a mile until Chapel Street on the right. Wincham Park is a quarter of a mile along this road.

The 2003/04 season was my first visit to Witton Albion's Wincham Park Stadium and I hope it will not be my last as I felt really at home. The ground is of a high standard and its cleanliness was matched by the excellent food and programme. I would suggest getting to the ground early to have a drink in the nicely presented bar before looking around the club shop, which doubles up as a memorabilia museum packed full of old Witton Albion memories, before watching the match. AP

Review

Witton Albion had a strong season in the Unibond First Division and finished a comfortable fifth place, though they finished eight points behind fourth placed Lincoln United due, in many ways, to too many draws at home. While they were hard to beat at home, Witton did have a good away record. Infact, they picked up one more win on the road than they managed at home.
However, Albion got off to a bad start as a 4-1 defeat at Lincoln United was followed by a 1-0 home defeat against Colwyn Bay. Another home reverse came against Stocksbridge Park Steels on the second Saturday of the season. Their campaign was finally given a kick-start against North Ferriby when a 3-1 win on the road finally put some points on the board. Simon Burton, Mike Moseley and David Eaton shared the goals that gave the club some much needed morale to push onwards and upwards.
However, disappointment was found in the FA Cup as Witton were dumped out in the Second Qualifying Round to Unibond Premier Division strugglers Wakefield & Emley - and this after two impressive performances in previous ties. Their Preliminary Round draw saw them clinch a 4-1 win over Nelson (which saw Burton add four goals to his season's tally) while a 7-0 win against Holker Old Boys in the First Qualifying Round saw Darren Dicken also net four. Fortunes were equally below par in the FA Trophy as they failed to make it to the First Round after Bamber Bridge squeezed through with a 4-3 win. Despite two goals by Moseley and another by Sargeson, two goals by Bamber Bridge in the last five minutes sealed the win. AP

The Albion

Workington

Address: Borough Park, Workington, Cumbria CA14 2ED

Tel: 01900 602871

Officials: Chairman: Dave Brotherton
Secretary: Dave Brotherton
Manager: Tommy Cassidy

Borough Park

Directions

Take the A66 to Workington. At the first set of traffic lights, turn right towards Maryport. After about half a mile you will come to another roundabout - take the fourth exit. The ground is half a mile on the left.
By train: The ground is approximately a five minute walk from Workington main station. Turn left out of the station and the ground is a quarter of a mile down this road on the right hand side.

Borough Park might have limited parking space but there are plenty of spaces over the road at the supermarket. The inside of the ground has plenty of terracing, most of which is covered, and it provides good shelter if it rains. The bar is a good size and supplies the supporters with both food and drink before and after the match. AP

Review

Workington finished in a positive seventh position at the end of the 2003/04 season, a position that comfortably secured them a place in the Unibond Premier Division. They certainly didn't mind entertaining the crowd along the way - scoring four or more goals in a match on six separate occasions throughout the league season. This is one statistic that will undoubtedly give them hope that they can build on those performances this term as they take a step up the ladder.
Workington were definitely not slow to come out of the blocks as they wrote the headlines on the opening day. Ossett Town were the visitors to Borough Park, although by the final whistle they may have wished that they had stayed at home for a bit of extra pre-season training. Workington netted four times in the first half and added another three in the second to make the final score 7-0, their biggest win of the season.
Workington were also involved in one of the biggest away wins of the season as well. In March they defeated their local rivals Kendal Town 5-0.
However, despite this entertaining form, Workington suffered an early exit from the FA Cup after Northern League outfit Shildon got the better of them at their Dean Street ground. Workington didn't fare much better in the FA Trophy either, despite beating Lincoln United in a replay to get to the First Round. Spennymoor United travelled to Borough Park and won, scoring three goals without reply.
Workington were also denied a slice of glory in the cruellest way after they were beaten in the Final of the Unibond President's Cup. Workington took on Premier Division Barrow in a two legged affair and, with the aggregate scores level after 90 minutes, the Final entered extra-time. Despite another goal from both sides during the extra half an hour, the two teams still could not be separated, meaning that Barrow lifted the trophy on the away goals rule. AP

The Reds